BUSINESS
ECONOMICS

BUSINESS ECONOMICS

BRIAN ATKINSON AND ROBIN MILLER

ADDISON-WESLEY

Harlow, England ● Reading, Massachusetts ● Menlo Park, California

New York ● Don Mills, Ontario ● Amsterdam ● Bonn ● Syndey ● Singapore

Tokyo ● Madrid ● San Juan ● Milan ● Mexico City ● Seoul ● Taipei

Addison Wesley Longman Ltd, Edinburgh Gate, Harlow,
Essex CM20 2JE, England

and Associated Companies throughout the World.

Published in the United States of America
by Addison Wesley Longman Inc., New York.

Text design by Claire Brodmann
Typeset by 43
Typeset in 9.5 point Garamond Light
Produced by Longman Singapore Publishers, Pte
Printed in Singapore
First printed 1998

ISBN 0-201-40351-X

British Library Cataloguing-in-Publication Data
A catalogue for this book is available in the British Library

Library of Congress Cataloguing-in-Publication Data is available

Contents

Preface

Why do some firms succeed while others fall by the wayside? This is a simple question, but the answer is far from simple; if it were, then businesspeople would only have to obey the rules and success would follow.

Consequently, this book cannot claim to answer the question, but what we can do is to help you understand the ways in which economic factors affect the business world. For example:

- How do governments' budget decisions affect firms?
- How do firms decide how much to produce?
- Why is the typical firm very large in some industries, but small in others?
- When should the government intervene in a market, and when should it leave well alone?

If you use other Economics textbooks, you may find that the contents of our book look very similar to those of others; but we hope that you will find our approach is different. That is because we are writing for a special audience; students such as you who are not really interested in Economics for its own sake, and do not want to make a career as an economist, but who want to know about the economic aspects of business as a basis for a successful career in industry.

Our book is divided into modules which in turn are sub-divided into units. Each module is concerned with a particular area of Economics and begins with a list of the things you will understand after you have read the module.

We have tried to include many examples to illustrate the relevance of the points made in the text, and these are supplemented with activities and exercises both within and at the end of each unit. You will also find Review Questions at the end of each unit. These are intended to help you understand and summarise the main points. In addition, each unit has essay type questions and a summary. We have put a glossary at the end of the book which explains the main terms (these are emboldened the first time that they appear in the book).

We hope that you will like our book, find it both interesting and helpful, and that if you don't you will write to us and tell us how to improve it. If you have questions, comments, or suggestions for improvement, you can submit them via email to us at b&e.feedback@awl.co.uk.

Robin Miller
Brian Atkinson
University of Central Lancashire
Preston PR1 2HE

Acknowledgements

The publisher would like to acknowledge: The Guardian, IMF, Jobwatch Manchester, HMSO, Causeway Press, The Bank of England, Economics Journal, National Westminster Bank, IEA, MIT Press, OUP, Blackwell Publishers, Paul Chapman Publishing Ltd, Chapman & Hall Publishers, American Economics Association, Scott Bader, MacMillan Press and the Society of Motor Manufacturers.

The Publisher has made every attempt to obtain permission to reproduce material in this book from the appropriate source. If there are any errors or omissions please contact the publisher who will make suitable acknowledgement in the reprint.

To: Di and Mark; Kath and Laura

MODULE A

Firms

After reading this module, you should be able to:

- discuss the advantages of organising production through firms;

- appreciate the relative importance of small and large firms in the economy;

- explain the importance of profits in the economy;

- discuss competing explanations of firms' objectives;

- understand the advantages and disadvantages of different legal structures for firms; and

- understand why most firms have hierarchial structures.

Firms and their objectives

In the first place, I was removed from all the wickedness of the world here. I had neither the lust of the flesh, the lust of the eye, or the pride of life. I had nothing to covet; for I had all that I was now capable of enjoying; I was lord of the whole manor ... I might have rais'd ship loads of corn, but I had no use for it; so I let as little grow as I thought enough for my occasion. I had tortoise or turtles enough; but now and then one was as much as I could put to any use. I had timber enough to have built a fleet of ships. I had grapes enough to have made wine, or to have cur'd into raisins, to have loaded that fleet when they had been built.

But all I could make use of was all that was valuable. I had enough to eat and to supply my wants, and what was all the rest to me?

Source: Daniel Defoe, *Robinson Crusoe*, 1719, Everyman edition, p. 95.

Why do firms exist?

Try to imagine a society without any firms.

Instead of, say, an engineering firm with managers, engineers, accountants, marketing staff, a drafting department and so on, it would be possible to imagine a system made up of many individuals, each having separate contracts for their services as independent consultants. The relationship between these independent consultants would be decided entirely by market forces. Consultants in huge demand, like pop stars, would earn large sums of money. Those with skills that were not really wanted, or which most people had, like cleaners, would earn little. The market would decide.

At the other extreme from this scenario, we could imagine an economy which was centrally planned and where there were no independent firms. Instead, the entire economy would be like one giant firm directed by a central planner. In this case, wages, the number of people employed and the quantity of goods produced would not depend on market forces, but would be decided by the planner.

Neither of these two extremes is possible. Thus we will spend a large part of the rest of this book examining how markets work – and sometimes fail to work (e.g. in Units 7 and 8). But here we want to ask a very basic question: Why do we have firms? We can define a **firm** as an organisation consisting of one or more individuals working as a decision-making unit to produce goods or services. The main reason why it is profitable to establish a firm is that there are costs involved in using markets to allocate resources. Organising production under the control of an entrepreneur – the decision maker in a commercial enterprise – can cut costs. For example:

- **Costs related to discovering the relevant market price**
  Someone wanting to buy a good or service needs to find out the price. In everyday life we do not bother much about this – we just go along to the supermarket and pay the price asked. But if we want to buy a more expensive item such as a car, we shop around; for example, we look at the motoring press and local papers, or go round garages. This incurs costs of time and money. When production is organised *within* firms, the firm supplies itself, and therefore information is more readily available.

- **Costs of negotiating contracts**
  In many markets, considerable expenses are incurred when contracts have to be negotiated. When transactions take place within a firm, these costs are minimised. For example, workers within a firm do not have to negotiate a contract with each other. Instead, they each have a contract with the firm, which normally lasts a long time and thus reduces the costs of negotiating a new one.

- **Uncertainty costs**
  A good example of uncertainty/risk cost occurs when buying a second-hand car. Such cars may prove to be very good value for money, but it is also possible that a second-hand car will have many defects. The risk can be reduced by paying for an inspection from the RAC or AA, but this increases the costs of the transaction. An industrial example of uncertainty costs occurs when firms making aluminium buy bauxite, its raw material. Bauxite varies considerably in quality, so that the aluminium-making firm is taking a risk every time it buys. Consequently, aluminium firms often try to reduce these uncertainty costs by owning the bauxite mines.

The costs we have just described are examples of **transactions costs**, which are incurred when goods or services are bought or sold. We can therefore summarise by saying that the main reason for the existence of firms is that they cut transactions costs. These costs also have an important influence on determining the size of firms (see Unit 4).

However, there is another reason why firms exist, namely, because efficient production often involves people working together as a team. When people work together, it is not always possible to identify the contribution made by each member of the team. Consequently, individuals may have an incentive to shirk since they may get the same reward as others, but contribute less. As this may not be identified, shirking may become widespread, so greatly reducing output. The solution to this difficulty is to appoint a person – a boss – who will observe behaviour and decide what rewards are appropriate. In order to do this, the person monitoring behaviour needs to have the power to discipline lazy members. Moreover, in order to prevent the monitor/boss from shirking, all residual rewards should go to the boss.

In this way we can see why the modern firm has arisen. An entrepreneur employs workers, monitors the productivity, and receives the profits. In the case of Robinson Crusoe, the individual was the firm, making all the decisions, taking the risk that his projects might fail, but receiving the rewards when they succeeded.

Number of firms

In pre-industrial times, the typical firm was very small; the owner also managed the firm and had daily and close contact with the workers. Manufacturing establishments tended to be craft shops where the owner was a master who supervised journeymen and apprentices. Until the Industrial Revolution, most business enterprises were engaged in servicing an agrarian economy, for example by selling clothing to farm labourers. Firms bought their raw materials locally and also sold their products in the neighbourhood.

The industrial revolution changed all that. Beginning in the textile industry, entre-preneurs built large factories, first using water power, and later steam and electricity to power machinery. Power made it possible to use more complex machines and to increase output. This higher production necessitated larger markets, and the development of steamships and railways made it possible to supply the whole world. The market was no longer local, but global.

The key person in these developments was the industrial capitalist. He – for very few, if any, were women – employed managers to solve day-to-day problems inside the factory. This left the entrepreneur free to oversee the whole enterprise, constantly seeking ways to increase productivity, raise capital and develop new markets.

The growth of industrial capitalism brought about a profound change in the form of business enterprise and also in the structure of markets. In manufacturing and transport, large-scale enterprise became common because small firms could not raise the capital needed, for example to build railways. In distribution, the small shop remained the norm. Indeed, it was not until after the Second World War that large chains of shops such as Marks & Spencer or Sainsburys became established.

At the same time, there were significant changes taking place in the structure of industry. In the nineteenth century, manufacturing grew and agriculture declined as a share of total output. In the last few decades manufacturing has become relatively less important as

Table 1.1: Industry output as a percentage of UK gross domestic product

	1980	1990	1995
Agriculture, forest and fishing	2.1	1.5	2.1
Energy and water supply	9.7	5.1	2.8
Manufacturing	26.7	22.4	20.1
Construction	6.1	7.6	5.4
Service industries	55.1	57.7	68.6

Source: Calculated from *Great Britain Annual Abstract of Statistics* (1997), table 14.7.

Table 1.2: Percentage of businesses, employment and output, UK manufacturing 1990

Size, by total employment	% of business	% of employment	% of output
1–99	90.5	25.0	19.2
100–999	5.5	24.0	22.0
1000–4999	2.4	19.7	21.0
5000–49,999	1.8	24.8	30.3
50,000 and over	0.1	6.5	7.5

Source: Based on *Business Monitor PA1002, Report on the Census of Production 1990,* Central Statistical Office (1992).

service industries have become dominant in all European economies. Table 1.1 shows the current position in the UK; other developed economies show similar trends.

The results of the most recent census of manufacturing, summarised in Table 1.2, show that most firms remain small – 90 per cent of businesses employ less than 100 people. These firms produce less than a fifth of total output, though they employ a quarter of all

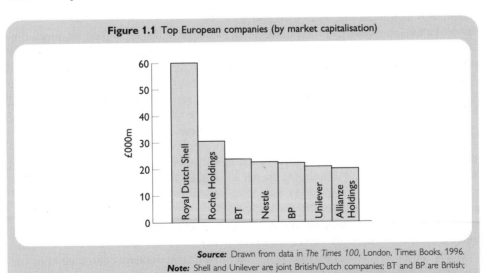

Figure 1.1 Top European companies (by market capitalisation)

Source: Drawn from data in *The Times 100,* London, Times Books, 1996.
Note: Shell and Unilever are joint British/Dutch companies; BT and BP are British; Roche and Nestlé are Swiss; and Allianze is German.

workers. In contrast, large firms produce most output and employ most people. The very largest firms, less than one-tenth of 1 per cent of the total, employ over 6 per cent of the workers and produce over 7 per cent of total output.

Because information supplied to the census is confidential, it does not give information about individual businesses. However, information is available from other sources. As Figure 1.1 shows, some European firms are very large indeed.

Firms' objectives

Economists – like other scientists – develop theories. Since the real world is far too complex for any theory to explain completely, we make use of assumptions. This is something we all do in everyday life. If the sun is shining, I often assume that it is not going to rain, and so I go out without a raincoat. Similarly, when I go to work, I assume that the shops will be open to enable me to buy some lunch.

In analysing the behaviour of firms, economists often assume that firms seek to maximise **profits**. As we will see, especially in Modules C and D, this makes it possible to develop elegant and persuasive explanations of how firms operate. But is the assumption true? What are firms' objectives?

Maximising profits

The meaning of profit

In order to examine the assumption of profit maximisation, we need first to be precise about what we mean by profit. This can be defined in various ways, but the simplest is to say that profit is the difference between total revenue and total cost. We can show this in symbols:

Profit $= TR - TC$

where TR is total profit and TC is total cost.

Hence if a firm receives £1,000,000 from selling its output and spends £900,000 producing this output, its profit is £100,000. We can show the relationship between costs, revenue and profit in a diagram. This is done in Figure 1.2. Here, costs rise with output, since it costs more to produce more. Up to a point, revenue also rises with output, but there may come a point where the firm will have to cut its prices to sell more, so that its total revenue actually declines. In the real world, a firm would not produce at this level of output, but we show it in the figure to make it complete.

In Figure 1.2 the firm will maximise profit if it produces at output q since this is the level of output where there is the greatest difference between the total revenue and total cost curves. Profit will fall if output is greater or smaller than this.

The importance of profits

Although Marxists might criticise profits, since they can be regarded as surplus value created by the workers and taken by the owners, they are essential in a capitalist economy. In the first place, profits create *incentives*. Entrepreneurs contribute time and skill to run a firm efficiently. They take risks, and profit is the reward they receive. If there were no profits, there would be no incentive for entrepreneurs to work, so that the

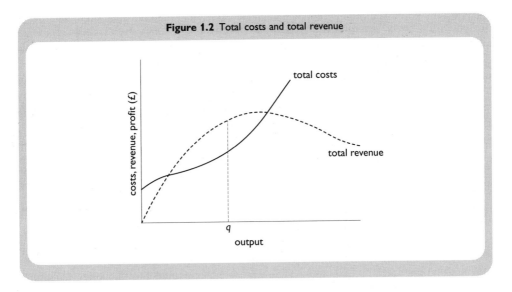

Figure 1.2 Total costs and total revenue

business would collapse. Since firms play a fundamental part in determining living standards, the ability to make a profit is an essential foundation.

Society also benefits because rising profits act as a signal to the entrepreneur that output should be increased. This will benefit consumers since more goods will be available. At the same time, profits provide a source of revenue that makes it possible for entrepreneurs to invest in new factories and machines, thus making this higher output possible. Moreover, profits also benefit society because they encourage innovation, both in new products and in new ways of producing existing products. Customers then gain from these innovations.

When profits are either low or falling, this is often a signal that the firm is inefficient or that it is making a product which people do not want to buy. In the latter case, resources should be allocated to make other goods and services that people do want.

One of the strongest arguments for profits is that firms which are losing money or making only low profits cannot afford to innovate, pay high wages or offer new jobs, which means that both existing and potential workers suffer. Firms making high profits can afford to pay high wages and to take on new workers.

So profits are essential in a modern economy. Nevertheless, as we will see, high levels of profit may not be desirable if they derive from a monopolist's ability to exploit consumers.

Do firms try to maximise profits?

We have seen that profits are essential in a capitalist society, but the question remains: Do firms try to maximise profits? The argument that they do rests on two assumptions:

1. That owners are in day-to-day control of the business.
2. That the main desire of owners is to maximise profits.

Both these assumptions are questionable. Very large firms such as Shell, Marks & Spencer and Ford are run by managers. There may be thousands of shareholders – the legal owners of the firm – but each will typically own only a few shares, which means that the typical owner has little or no power.

This division between owners and shareholders gives rise to what is called the **principal–agent problem**. In this case, the principal (i.e. the owner) hires agents (the managers) to run the business. However, the goals of the owners may differ from those of the managers. Principals may indeed wish to maximise profits so that their income rises, and this will probably also cause the value of their shares to rise. However, the managers may have other goals such as maximising sales or, indeed, increasing the size of their department so that their status (and probably their salary) increases. When this is the case, profit maximisation may not be the prime goal of those who actually run the business.

However, there are strong arguments to suggest that in practice firms may indeed adopt some strategy such as profit maximisation:

● Given the choice between less profit and higher profit, both owners and managers would choose higher profits.

● Competition forces firms to adopt a profit-maximising policy. Where competition is fierce, only the most efficient will survive, which ensures that they will try to maximise profits.

● The best test of theory is its predictive power. Assuming a policy of profit maximisation on the part of firms has made it possible for economists to predict the price and output of those firms.

However, empirical evidence suggests that these arguments are not conclusive. Shipley surveyed 728 UK firms and asked the two questions shown in Table 1.3. The resulting data can be interpreted in two ways. Supporters of the profit-maximising assumption can argue that nearly 90 per cent say that achieving a target profit is very important or of overriding importance. Critics can point out that 'target profit' is not the same as profit maximisation, and that less than half the firms said that they tried to maximise profits.

So, if firms do not always try to maximise profits, what other goals might they have?

Table 1.3: Survey of firms' goals

	%
1. Does your firm try to achieve	
(a) maximum profits	48
(b) satisfactory profits	52
2. Compared to your firm's other objectives, is the achievement of a target profit . . . regarded as being	
(a) of little importance	2
(b) fairly important	13
(c) very important	59
(d) of overriding importance	26

Source: Shipley D.D. (1981) 'Primary objectives in British manufacturing industry' *Journal of Industrial Economics*, vol. 29 no. 4, June.

Satisficing

One suggestion is that managers set themselves a minimum acceptable level of profit – in other words, a satisfactory level of profits. The advocates of this view suggest that managers in large firms in particular try to achieve profits that are always rising: that is, next year's profits should be higher than this year's. This policy will probably satisfy shareholders, and it may be safer than taking risky measures that might maximise profits. It will probably also satisfy the workers, who also have a stake in the business, since the firm will also be able to pay higher wages. Firms which set themselves such targets are said to 'satisfice' rather than 'maximise'. This kind of objective may also apply to small family firms where maximising profits may require more effort and more risk. Consequently, if they think that their income is adequate, the owners may choose less work and more leisure, even though this means lower profits. This was the case with Robinson Crusoe in the article which introduced this unit; he could be said to be satisficing rather than maximising.

Maximising sales revenue

One reason that large firms may seek to maximise sales rather than profits is that managers' pay may be directly related to sales. Thus higher sales equals higher pay. There is some evidence to support this argument. Shipley's research, summarised in Table 1.3 showed that nearly half the firms included maximising sales revenue as part of their overall objectives. Moreover, maximising sales revenue may, in the long run, lead to maximising profits, because higher sales revenue generates funds which can be used to increase investment and hence future profits.

Growth

Very similar factors apply to firms which have maximum growth as their prime objective. Managers often increase their status (and salary) when their departments are large. Furthermore, outsiders such as potential shareholders may be more impressed by a firm which is growing, rather than by one which seems to be stagnating. In addition, growth may give a firm *power*. A firm which has only 10 per cent of the market will often have to follow the price changes of the market leader; one which has 90 per cent can often make decisions which tiddlers in the industry have to follow.

At the same time, while growth may lead to higher profits, the evidence is not convincing. Many large firms report lower rates of profit than small firms. One reason for this is that large firms may become too bureaucratic. This line of argument has caused some large firms to sell off some departments. A notable example is ICI, which split off its medical products department and created a new firm called Zeneca to handle that business.

In practice, therefore, it may be that managers in different firms have different objectives. Some will seek to maximise profits, some to maximise growth or sales, and some simply to produce a satisfactory level of profits. However, profit maximisation may be sufficiently widespread that it is a reasonable assumption, and, as we will see in later units, this assumption makes possible perceptive analyses of firms' behaviour.

Exercise

XYZ is a firm which makes artificial smiles for politicians. As you can imagine, it is a thriving business and details of its output, costs and revenue are:

Output (No. of smiles per month)	Total revenue (£000)	Total cost (£000)
1	10	6
2	20	10
3	30	18
4	40	28
5	50	40
6	60	60

1. What is the firm's profit at each level of output?
2. At what level of output will the firm maximise its profits?
3. What reasons might the firm have for producing more or less than this level of output?

Objectives in the public sector

So far we have been talking about the objectives of firms in the private sector of the economy. In recent years, many industries in the public sector have been privatised (e.g. coal, water and electricity). These industries are now owned by shareholders and have similar objectives to firms which have always been in the private sector, though since some of them are monopolies – for instance, you cannot choose your water supplier as you can your supermarket – they are heavily regulated.

Despite this trend towards privatisation, however, the public sector remains important. The Post Office is a notable example of an industry that is still in public ownership.

It is rather easier to be clear about the objectives of nationalised industries since these objectives are often laid down by law or by ministerial regulation. Although the objectives vary over time, they do not include profit maximisation. They have included the following:

● **Providing a service for the nation**
For example, the Royal Mail delivers letters to rural areas even though this service is so costly that it is loss making.

● **Making a reasonable return on investment**
Maximising profits was not a reasonable aim of the nationalised water, gas or electricity industries. They were monopolies, and any attempt to increase profits would have penalised customers who had no other choice of supplier. Instead, they were often given a target, such as making a 5 per cent return on investment.

● **Keeping prices down**
In some periods, governments forced nationalised industries to keep down prices as part of an anti-inflation policy. This meant that the industries made losses.

Public sector organisations

In recent years, large parts of the economy such as health and education have been opened up to market forces, though they still remain in the public sector. In the health service, most general practitioners buy health care for their patients from hospitals, and so have an incentive to buy cheaply since they can use any surplus to improve their practice. Schools and colleges receive money for each student, and therefore have an incentive to attract more students, just as a shop aims to attract customers.

Despite the introduction of some market forces, neither schools nor hospitals have profit maximisation – or even satisficing – as an objective. They are more concerned to provide a service, and income generation is needed to achieve this. Similarly, other areas of the economy such as defence, law and order and social services are not concerned with making profits; their objectives are different, though they should all seek to improve their efficiency. Charities also provide a service, and in many cases they do try to increase their income, although this is to enable them to provide more and better services and not to make a profit.

Summary

Firms' objectives are important. A firm which seeks to maximise profits will choose different prices and levels of output from one which has other objectives. In Figure 1.3, a firm wishing to maximise profits will produce a level of output q_1. One trying to maximise sales revenue will produce at q_2. As this figure shows, the firm which tries to maximise sales will produce a larger output. In order to sell this output it will have to cut its prices.

It is clearly not always the case that firms try to maximise profits, but it is an assumption that fits the behaviour of many firms, and one which economists have usually accepted as a simplifying device.

Figure 1.3 Maximum sales and maximum profit

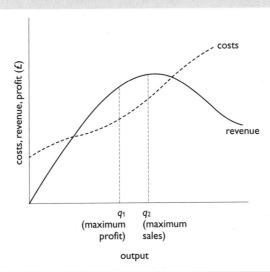

costs

revenue

costs, revenue, profit (£)

q_1
(maximum profit)

q_2
(maximum sales)

output

Review questions

1. Explain why costs can be cut when decisions are made within firms.
2. What are the functions of an entrepreneur?
3. Outline the changes in the structure of British industry in recent years.
4. Summarise the reasons why it is reasonable to assume that firms attempt to maximise profits.
5. Discuss the other objectives that a firm might have. What implications do the varying objectives have for the level of output and profit?

Essay questions

1. Why is most production organised through firms?
2. Critically discuss the validity of the assumption that firms attempt to maximise profits.

Reading 1.1

Scott Bader Ltd

Scott Bader Ltd is wholly owned by the Scott Bader Commonwealth Ltd. The company's history goes back to 1920 and it makes polyester and similar products. Everyone working at Scott Bader can become a member of the Commonwealth and, by this means, a joint owner of the company. There are no outside shareholders. The company philosophy is that of the founder Ernest Bader, and can be summarised as follows:

1. Labour should employ capital and not capital employ labour.
2. We are all equal as human beings and therefore we all have the right of human dignity.
3. A minimum of 60 per cent of profits must be ploughed back into the company for future development and investment. Of the remaining 40 per cent, a maximum of 20 per cent can be paid as a bonus to staff. Whatever percentage is set as a bonus, a roughly equal amount must be given to charity.
4. In the event of a downturn in trade, all remaining work is shared rather than making any employee redundant – even if this means a cut in pay.
5. Scott Bader limits production to products which are beneficial to the community. In particular, it excludes any products for the specific purpose of manufacturing weapons of war.

▷

6. Industrial democracy is an important aim, and all employees are consulted on decisions which may affect their interests. Most of the board of management are elected by the members of the Commonwealth.

Source: Jones M. (1991) *The History and Philosophy of the Scott Bader Commonwealth*, Scott Bader Commonwealth, Wollaston.

Questions

1. Summarise the arguments given in the unit in favour of profits. Do you think that these arguments apply to Scott Bader?
2. What are the advantages and disadvantages to the workers of a company run on Scott Bader principles?
3. Why do you think that few other companies are run on Scott Bader lines?

The internal organisation of firms

Accountants go public

Everyone knows that accountants are rich – and the largest accountancy firms are richer than most, so it is difficult to feel sorry for them when they run into trouble. Yet the big six accountancy firms – Coopers & Lybrand, KPMG, Price Waterhouse, Arthur Anderson, Touche Ross, and Ernst & Young – feel that they are being hounded when the firms that they have audited run into difficulties. That is because they become the targets for lawsuits which can cost millions of pounds.

The obvious solution to this problem is to take out insurance, but insurance companies are often reluctant to offer insurance cover when the bill might be so large. Hence they charge high premiums, amounting to about 8 per cent of the accountant's income from fees.

The problem is particularly acute for accountants because the large firms are partnerships, and in partnerships the partners cannot claim limited liability since they operate under the principle of joint and several liability. If the company becomes bankrupt, all the partners' assets – including their homes – have to be sold to pay off the company's debts. Thus, in the case of accountants, should a company they audit collapse, the accountants may be sued if they were negligent, even though others may have also been inefficient.

KPMG, the third largest accountancy firm in the UK, today announced its solution. In future it will cease being a partnership and become a limited liability company. This means that its partners will no longer be liable to lose all their assets, but it also means that the firm's accounts will be open to public examination, something that accountancy firms have resisted until now.

Businesses are as diverse as people. However, it is possible to categorise firms according to their legal status, and as we will see, each type of business organisation has its advantages and disadvantages.

In order to decide the most appropriate legal status, the entrepreneur must answer such questions as:

● How much money is needed to finance the business?

● How can this money be found?

● How much money am I willing to risk?

● Who will make the major decisions – the owners or managers?

● What legal obligations will be incurred?

Figure 2.1 shows the main types of firm. The basic distinction is between firms that are incorporated and those that are not incorporated:

1. **Unincorporated businesses** are businesses where there is no legal difference between the owner and the firm. Everything is done in the name of the owner. If the firm is sued, the owner is responsible for any damages. Most unincorporated businesses are relatively small, and this type of organisation is common in such industries as hairdressing, window cleaning and the retail trade.

2. An **incorporated business** has a separate legal identity from its owners. Thus the business can be taken over, liquidated or sold. Most of the large familiar names in the economy are incorporated businesses.

The main reason for firms to be incorporated is that the owners then have **limited liability**. The background to this is that as the Industrial Revolution developed, owners of businesses needed more capital, for example to build bigger factories. However, people buying shares in the business were also taking on a big risk – if the firm became bankrupt, they could lose everything that they possessed, including their home. Limited liability changed this. Shareholders in a firm with limited liability can only lose the money that

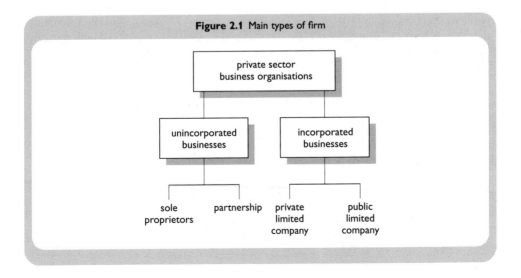

Figure 2.1 Main types of firm

they have invested in the firm; their other possessions are safe. Hence the introduction of limited liability meant that many investors could be found for growing firms. The shareholders could benefit from any profits, while their risks were limited. It was the advent of limited liability that led to the growth of large firms such as BP and Unilever, which have many thousands of shareholders.

Unincorporated businesses

The sole proprietor

This is the oldest, simplest and most common form of business organisation. Table 2.1 shows their distribution across the economy.

The type of business here called 'sole proprietor' is sometimes called 'sole trader'. However, this can be misleading, because although many of these firms consist of one person who does everything, many of them employ other workers – the emphasis is on one owner.

Sole proprietorships are found throughout the economy, but they are most common in those areas where there are few advantages to be had in being big. Hence it is the form of organisation preferred by, for example, small shopkeepers, gardeners and building repairers.

Advantages of sole proprietorships

The main advantages of this form of organisation are:

- **Ease of formation** It is the easiest form of business to create. Legal requirements are minimal: for example, the owner has to pay income tax, and VAT has to be paid once the threshold is reached, but there are few other legal requirements.

- **Retention of profits** Since there is only one owner, this person keeps all the profits. This implies that the owner has a great incentive for the business to do well.

Table 2.1: Sole proprietors in the British economy

Industry	% of total
Finance, property and business services	17.7
Retail	15.7
Construction	14.9
Agriculture	11.3
Manufacturing and mining	6.4
Wholesale	5.5
Transport	5.4
Other	23.1
Total number of sole proprietors	598,170

Source: Calculated from Size Analysis of UK Business, Business Monitor PA 1003 (1996), Office of National Statistics.

- **Quick decision making** In other forms of business enterprise, other people need to be consulted. Here there is only one owner, so decisions can be made quickly, without the need for consultation.
- **Personal satisfaction** Many sole proprietors gain great satisfaction from owning their own business.
- **Flexibility** The owner has flexibility to decide what hours will be worked, and what holidays to take.
- **Personal service** Because they are usually small, this form of business organisation can offer a personal service to customers.
- **Ease of dissolution** A sole proprietorship can easily be wound up if the owner no longer wishes to run the business.

Disadvantages of sole proprietorships

Despite their many advantages, sole proprietors have many disadvantages:

- **Unlimited liability** Since in the eye of the law, there is no difference between the owner and the firm, the owner is liable for all debts incurred by the business. This means that all the owner's assets are at risk if the business goes bust.
- **Limited funds for expansion** Since there is only one owner, it is difficult to raise funds for expansion. The owner will have limited personal assets, and banks will often be reluctant to lend money, since if the owner is ill, incompetent or unlucky, they may not get their money back. Even when they are willing to lend, they may demand assets such as the owner's house as security for the loan.
- **Lack of management skills** No single person can have all the skills needed to run a business, so success may be restricted by the owner's limitations.
- **Personal time demands** Because they are solely responsible, many sole proprietors work very long hours and have very few holidays.
- **Illness** Where the owner is the only worker, illness means no income.

Partnerships

A **partnership** is similar in many ways to a sole proprietorship except that it has more than one owner. A partnership can be defined as an association of two or more people who are co-owners of a business run for profit. They are common in professional services such as lawyers and accountants, but as Table 2.2 shows, they are also found in many other areas of the economy.

Advantages of partnerships

- **Ease of formation** There is no need to sign any legal agreement to form a partnership, though, normally, partners do sign a document which sets out the duties of each partner such as the amount of capital they will invest and how conflicts will be resolved.

Table 2.2: Partnerships in the British economy

Industry	% of total
Retail	20.6
Agriculture	19.8
Finance, property and business services	12.9
Hotels and catering	10.9
Construction	8.8
Manufacturing and mining	7.2
Other	19.8
Total number of partnerships	388,130

Source: Calculated from *Size Analysis of UK Business, Business Monitor PA 1003* (1996), Office of National Statistics.

- **Pooling of knowledge and skills**   Partners may have different skills which can be pooled to form an effective business. For example, one partner may specialise in the financial aspects of the business, another in marketing or production. In a very large partnership such as the one described at the beginning of this unit, the partners can offer a very wide range of expertise.

- **More funds are available**   Each partner will usually have financial resources to contribute, and they also find it easier than single proprietorships to borrow.

- **Sharing**   Partners can share the work and the risks. The business can still be earning even if one partner is ill or on holiday.

Disadvantages of partnerships

- **Partners may disagree**   Business marriages, like personal ones, can easily fall apart. One partner may feel that others are not pulling their weight, or they may disagree about such matters as pricing policy or whether to take on more employees.

- **Unlimited liability**   If one partner makes a bad decision, the others have to pay their share of the resultant losses. In extreme cases, since there is unlimited liability, they may lose all their possessions to pay off the debts incurred by another's poor judgement. It is this unlimited liability which makes partnerships a risky form of business organisation, and why it is most likely to be found in fields where risk is relatively small such as accountancy, medicine and the legal profession. As the article at the beginning of this unit showed, there is risk even in these professions that cause accountancy firms such as KPMG to change their status.

- **The partnership ends when a partner dies**   This can cause problems to the remaining partners since the heirs of the deceased often want the money their relative has invested in the business, and this can cause financial problems if the business has to find this money at short notice.

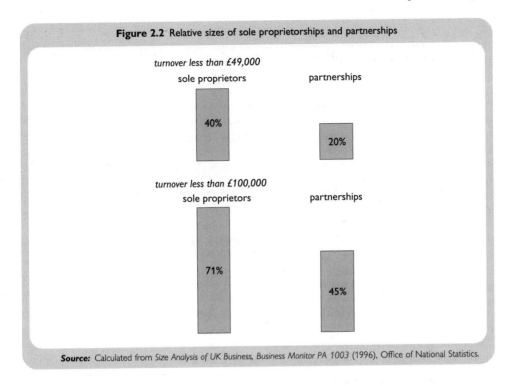

Figure 2.2 Relative sizes of sole proprietorships and partnerships

turnover less than £49,000

sole proprietors

partnerships

40%

20%

turnover less than £100,000

sole proprietors

partnerships

71%

45%

Source: Calculated from *Size Analysis of UK Business, Business Monitor PA 1003* (1996), Office of National Statistics.

Comparing sole proprietorship and partnership

There are many similarities between these two kinds of firms, but as might be expected, partnerships tend to be larger, as Figure 2.2 shows.

Incorporated companies

Sole proprietorships and partnerships are relatively simple forms of business organisation, but incorporated companies are much more formal, largely because they possess limited liability and have their own legal identity. They can therefore own their own assets, employ people, and be sued quite separately from the people who actually own the company. The owners are the people who own shares in the company, which gives them the right to vote, the number of votes depending on the number of shares.

Because a limited company has its own legal identity, it must be set up formally with legal documents that set out such matters as its aims, the amount of capital and the procedures for appointing directors to run the company. These documents have to be sent to the Registrar of Companies, and can be seen by the general public.

Limited liability is a form of organisation that is found all over the world, though, as Table 2.3 shows, each country has its own name and abbreviation for this format.

Private limited companies

These are usually the smaller kind of incorporated company, and their shares are not bought and sold on the open market. Instead, they can only be sold privately and all

Table 2.3: Incorporated companies

Country	Abbreviation	Meaning
USA	Inc.	Incorporated
Germany	AG	Incorporated (Aktiengesellschaft)
Germany	GmbH	Limited liability company (Gesellschaft mit beschrankter Haftung)
Spain	Cia	Company (Compania)
Netherlands	NV	Incorporated (Naamlose Vennootschap)
Italy	SPA	Incorporated (Societa per Azioni)
Australia	Pty	Proprietary

shareholders must agree about the sale. This makes them suitable for family firms where the owners want to keep the business in the family. Private limited companies can be identified by the abbreviation 'Ltd' – short for 'limited'. This is a warning to those dealing with the company that the owners are not legally responsible for the debts of the company.

Advantages

- The principal advantage is limited liability. It was to gain this advantage that KPMG, the accountancy firm discussed in the introduction to this unit, decided to cease being a partnership.
- Control of the business can be kept within a small group.
- The company continues in existence even if some owners die.
- The company can have many shareholders, making it relatively easy to raise money.

Disadvantages

- Setting up the business involves some costs.
- Because shares cannot be sold to the general public, it has limited ability to raise money.
- It can be difficult to sell the shares.
- Some financial information has to be made public.

Most private limited companies are relatively small, but two that are well known are C & A and the Littlewoods pools and mail order business.

Public limited companies

These are the giants of the economy. Almost all the large firms in the economy are public limited companies, and are recognisable by the abbreviation 'plc' after their name. Shares in these companies can be bought and sold by the general public

The advantages of a public limited company are very similar to those of a private limited company. But it has one other particularly important advantage: it can have many shareholders, and so can raise large sums of money. It is this factor which explains the dominance of this type of company in the modern economy.

The disadvantages of public limited companies are that they are expensive to set up, a large amount of information has to be made public, and the company can be taken over by outsiders. Some would argue that the last point is an advantage for the economy as a whole, since if a company is underperforming, outside entrepreneurs may see this, buy shares and then run the company more efficiently.

Exercise

Rembrandt, Turner and Picasso were a firm of painters and decorators in Scunthorpe. They were confident of their abilities and joined together to form a partnership. For several years the firm grew. Sometimes the partners all worked together on a large project with their employees, and sometimes they worked on their own.

Then Rembrandt suggested that they expand and move into new offices. After much discussion and disagreement he signed a long lease and borrowed money from the bank for new equipment and transport. Unfortunately, this coincided with the recession. The business went into decline and they could pay neither the rent nor the interest on the bank loan. They then went out of business.

1. Explain how this illustrates the advantages and disadvantages of a partnership.

2. Do you think it would have been better for them to have worked as sole traders?

3. If the business had succeeded and grown, what form of organisation do you think would have been most suitable?

Ownership and control

Unit 1 described the principal–agent problem. In theory, public limited companies are run in the interests of their owners – the shareholders – who are the principals in this case. The managers – the agents – are expected to act in the interest of the owners. But who exactly are the owners?

Historically, the owners were hundreds, occasionally thousands, of small shareholders – perhaps with the descendants of the original founders owning a relatively large number of shares. That is no longer the dominant pattern. Direct investment by individuals in the stock market has fallen dramatically as a proportion of total shares. Forty years ago private individuals owned about two-thirds of shares; now the figure is less than 10 per cent. Although more people now own shares, largely because of privatisation, they typically own only a few shares, and this gives them no power over the decisions made by the company in which they hold those shares.

Private investment is now increasingly channelled through pension funds, insurance companies and unit trusts. For example, the Prudential has £74,000m. under its control, within which is included 5.6 per cent of Marks & Spencer, 3.7 per cent of BT, and 3.6 per cent of British Gas, plus significant shares in many other firms. This gives the Prudential and other big insurance companies with equally large holdings considerable power. One criticism that is levelled at insurance companies is that they are constantly seeking higher dividends so that they can pay out more to the people who invest with them. This, in turn, puts pressure on the companies whose shares they hold to go for quick returns rather than long-term growth.

The hierarchical structure of firms

We saw in Unit 1 that firms exist because in some circumstances they can be more efficient than markets in allocating resources. The concept of efficiency in the form of economising on transactions costs can be used to explain why different forms of organisational structure have developed.

Non-hierarchical structures

Non-hierarchical structures – sometimes called peer groups – are one possible form of organisation. They are particularly suitable for cooperatives, where every member has an equal say in the firm's decision making. One advantage of this form of organisation can be that all members feel a commitment to the success of the project.

Another advantage of peer group organisation is that they can take advantage of **indivisibilities**. These exist when production requires the use of a large asset which cannot be divided up. An example would be an X-ray machine in a medical practice. Such a machine might be too expensive for a single doctor, but several doctors sharing a practice can also share the use of expensive machines.

One problem with non-hierarchical structures, illustrated in Figure 2.3, is that communication becomes difficult as firms grow. If there are five participants in the organisation, and all participate equally in decision making, then all members need to be informed. This means that there have to be 10 flows of information. If the number of participants increases to six, then 15 flows of information are required, and for seven participants, 21 flows. Hence as the organisation grows, more time has to be spent in meetings, and much time is wasted in communicating everything to everybody. Furthermore, sometimes the flows will fail to operate properly, so that people feel left

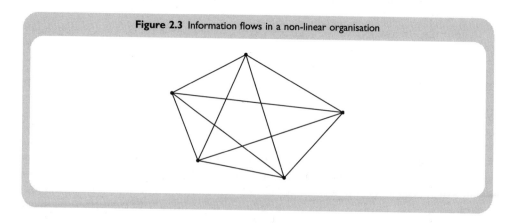

Figure 2.3 Information flows in a non-linear organisation

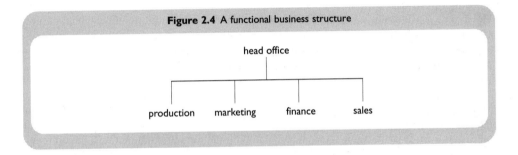

Figure 2.4 A functional business structure

out. This problem of communication is one reason why non-hierarchical groups are rare in large-scale institutions.

Hierarchical structures

Figure 2.4 shows one possible form of large-scale organisation. The head office coordinates the specialist areas such as production or sales, while finance collects and records financial information and reports to head office. This seems a logical structure, but it proved to be inadequate in many cases where the firm made several products. This problem was overcome by one of the great managerial innovations, which was made at General Motors at about the time of the First World War.

The problem at the time was that General Motors made several different cars, so that 'production' covered many different products. The result was that many different people were involved in making decisions about a single model. General Motors' solution was to introduce a divisional structure as shown in Figure 2.5. Each division was responsible for a particular product – in this case, a particular car model. Divisions therefore had many of the characteristics of an individual firm, but instead of reporting to a board of directors, they reported to head office. This left head office free to concentrate on formulating policy, setting targets, and monitoring the divisions. This divisional form of structure has proved remarkably efficient over the years, and it is commonly found in large firms which produce many products.

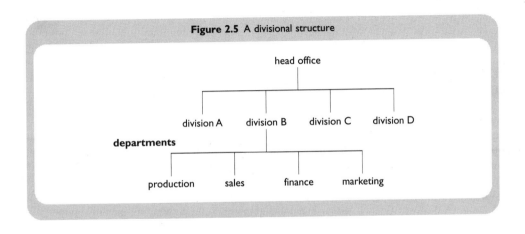

Figure 2.5 A divisional structure

Summary

There is no perfect form of organisation for a firm. Pre-industrial revolution, the typical firm was tiny; now, multinational giants can have revenues larger than many countries.

Nevertheless, most firms remain small, and many of these are owned by one person. This creates incentives for the owner, but such firms have limited ability to expand. Partnerships tend to be larger, but still suffer from unlimited liability.

Incorporated businesses do not have these disadvantages, and the public limited company is the dominant form of business organisation in modern economies. Their internal organisation varies, but most large firms are hierarchial and many have a divisional structure to facilitate efficient decision making.

Review questions

1. Explain the difference between incorporated and unincorporated businesses.
2. Summarise the main advantages and disadvantages of sole proprietorship as a form of business organisation.
3. Why do people form partnerships as opposed to any other form of business organisation?
4. Why do private limited companies not become public?
5. Why is the public limited company the characteristic form of business organisation in a modern economy?
6. Why do many large firms adopt a divisional structure?

Essay questions

1. What is meant by 'limited liability'? Explain with examples why certain firms have unlimited liability and others limited liability.
2. Why do you think that the public limited company has become the dominant form of business organisation?

Reading 2.1

Why Preston are joining Spurs on the market

One of the most venerable names in English soccer, Preston North End, will be changed today, assuming that all goes to plan at the club's annual meeting. Don't panic, the change will be minor. The company is merely becoming Preston North End plc, not something appalling such as Baxi Preston Panthers.

▷

But whereas the name change will be minor, the effect will be substantial since it indicates that the club are to join the elite band floated on the stock market. Once again the club will be joined with such greats as Manchester United, Arsenal, Tottenham, Aston Villa and Liverpool, just as they were in the glory days when they were among the league leaders.

The route to the stock market began last year with the club's takeover by Baxi. The Preston chairman, Bryan Gray, explained that Preston's flotation has been driven by the same financial necessity that has brought most clubs to market. Selling shares will put Preston in 'a very strong financial position', Gray said, and help to finance redevelopment of the ground.

A share issue makes it possible to raise money from a wider group of subscribers . . . though only Manchester United, with a stock market valuation of almost £100 million, are large enough to interest investment funds . . . The fear of losing control has discouraged many clubs from joining the stock market.

Source: *Guardian*, 5 September 1995, p. 22.

Questions

1. Explain what is meant by 'plc'.
2. Summarise the arguments for football clubs becoming public limited companies. Why do many not do this?
3. Why do you think people might buy shares in Preston North End plc? Do you think that the same reasons would apply to other, non-sporting companies?

Production and costs

After studying this module, you should be able to:

- recognise the costs that firms have to meet;
- understand the response of these costs to changes in output;
- understand the concept of economies of scale and why they arise;
- appreciate the drawbacks that larger firms experience;
- appreciate the role and contribution that smaller firms can make to the economy;
- comprehend the reasons why firms grow in size; and
- understand the ways in which firms may grow.

Firm's costs

Shire horses replace tractors

The parks and gardens departments of many towns and cities are turning to shire horses as a replacement for tractors. They are mainly used to pull lawnmowers, trailers, flower-watering machines and street-cleaning equipment

The use of shire horses is not merely a gimmick aimed to boost tourism; they also make sound economic sense. Bracknell Forest Borough Council, in Berkshire, purchased two shire horses for £4,000 each as an alternative to spending more than £20,000 on a new tractor or lorry. While the upkeep of each horse can amount to around £150 per week, this still compares favourably with the running costs of tractors. There is no need to purchase a road fund licence, insurance premiums are lower, and each horse produces manure to the value of around £70 per year.

The horses are particularly economical when they are used for light jobs with frequent stops.

Understanding costs is of considerable importance to a firm. A firm needs to know whether it is operating efficiently. Rising costs can lead to lower profits. If increases in costs are passed on to the consumer in the form of higher prices, then sales may fall. Firms therefore must be able to control their costs and to understand the relationship between costs and output.

Short run and long run costs

In the field of production, we need to distinguish between that time period which economists refer to as the 'short run' and that which is known as the 'long run'. The concepts of **short run** and **long run** are not fixed in terms of weeks or years, but will vary from firm to firm and from industry to industry. In an industry such as mining, it may take several years to open up a new mine, hence the long run can be measured in years, but in other industries, it may take much less time to increase the scale of operations.

In the long run, all **factors of production**, such as land, buildings, workers and machinery, are variable. Hence the firm is able to vary all production inputs and increase the *scale* of its operations (see Unit 4). In the short run, however, at least one factor of production remains fixed and cannot be altered. It is not possible in the short run to increase the scale of the firm by, say, building a larger factory. The scale of the firm can only be altered in the long run. In the short run, therefore, a firm can only increase output within its existing scale, for example by employing more workers, or by getting more work out of existing workers. An increase in output in the short run therefore requires an increased input of some factors while other inputs remain fixed.

The extra output produced as a result of employing one more factor, for example, the increase in output from employing one more worker, is referred to as the **marginal product (MP)**. The firm will want to know how varying one input while another remains fixed affects efficiency; inputs might start to be combined in inefficient proportions. While one input remains fixed, this gives rise to the concept known as the **'law of diminishing marginal returns'**. This law states that if increasing quantities of a variable input are employed while another input remains fixed, there eventually comes a point at some level of output when the marginal return of the variable input will start to decrease.

The concept dates back to agricultural production. Consider agricultural workers working on a given piece of land, the **fixed factor**. It should be fairly evident that as the number of workers employed is increased, it will not be possible for each additional worker to increase output by the same amount. The piece of land will start to become overcrowded, or saturated, with too many workers being employed in proportion to the piece of land. The same principle can be applied to other types of production. For example, the demand for drinks in a pub is likely to be higher on Friday and Saturday evenings than on other nights of the week. The publican can cater for this by employing additional bar staff, but there remains the same number of beer pumps and drink dispensers, the fixed factor in this case. At times, therefore, the area behind the bar will be overcrowded and the bar staff will have to wait to gain access to the pumps, and thus will not be working as efficiently as they might.

The **average product (AP)** measures how much output, on average, each unit of the variable factor is producing. It is calculated by dividing total output by the number of units of the variable factor:

$$\text{Average product} = \frac{\text{Total output}}{\text{Quantity of the variable factor}}$$

Now consider Table 3.1, which illustrates the effect on output as a firm employs additional workers. As the firm employs extra workers, initially the marginal output of each worker increases, as there are some tasks that can be performed more efficiently with two or more workers. However, there eventually comes a point, at the fourth worker, when the output of additional workers starts to fall. Thus in Table 3.1, the firm experiences increasing marginal returns to labour over the first three workers, but diminishing returns to labour after the third worker. Using the data from the table, the marginal and average product curves may be plotted on a graph (see Figure 3.1). Note that the values for marginal product are plotted at intervals of $\frac{1}{2}$, $1\frac{1}{2}$, $2\frac{1}{2}$, and so on, along the horizontal axis. This is to show that it represents the extra output when increasing the number of workers from one quantity to another. Also you will see that when the *MP* curve is above the *AP* curve, the *AP* curve is rising, but once the *MP* curve falls below the *AP* curve, the *AP* curve starts to fall. This is because the 'average' is derived from all the 'marginal' outputs. If a marginal output is above the current average output, it will pull the average up, but if the marginal output is below the average, it will pull the average down. It therefore follows that the *MP* curve will intersect the *AP* curve at the maximum of the *AP*.

If the relationship between average and marginal product still causes some confusion, it can be further explained by considering an example that examines the heights of

Table 3.1: The effect on output of employing additional workers

Number of workers	Total output	Marginal output	Average output
		10	
1	10		10.0
		15	
2	25		12.5
		20	
3	45		15.0
		19	
4	64		16.0
		16	
5	80		16.0
		10	
6	90		15.0
		8	
7	98		14.0
		6	
8	104		13.0
		4	
9	108		12.0
		2	
10	110		11.0

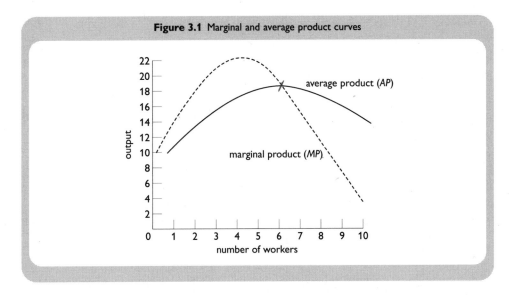

Figure 3.1 Marginal and average product curves

students in a particular class. Starting with the average height of all the students currently in the class, any additional student entering the class who is taller than the average would bring the average height up, while any student entering the class who is shorter than the average would lower the average height. A student who enters the class whose height is the same as the average height will not have any effect on the average. Thus, returning to the example of our firm, if the additional, or marginal, output of an extra worker is more than the average output, the average will rise, but if it is less than the average, the average will fall.

Short-run costs

Firms will incur many different costs in the production process. The relative importance of different costs will vary depending on the size of the firm and the industry it is operating in. However, a useful distinction can be made between fixed costs and variable costs.

Fixed costs

As some inputs remain fixed in the short run, the costs associated with these inputs will also remain fixed and will not vary as the level of output changes. **Fixed costs** will have to be met even if output is temporarily halted due, for example, to closure for holidays or a strike. Typical examples are rent, interest on a bank loan, and some administrative costs. These are also often referred to as overhead costs. As fixed costs are not related to output in the short run, they may be depicted graphically as a horizontal line, as shown in Figure 3.2.

In the long run however, as the firm is able to increase the scale of its operations – for example, by building a new factory – fixed costs will rise. A longer-term view of fixed costs is shown in Figure 3.3.

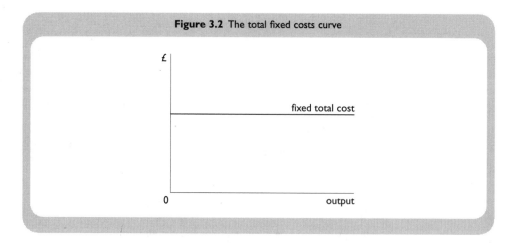

Figure 3.2 The total fixed costs curve

Average fixed cost or fixed cost per unit can be calculated by taking the total fixed cost and dividing by the number of units produced:

$$\text{Average fixed cost} = \frac{\text{Total fixed cost}}{\text{Output}}$$

For example, if a firm has fixed costs of £10,000 per month and produces 200 units per month, the average fixed cost is £50 per unit. As the level of output rises, the total fixed cost will be spread over a larger volume of output, and hence the average fixed cost will fall as output rises (see Figure 3.4). Thus, if this same firm were to increase output to 250 units per month, the average fixed cost would fall to £40 per unit.

However, if the firm were to increase the scale of its operations, the average fixed cost would rise again. In Figure 3.5, at an output level of 0Q, the firm has increased the scale of its operations and hence fixed costs have risen.

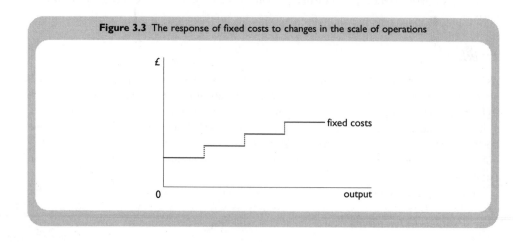

Figure 3.3 The response of fixed costs to changes in the scale of operations

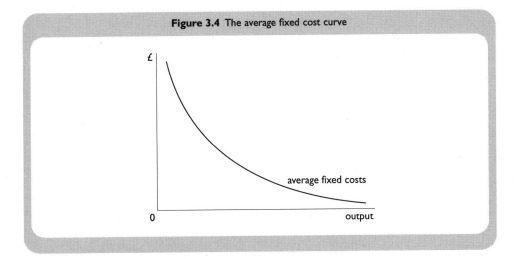

Figure 3.4 The average fixed cost curve

Variable costs

Variable costs are those costs which alter as output changes: the cost of materials is a typical example. Thus a furniture manufacturer which increases its production of tables will need more wood. A simple linear representation of variable costs is shown in Figure 3.6. This means that variable cost rises by the same amount as output increases, whatever the level of output. The variable cost graph starts from the origin, as when output is zero, no variable costs are incurred. However, due to the concept of diminishing marginal returns, discussed earlier in this unit, variable costs are usually shown as in Figure 3.7. During that output range when the firm is enjoying increasing marginal returns, variable costs will rise at a decreasing rate, but once the firm starts to experience diminishing marginal returns, variable costs will rise more rapidly.

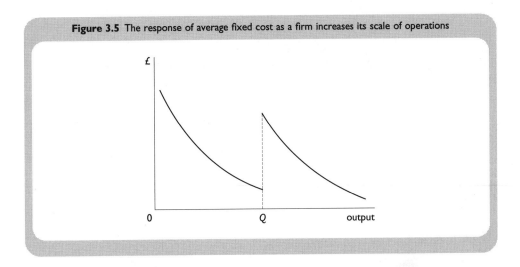

Figure 3.5 The response of average fixed cost as a firm increases its scale of operations

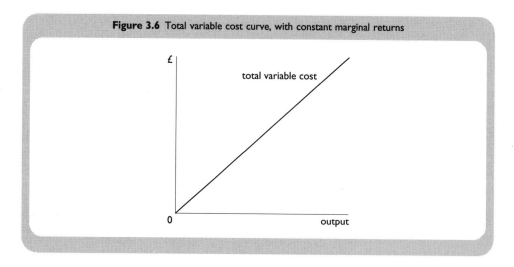

Figure 3.6 Total variable cost curve, with constant marginal returns

Average variable cost or variable cost per unit is calculated by dividing total variable cost by the number of units produced:

$$\text{Average variable cost} = \frac{\text{Total variable cost}}{\text{Output}}$$

Thus if the total variable costs incurred in producing 200 units are £30,000, then the average variable cost is £150 (i.e. £30,000/200). Again, due to diminishing marginal returns, average variable cost typically falls then rises, as shown in Figure 3.8, rather than remaining constant at all levels of output.

Total costs can therefore be subdivided into fixed and variable, and can be illustrated as shown in Figure 3.9.

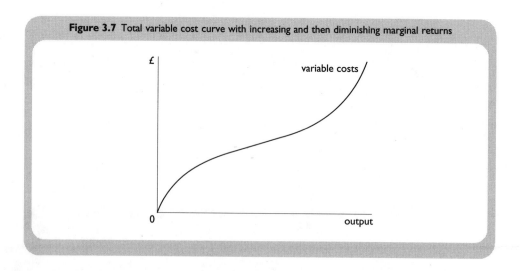

Figure 3.7 Total variable cost curve with increasing and then diminishing marginal returns

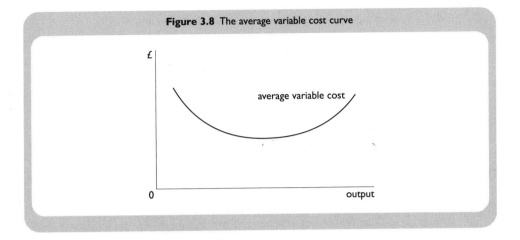

Figure 3.8 The average variable cost curve

It is important to realise however that this distinction is rather a simplification. Many costs incurred by firms may not fall neatly into either the fixed or variable category but may be **semi-variable costs** (e.g. administration costs). These may not vary directly with output, but may have a tendency to increase as output increases. Costs could therefore be represented on a scale, with one extreme being highly fixed, the other highly variable, with many costs falling somewhere in between the two categories (see Figure 3.10).

Average total cost can be calculated by dividing the total costs by the number of units produced, or by adding average fixed costs to average variable costs. The short-run average total cost curve is usually depicted as a U-shape. Initially it falls, as the average fixed cost falls steeply and the firm may also be experiencing increasing marginal returns.

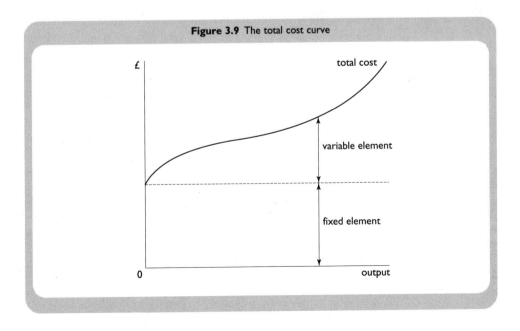

Figure 3.9 The total cost curve

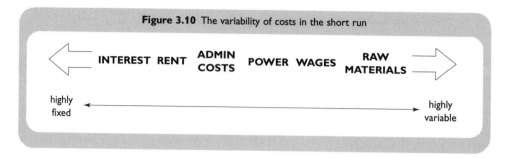

Figure 3.10 The variability of costs in the short run

However, eventually the increase in the average variable cost, due to diminishing marginal returns, overrides the fall in the average fixed cost and the average total cost starts to rise.

You should be able to realise that the vertical distance between the average variable cost and the average total cost is the average fixed cost. Thus, in Figure 3.11, at an output of 0Q, the average fixed cost can be measured in two ways (distance *x*). Note that as the average fixed cost approaches zero, so the average variable cost and the average total cost will converge.

The firm is at its most efficient at any given scale when the average total cost is at a minimum, an output of Q in Figure 3.12. This is referred to as the **optimum output**.

Marginal cost

The **marginal cost** is the extra cost incurred as a result of producing an additional unit of output. If total costs rise from £1,600 to £1,620 as a result of increasing output from 50 to 51, for example, the marginal cost of the 51st unit is £20. It may be that output can only be increased in stages; in this case, the marginal cost is the increase in total costs divided by the

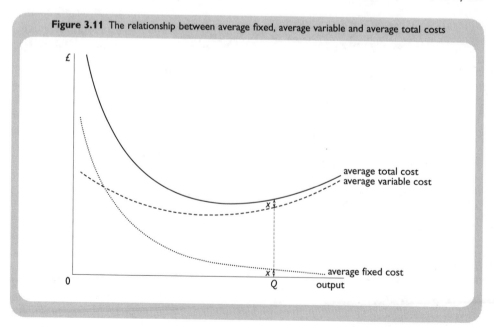

Figure 3.11 The relationship between average fixed, average variable and average total costs

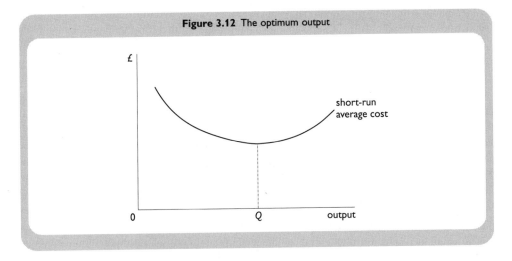

Figure 3.12 The optimum output

increase in output. For instance, if a firm increases production from 50,000 units to 51,000 units and as a result the total costs rise from £600,000 to £610,000, then the marginal cost in this output range is £10. The formula for marginal cost can be expressed as:

$$MC = \frac{\Delta TC}{\Delta Q}$$

where Δ represents 'the change in'.

As fixed costs remain constant as output increases, marginal costs are always marginal variable costs (unless an increase in output necessitates an increase in the scale of production and therefore an increase in fixed costs). Due to the concept of diminishing marginal returns, explained earlier in this unit, there comes a point when the marginal cost will rise, and the marginal cost curve is usually depicted as in Figure 3.13. Compare this with the marginal product curve shown in Figure 3.1. The marginal cost curve is the

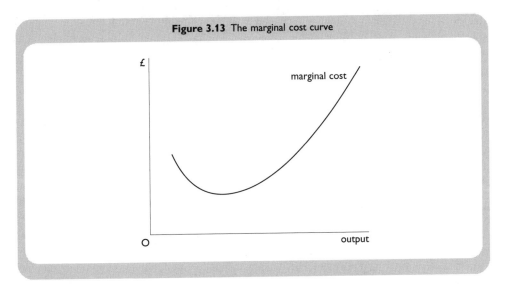

Figure 3.13 The marginal cost curve

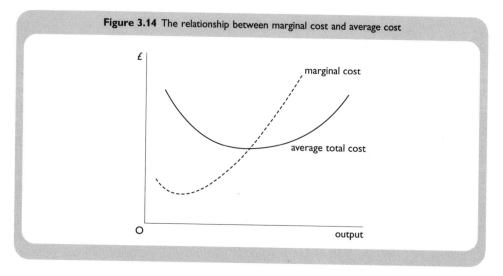

Figure 3.14 The relationship between marginal cost and average cost

inverse of the marginal product curve and the upturn in marginal cost arises because of the decline in marginal product.

Relationship between marginal cost and average cost

The marginal cost curve intersects the average variable and the average total cost curves at their minimum point. This is for the same reason that marginal product intersects average product at its maximum point, explained earlier in this unit. Provided the marginal, or 'extra', costs are below the average this will cause the average to fall, but once the marginal, or 'extra', costs are above the average, the average will rise. Figure 3.14 shows the relationship between the marginal cost and the average total cost curves, while Figure 3.15 depicts typical marginal cost, average variable cost, average fixed cost

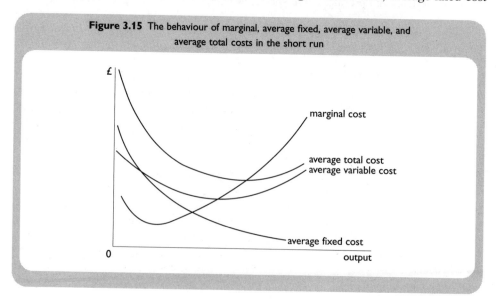

Figure 3.15 The behaviour of marginal, average fixed, average variable, and average total costs in the short run

and average total cost curves, demonstrating that the marginal cost curve intersects both the average total cost curve and the average variable cost curve at their lowest points.

Exercise

The table below represents the costs for various levels of output for a firm manufacturing dining-room chairs.

Output	Fixed cost	Variable cost	Total cost	Average fixed cost	Average variable cost	Average total cost	Marginal cost
0	10,000		–	–	–	–	
100		16,000					
200		22,000					
300		26,000					
400		38,000					
500		60,000					

1. Complete the table of costs.
2. Using graph paper, plot the average fixed cost, average variable cost, average total cost and marginal cost curves, with costs on the vertical axis and output on the horizontal axis. (Plot marginal cost at intervals of 50, 150, 250, 350, 450.)

Limitations of traditional theory

The analysis of costs so far presented involves a number of simplifying assumptions, and in real life, firms may find that their costs do not follow the pattern predicted by traditional economic theory. We have assumed, for example, that a firm is able to anticipate correctly the various costs associated with any level of output, but there exist many uncertainties; firms do not have perfect knowledge of their costs at different levels of output. We have assumed that it is possible for a firm to produce over a fairly wide range of outputs, making small variations to the amount produced. In reality, firms may not be quite so flexible; it may not be possible to make small adjustments to the number of factor inputs used. It is also assumed that the prices of inputs remain constant, but it may be that, for example, in order to employ more workers, higher wages would have to be offered. We have assumed that technology and the techniques of production remain constant. Changes in production methods, however, would result in a new set of cost curves.

The law of diminishing returns as used in traditional economic analysis implies that marginal cost and average variable cost will rise eventually as output increases. Evidence suggests that this is not always the case, and the response of these costs to changes in output may be as shown in Figure 3.16. This representation of marginal cost suggests that extra units of output may cost just as much to produce as previous units, up until the plant is operating at or near full capacity. Thus the marginal cost curve and the average variable cost curve may be horizontal over a wide range of output, and not the traditionally assumed U-shape.

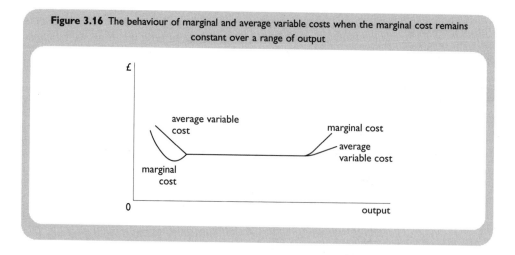

Figure 3.16 The behaviour of marginal and average variable costs when the marginal cost remains constant over a range of output

However, it is important for a firm to have some understanding as to how its costs are likely to react to changes in output, and traditional economic theory provides a basic tool of analysis.

Summary

In the short run at least one factor input remains fixed in supply and cannot be altered. The costs associated with this fixed input are termed 'fixed costs' and total fixed costs remain the same as output varies. Average fixed costs fall as output increases, as the total fixed cost is being spread over a greater number of units of output. Output in the short run can be increased by adding to the number of variable inputs employed. The costs associated with these inputs are termed 'variable costs'. As more is produced, variable costs will increase less rapidly at first since the firm enjoys increasing marginal returns, but a point will be reached when the firm starts to experience diminishing marginal returns and variable costs will start to rise more rapidly.

Review questions

1. Define and explain how you would calculate the following costs of a firm:
   (a) total cost;
   (b) total fixed cost;
   (c) total variable cost;
   (d) average fixed cost;
   (e) average variable cost;
   (f) average total cost;
   (g) marginal cost.

2. What is meant by the term 'semi-variable' cost?

3. Would you classify the following costs of a firm as fixed, variable, or semi-variable? Explain your answer.
   (a) electricity;
   (b) marketing costs;
   (c) insurance;
   (d) depreciation.

4. Identify an industry in which a high proportion of its costs are likely to be:
   (a) fixed costs;
   (b) variable costs.

5. (a) How does the determination of short-run costs differ from that of costs in the long run?
   (b) Explain why, in the short run, a firm is likely to experience diminishing marginal returns.
   (c) What is the implication of diminishing marginal returns for a firm's costs as it increases output?

6. The short run total cost curve of a firm is given by the formula:

   $$TC = 1500 + 20q^2$$

   where q equals the level of output.
   (a) What element of the formula represents the firm's variable costs?
   (b) How much are the firm's fixed costs?

7. The average fixed cost of producing two products in a workshop is £600 while the average variable cost is £140. For an output of three products, the average fixed cost is £400, while the average variable cost is £120. Calculate the marginal cost of increasing production from two to three products.

8. If an airline is flying half-empty planes from London to New York, what is the marginal cost of carrying extra passengers?

9. A carpenter manufactures chairs. His fixed costs are £250 per week, and his variable costs are £50 per chair. He has a contract to make ten chairs per week, sells them for £100 each, and thus makes £25 profit per chair. He is offered another contract to make an additional four chairs a week, for a price of £66 per chair. Should he accept this contract? Explain your answer.

Essay questions

1. Explain what is meant by 'diminishing returns' and why they arise. Illustrate the effect they have on a firm's cost curves? How might a firm try to avoid the problem of diminishing returns?

2. Explain and account for the response of the *average total cost, average variable cost* and *marginal cost* to changes in output, and the relationship between these costs.

Reading 3.1

Maggie's magic mirrors

Maggie makes magic mirrors (shaped to make you look thinner). The size of her workshop is fixed, but she can vary the number of workers employed, which varies the number of mirrors produced as follows:

Labour (no. of workers)	Output (no. of mirrors)
4	10
5	15
6	22
7	28
8	32
9	34

1. Calculate the average and marginal products, and draw them on a diagram.

2. What is the relationship between the average and marginal product curves at outputs less than 28 mirrors? Why?

3. What is the relationship between the average and marginal product curves at outputs above 28 mirrors? Why?

4. What would you expect to happen to output if Maggie employed more than 9 workers? Explain your answer.

Reading 3.2

The following data applies to a toymaker manufacturing rocking horses:

Units of output per week	Marginal cost
1	80
2	60
3	80
4	120
5	160
6	200

Fixed costs are £200 per week.

1. Calculate:
   (a) the total variable cost at each level of output;
   (b) the total cost at each level of output;
   (c) the average variable cost at each level of output; and
   (d) the average total cost at each level of output.

2. What is the optimum level of output?

3. If the rocking horses can be sold for £150 each, and assuming that he wishes to make a profit, between which levels of output each week should the toymaker aim to produce?

Size of firms

Stagecoach takes over Busways

The Scottish-based bus group Stagecoach is considering buying up the Newcastle-based company Busways, to add to their other acquisitions. They believe that acquiring other bus companies will enable them to become more profitable, due to the economies of scale that they would be able to enjoy in the purchase of fuel, insurance, spare parts and other supplies.

Companies cleared over high CD prices

The Monopolies and Mergers Commission has cleared UK companies of making excessive profits by charging too much for compact discs. Even though compact disc prices are considerably higher in the UK than in the US, the difference could largely be explained by the existence of economies of scale in the US, said the Commission's chairman.

An end to the large corporation?

Many large corporations are breaking up. This is not due to competitive pressures, or the effects of the recession, or even government regulation. It is being brought about by the companies themselves. Many managers believe that large companies are too bureaucratic and not sufficiently responsive to the market to be able to compete effectively. The fashion is therefore for restructuring, rationalisation and demergers. IBM provides a good example. From a position of having over 400,000 employees in the mid-1980s, it now has less than 250,000.

Throughout the twentieth century, there has been an increasing domination of markets by large business enterprises. The number and the size of large firms seem to be increasing. In the UK in the early 1900s, for example, the top 100 manufacturing firms accounted for 16 per cent of output; by 1950, this figure had risen to 22 per cent, and by 1975, it had reached 42 per cent. It has since fallen back, however, and in the 1990s, the largest 100 manufacturing firms accounted for approximately 36 per cent of output.

In Unit 3 we saw that when a firm operates on any given scale with at least one factor of input fixed, if it wishes to expand its output there comes a point where diminishing marginal returns start to occur and the cost of producing additional units increases. However, a firm can choose to operate on any particular scale and may choose to increase its scale of operations. In the first news item above, economies of scale are used as an explanation for taking over other firms, while the second item uses them to explain the existence of price differences. The third news item, however, suggests that large firms may be a thing of the past.

One reason for the dominance of large firms is the existence of 'economies of scale'. But before discussing why the size of a firm is important, it is necessary to explain what criterion we may use to define a 'large firm'. The size of a firm may be classified according to the following:

- size of workforce
- annual turnover (£m.)
- value of assets (£m.)
- market share (%)

It is necessary to have more than one criteria on which to judge the size of firm as, for example, a large capital intensive firm might have a relatively small workforce.

If we consider Table 4.1, which refers to three of the largest companies in Europe, BP is the largest of the three firms in terms of turnover, but EDF is the largest in terms of capital employed, while VW is the largest when using the number of employees as the measure.

Other criteria that could be used to judge the size of a firm include:

- The number of outlets or branches.
- The floorspace (square metres).
- The quantity of output (only when comparing firms in the same industry).
- The range and variety of products produced.

Table 4.1: Size of firm by turnover, capital and number of employees

	Turnover (£m.)	Capital employed (£m.)	Employees
British Petroleum	33,116	20,777	66,550
Electricite de France	21,596	45,016	118,146
Volkswagen	32,270	21,992	243,638

Source: The Times 1000 (1996).

Economies of scale

Economies of scale can be classified as **external economies** or **internal economies**. External economies of scale are the advantages that a firm gains from the expansion and size of the industry as a whole, rather than from the size of the firm: that is, the advantages accrue from outside influences. For example, a firm operating in a well-established industry (e.g. the construction industry) is likely to be able to take advantage of a labour force which already has skills specific to that industry (e.g. bricklaying), rather than having to devote resources to training its labour force itself. Support services which the firm requires (e.g. suppliers of building materials) are also likely to be well established.

Internal economies of scale are the advantages that a firm gains from increasing the scale of its production. These advantages result from the activities of the firm itself. In this unit, we are more concerned with internal economies of scale. If a firm is benefiting from economies of scale, it means that it becomes more efficient as the scale of production increases: that is, the cost per unit falls as the scale of production rises.

Consider the following numerical example. The total cost for a firm producing 100,000 units per year is £1m. The average cost per unit is therefore £10 each. The firm estimates that if it were to operate on a much larger scale, producing 200,000 units per year, then its total costs would rise to £1.8m. The cost per unit would therefore be reduced to £9 each: that is, it would be cheaper to produce goods on a larger scale. This is illustrated in Figure 4.1.

We now need to consider why the firm becomes more efficient as the scale of production rises. There are many different economies of scale, but they may be grouped into several categories.

Technical economies

Technical economies relate to the process of production:

- Indivisibilities: machinery and equipment often has to be purchased in fixed amounts or it has a given capacity. The firm which is producing a large output is more likely to fully utilise its machines, thus enabling the overhead costs to be

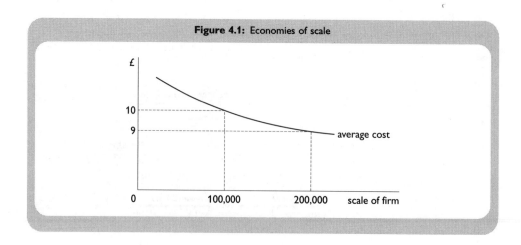

Figure 4.1: Economies of scale

spread. Firms with large outputs may even be able to use the equipment 24 hours a day through shift work. Smaller firms would still need to purchase the equipment, but it would be underused. For example, a building firm would have to purchase a cement mixer. A small builder with a limited amount of business would not get as much use out of the cement mixer as a larger firm which carried out more business. Thus more use of the cement mixer can be made by the larger firm, spreading its cost over more jobs.

- A larger output also makes it worthwhile for a firm to purchase more sophisticated and superior equipment which can help to bring down the cost per unit. Capital intensive methods of production may only become economic at high levels of output, as some machines are only worth using beyond a minimum level of output. For example, a large motor manufacturer would utilise a high proportion of automated robotic equipment.

- Specialisation of workforce: assuming that specialists are more efficient, thus reducing the cost of producing each unit, as the size of the workforce increases so does the scope for employing specialist workers. A small firm, for example, cannot afford to employ specialists in financial management.

- A large firm can set up a research department devoted to finding ways of reducing the costs of production.

Marketing economies

Marketing economies are advantages that accrue in the area of buying and selling:

- A firm which is producing a large output will require larger quantities of inputs, and will therefore qualify for bulk-buying discounts. Hence large firms can negotiate lower prices for their purchases of gas. Supermarkets such as Sainsbury or ASDA can sell more cheaply than a small corner shop as a result of obtaining their supplies more cheaply.

- The firm that purchases a large quantity of inputs will also be able to exert some influence over its supplier, dictating quality, specifications, and so forth, as it will be in a strong bargaining position. For example, Marks & Spencer exerts great pressure on its suppliers, forcing down prices and insisting on certain conditions and quality of goods, with the threat of withdrawing an order if these conditions are not met.

- The employment of specialist buyers, who can negotiate the best deals and buy at the best times at the best prices.

- The employment of specialist sales staff.

- The cost of advertising can be spread over many units, reducing the advertising cost per unit to a minimum. A firm producing several brands can market goods together, resulting in little additional cost to the marketing of a single product.

- The larger firm can set up a market research department, looking, for example, into consumer spending patterns. The smaller firm would not be able to devote resources to a market research department.

- A large output should make it possible to make more economical use of transport, as it is more likely that the firm can ensure full loads. A large firm may even set up its own transport and distribution fleet, which may be a cost saving.

Financial economies

- Larger firms can obtain loans more easily and at preferential rates of interest, as they have greater reserves and may be viewed as less risk by potential lenders. If the smaller firm is perceived to be a greater risk, the lender will not be so willing to grant the loan, or will require a higher rate of interest to compensate for the increased risk. Thus a small house builder will find it more difficult to borrow than a large firm such as Tarmac or Wimpey, and it will have to pay higher rates of interest.
- Raising finance through a share issue. The stock market is not generally a source of finance for the smaller firm.
- The use of retained profits as a source of finance.

Managerial economies

- The larger firm has the scope to employ specialist managers.
- As the size of a firm increases, the number of managers required will probably not increase in the same proportion. A firm increasing output by 20 per cent may not need any more managers, so average cost will fall.
- A larger firm may be in a better position to attract and retain the best staff.

Risk-bearing economies

- Diversification of markets: if a firm has a large output, it may be in a position to sell to a range of different customers in a wide variety of markets. Therefore, if demand drops in one market, it still has sales elsewhere to fall back on. For instance, in the opening commentary at the start of this unit, Stagecoach, a Perth-based bus group, has expanded into the Newcastle area, widening the geographical range of its operations.
- Diversification of products: likewise, the larger firm is in a better position to produce a range of different products, again spreading risks if demand falls for one particular product, since it has other products to fall back on.
- The larger firm can employ a research department to minimise risks.

Administrative economies

- A larger firm can enjoy advantages in the area of administration, for example by utilising the best computerised systems.

The existence of economies of scale means that in the long term, as the firm increases its scale of operations, the average cost of production falls. Each individual scale of the firm

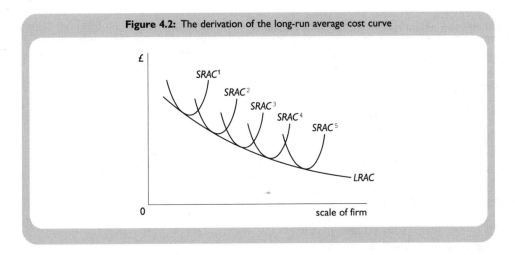

Figure 4.2: The derivation of the long-run average cost curve

will still be subject to diminishing returns (see Unit 3) and will have its own U-shaped short-run average cost curve (*SRAC*), but due to economies of scale, as the scale of the firm increases, each successive *SRAC* will not only be to the right but also below the previous *SRAC*. The **long-run average cost curve** (*LRAC*) is derived from tracing the path of the *SRAC* curves. Figure 4.2 shows five alternative scales of operation, each with its own *SRAC* curve.

Minimum efficient scale

A firm cannot expect always to achieve economies of scale when it expands. There are limits, and it is likely that the firm will eventually reach a scale of production where a further increase in its size does not produce any reduction in the average cost per unit. This scale of production is known as the **minimum efficient scale** (*MES*) and can be identified in Figure 4.3 as that point at which the *LRAC* first becomes horizontal.

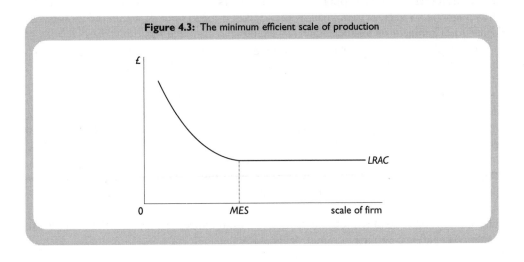

Figure 4.3: The minimum efficient scale of production

Table 4.2: Minimum efficient scale for plants in various industries

Industry	MES	MES as a % of UK output	MES as a % of EC output	% increase in costs at $\frac{1}{3}$ MES
Refrigerators	1.2m. units per year	85.0	11.0	6.5
Steel	12m. tons per year	72.0	10.0	10.0
Washing machines	800,000 units per year	57.0	10.0	7.5
TV sets	1.2m. sets per year	40.0	9.0	15.0
Cigarettes	36bn per year	24.0	6.0	2.2
Beer	4.5m. barrels per year	12.0	3.0	5.0
Paint	10m. gallons per year	7.0	2.0	4.4
Shoes	4,000 pairs per week	0.3	0.03	1.5

Source: C. Pratten, *A Survey of the Economies of Scale in Research on the Costs of Non-Europe* (1988), vol. 2, pp. 2.76–2.80, Office for Official Publications of the European Community.

The *MES* for firms will differ according to the industry in which they operate. Table 4.2 shows estimates of the *MES* for plants in various industries, and expressed as a percentage of both UK and EC output. In some industries (e.g. shoe manufacturing), the *MES* is very small compared with the total output of the industry. This is because economies of scale are not so evident in an industry such as shoes, and any which do exist are exhausted when a firm reaches a size which is still only a tiny percentage of UK or EC output, allowing numerous firms to operate within the market. In other industries, however, the *MES* might be so large as to only allow one or two firms to operate within the industry. In order for a refrigerator manufacturer, for example, to achieve full economies of scale, it would need to produce an output that represents 85 per cent of total UK output, which means that there is not room for more than one firm to achieve maximum economies of scale.

When the *MES* is a very high proportion of UK output, say, approaching 100 per cent, and there can only be one firm operating if it is to achieve production at or near the lowest possible cost, such situations are known as a **natural monopoly**. A natural monopoly is an industry which is characterised by a high proportion of fixed costs and low marginal costs, and where competition would be wasteful and inefficient due to duplication of substantial fixed overhead costs. Industries such as electricity and water fall into this category. Natural monopolies will be discussed in more depth in Unit 9. Alternatively, if there is more than one firm operating in an industry where the *MES* is a high proportion of total output, the firms might have to seek overseas markets if they are each to operate around the minimum efficient scale.

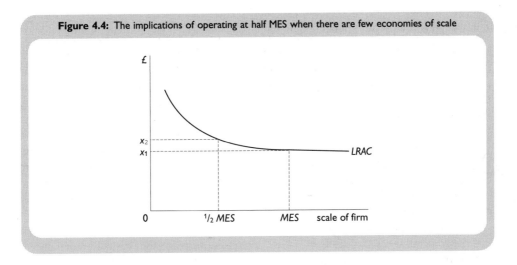

Figure 4.4: The implications of operating at half MES when there are few economies of scale

Table 4.2 also shows the percentage increase in costs when operating below the *MES*. In some industries, average costs may not be significantly higher, even when the firm is operating below the *MES*. Thus, in the case of the refrigerators, although the *MES* is 85 per cent of UK output, permitting only one firm to achieve maximum economies of scale, costs are only 6.5 per cent higher if a manufacturer operates at an output which is one-third of the minimum efficient scale, thus allowing several firms to operate in the industry. But for a firm manufacturing TV sets, if it operates at one-third of the *MES* for the industry, it faces an increase in costs of 15 per cent. These situations are illustrated in Figures 4.4 and 4.5. In Figure 4.4, a firm producing at *MES* would have costs of x_1 while a firm producing at half this output would face costs of x_2, not much higher. However in Figure 4.5, a firm producing at *MES* would have costs of x_3, while in this industry, a firm producing at half *MES* would have costs of x_4, substantially higher.

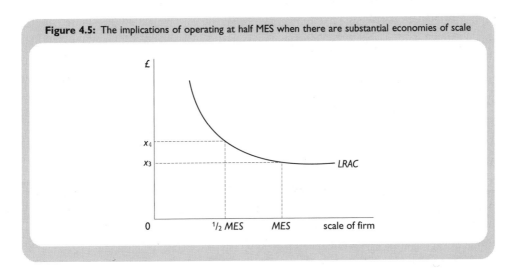

Figure 4.5: The implications of operating at half MES when there are substantial economies of scale

Diseconomies of scale

Is it possible for a firm to grow too large? The firm may reach a situation where increasing the scale of operations results in a decrease in efficiency: that is, the cost per unit begins to rise as the scale of the firm increases. When this occurs, the firm is said to be experiencing **diseconomies of scale** and this helps to explain why many large firms are being dismantled, as described in one of the commentaries at the start of this unit.

A possible scenario is shown in Figure 4.6, where initially, as the firm increases the scale of its operations, it experiences economies of scale. There is then a range of outputs at which, having reached the minimum efficient scale, the average cost per unit remains fairly constant. Having reached the size represented by point Q, however, the firm starts to become less efficient as it continues to increase its size and the long-run average cost curve (*LRAC*) starts to rise.

Diseconomies of scale do *not* usually arise for technical reasons: these aspects are invariably positive as the scale of a firm increases. Instead, they usually arise due to the problems associated with managing and coordinating a large workforce. Eventually, these problems and drawbacks might start to outweigh the technical economies gained from operating on a larger scale and the net result will be a decrease in efficiency and a rise in the *LRAC*. Some examples of such problems are as follows:

- It is more difficult to ensure good communication in a larger firm – possibly due to the fact that the firm is geographically dispersed or simply because of the large number of employees, resulting in excessively long chains of communication. Communication breakdown will inevitably result in inefficiency.

- Similarly, as the size of the workforce increases, control becomes more problematic. It may be increasingly difficult to check that all the workers are doing exactly what they should be doing.

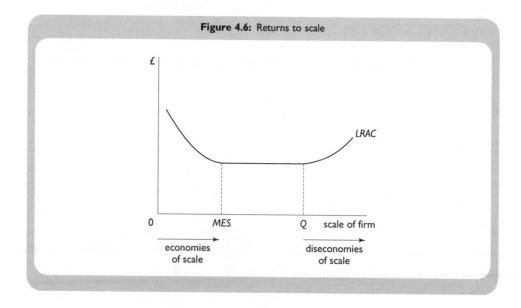

Figure 4.6: Returns to scale

● A large firm will inevitably have to be divided up into departments. An added danger here is that a department will pursue its own goals and objectives, instead of those of the company. There may be a lack of coordination and even conflict between departments, adding to the inefficiency.

● A firm employing many workers may find that the workers find it difficult to identify with the firm, becoming alienated and suffering from a lack of morale. The poorer labour relations may lead to an increase in industrial stoppages, absentee rates, lateness, petty theft or hostility at work. All this will add to costs and reduce efficiency.

For these reasons, large firms may be less efficient than small ones, particularly in those industries where the product is individualised and economies of scale are limited: in decorating, or in hairdressing, for example, where each haircut is a separate job and cannot be mechanised.

Exercise

At a board meeting of Balshaw's Bearings, the production manager argued that if the firm were to expand and increase the scale of its operations by 50 per cent, it would benefit from technical, marketing, financial and managerial economies. This would then enable the firm to reduce its prices, giving it a competitive advantage and enabling it to increase profits. However, the sales manager urged caution. She argued that if the firm were to increase output by 50 per cent, the market would become saturated. There was also the danger that the firm might experience diseconomies of scale, which would reduce profitability. 'It is important', she said, 'that we do not expand beyond our optimum size.'

1. Give two examples of each of the economies of scale mentioned by the production manager.

2. What does the sales manager mean by the phrase 'the market would become saturated'?

3. Explain the concept of diseconomies of scale and provide four reasons why these might occur.

4. What is meant by the 'optimum' scale of production?

Economies of scope

Although economies of scale are an important concept and give large firms a competitive edge by lowering the average cost of production, in recent years attention has shifted to the concept known as the **economies of scope**.

In order to benefit from the economies of large-scale production, and to reduce the cost and therefore the price of the product, it was traditionally necessary to set up long production runs on equipment usually dedicated to just one product, thus mass producing fairly standardised products which sometimes had a reputation for quality defects. Henry Ford was able to reduce the price of a car significantly through mass production of the

Model T, although the product was standardised even to the extent that the only colour available was black. Changes in the market, however, have meant that this is no longer necessarily the best approach for a firm to adopt if it wishes to gain a competitive edge. The rapid pace of technology has meant that products now tend to have shorter life spans; they become obsolete more quickly. Consumers, meanwhile, have started to demand high-quality products and are no longer happy to accept mass-produced, standardised goods (e.g. in the design of clothes).

In order to be competitive, therefore, firms must be able to respond quickly to market changes, providing what the customer wants at the required quality. They have to have the 'scope' to be able to switch production from one product to another in response to changes in market demand, and can no longer afford simply to churn out vast quantities of a standardised product. Instead, they must be able to produce several different outputs from a common set of resources. For example, a car manufacturer may produce a range of models using common components and even the same production line. New technologies have helped firms to do this. Flexible manufacturing systems (FMS), utilising computer-aided design (CAD) and computer-aided manufacturing (CAM) have provided firms with much greater flexibility, enabling them quickly to swap production from one product to another. This is not to say that economies of scale are no longer important, as producing goods on a large scale can still help to bring down the average cost of production. Nevertheless, cost advantages can also be gained from economies of scope, where a firm is able to produce a range of products from the same set of resources. This does, however, lead to considerable uncertainty for the firm. Should it mass produce in order to take advantage of economies of scale, or should it maintain its flexibility?

The small firm sector

Despite the advantages to be gained from producing goods on a large scale, there still remain many small firms operating within the economy. How do these small firms manage to survive alongside their larger competitors, and what role and contribution can they make to the economy?

In the 1960s, 'Big is Beautiful' seemed to be the philosophy when considering the optimum size of firms, with small firms widely regarded as being inefficient. However, by the 1970s, concern was starting to be expressed at the increasing domination of big business and the decline of the small firm. Small firms appeared to play a lesser role in the UK than in comparable countries, with a smaller proportion of the workforce employed in the small firm sector.

Figure 4.7 shows that small and medium-sized firms make a smaller contribution to gross domestic product (GDP) in the UK than do such firms in competing countries, while Table 4.3 demonstrates that although firms with under 100 employees make up 96 per cent of the total number of firms in the manufacturing sector, they employ only 27 per cent of the workforce in this sector.

Could the size of the small firm sector have been a contributory factor to the relatively poor economic performance of the UK? Perhaps a strong small firm sector is an important requirement for a successful economy.

As a result of this concern, the Bolton Committee was set up in 1971 to consider the role of small firms in the national economy. Initially, their brief was to investigate small

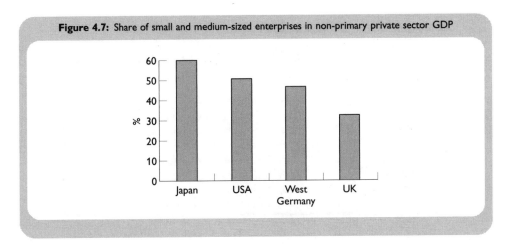

Figure 4.7: Share of small and medium-sized enterprises in non-primary private sector GDP

firms defined as those having less than 200 employees, but they found this definition inadequate. The definition of a small firm depends on which industry it is in. For example, a manufacturing firm employing 150 workers might be regarded as a small enterprise, but a construction firm employing the same number would not. Table 4.4 shows the different classifications used by the Bolton Committee for defining a small firm. Note that the figures for turnover need to be adjusted to account for the inflation that has occurred since the *Bolton Report* was published.

The Bolton Committee also suggested that there were three main characteristics of a small firm:

1. It should have a relatively small share of the market.

2. It should be managed by its owners in a personalised way and not through the medium of a formalised management structure.

3. It should be independent, so that its owner-managers are free from outside control when taking their decisions.

Table 4.3: Number of legal units in UK manufacturing, 1994

Employment size band	Number of units	%	Total employment (000s)	%
1–9	114,293	72.9	293.0	5.5
10–19	16,827	10.7	232.4	4.4
20–49	14,235	9.1	481.3	9.1
50–99	5,365	3.4	423.5	8.0
100–199	2,965	1.9	492.4	9.3
200–499	1,935	1.2	720.8	13.6
500–999	615	0.4	578.0	10.9
1000+	450	0.3	2085.4	39.2

Source: Business Monitor PA 1003.

Table 4.4: Bolton Committee definitions of a small firm

Industry	Definition
Manufacturing	200 employees or less
Construction	25 employees or less
Mining/quarrying	25 employees of less
Retailing	Turnover of £50,000 or less
Wholesale trades	Turnover of £200,000 or less
Motor trades	Turnover of £100,000 or less
Miscellaneous services	Turnover £50,000 or less
Road transport	5 vehicles or less
Catering	All establishments, excluding multiples and brewery managed houses

Source: Bolton Committee Report (1971).

The Bolton Committee concluded that the small firm sector was in a state of decline, but argued that it had an important role to play in the economy. The committee therefore recommended action by the government.

The role of small firms

The contribution that small firms can make to the economy is wide and varied:

- **Job creation** Small firms are an important source of employment, particularly during a period of time when larger firms are rationalising and shedding labour.

- **Competition** Small firms help to maintain a competitive environment by providing an alternative source of supply. They are a check on the monopoly power of large firms.

- **Flexibility** Small firms tend to be far more flexible. They are able to take decisions more quickly, due to the lack of a bureaucratic management structure and can thus respond much more quickly to market changes.

- **Quality of service** The smaller firm is often able to provide a much more personalised service. Small firms therefore have an important role to play in service industries, where the scope for economies of scale is not so great.

- **Customised products** Exclusive, one-off products are usually produced by the smaller firms, supplying niche markets. Larger firms are generally only interested in long production runs.

- **Innovation** Although research and development is normally associated with the larger firm, many smaller firms have a good record in the area of innovation, and often get a better return for their money invested. For example, Microsoft developed MS-DOS when it was a small firm.

- **A training ground for managers** Small firms provide a seed-bed for entrepreneurs, enabling managers to gain experience in a range of managerial functions.

- **Foreign trade** Small firms can help contribute to Britain's balance of trade position. Many have a good export record, the Queen's Award for Exports often being given to the smaller firm.
- **Suppliers** Larger firms often rely on smaller firms as suppliers of components, or use them as subcontractors for work of a specialist nature or if they are faced with a heavy demand.
- **Potential for growth** Small firms may grow into larger ones (e.g. Body Shop).

Exercise

Select a small business with which you are familiar.

1. Identify any competitive advantages that this business might have over its larger rivals.
2. What drawbacks might the firm face as a result of its size?
3. What measures could the government take to assist this particular firm?

From the 1970s onwards, there has been a trend in the UK for the number of small businesses to rise. There are several factors which might have contributed to the rising number of small firms, as follows:

- **De-industrialisation** The UK economy is going through a period of 'de-industrialisation'. There has been a decline in manufacturing industries and a relative rise in the service sector. Large firms are more likely to be found in manufacturing, while smaller firms are more suited to service industries. Thus it follows that de-industrialisation is likely to result in an increase in the number of small firms. The closure and rationalisation of many large firms has resulted in redundancies and reduced employment opportunities in these establishments. Therefore, many people have turned to setting up their own business as an alternative source of employment, making use of redundancy payments to help set up the business. At the same time, there has been an increase in the popularity of business units which are suited to the small business, such as franchises, worker cooperatives and management buy-outs.
- **Government support** The government in recent years has also promoted the growth of the small firm, which it sees as an important source of employment and a means of regenerating inner-city areas and depressed regions. In addition to offering a whole range of advisory and financial packages, examples of which are shown in Table 4.5, policies such as deregulation and the increased contracting-out of services have provided many opportunities for the small firm.
- **European Union** The European Union is also committed to promoting a favourable environment for small firms, acknowledging that small and medium-sized firms have an important role to play in helping to realise the benefits of the Single European Market.

Table 4.5: Examples of government schemes to assist small firms

Scheme	Nature of assistance
Business Start-Up	Grants offered to unemployed individuals to start their own business
Loan Guarantee Scheme	Up to 70 per cent of a loan made by a bank to a small business is guaranteed by the government, for a premium payable by the firm
Enterprise Initiative Scheme	Income tax relief for investors who invest in smaller companies
Unlisted securities market (USM)	Gives smaller companies access to share capital on the Stock Market without having to incur the costs of a full listing
Lower corporation tax	Smaller companies pay a lower rate of corporation tax
Training and Enterprise Councils (TECs)	Agencies, organised on a local basis, which provide training, advice and finance for smaller businesses

- **More financial support** Banks now take a more positive attitude towards the small firm, with high-street banks more willing to give advice to and arrange loans for the small business than they were in previous years.

- **Niche markets** We saw in addition, when discussing 'economies of scope', that there is some evidence to suggest that consumers are no longer content with standardised, mass-produced items but are looking for more exclusivity. This too provides opportunities for smaller businesses which can establish themselves as suppliers to niche markets.

- **Enterprise culture** It is also believed by many that the 1980s saw the development of an 'enterprise culture', whereby there was a marked change in attitudes and people were more keen to work for themselves. Figure 4.8 shows the rise that has occurred in the percentage of the UK workforce which are self-employed.

Problems faced by small firms

Despite the range of government schemes to assist small firms, and despite the apparent rise in the small-firm sector, small firms are still faced with a great many difficulties. Evidence seems to suggest that a high proportion of small firms collapse within the first two or three years of being set up. Thus, although there are many new businesses being created, there are also many that are closing, creating a 'throughput' rather than an increase in the number of small firms. There have been over one hundred government schemes introduced since 1979 aimed at helping the small firm, but many of these have been complex and cumbersome, and critics claim that small firms still face too much bureaucratic regulation. Recent government policy has concentrated on deregulation and

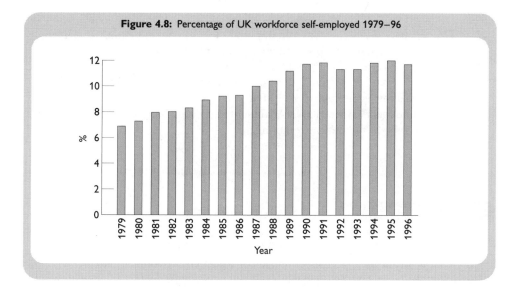

Figure 4.8: Percentage of UK workforce self-employed 1979–96

reducing the amount of red-tape that small firms have to deal with, but in 1996, the NatWest's quarterly small-business opinion survey found that government regulations and the associated paperwork were still regarded as the most serious problems facing small firms.

Small firms are also faced with other problems. For example:

- Lack of specialist knowledge and skills.
- They still rely heavily on bank lending as a source of finance and therefore suffer greatly if there is a restriction placed on bank lending or a rise in interest rates.
- Their limited financial resources also means that late payment can cause serious cash-flow problems, leading to closure.
- Small firms also suffer disproportionately during a recession, as they often rely on only one product and do not have the advantages of a diversified output or diversified markets.
- They also tend to be found in industries which are highly saturated and therefore highly competitive, such as window cleaning and car repair, making survival that much more difficult.

Summary

Large firms, through their use of economies of scale, have many competitive advantages over small firms. They are able to bring down the average cost of production and therefore the price. In some industries, the minimum efficient scale is such that only one or two firms are able to operate. Large firms may, however, experience diseconomies of scale, reducing their efficiency, and changes in the market have meant that large firms now need to be far more flexible. Since the 1970s there has been a renewed interest in the role of small firms. ▷

It is now recognised that they have an important role to play in helping to maintain an efficient economy and the government has introduced a wide range of measures to encourage their growth and development. However, small firms still face many problems. Perhaps what is needed most to enable the small-firm sector to flourish is a generally healthy economic climate, but even given this, the small-firm sector would have to expand by a remarkable amount in order to help reduce the levels of unemployment by any significant amount.

Review questions

1. What criteria can be used for measuring the size of a firm?

2. What is meant by 'external economies of scale'? Give two examples.

3. What is meant by 'internal economies of scale'? Give two examples of each of the following:
   (a) technical economies
   (b) marketing economies;
   (c) financial economies;
   (d) managerial economies;
   (e) risk-bearing economies.

4. How is the long-run average cost curve derived?

5. What is meant by 'minimum efficient scale' (*MES*)?

6. What happens when a firm experiences 'diseconomies of scale'?

7. Give four reasons that could account for diseconomies of scale arising.

8. Explain what is meant by 'economies of scope'.

9. How might one define a small firm?

10. Outline five contributions that small firms can make to the economy.

11. Identify five reasons why the number of small firms might have increased over the past twenty years.

12. Outline the problems that are specifically faced by small firms.

Essay questions

1. What is meant by the concept of 'economies of scale'? Explain, with the use of examples, why they may arise. What factors might limit the size and growth of a firm?

2. Why is the average size of firms *large* in some industries, but *small* in others?

Reading 4.1

The manufacture of vehicles can be divided into a number of distinct operations, each with its own optimum scale (see Table 4.6). However, as well as technical economies of scale, opportunities for lowering unit costs also stem from scale economies in advertising, sales, finance, and research and development (see Table 4.7).

Table 4.6: Optimum scale in various car making activities

Activity	Output per year (volume)
Casting of engine block	1,000,000
Casting of various other parts	100,000–750,000
Power train (engine, transmission, etc.) machining and assembly	600,000
Pressing of various panels	1–2,000,000
Paint shop	250,000
Final assembly	250,000

Table 4.7: Non-technical economies of the firm

Activity	Optimum output per year (cars)
Advertising	1,000,000
Sales	2,000000
Finance	2,500,000
Research and development	5,000,000

Where technical economies of scale are concerned and in terms of similar units, the most efficient car firm would, for instance, need to produce between one and two million units using common body panels. In practice, no such volumes per model are achieved anywhere, but firms try to approach the optimum by using as many common panels as possible over a range of vehicles. Similarly, one type of engine is used over a variety of models. Another approach is for firms to collaborate and cooperate, so that the different manufacturers use the same basic components. This turns an 'internal' into an 'external' economy of scale. Table 4.7 demonstrates why so many different firms try to collaborate on marketing, and on research and development.

At present it is felt that technological change may reduce the optimum size of car firms. However, so far, this merely means that new flexible production equipment in assembly plants facilitates the manufacture of a wide range of models on the same assembly line. This reduces the model-specific optimum, but not the overall assembly optimum. Indeed, robots can actually increase the latter. In addition, new types of equipment, that can be used over a variety of models and over time, reduce the fixed cost per model. This reduces the numbers of a particular car that have to be made to recoup tooling and development costs. Similarly, the use of computer-aided design (CAD) might reduce the R&D costs per car. However, in other areas of technical and non-technical activity, the optimum has not yet been reduced by new technology. ▷

Table 4.8: Gains from scale (cars)

Output per year	Index of unit average costs (cars)
100,000	100
250,000	83
500,000	74
1,000,000	70
2,000,000	66

Table 4.9: Gains from scale (commercial vehicles)

Output per year	Index of unit average costs (commercial vehicles)
1,000	150
10,000	132
25,000	120
50,000	110
100,000	100
200,000	85

The gains from scale in car and truck manufacture are considerable and are as shown in Tables 4.8 and 4.9. The figures in these tables suggest that the long-run average cost curve for the motor industry is L-shaped, rather than U-shaped. Despite labour relations problems in some large firms, there are no overall diseconomies of scale. Table 4.9 suggests that the minimum efficient scale (*MES*) for truck production is way beyond the present scale of any truck manufacturer. In the case of cars, there are a number of firms which exceed 2 million units, beyond which point, cost reductions seem limited. Table 4.7 however, shows that the research and development optimum is much greater than 2 million units. Hence the interest shown by all large car manufacturers in joint ventures geared to cost sharing, and therefore cost savings.

Source: Adapted from Garel Rhys, 'Competition in the Car Industry', in Brian Atkinson (ed.) *Developments in Economics*, vol. 9 (1993), Causeway Press.

Questions

1. What technical economies of scale might arise in car manufacturing?

2. Identify the external economies of scale that might occur in the car industry.

3. In view of the considerable economies of scale which exist in the car industry, how do you account for the continued existence of relatively small car firms?

4. Why do you think that the minimum efficient scale for truck production is well beyond the present scale of any truck manufacturer?

How firms grow

Cadbury-Schweppes expands in North American markets

In January 1995, Cadbury-Schweppes entered the large North American soft drinks market by taking over the Dr Pepper group. Cadbury-Schweppes previously supplied only 3.5 per cent of the North American market but the takeover deal increased that share to 15 per cent, and placed them in third position behind Coca-Cola and Pepsi. Cadbury had to borrow extensively to finance the takeover, which is likely to result in job losses and plant closures, but the Chairman, Dominic Cadbury, believes that it was an important strategic move. The soft drinks market has shown signs of moving away from cola products and towards the type of brands that Dr Pepper produces. Dr Pepper itself is the fourth most popular brand in the US, while another of its brands, 7-Up, is the eighth most popular.

Later the same year, Cadbury also made a bid for Canada's largest chocolate bar producer, Neilson, strengthening its position as the fourth largest producer of confectionery products in the world. Neilson produces seven of the top twenty brands in Canada.

Why was Cadbury Schweppes so keen to expand? The idea that growth might be a principal objective for a firm was introduced in Unit 1. Theorists such as Baumol, Marris and Williamson have suggested that growth may even have replaced profit maximisation as the main objective of firms, as the salaries, status, power and job security of managers are closely linked to the growth and size of the firm. Growth is also important for a firm as it enables it to take advantage of the economies of large-scale production which help to lower costs and therefore increase profit (see Unit 4). As a firm grows it should also be able to increase its market power as its share of the market increases, leading to a degree of monopoly power and again an increase in profits. Cadbury's bid for Dr Pepper increases its share of the US market from 3.5 per cent to 15 per cent. Growth is also seen as a strategy for achieving security. As a firm grows and diversifies, this spreads its risks.

Methods of growth

Firms can grow through internal expansion, or through external expansion by takeover or merger.

Internal expansion

Firms can grow simply through internal growth and development, independent of any other firm. A firm could, over time, gradually build up its resources of plant and machinery, and increase its labour force. This would enable it to increase its production and sales of existing products, or diversify its output to produce a wider range of goods. Internal growth can be financed by ploughing back profits, by external borrowing or by share issue. This is the way in which many firms have grown: the Ford Motor Company started in a small workshop and gradually grew; Marks & Spencer started life as a market stall; Amstrad experienced rapid internal growth through producing competitively priced personal computers.

Internal expansion, however, is usually a relatively slow method of achieving growth; there are limits to the amount of finance a firm can acquire. It also takes time to increase market share, though it is easier to grow if the firm is operating in a market which is rapidly expanding.

External expansion

Because of the drawbacks associated with internal expansion, most of the large firms that exist today have reached their present size through merger, takeover or acquisition of other firms: that is, the combination of two or more firms into one. A 'merger' is usually where firms agree to join, whereas a takeover is where one firm acquires a controlling interest in another firm. Sometimes the distinction between the two is clear – for example, in a situation where an acquired firm has put up a fight to try to prevent the merger – but often it is difficult to distinguish between the two. For our purposes here, there is little difference, and either may be referred to as an acquisition. This enables a rapid, even instantaneous increase in size, and gives a firm immediate access to resources that it might currently be lacking, for example managerial expertise, new technology or recognised brand names. Thus Nestlé's acquisition of Rowntree enabled them to gain ownership of

Table 5.1: Mergers and takeovers in the UK 1980–95

	Number (annual average)
1981–85	481
1986–90	1197
1991–95	528

brand names such as Kit Kat, Polo and Aero. The problems occur, however, in the integration of two or more organisations that have different identities, different cultures and different values, which can lead to conflict and hostility. Nevertheless, external growth has been a very prominent feature of industry, both in the UK and in the European Union.

Merger activity often goes in phases, as demonstrated in Table 5.1. There may be little merger activity at times, only to be followed by a period of many takeovers and mergers. The late 1980s was a period when there was a great deal of merger activity. This coincided with a period of growth in the economy, and as this growth slowed down as we moved into the 1990s, so merger activity also lessened.

It is possible to identify different forms of merger, depending on the nature of the business of the two firms coming together. The categories which follow may also be applied to internal growth.

Horizontal merger

A **horizontal merger** occurs when two firms which are in the same industry and at the same stage of production merge together (see Figure 5.1). For example, one brewery may take over another brewery, or two building societies may merge. BMW's takeover of Rover and Ford's acquisition of Jaguar are two examples of horizontal merger that have occurred in the motor industry. Most the mergers which take place are of this type (see Table 5.2). Sometimes the firms may still keep their separate identities, despite joining together. Thus when the Dixons electrical retail chain took over Currys, they retained both the Dixons name and Currys name.

The reason for a merger of this type is to enable the firm to take advantage of economies of scale, which were identified in Unit 4. In particular, the firm will find that marketing and R&D activities are more cost effective. A horizontal merger will also eliminate some of the competition, and provides an instant increase in market share, which can be of particular importance if the market demand for a product is falling: by taking over a competitor, the firm is able to maintain its level of sales. It also gives the firm more control over the market and perhaps a degree of monopoly power. Claims are often

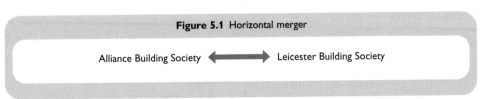

Figure 5.1 Horizontal merger

Alliance Building Society ⟷ Leicester Building Society

Table 5.2: Percentage of proposed mergers in the UK (yearly average)

	1965-69	1970-77	1978-84	1985-89	1990-94
Horizontal	82	71	62	62	87
Vertical	6	6	6	3	4
Conglomerate	12	23	32	35	9

Source: Adapted from the *Annual Reports* of the Director General of Fair Trading.

made that a merger between two companies will lead to synergy: that is, that the profits of the merged companies will be greater than the sum of the profits of the two separate companies. If this does occur, however, it may not be due to improved efficiency, resulting in lower costs, but rather to an increase in market power which has enabled the merged company to charge higher prices. Should this be the case, such a merger may be referred to the Monopolies and Mergers Commission. This aspect is discussed in more detail in Unit 11.

Horizontal mergers will often have to be accompanied by a rationalisation process, as the firm will find that many of its facilities are duplicated (e.g. two Head Offices). There is also the danger that the firm might experience diseconomies of scale (see Unit 4).

Vertical merger

A **vertical merger** occurs when firms which are in the same industry but at different stages of production merge together. For example, a brewery may take over a chain of public houses, or a car manufacturer may take over a steel plant which produces the pressed-steel car bodies. If the firm being taken over is closer to the end product/customer in the chain of production, this is known as forward integration, while if the expansion is towards the beginning of the production process, further away from the customer, it is known as backward integration (see Figure 5.2).

The package holiday industry in the UK provides a good example of vertical integration, where the tour operator Thomson also owns a chain of travel agents (Lunn Poly) and an airline (Britannia). The main advantage of vertical growth is that it reduces a firm's dependence on other firms. An organisation may even be able to handle the production of a product from start to finish. For example, in the oil industry, a firm may

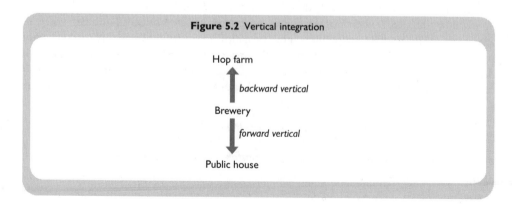

Figure 5.2 Vertical integration

Hop farm

↑ *backward vertical*

Brewery

↓ *forward vertical*

Public house

extract the oil, then refine and process the crude oil into products, finally selling the product to customers through its own petrol stations.

Backwards integration gives a firm greater control over its source of supply and makes it easier to keep a check on quality, or to ensure that the materials are supplied to meet exact specifications. It can also mean that supplies can be obtained more cheaply, as the profit margin that the supplier would normally include in the price is eliminated. Control over raw material supplies also puts the firm in a strong position vis-à-vis its competitors, as the firm may be able to secure sole ownership of the source of supply and deny competitors access to that source, or at least sell to them at inflated prices. For example, two firms, ICI and British Salt have 95 per cent of the British market for salt between them. One way in which they continue to dominate the market is by owning the salt beds used to manufacture salt.

Forward integration helps to ensure that a firm has an outlet for its product, and may also have the effect of depriving rival firms of retail outlets for their products. By taking over a chain of public houses, not only does a brewery have somewhere to sell its product, but it can also refuse to sell the products of other breweries. This also makes it easier to control the marketing of the product to the consumer. Thus, in the above example, the brewery can control the price of its products, promote its products over other products, and ensure both that the quality of the product is maintained at the point of sale and that the product is sold in comfortable surroundings – all helping to increase sales. The brewery is also able to enjoy the profit margin that would normally go to the retailer, and gain improved access to valuable information, such as market research data about customers' tastes and requirements.

There are, however, some risks and drawbacks associated with vertical expansion:

- There is the danger of investing heavily in a source of supply, only for that supply to become obsolete due to the development of a superior and cheaper alternative. Imagine a tyre manufacture investing heavily in rubber plantations, only to find that within a few years, supplies of cheaper synthetic rubber were available.

- The price of raw materials can also fluctuate widely. During a world recession it may be more economical to buy in supplies from outside, at a lower price, rather than have one's own source of supply.

- The firm which pursues a vertical expansion strategy is also risking becoming heavily involved in different stages of the same industry, and as a result, if the industry collapses, the firm has that much more to lose.

- Despite the fact that the expansion is within the same industry, because it involves a different stage of production, the skills and expertise required to run one part of the industry may be quite different from those required elsewhere in the industry. For example, a firm which is successful at *brewing* beer will find that the skills required to run a chain of public houses and *sell* beer are quite different, and are not something that it is suited to.

- The optimum scale of production is also likely to be different at different stages of production, meaning that the firm may find itself with overcapacity in one of its stages of production.

Many firms therefore decide to limit the scope of their activities. Marks & Spencer, for instance, have not ventured into producing their own knitwear and clothing; they continue to rely on outside suppliers to produce the products, while they concentrate on retailing. Vertical mergers are therefore relatively few in number, as demonstrated by the figures in Table 5.2.

Finally, where vertical merger leads to a firm controlling a significant share of the supplies of raw materials/components, or the distribution channels in its field, this could be perceived as being against the public interest, and again could be referred to the MMC.

Exercise

Firefly Fashions is a clothing manufacturer which specialises in the production of an exclusive range of high-quality clothing. It relies primarily on department stores to stock and sell its products. Over the past few years however, sales have declined. The firm is therefore considering opening up a number of its own retail shops, under the 'Firefly Fashions' name, where it would sell its own garments.

Task: Advise the firm as to the possible strengths and weaknesses of this strategy.

Conglomerate merger

This is where a firm joins with another firm which is producing different products. The reason for this is to diversify and spread risks if demand for the original market declines. It also provides a means of growth for those firms whose existing market is saturated. Hanson is a diversified industrial company with major interests in mining, chemicals, building materials and tobacco. Its established brand names include products as diverse as Seven Seas vitamin supplements, Jacuzzi whirlpool baths and spas, and Regal and Embassy cigarettes. The Unilever Group has interests in a wide range of branded and packaged consumer goods including soaps and detergents, tea, frozen meals, ice-cream, margarine and cosmetics. Its brand names include Liptons, Brooke Bond, Birds Eye, Flora, Oxo, Elizabeth Arden, Boursin Cheese and Batchelors Soups.

Conglomerate mergers became increasingly popular. In the 1960s they accounted for around 10 per cent of all mergers in the UK, but by the 1980s, they represented over 30 per cent of all mergers (see Table 5.2). The recession of the 1990s, however, has seen the popularity of this type of merger fall again to less than 10 per cent of all mergers, as companies seek to concentrate on 'core' business areas. There is a widely held belief that managers based in one industry may not have the skills and expertise to manage firms in other industries, resulting in some poor performances from conglomerate firms. For this reason, conglomerates such as ICI and BAT have been broken up into smaller units.

Much diversification which takes place is in related fields and such growth is sometimes referred to as 'lateral growth'. In a lateral merger, there is some connection between the firms, even though they are producing different products: for example, a brewery might takeover a crisp manufacturer (see Figure 5.3).

Overseas growth

Opportunities for growth in the home market may be limited, perhaps due to the size of the market or by government competition policy which might prevent any further increase in market share. An alternative is therefore for firms to grow through overseas expansion. Multinational enterprises are examined in detail in Unit 13.

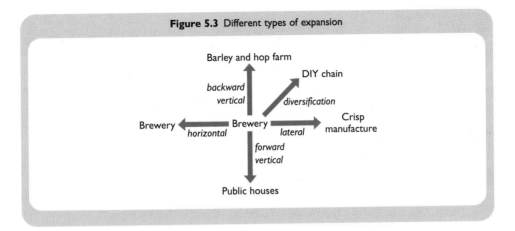

Figure 5.3 Different types of expansion

Ansoff matrix

A useful way of summarising the different growth strategies available to a firm is through the **Ansoff matrix**, developed by H.I. Ansoff (see Figure 5.4). *Market penetration* involves selling more of your present product to existing customers. This might be achieved through a new advertising campaign, or price cuts. *Market development* involves selling the existing product to a new group of customers. These might be overseas customers, or customers from a different age range. Guinness, for example, targeted younger drinkers as a means of increasing sales. *Product development* involves selling new or modified products to existing markets. These products are often complements to the existing product, while *diversification* involves selling a new product to a new market.

Exercise

Using as an example a firm such as Gillette, whose core business is the production of men's razors, outline four different growth strategies that the firm could pursue, using the options identified by the Ansoff matrix, identifying clearly for each strategy the nature of the product and the market that it would be sold to.

Figure 5.4 Ansoff matrix

	Existing products	New products
Existing markets	Market penetration	Product development
New markets	Market development	Diversification

Summary

Firms may grow through internal expansion or by merger. The motives for merger are wide and varied. Mergers may be classed as horizontal, vertical or conglomerate. Merger activity tends to occur in cycles, depending on the level of economic activity.

Review questions

1. Why might growth of the firm be a primary objective for managers?
2. Explain three methods a firm might use to finance internal expansion.
3. What are the problems and drawbacks associated with internal expansion?
4. Distinguish between vertical and horizontal expansion.
5. Why might a firm decide to merge with (a) its supplier, and (b) its customer?
6. Identify the economies of scale that a firm is likely to enjoy as a result of (a) horizontal growth, and (b) vertical growth.
7. What problems might a firm face following a takeover of another company?

Essay questions

1. Explain and evaluate the alternative ways in which a company might increase the scale of its operations, making reference to current examples where appropriate.
2. Many of Europe's car makers have opted to cooperate with each other and work together as a means of survival. Explain the reasons why they might have decided on joint ventures, rather than to pursue out-and-out takeovers and mergers.

Reading 5.1

The building society industry in the UK has provided a good example in recent years of growth through merger. Responding to rumours that it was considering merging with the Nationwide Building Society, a spokesman from the Alliance and Leicester Building Society (which is itself the product of a merger between two smaller societies) declared that 'Building societies are looking for economies of scale. But mergers have to be entered into very carefully; cultural differences between institutions can present a major obstacle.' ▷

Questions

1. Why might the building society industry be looking to grow through merger? What economies of scale could be achieved through such mergers?

2. Outline and explain the drawbacks that could result from mergers such as these.

Reading 5.2

The BMW takeover of Rover

In 1994, Rover, the last remaining large British-owned car manufacturer, was sold to BMW of Germany. The takeover provoked many protests, not only for nationalistic reasons, but also because of fears that the rationalisation that was bound to follow the takeover would result in plant closures and job losses, despite promises by BMW that the 30,000 jobs at Rover would be safe.

The possible motives for the takeover by BMW were as follows:

- It would allow them to take advantage of economies of scale in areas such as research and development, the distribution of cars and the purchasing of components.

- It would allow them to take advantage of the lower production costs in the UK, where labour costs in the car industry were almost half those in Germany.

- It represented an opportunity to enter market segments in which they did not have a product, such as Land Rover and Range Rover. It would have taken several years and have been very costly for BMW to develop their own 4×4 vehicle. The takeover of Rover permitted a rapid entry into this market.

Despite the protests of those concerned for the company's future, Rover too could derive benefits from the takeover. They would now be able to utilise BMW's extensive dealer networks in overseas markets such as Italy and Spain. BMW, as car manufacturers of some repute, were thought to have a better understanding of the car market than Rover's previous owners, British Aerospace. The synergy that had been expected following the merger of British Aerospace and Rover in 1988 had not materialised. Lower UK labour costs and the greater flexibility of the UK labour market might even encourage BMW to increase production within the UK, resulting in an expansion of jobs.

Questions

1. Why might it be considered important to keep Rover as a British-owned company? What would have been the dangers of not allowing the takeover to take place?

2. Why do you think BMW was keen to purchase Rover?

3. What difficulties might BMW face as a result of the takeover?

Markets

After studying this module you should be able to:

● understand the factors which determine the demand and supply for products;

● explain how prices are determined in a market economy;

● understand the concepts of elasticity of demand and supply;

● identify the benefits of the market mechanism;

● explain why market failure arises; and

● identify the reasons for and evaluate government intervention in the market.

Demand and supply

When the original bridge which carried the M4 motorway across the River Severn was privatised, the French-owned company, Cofiroute, imposed substantial government-sanctioned toll increases. The previous 'each-way' tolls of £1 for cars and £2 for lorries were raised to 'return-ticket' prices of £3.70 for cars and £11.10 for heavy-goods vehicles and buses. The justification for the increased tolls was to help finance the construction of the second motorway bridge to cross the river.

However, the increased tolls resulted in increased congestion on alternative routes into Wales by traffic seeking to avoid the higher charges. According to Gloucestershire County Council, the bridge company themselves also suffered from the new pricing policy, as the effect of those seeking to avoid the higher prices resulted in a loss of toll revenue of up to £3 million a year.

Firms operate within a market that consists of buyers and sellers. We need to understand how these markets work. A market is more than simply a geographical location: it is any situation that brings potential buyers and sellers together. A market may be localised, such as the market for second-hand cars, or it may be worldwide, as is the case for the foreign currency market and for commodities such as oil and wheat.

In this unit, we look at the fundamentals of demand and supply, while in the following units in this module we look at why markets may fail to perform as efficiently as they might, and the ways in which government intervenes in markets.

Demand

In order to be successful, firms need to have some knowledge of the factors which influence the demand for their products. It would be very useful for them to know how sales might be affected by changes in consumers' income, or how a change in the price of a rival's product might affect the demand for their product.

In economics, in order for demand to be 'effective', it must be backed by the willingness and ability to pay for the product. Many people would like luxury cars or expensive holidays, but this does not mean there is a high **demand** for these products.

Demand is usually expressed at a particular price, over a given time period. For example, the demand for cars at £15,000 might be 1,000 per month.

The basic rule of demand is that it varies inversely with price. In the opening extract, an increase in the toll charge for the Severn Bridge resulted in a decrease in bridge crossings. This is the case for most products: more will be demanded at a lower price than at a higher price. We can demonstrate this in Table 6.1, which looks at the **demand schedule** for compact discs.

This information can also be illustrated graphically (see Figure 6.1). Price can be plotted on the vertical axis, while quantity demanded can be plotted on the horizontal axis. The **demand curve**, D, demonstrates the different quantities of compact discs that will be demanded at various prices, assuming that other factors which might influence their demand remain constant (a condition which is referred to as **ceteris paribus**). This can then be used as the model for the vast majority of goods (see Figure 6.2). As the price changes from P_1 to P_2, the quantity demanded changes from Q_1 to Q_2, that is, there is an inverse relationship between price and the quantity demanded.

There are, however, some products where this relationship between price and the quantity demanded might not exist. It is possible that for some products, a lower price

Table 6.1: Demand schedule for compact discs

Price (£)	Quantity demanded (per week)
18	20
14	60
10	100
6	140
2	180

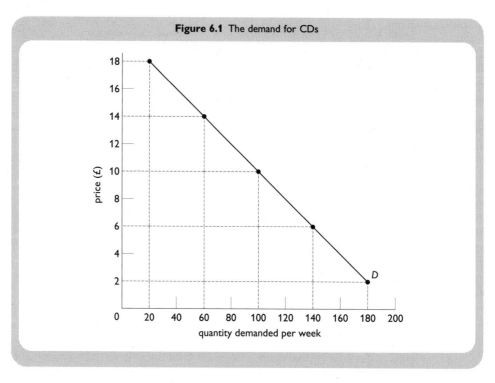

Figure 6.1 The demand for CDs

could lead to a fall in the quantity demanded, while a higher price might lead to an increase in demand. This could be true of shares, where if the price rises, there may be an increase in demand as people are anticipating a further rise in price, while if price falls, demand may also fall as people are expecting a further fall in price. If the price of a product is very low, demand may also be low, as buyers may associate the low price with poor

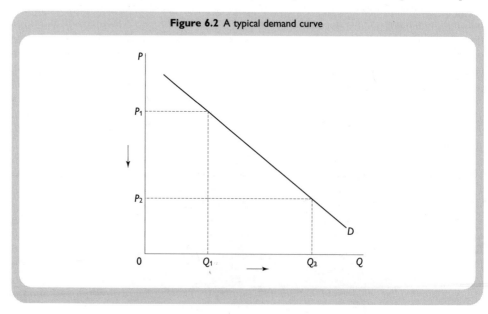

Figure 6.2 A typical demand curve

Table 6.2: Effect of advertising campaign on the demand for compact discs

	Quantity demanded	
Price (£)	Before campaign	After campaign
18	20	50
14	60	90
10	100	130
6	140	170
2	180	210

quality. There are also some products which are consumed because of their high price: 'conspicuous consumption' or 'snob value' means that demand may rise when price rises.

In these latter cases, the demand curve would be upward sloping, indicating that more is demanded at a higher price than at a lower price. However, these are exceptions and in the vast majority of cases, the demand curve has a negative slope, sloping down from left to right.

Changes in the conditions of demand

We have seen that the demand curve is drawn on the condition that all other influences on demand remain unchanged (i.e. 'ceteris paribus'). However, there may be a change in these other influences, that is, a change in the 'conditions' of demand:

- A successful *advertising* campaign would increase the demand for a product, at each and every price. Table 6.2 shows the effect on the demand for compact discs following an extensive advertising campaign. The effect of this is to shift the demand curve to the right, as illustrated in Figure 6.3, showing that more will be demanded at every price.

Figure 6.3 An increase in demand

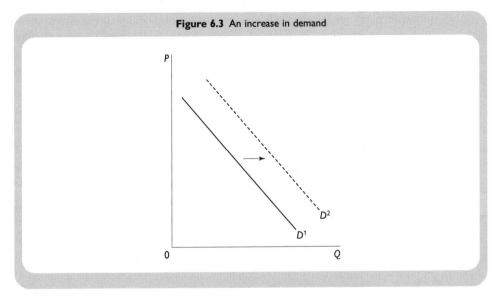

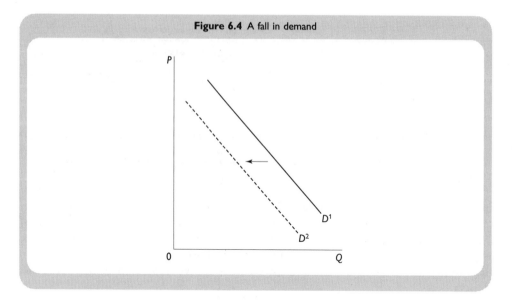

Figure 6.4 A fall in demand

- A change in the size of the *population* is also likely to affect the demand for a product. Likewise, a change in the age distribution of the population will affect the demand for many products. Thus there is an increased demand for health care as a result of an ageing population in Britain.

- Demand will be affected by changes in *tastes and fashion*. This is particularly true of the clothing industry. If a product goes out of fashion, this would be illustrated by a shift in the demand curve to the left (see Figure 6.4), showing that less will be demanded at every price.

- The demand for a product is also likely to be affected by the *price and availability of other goods*. These goods may be 'complements', as is the case in the relationship between compact discs and compact disc players, or substitutes, as is the case in the relationship between compact discs and cassette tapes. A change in the price of compact disc players or cassette tapes is likely to affect the demand for compact discs, even though the price of the compact disc itself has not changed.

- A change in *disposable income* is also likely to affect the demand for products. For most products, an increase in income will lead to an increase in the demand for the product, shifting the demand curve to the right. Thus, if a student receives a larger grant, the number of compact discs which he or she purchases is likely to rise. However, for some goods, a rise in disposable income could lead to a fall in demand, shifting the demand curve to the left. These goods are referred to as 'inferior' products. Public transport is an example, as an increase in incomes could lead to more people travelling by private car. The relationship between changes in income and changes in demand is examined in more detail later in this unit, under the heading of **income elasticity of demand**.

- The *price and availability of credit* can also affect the demand for products, particularly consumer durables such as cars or electrical goods. If credit facilities are readily available at reasonable terms, then the demand for these products is likely to rise. Car dealers, for example, often try to increase the demand for their cars by offering '0 per cent finance'.

● Demand for some products will be influenced by the *weather* and *season*. Ice-cream, for instance, will be in much greater demand during warm weather, irrespective of price.

You should now be quite clear about the distinction between a movement along a demand curve and a shift in the curve. Any demand curve is drawn on the assumption that all influences on demand other than price remain unchanged ('ceteris paribus') and therefore a change in price is illustrated by a movement along the same demand curve, as shown in Figure 6.2. However, any change in the conditions of demand means that we have to construct a new curve, by shifting it to the right if it is an increase in demand, or to the left if it is a decrease in demand, as illustrated in Figures 6.3 and 6.4.

Exercise

Illustrate, using demand curves, the effect of each of the following:

1. The demand for cross channel ferries following the opening of the channel tunnel.
2. The demand for ice-cream from winter to summer.
3. The demand for ice-cream following a rise in its price.
4. The demand for computer software following a fall in the price of home computers.

Supply

The supply of a product refers to the amount of a product which suppliers are willing and able to supply at any particular price, over a given time period. The basic rule of **supply** is that as the price of a product rises, more will be supplied to the market, because, at a higher price, firms will find that the production and sale of the product is more profitable. Thus existing firms are likely to produce more of the product and new firms will enter the market and start production. Table 6.3 represents the **supply schedule** for compact discs. As the market price of CDs rises, so more are willing to supply them.

Table 6.3: Supply schedule for compact discs

Price (£)	Quantity supplied (per week)
18	180
14	140
10	100
6	60
2	20

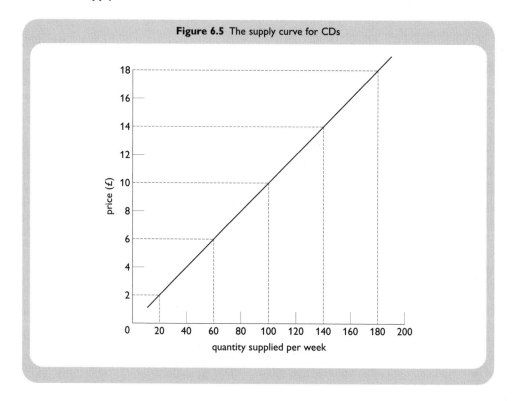

Figure 6.5 The supply curve for CDs

Figure 6.5 illustrates the **supply curve** for compact discs, derived from Table 6.3, while Figure 6.6 represents a typical supply curve.

As is the case with demand, this curve is drawn under the assumption of 'ceteris paribus', that is, that all other factors remain constant. However there may be a change in the *conditions of supply*, which will cause firms to supply more or less of the product at any given price:

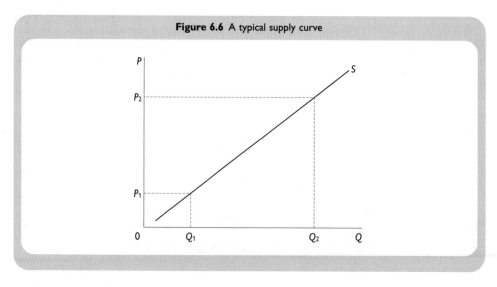

Figure 6.6 A typical supply curve

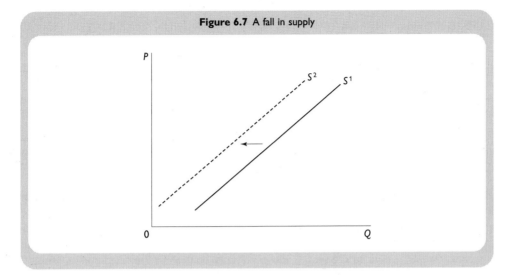

Figure 6.7 A fall in supply

- If there is a change in the *costs of production* this will affect profitability, which will influence the willingness of firms to supply the product. Thus an increase in wage costs, or the costs of raw materials will mean that less will be supplied at any given price. This will cause the supply curve to shift to the left, as illustrated in Figure 6.7. A fall in the costs of production will encourage firms to produce more at any given price, thus shifting the supply curve to the right, as shown in Figure 6.8.

- *Improvements in technology* might cause a rise in productivity, thus reducing costs per unit. This too would cause a shift in the supply curve to the right.

- A *tax* placed on a product would mean that the firm receives less from the sale of the product at any given price, and this will reduce supply, causing a shift of the supply curve to the left.

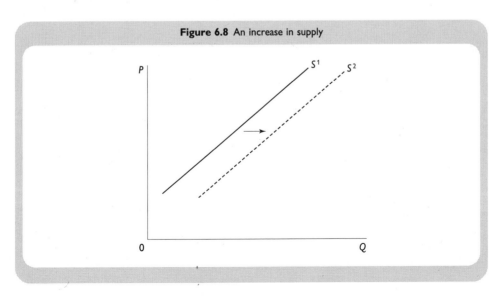

Figure 6.8 An increase in supply

● A *subsidy*, meanwhile, would encourage production and shift the supply curve to the right.

● It is possible that changes in the *price of other goods* might affect the supply of a product. If the price of another good rises, a firm might find it more profitable to switch production to this good, causing supply of the original good to fall, even though its price had not changed.

● In the case of agricultural produce, the *weather* and *season* can affect supply. Thus the supply of strawberries will be much greater at certain times of the year than at others.

As is the case with demand, you should now be quite clear about the distinction between a movement along a supply curve and a shift in the curve. A supply curve is drawn on the assumption that all influences on supply other than price remain unchanged ('ceteris paribus'), and therefore a change in price is illustrated by a movement along the same supply curve, as shown in Figure 6.6. However, any change in the conditions of supply means that we have to construct a new curve, by shifting it to the left if it results is a decrease in supply, and to the right if it results in an increase in supply, as illustrated in Figures 6.7 and 6.8.

Exercise

Illustrate, using supply curves, the effect of each of the following:

1. The supply of apples following a bumper harvest.
2. The supply of books following the imposition of VAT.
3. The supply of coal following the introduction of more efficient power drills.
4. The supply of coal following a fall in its price.

Finally, Table 6.4 summarises the factors that cause shifts in demand and supply.

Table 6.4: Summary of factors causing shifts in demand and supply

Demand	*Supply*
Advertising	Changes in the costs of production
Population changes: size and structure	Technological developments
Income	Taxes and subsidies
Changes in the price and availability of	Changes in the price of other products
substitute and complementary products	Seasonal factors
Price and availability of credit	
Seasonal factors	
Fashion	

Price determination

If we combine demand and supply, we can determine the market price of the product. Table 6.5 combines the demand and supply schedule for compact discs, while Figure 6.9 combines the demand curve and supply curve on the same diagram.

At a price of £10, the quantity demanded equals the quantity supplied. This price is called the **equilibrium price**. It is the only price at which demand equals supply. At this equilibrium price, the market will 'clear'. There will be no shortages and no surpluses.

Table 6.5: Combined schedule for compact discs

Price (£)	Quantity Demanded	Quantity Supplied
18	20	180
14	60	140
10	100	100
6	140	60
2	180	20

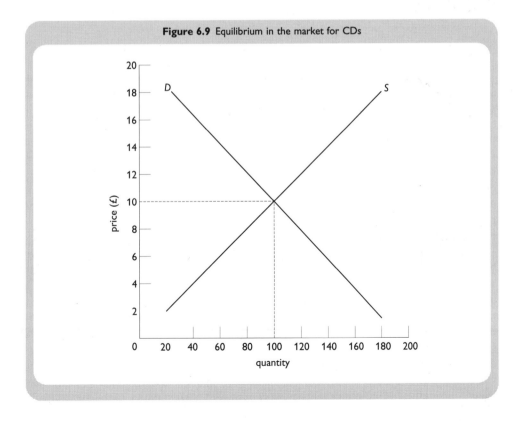

Figure 6.9 Equilibrium in the market for CDs

Figure 6.10 Excess supply

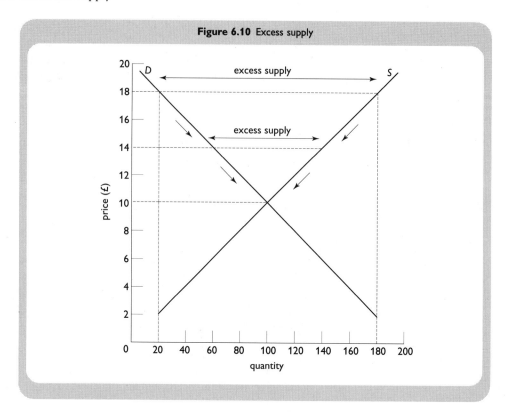

The laws of demand and supply will usually ensure that markets will settle at an equilibrium. Consider what would happen if the price was above the equilibrium, say at £18, as illustrated in Figure 6.10. At this price, the quantity demanded is less than the quantity supplied. There is excess supply, or a surplus. The market is in disequilibrium. However, the workings of the price mechanism should ensure that the market returns to equilibrium. Because suppliers will find themselves with a surplus of compact discs, they will lower the price in order to encourage sales. As the price is lowered, the quantity demanded will increase, while at the same time, the quantity supplied will decrease, as some suppliers will decide it is not worth while supplying the CDs at the lower price. The price may fall to £14, at which price there is still an excess supply, so the process described above will continue until the price returns to the equilibrium price of £10.

Now consider what happens if the price is below the equilibrium, say at £2, as shown in Figure 6.11. At this price, the quantity demanded is greater than the quantity supplied. There is excess demand, or a shortage. Some consumers demand compact discs but are unable to purchase them. The price will therefore be bid higher as they attempt to buy a CD. As the price rises, the quantity demanded falls, as some consumers are unwilling pay the higher price, while at the same time, the quantity supplied rises, as suppliers find that it is now more profitable to supply CDs. The price may rise to £6, but there is still excess demand. The process will therefore continue until the price rises to the equilibrium, where the quantity demanded equals the quantity supplied. Thus the price mechanism should ensure that shortages or surpluses are removed fairly rapidly.

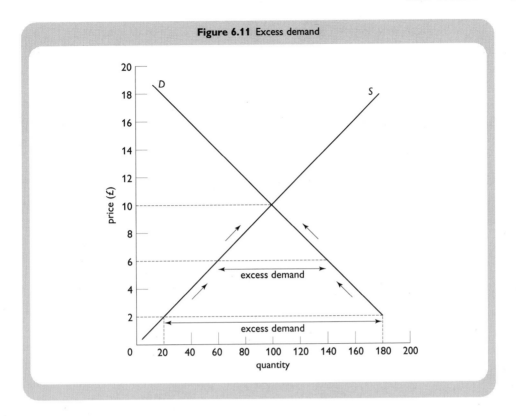

Figure 6.11 Excess demand

Changes in equilibrium

While price returns to equilibrium in a free market, the equilibrium will not stay the same for ever. Any change in the conditions of demand or supply will cause a shift in the demand or supply curve and this will result in a new equilibrium. Let us consider what happens if a product becomes more fashionable. The increased popularity of the product will lead to an increase in demand, which is represented in Figure 6.12 by a shift in the demand curve to the right. As a result there is a new equilibrium, with equilibrium price rising from P_1 to P_2, while output rises from Q_1 to Q_2. A change in the conditions of demand which causes a shift in the demand curve to the left would result in a lower equilibrium price and a lower output. You should draw a diagram to illustrate this yourself. Figure 6.13 illustrates the effect on equilibrium price and output of a shift in the supply curve to the right, which could be caused by a government subsidy on the product. The price has fallen from P_1 to P_2, while output has risen from Q_1 to Q_2. A change in the conditions of supply which shift the supply curve to the left would result in a higher equilibrium price and a lower output. Again, you should draw a diagram to illustrate this.

   In the above analysis, we have assumed that only the demand curve or the supply curve has shifted. Over time, however, there may be changes in the conditions of both demand and supply, causing both the demand curve and the supply curve to shift, thus resulting in frequent changes to equilibrium price.

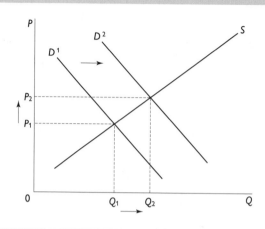

Figure 6.12 The effect on equilibrium price and output of an increase in demand

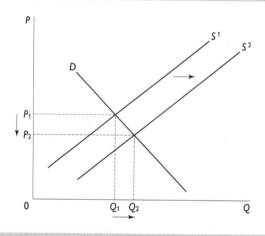

Figure 6.13 The effect on equilibrium price and output of an increase in supply

Exercise

Figure 6.14 represents the market for wind-surf boards.

1. From the graph, estimate:
   (a) the equilibrium price of wind-surf boards;
   (b) the quantity that will be sold at this price;
   (c) the total revenue gained from the sale of wind-surf boards.

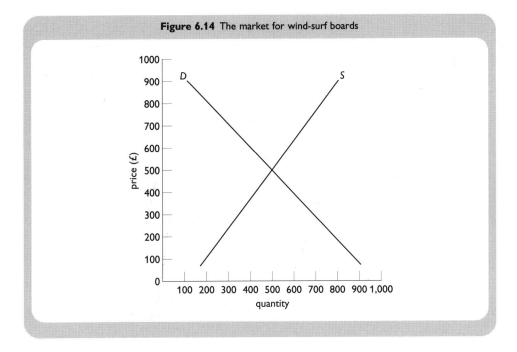

Figure 6.14 The market for wind-surf boards

2. Making use of demand and supply diagrams, illustrate the likely effect on equilibrium price and quantity of each of the following events:
   (a) wind-surf board manufacturers discover a cheaper material with which to make the boards;
   (b) a number of accidents at seaside resorts reduces the popularity of wind-surfing;
   (c) the government places an additional sales tax on wind-surf boards.

Elasticity of demand

We have seen that there are numerous factors which can affect the level of demand. **Elasticity of demand** measures the *extent* to which a change in these factors influences the level of demand. The main measures that we shall look at are **price elasticity of demand**, **income elasticity of demand** and **cross-elasticity of demand**, although the concept can also be applied to examine the extent to which other factors (e.g. advertising expenditure) affect demand.

Price elasticity of demand

In the vast majority of cases, there is an inverse relationship between price and the quantity demanded. If a firm puts the price of its product up, other things remaining equal, it can expect sales to fall, while if it lowers price, it can expect sales to rise.

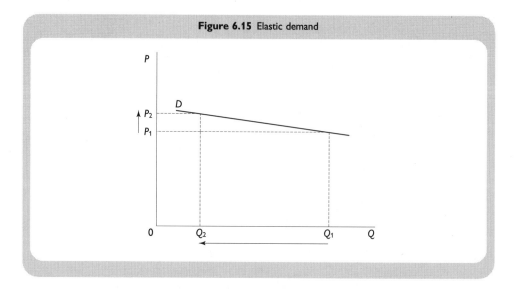

Figure 6.15 Elastic demand

However, a firm will want to know more than this. It will want to know the *extent* to which demand changes as price changes. In other words, how sensitive is the demand for its product to changes in price?

Consider for example two products, salt and chocolate biscuits. If the price of salt were to rise by 50 per cent, or even fall by 50 per cent, one would not expect there to be a very significant change in the demand for salt. However, if the price of chocolate biscuits were to rise or fall to the same degree, one might predict a significant change in the quantity demanded because people would buy other kinds of biscuits. The demand for salt, in the above example, is therefore said to be price inelastic, as demand does not respond much to changes in price, while the demand for chocolate biscuits is said to be price elastic, as a change in price causes a sizeable change in the quantity demanded.

A convenient way to illustrate price elasticity of demand is through the gradient of the demand curve. In Figure 6.15 a small change in price from P_1 to P_2 has resulted in a significant change in the quantity demanded, thus illustrating demand that is price elastic, while in Figure 6.16 a fairly substantial price change from P_1 to P_2 has had little effect on the quantity demanded, thus illustrating demand that is price inelastic.

However, diagrams can be misleading, because, for example, the slope depends on the scale of the axes used in the diagram (see 'Words of warning' on page 94 for a more detailed discussion). An alternative is to calculate elasticity mathematically.

Measurement of price elasticity of demand
Price elasticity of demand can be measured through using the formula:

$$\text{Price elasticity of demand} = \frac{\text{Percentage change in quantity demanded}}{\text{Percentage change in price}}$$

or, using symbols:

$$\frac{\Delta Q}{Q} \div \frac{\Delta P}{P}$$

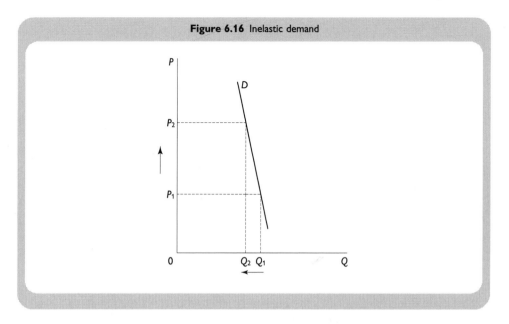

Figure 6.16 Inelastic demand

where:

ΔQ = change in quantity;
Q = original quantity;
ΔP = change in price; and
P = original price.

If the value for price elasticity is greater than one, then demand is said to be price elastic, while if the value is less than one, demand is said to be price inelastic. The higher the value of price elasticity, the more elastic demand is said to be. Note that as there is an inverse relationship between price and the quantity demanded, the value for price elasticity of demand will be negative. However, for brevity the minus sign is often omitted.

Consider the following examples. A firm raises the price of its product from £2 to £2.20, and as a result, sales fall from 400 per week to 320. What is the price elasticity of demand? Using the formula:

$$\frac{\text{Percentage change in quantity demanded}}{\text{Percentage change in price}}$$

price elasticity of demand:

$$= \frac{(-)20\%}{(+)10\%} \quad \begin{array}{l}\text{(a decrease from 400 to 320)}\\ \text{(an increase from £2 to £2.20)}\end{array}$$

$$= (-)2$$

Thus demand is elastic over this price range.

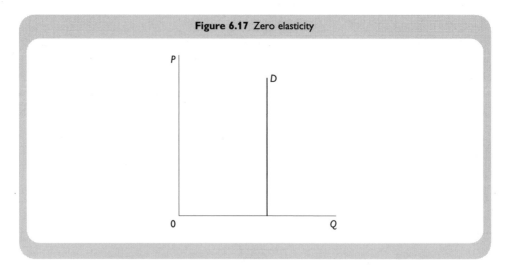

Figure 6.17 Zero elasticity

However, when the firm raises the price of another product, from £1 to £1.10, sales fall from 1,000 per week to 960 per week. In this case, the price elasticity of demand:

$$\frac{(-)4\%}{(+)10\%} \quad \begin{array}{l}\text{(a decrease from 1,000 to 960)} \\ \text{(an increase from £1 to £1.10)}\end{array}$$

$$= (-)0.4$$

In this case demand is price inelastic.

If price elasticity of demand has a value of one, then demand is said to have unit elasticity. (A demand curve of unit elasticity is illustrated in Figure 6.22.) The two extreme cases are where the price elasticity of demand is equal to zero (perfectly inelastic) or is equal to infinity (perfectly elastic). These are illustrated in Figures 6.17 and 6.18).

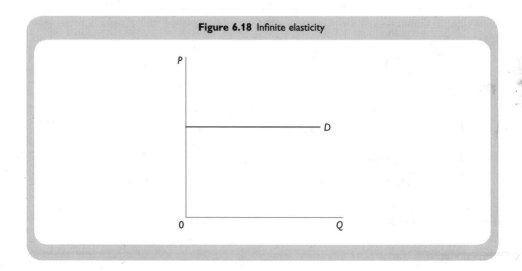

Figure 6.18 Infinite elasticity

Factors influencing price elasticity of demand

There are several factors which may determine the price elasticity of demand of a product. The *availability of substitutes* will have an influence. If there are many close substitutes or alternative products available, then demand is likely to be price elastic, but if there are few alternative products, as in the case for salt, then demand is likely to be price inelastic. Note, however, that the demand for petrol can be considered to be price inelastic as there are no substitutes available, but the demand for a particular brand of petrol will be elastic.

Whether the product is a *necessity* or a *luxury* will also have an influence on the price elasticity of demand. If the product is a luxury, as in the case of chocolate biscuits, consumers may decide to forgo the product following an increase in price, but if the product is a necessity they may still continue to demand the product despite a price increase. This explanation, however, produces the problem of defining what is a necessity and what is a luxury. Products do not always fall neatly into these two categories: for instance, food is clearly a necessity and the demand for this as a whole is therefore inelastic, but the demand for fillet steak is elastic. The *proportion of a person's income* spent on a product will also influence the price elasticity of demand. If the price of a box of matches were to double, the demand is not likely to change much as, despite the 100 per cent increase in price, it represents such a small proportion of a person's budget. If a product taking up a much larger proportion of one's budget increased in price, it is likely that demand for this product would have to be reduced considerably. Goods which are bought through *habit*, or which have *addictive properties*, will tend to be price inelastic.

Time can also have an effect on price elasticity of demand. When the price of cigarettes is raised in the budget, many smokers decide to cut back on demand, unwilling to pay the higher price. However, as time passes, people become accustomed to the higher price and demand reverts back to its original pre-budget level. In this example, the passing of time has made demand less price elastic. However, time also provides consumers with more time to search for alternative products. Thus, for example, if the price of petrol rises, motorists have little choice but to continue buying petrol at the higher price as their car will not function on any other fuel. But over time, there is the opportunity to switch to a diesel-engine car, so in time the demand for petrol may fall in response to the higher price. In this example, the passing of time has made demand more price elastic.

The relationship between price elasticity of demand and revenue

The sales revenue of a firm is determined by multiplying the price of the product by the number of units sold, and this can be illustrated by the rectangle shown in Figure 6.19.

The effect on a firm's revenue of a change in price depends on the price elasticity of demand for its product. When demand is elastic, an increase in price will lead to a fall in the firm's revenue, while a reduction in price will lead to an increase in revenue (see Figure 6.20). This is the basis of the argument put forward by Gloucestershire County Council in the opening extract to this unit, when considering the pricing strategy for the Severn Bridge. They argued that by raising the bridge toll, the company received less income, as there was a significant drop in the number of vehicles crossing the bridge. If demand, on the other hand, is inelastic, a rise in price results in an increase in the firm's revenue, while a decrease in price results in a fall in revenue, as illustrated in Figure 6.21.

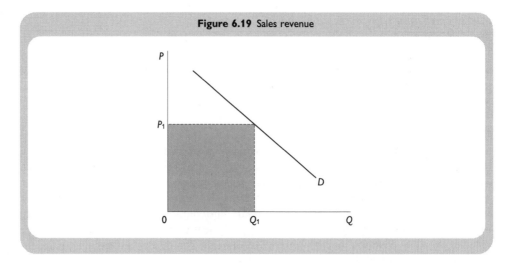

Figure 6.19 Sales revenue

If demand has unit elasticity over a price range, a change in price will leave revenue unchanged. This is illustrated in Figure 6.22, which shows a demand curve that has unit elasticity along its entire length. This curve is called a rectangular hyperbola. Whatever the price charged, the revenue remains the same, so that the area bounded by $0P_1AQ_1$ is the same as that bounded by $0P_2BQ_2$.

Knowledge of the price elasticity of demand for their product is therefore important for firms when considering their pricing policy. The argument that a firm needs to raise price in order to increase revenue does not hold true if the demand for the product is elastic;

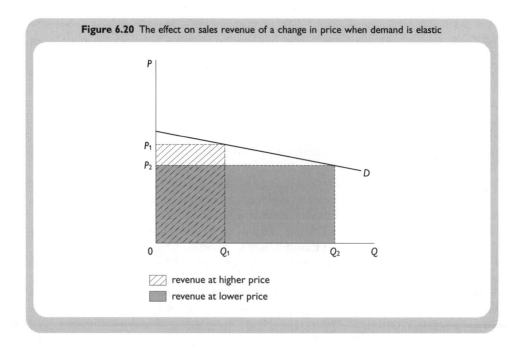

Figure 6.20 The effect on sales revenue of a change in price when demand is elastic

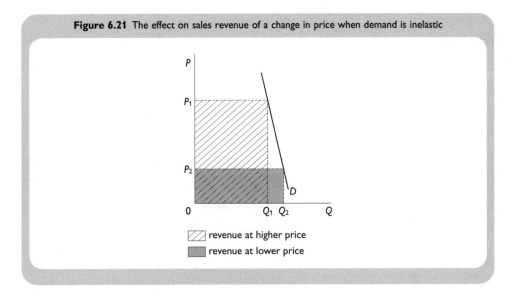

Figure 6.21 The effect on sales revenue of a change in price when demand is inelastic

a better policy may actually be to lower price. If demand is inelastic, however, there is little to be gained from a price cut.

Knowledge of the price elasticity of demand for products is also important for the Chancellor of the Exchequer, who needs to know the effect that a change in tax rates will have on the demand for products when calculating total tax yields. If the aim of the Chancellor is to raise as much revenue as possible from indirect taxes, then he or she would be advised to tax products which have an inelastic demand, as consumption will remain high, despite the imposition of a sales tax.

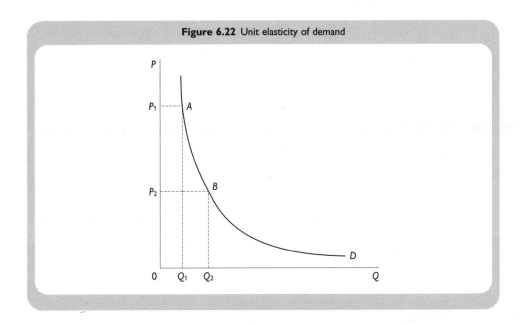

Figure 6.22 Unit elasticity of demand

Case study

Price elasticity of demand: some words of warning

1. We have shown that a convenient way to illustrate price elasticity of demand is to vary the slope of the demand curve. This is not strictly accurate, however. Consider Figure 6.23: at a price of £20, a decrease in price of £2 leads to an increase in demand of 20, from 60 to 80 units, while at a price of £10, a decrease in price of £2 also leads to an increase in demand of 20, from 160 to 180 units, demonstrating that the slope of the demand curve is constant.

Figure 6.23 A linear demand curve with differing elasticities

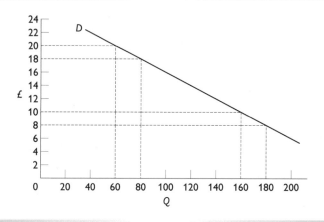

Figure 6.24 How elasticity varies along a linear demand curve

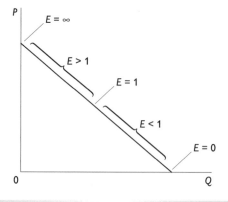

However, if we calculate the price elasticity of demand using the formula:

$$\frac{\text{percentage change in quantity}}{\text{percentage change in price}}$$

as the price falls from £20 to £18, price elasticity is (−)3.3 (33.3 per cent/10 per cent) while as the price falls from £10 to £8, price elasticity is (−)0.625 (12.5 per cent/ 20 per cent), resulting in entirely different values, despite the fact that the gradient of the demand curve is constant. In fact, the price elasticity of a demand curve which is a straight line varies along its entire length, from being highly elastic close to the price axis to very inelastic close to the quantity axis. This is illustrated in Figure 6.24, which shows the extreme ends of the demand curve having price elasticity of zero and infinity.

Nevertheless, although not strictly accurate, it is still useful to illustrate the concept of price elasticity by varying the gradient of the demand curve.

2. The formula that we have used to measure price elasticity of demand produces an inconsistency. Consider Figure 6.25, in which a firm has raised the price of its product from £4 to £5 and, as a result, sales have fallen from 200 units per week to 100 units.

    Calculating the price elasticity of demand, using our formula:

$$\frac{\text{percentage change in quantity}}{\text{percentage change in price}}$$

the price elasticity of demand as the price is increased from £4 to £5 is (−)2 (50 per cent/ 25 per cent). But if the firm were to lower price again, from £5 to £4, and demand were to revert back to its original level, from 100 units back to 200 units, the price elasticity of demand as price changes from £5 to £4 is (−)5. Thus, using our method of calculation, the price elasticity of demand is different depending on whether the price has risen or fallen. To overcome this problem, we can use a different formula, which does not depend on the direction of movement along the demand curve. This method takes the change in values

Figure 6.25 The value of elasticity can depend on the direction of movement

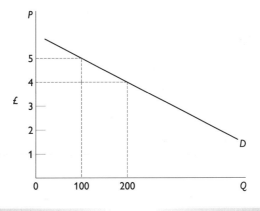

continued

as a percentage of the midway point between the old and new value. The formula becomes:

$$\frac{\Delta Q}{\frac{1}{2}(Q_1 + Q_2)} \div \frac{\Delta P}{\frac{1}{2}(P_1 + P_2)}$$

Therefore, whether price has changed from £4 to £5, or £5 to £4, using this method of calculation, the price elasticity of demand $= (-)3$.

Income elasticity of demand

We have seen when discussing demand that income is an important factor influencing the level of demand. In most cases, an increase in income leads to an increase in the demand for a product. However, it would be useful to know the *extent* to which demand changes as income changes. Income elasticity of demand measures the sensitivity of demand to changes in income. If consumers get an increase in income, their demand for some products may rise substantially, but their demand for other products may rise only very slightly, if at all.

Income elasticity of demand can be measured by using the formula:

$$\frac{\text{Percentage change in quantity demanded}}{\text{Percentage change in income}}$$

If the value is more than one, demand is said to be income elastic, and if the answer is between zero and one, demand is said to be income inelastic. Most goods will fall into this range: that is, their income elasticity of demand will be positive, and the higher the value of the income elasticity of demand, the stronger the relationship is between changes in income and changes in demand. Luxury products tend to have a high income elasticity, while necessities have a low income elasticity. Thus the demand for foreign holidays or eating out is likely to be fairly responsive to changes in income, but the demand for bread is unlikely to change by much as income changes.

For some products, however, the income elasticity of demand is negative, and these are referred to as inferior products. For these products there is an inverse relationship between income and demand, and an increase in income will lead to a fall in demand. The explanation for this is that as their income rises, consumers substitute better products in place of the 'inferior' products. Typical examples are public transport or cheap cuts of meat.

Knowledge of the income elasticity of demand is important as it can help us to predict what will happen to demand as income levels change. Over time, living standards and the level of income have a tendency to rise. Using data on the income elasticity of demand for products, we can predict changes in spending patterns. We can expect to see a rise in spending on those products which have a high income elasticity of demand, such as eating out, electrical goods, foreign holidays and leisure activities, whereas for those products which have a low income elasticity of demand – for example, necessities such as bread, toothpaste, washing-up liquid – demand will rise only slightly. Expenditure on

Table 6.6: Price and income elasticities for various food products

	Price elasticity of demand	Income elasticity of demand
Bread	−0.09	−0.25
Milk	−0.19	−0.02
Potatoes	−0.21	−0.48
Fruit	−1.05	+0.48
Cheese	−1.20	+0.19
Beef and veal	−1.25	+0.08

those products which have a negative income elasticity will fall. Thus the demand for public transport may fall as people switch to private cars.

Firms may therefore want to consider selling products with high income elasticities of demand, as when living standards are rising, peoples' expenditure on these goods will be rising more rapidly than on those goods with low income elasticities of demand. On the other hand, those firms which produce goods with low income elasticities of demand will be less affected in times of recession as, despite the fall in income levels, demand for these products will remain fairly stable.

A particular problem for the UK economy is that many of the products which it imports have a high income elasticity of demand. Therefore, as the level of national income rises, this leads to an influx of imports. The products which the UK exports, however, tend to have a much lower income elasticity of demand, and so, as world income rises, the level of exports does not increase to the same extent, which results in **balance of payments** problems for the UK.

In practice, it might be difficult to calculate accurately the elasticity of demand for a product. A firm could attempt to determine the price elasticity of demand for its product by varying the price it charges and examining the extent to which demand changes. In the UK, the Ministry of Agriculture, Food and Fisheries has estimated the price elasticities and income elasticities for various food products, and these are shown in Table 6.6. The figures demonstrate that the demand for bread, milk and potatoes is inelastic with respect to price, and that they are 'inferior' products, as their income elasticty of demand is negative, while the demand for fruit, cheese, beef and veal is price elastic and has a positive income elasticity of demand.

Cross-elasticity of demand

Cross-elasticity of demand examines the nature and the extent of the relationship between two products. In particular, it examines the extent to which a change in the price of one product affects the demand for another product. To measure the cross-elasticity of demand, we can use the formula:

$$\frac{\text{Percentage change in demand for product X}}{\text{Percentage change in price of product Y}}$$

The value of the cross-elasticity of demand may be positive or negative, depending on the nature of the relationship between the two products. If the value is positive, this indicates that the two products are substitutes. Thus, a 10 per cent increase in the price of gin might lead to a 5 per cent increase in the demand for whisky. Using the formula above, the cross-elasticity of demand:

$$= \frac{+5\%}{+10\%}$$

$$= +0.5$$

However, if the cross-elasticity of demand between two products is negative, this indicates that they are in joint demand or complementary products. Thus a 10 per cent increase in the price of gin might lead to a 5 per cent decrease in the demand for tonic water. Using the formula, the cross-elasticity of demand in this case:

$$\frac{-5\%}{+10\%}$$

$$= -0.5$$

The further the value is away from zero, either positive or negative, the stronger the relationship is between the two products. If, however, the value of the cross-elasticity of demand between two products is zero, then this indicates that there is no apparent relationship between the two products. Thus one would expect the demand for bread to remain unchanged following an increase in the price of gin.

As well as helping us to forecast the effect on demand of a change in the price of another product, cross-elasticity of demand can also be used to help assess the extent of competition in an industry. If the cross-elasticity of demand between two products is high, this indicates that the products are close substitutes and are competing within the same market. This might then influence whether the government feels it is necessary to intervene to ensure competition (see Unit 11 on competition policy).

Elasticity of supply

We have seen that there are numerous factors which influence supply. **Elasticity of supply** measures the *extent* to which a change in these factors influences supply. We shall concentrate here on the price elasticity of supply.

Price elasticity of supply

Price elasticity of supply measures the responsiveness of supply to changes in price. In the case of some products, it may be relatively easy to increase supply, but for other products, there may be great difficulties in supplying more, even though the market price might have risen considerably. The formula used to measure the price elasticity of supply is similar to that for the price elasticity of demand:

$$\frac{\text{Percentage change in quantity supplied}}{\text{Percentage change in price}}$$

or, in symbols:

$$\frac{\Delta Q}{Q} \div \frac{\Delta P}{P}$$

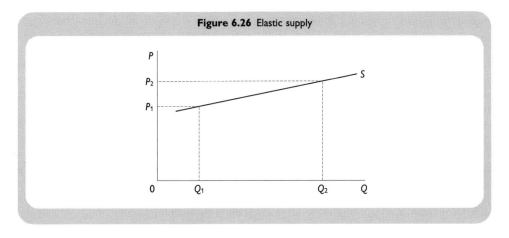

Figure 6.26 Elastic supply

where:

ΔQ = the change in quantity supplied;
Q = the original quantity supplied;
ΔP = the change in price; and
P = the original price.

As an increase in price usually leads to an increase in the quantity supplied, the value of the price elasticity of supply will be positive. If supply is elastic, the value will be greater than one, whereas if supply is inelastic, the value will be between zero and one. A convenient way to illustrate the concept of price elasticity of supply is through the slope of the supply curve. Figure 6.26 is an example of elastic supply, where a slight increase in price results in a significant increase in the quantity supplied. This would be the case for many manufactured goods when firms are producing at less than capacity output. Figure 6.27 is

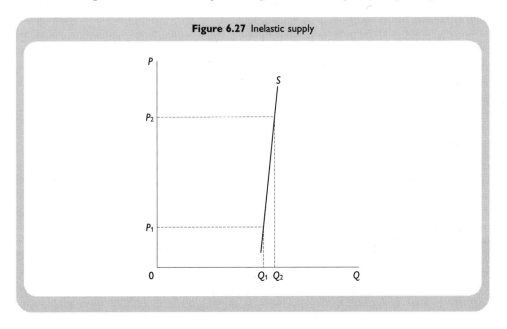

Figure 6.27 Inelastic supply

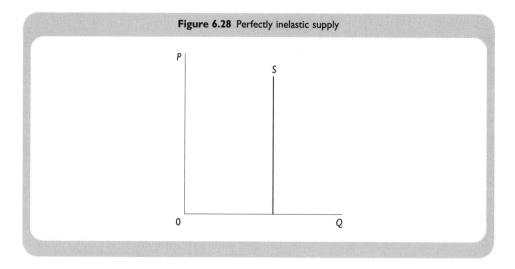

Figure 6.28 Perfectly inelastic supply

an example of an inelastic supply curve where, despite the increase in price, the quantity supplied has only slightly increased, as may be the case with agricultural products.

In extreme circumstances, supply may be perfectly inelastic, meaning that supply is fixed and cannot be increased. This applies to Van Gogh paintings, or the capacity of a football stadium on matchday. In this case, elasticity of supply has a value of zero. This is illustrated in Figure 6.28.

Factors determining elasticity of supply

Elasticity of supply is dependent on how easy it is for firms to adjust supply. The *availability of raw materials and components* can have an important effect. If materials are readily available, the firm may easily be able to increase supply, thus making supply elastic, but if access to materials is limited, the firm may experience difficulty in increasing supply. Likewise, the *availability of workers* can affect elasticity of supply. If the production process requires a highly skilled workforce, the firm may find it difficult to hire additional workers to increase supply, and so supply will be inelastic, but if the production process relies on unskilled workers, the firm will find it much easier to hire additional workers and so supply will be more elastic. The *level of unemployment* in the economy can also have a bearing on how easy it is for the firm to recruit additional workers, so supply will tend to be inelastic during times of full employment. If the firm has spare capacity, supply will tend to be elastic. If, for example, the Ford Motor Company is working 24-hour shifts, seven days a week, it would find it extremely difficult to increase supply, but if it were only working a four-day week, it would be much easier to increase supply, making supply elastic.

The *ease with which new firms can enter the industry* will also have an influence on elasticity of supply. If it is relatively simple and straightforward for new firms to enter the industry and start supplying the product, supply will be more elastic than if there are barriers preventing new firms from entering the industry. (Barriers to entry are covered in more detail in Unit 9.)

The *existence of stocks* held in reserve will make supply elastic, as the stocks can simply be released on to the market to increase supply if necessary. This means that those products that can be stored easily will tend to have an elastic supply, but for those products which have poor storage properties (e.g. fresh food or fresh flowers), supply will tend to be inelastic. If a firm *supplies the product in more than one market* supply will be elastic in any one market as supplies can be diverted from one market to another. For example, if a firm is supplying a product to more than one country, supplies to one country can be increased relatively easily by using some of the supplies that would have been sold elsewhere.

A crucial factor determining elasticity of supply is *time*. Given a longer time scale, it is easier to increase supply. This applies particularly to agricultural products: whatever the price, the supply of coconuts cannot be increased by very much for several years.

It is possible to identify three time periods. In the momentary period, supply is fixed, or perfectly inelastic. This is because at any moment in time there is only a given level of supply available. A music shop only has a fixed quantity of CDs at any moment in time. In the short run, it is possible to increase supply by employing more factor inputs. For example, manufacturers of CDs can employ more workers and use machinery more intensely through shift work. In the long run, supply can be increased by increasing the capacity of existing firms in the industry and by new firms entering the industry. (For a fuller discussion on the short run and the long run, see Unit 3.)

The relevance of elasticity of supply

Elasticity of supply has an important influence on what happens to the equilibrium price and quantity following changes in demand. If supply is inelastic, it will be extremely difficult to increase supply in response to a change in demand. Thus the effect of an increase in demand will be a relatively large increase in price but only a small increase in output, as illustrated in Figure 6.29. If, however, supply is elastic, it is much easier to accommodate an increase in demand, and output will rise with only a small increase in price, as illustrated in Figure 6.30. In the extreme case where supply is fixed, an increase

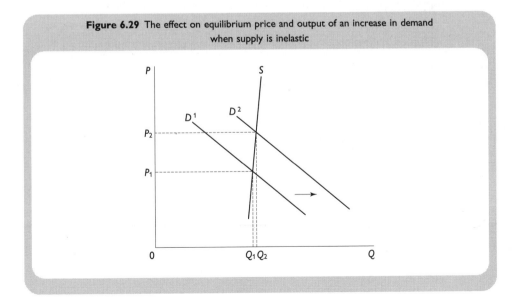

Figure 6.29 The effect on equilibrium price and output of an increase in demand when supply is inelastic

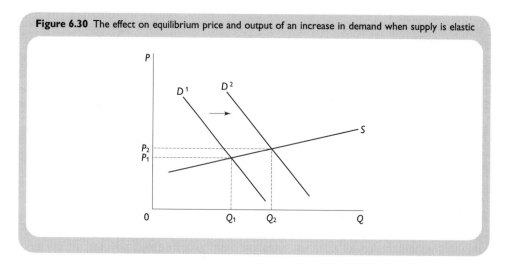

Figure 6.30 The effect on equilibrium price and output of an increase in demand when supply is elastic

in demand has no effect on output but results in a significant increase in price (see Figure 6.31). This would be the case, for example, for an event in the Olympic Games where local competitors are involved.

Elasticity of supply helps to explain why the price of agricultural products may fluctuate far more than the prices of manufactured goods. Not only is the supply of agricultural produce unpredictable due to bad weather or crop disease, but its supply also tends to be inelastic. It takes time to increase supply, so any increase in demand will result in a significant rise in price. In addition, agricultural products cannot be stored easily, so any fall in demand tends to be met by a fall in price as supply to the market cannot be reduced by putting it into storage. The supply of cars, however, could be increased in response to an increase in demand, through car manufacturers stepping up production or drawing on their reserve stocks of cars, thus making supply elastic, while if the demand for cars dropped, supply to the market could be reduced by storing the excess supply.

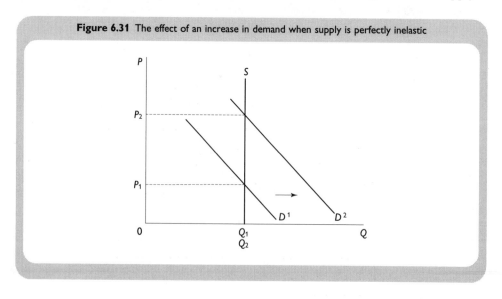

Figure 6.31 The effect of an increase in demand when supply is perfectly inelastic

Summary

In a market economy the price of products and the quantity sold are determined by the forces of demand and supply. Equilibrium occurs at that price at which the quantity demanded equals the quantity supplied. A change in the conditions of demand or supply will shift the curves, producing a new equilibrium. Elasticity measures the extent to which demand or supply changes in response to a change in any of the factors that influence demand or supply.

Review questions

1. What is a market?

2. Define demand.

3. What is the difference between a movement along a demand curve and a shift of the demand curve?

4. What factors are likely to influence the demand for new cars?

5. What is meant by an 'inferior' product?

6. The quantity demanded usually rises as price falls. Suggest three reasons why the quantity demanded might fall as price falls.

7. Suggest three reasons why the price elasticity of demand for product A might be greater than that for product B.

8. The demand for margarine has risen over the past decade, despite an increase in its price. Does this mean that the demand curve for margarine is upward-sloping? How else could you explain this phenomenon?

9. Illustrate, using demand and supply diagrams, the effect on the equilibrium price and output of beef of each of the following events:
   (a) the outbreak of 'mad cow disease' decreases the demand for beef;
   (b) cattle feed becomes more expensive;
   (c) the government decides to subsidise beef production;
   (d) there is an extensive 'Eat More Beef' advertising campaign.

10. The data below represents a demand and supply schedule for a product:

Price (£)	Quantity demanded (per week)	Quantity supplied (per week)
10	40	200
9	60	150
8	80	120
7	100	100
6	120	60
5	140	40

(a) What is the equilibrium price and output?

(b) What is the total revenue/expenditure at this price?

(c) If demand increases by 50 per cent at all prices, what will be the new market price?

(d) Returning to the original situation, if supply increases by 100 per cent at all prices, what will be the new equilibrium price?

(e) Provide sketches for (c) and (d).

11. A firm raises the price of its product from £1 to £1.20 and as a result, weekly sales fall from 1200 to 900. Calculate the price elasticity of demand, showing your method of calculation.

12. If a firm knows that its product has a price elasticity of demand of $(-)2$, what will be the percentage fall in sales if it raises its price by 10 per cent?

13. A firm's product has a price elasticity of demand of $(-)5$. With the price at £5 each, the firm is currently selling 240 items per week. It then lowers price and sales rise to 360 items per week. What is the new price?

14. A firm's product has a price elasticity of demand of $(-)0.25$. If 500 units are sold when the price is 50p each, how many units are likely to be sold if the price is lowered to 40p each?

15. The average income of consumers of a particular product increases from £500 to £540 per week, and demand for the product rises from 2000 to 2080 units per week. Calculate the income elasticity of demand.

16. The income elasticity of demand for a product is 1.5 at all prices. If real income rises by 6 per cent, what will happen to the demand for the product?

17. Would you expect the cross-elasticity of demand between the following products to be positive, negative or zero. Give reasons for your answer.

(a) Coca-Cola and Pepsi-Cola

(b) tea and coffee

(c) cars and petrol

(d) cars and public transport

(e) Rolls-Royce cars and Lada cars

18. What are the factors that determine the price elasticity of supply of a product?

19. What type of product might have a perfectly inelastic supply?

Essay questions

1. (a) Explain the concepts of price elasticity of demand, income elasticity of demand and cross-elasticity of demand.

(b) Examine the ways in which a business might use information about the different elasticities of demand for its product in its decision making.

2. Explain why the prices of agricultural products tend to fluctuate more than the prices of manufactured goods.

Reading 6.1

Potato shortages lead to increased prices

Potato shortages in the UK in the 1990s forced up supermarket prices and reduced the profits of Britain's fish-and-chip shops. Adverse weather conditions led to delays in the planting of crops and lower yields. Although potatoes were imported from countries such as Cyprus and Egypt, prices remained high.

Large potatoes used for baking or making chips were particularly scarce, leading to a doubling of prices. The National Federation of Fish Friers claimed that fish-and-chip shops were reluctant to pass on the extra costs to their customers as the takeaway food market is highly competitive. Shops were therefore having to cut their profits.

Questions

1. Illustrate, using a demand and supply diagram, the effect of the potato shortage on their equilibrium price.

2. Illustrate the effect of the arrival of imported potatoes. What effect is this likely to have on the equilibrium price?

3. Is the supply of potatoes elastic or inelastic? Give reasons for your answer.

4. According to the article, is the demand facing a takeaway food outlet likely to be elastic or inelastic?

5. If the price of a portion of chips rose by 20 per cent and, as a result, the demand for fish fell by 10 per cent, calculate the cross-elasticity of demand between fish and chips.

Reading 6.2

Barkers Bakers

Barkers is a small independent bakery who produce a range of bread loaves and rather delicious cakes. The average price, average weekly sales, and estimates of price elasticity and income elasticity of demand for loaves and cakes are as follows:

	Average price (£)	Average weekly sales	Price elasticity of demand	Income elasticity of demand
Loaves	0.80	1000	0.5	0.1
Cakes	1.00	100	2.0	2.0

▷

Questions

1. In an attempt to increase sales revenue, Mr Barker is considering raising the price of both loaves and cakes by 10 per cent. Using the information provided above, advise him of the consequences of this action, calculating the changes in sales revenue which are likely to occur.

2. Economic forecasts indicate that the average income of his customers is likely to rise by 5 per cent over the coming year. Estimate the level of sales of loaves and cakes that Mr Barker can expect if this forecast is to be believed.

Markets and market failure

Every individual is continually exerting himself to find out the most advantageous employment for whatever capital he can command. It is his own advantage, indeed, and not that of the society, which he has in view.... He generally, indeed, neither intends to promote the public interest, nor knows how much he is promoting it.... He intends only his own security,... only his own gain, and he is in this, as in many other cases, led by an invisible hand to promote an end which was no part of his intention. Nor is it always the worse for the society that it was no part of it. By pursuing his own interest he frequently promotes that of society more effectively than when he really intends to promote it.

Source: Adam Smith, *The Wealth of Nations* (1776), book IV, chapter 2

Customers sold unnecessary warranties

The Office of Fair Trading has declared that the extended warranties which are sold to consumers when they purchase electrical products represent poor value for money. The price of the warranties, which cover the cost of repairs for up to five years, are usually high compared with the costs of repairing the products should a fault arise. In any case, breakdowns are most likely to occur within the first year of purchase and would therefore be covered by the manufacturer's warranty that is included in the price of the product, rather than between years two to five. From now on, retailers must display the prices of the extended warranties in their shops for consumers to see, rather than putting pressure on the customer to buy the warranty at the time of paying for the product.

In the previous unit, we saw how the interaction of demand and supply resulted in an equilibrium price. In this unit we examine how well the market performs and why the market mechanism is regarded as an efficient way of allocating resources. We also look at those occasions when the market does not operate as efficiently as it might. These instances are referred to as **market failure**, and the example given in the article above concerning the sale of warranties for electrical products illustrates how the government may have to intervene to protect consumers.

One way of allocating resources is to have a centrally **planned economy**, where the state or its agencies plays a major part in deciding how resources will be used. It is the central state agency which decides what to produce, how to produce it and for whom the output is produced. This is the system that was associated with the Soviet Union for much of the twentieth century and was used in countries such as the UK during the Second World War.

In a free market, however, resources are allocated through the operation of the market forces of demand and supply with no government intervention (i.e. a **market economy**). Consumers demand those products which will give them the most satisfaction. Resources are owned by private individuals or groups of individuals and the owners of these resources use them to promote their own self-interest, which is to maximise the amount of profit they can make. In order to achieve this, they produce those goods and services which are in demand. It is the price mechanism which coordinates the decisions of all the individuals. The fact that the price mechanism works without any centralised planning means that it is sometimes referred to as a **laissez-faire system**, free from government intervention.

Consider the following scenario. Imagine that there is a change in consumer tastes, and that there is a switch in demand away from white bread and towards wholemeal bread. This can be illustrated in the diagrams below (see Figure 7.1a and b).

The increase in the demand for wholemeal bread will lead to an increase in its equilibrium price, while the fall in demand for white bread will lead to a fall in its price.

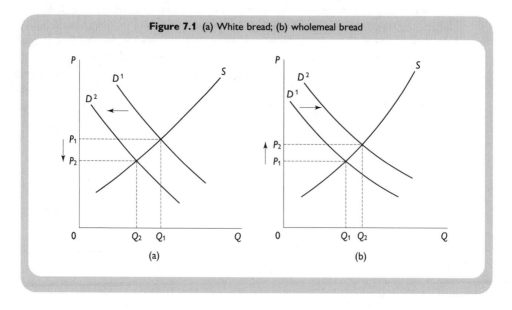

Figure 7.1 (a) White bread; (b) wholemeal bread

(a)

(b)

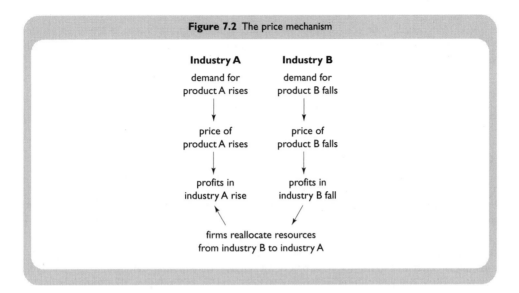

Figure 7.2 The price mechanism

Wholemeal bread will become more profitable to produce, while white bread will become less profitable. Bakers will therefore switch production to wholemeal bread and away from white bread. More resources will be used to produce wholemeal bread while fewer resources will be used to produce white bread. This transfer of resources from the production of white bread to the production of wholemeal bread has been brought about by the price mechanism. There is no central direction, telling bakers to produce less white bread and more wholemeal bread; the process has occurred automatically. Adam Smith, writing in *The Wealth of Nations* in 1776, and quoted at the beginning of this unit, referred to this process as the 'invisible hand' of the price mechanism. The price mechanism allocates the resources with no government intervention. Decision making is decentralised, with thousands of individuals taking decisions about consumption and production every day. The workings of the price mechanism are illustrated in Figure 7.2.

The price mechanism does not only work in the market for goods: it also operates in the labour market. Thus an increase in the demand for cars will lead to an increase in demand for car workers. This increase in demand for car workers will lead to a rise in their wages, and workers will be attracted into the motor industry. Meanwhile, if there is a fall in demand for coal, there will be a drop in demand for coal miners, the wages of miners will fall relative to those of other workers and people will leave the industry in search of more profitable employment. Again, there is no central planning authority telling workers to change jobs, to leave one occupation and enter another occupation. The process happens automatically through the price mechanism, with consumer preferences affecting wage levels in different industries and therefore reallocating labour to those industries where it is required.

Prices play a key role in the market mechanism. Prices are the signals that indicate to producers which goods and services are in demand and therefore which products to produce. If consumers express an increased demand for a product, the price of this product will rise and firms will be encouraged to produce it as there will be a greater reward. Likewise, if consumers stop buying other products, the price of these products will fall and firms will stop producing them, shifting their resources to the production of more profitable products.

Price also acts as a rationing system. If demand for a product is greater than supply, the price of the product will rise until only those prepared to pay the higher price obtain the good.

Advantages of the market system

In many respects the price mechanism works remarkably well – so much so, in fact, that we take it for granted. Shops are full of a vast variety of products at a range of qualities and prices, offering the consumer a wide choice. Very rarely are there any shortages, and this is because the price mechanism directs the economy towards the production of those goods and services which are in demand. Prices and output react quickly to changes in consumers' demand patterns. Ultimately, it is the consumers who determine which products are produced. Firms will not produce goods and services that consumers do not want; if they do, they will go out of business. Consumers' spending power therefore determines the allocation of resources. This concept is known as **consumer sovereignty**, and it is very different from having resources allocated by government officials, whose decisions may not reflect the preferences of the consumers.

The market system is said to be efficient in two ways. First, it promotes *allocative efficiency* (i.e. an efficient allocation of resources) because it ensures that resources are used to produce the goods and services that are in demand and are not wasted on products that are not in demand. The desire for profit means that firms will quickly change their production to adapt to the new demands. Resources are therefore shifted towards expanding sectors of the economy and away from declining industries. Secondly, the market system also promotes *productive efficiency*, which relates to the efficiency of the firm and the cost of making products. Due to the competition that exists between firms, they will have to produce goods and services at their lowest possible cost and of a high quality in order to survive. Inefficient firms will be driven out of the market by their competitors. Competition also promotes the innovation of new products and new production methods.

Living standards in market economies today are the highest the world has ever seen and this is largely the result of the market system. The search for profit leads to investment by firms, which, in turn, promotes economic growth. With many firms producing goods and services, consumers are also presented with a wide variety of choice of products.

Freedom of choice is often put forward as an advantage of the market system. Consumers are free to demand the products which they wish to buy, producers are free to decide the products they wish to produce, and workers are free to decide which industry they wish to work in. There is no direction of labour: people are free to work wherever they choose. There is thus no control by the government, and the market system therefore has no need for a central government agency to direct resources. This represents a saving for the taxpayer as there is no need for an expensive bureaucracy to be financed.

Hence, in many circumstances, the free-market system leads to a favourable and efficient allocation of resources.

Market failure

In practice, however, markets do not always make the most efficient use of resources. There are occasions and circumstances in which the market does not perform as efficiently as it might and does not result in an optimal allocation of resources. This is called market failure. In these circumstances it may be possible to justify government interference in the market mechanism in order to improve the allocation of resources.

Monopoly firms

The market mechanism depends on competition between firms, but in practice, the amount of competition might be limited. Industries may come to be dominated by large firms who have a degree of monopoly power. These firms may participate in practices which restrict the amount of competition. Without competition, many of the advantages of the market system cease to exist. Limited competition may mean that firms have no need to be as efficient as possible. Consumers therefore end up with a limited choice, and firms with monopoly power are able to restrict output and charge high prices. In the UK, consumers benefited from reduced prices and more choice in the supply of gas and telecommunications when competition was introduced to challenge the monopoly power of British Gas and British Telecom.

However, monopoly firms may become so powerful in the marketplace that the concept of 'consumer sovereignty' disappears. Instead of consumers expressing a demand for certain products and then firms producing these products, some argue that there exists instead 'producer sovereignty'. In other words, it is powerful firms who decide which products they are going to produce, and they then persuade consumers, through sophisticated and extensive advertising campaigns, to purchase these products. The American economist, J.K. Galbraith refers to this as 'revised sequence'. Under **monopoly**, it is the firms who decide the allocation of resources and what to produce, not the consumers. The problem of monopoly is discussed more fully in Unit 9.

Wasteful competition

While competition is generally deemed to be desirable, there are circumstances where competition leads to inefficiency. Small firms competing with each other might prevent the utilisation of economies of scale (see Unit 4), which are important in industries such as electricity supply, where duplication of services would be a waste of resources. Likewise, the duplication of research activities represents a waste of resources, and the competitive advertising which occurs in a market system could also be seen in this light.

Public goods

The market is unable to provide what are referred to as **public goods**. Public goods have two important characteristics. First, that of *non-rivalry in consumption*, which means that the use or consumption of the product by one individual does not reduce the amount available to other consumers. The second characteristic is that of *non-excludability*, which means that it is impossible to exclude non-payers. Individuals could refuse to pay for these products and yet still benefit from them. Those who benefit from the product but do not pay are termed **free-riders**. National defence is probably the best example of a public good. By taking advantage of a national defence system, I am not preventing others from benefiting from it. Also, if only half the population wished to finance a national defence programme, the other half of the population would still benefit, despite the fact that they had not helped to pay for it. But the market system operates on the basis of firms charging individual consumers for products. If firms cannot exclude non-payers from consuming the product, they will not produce it. Hence public goods have to be provided by the state and paid for collectively through taxation. Other examples of public goods are flood protection schemes and street lighting.

Merit goods

Merit goods are goods and services that can be, and indeed are provided through the market mechanism but which if left to be provided solely by the free market, would be underprovided. Education and health care are good examples of merit goods. If left to be provided by the free market, some individuals may choose not to consume these products, or may not be able to afford to consume them. In order to encourage consumption of these products, the government might subsidise them or provide them free of charge to the consumer. The provision of merit goods is largely a matter of values. The state might also provide facilities such as libraries, playing fields and swimming pools because of a belief that they are desirable additions to society.

Demerit goods are those products which are provided through the free market but which are not considered to benefit the individual or society. The government therefore discourages or prohibits the purchase of these goods and services through taxation or legislation. An example of such a product is tobacco. Figure 7.3 illustrates the effect of a

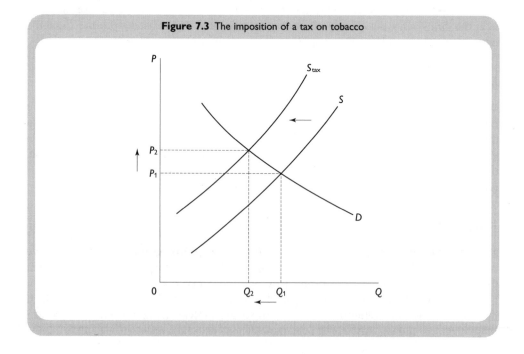

Figure 7.3 The imposition of a tax on tobacco

tax placed on tobacco. The supply curve shifts to the left, resulting in a higher equilibrium price and a smaller output than would have existed given a free market with no taxation. We will examine in more detail the use of taxes to modify behaviour in Unit 8.

Externalities

Market prices fail to take external costs and benefits into account, or what one might describe as 'spill over' effects. When making decisions concerning consumption or production under a market system, people are only likely to consider the costs and benefits to themselves of any decision. Consumers are interested in maximising their own satisfaction and will make their purchasing decisions based on what gives them the greatest benefit, while producers will produce those goods and services which maximise their personal profit. It is **private costs** and **private benefits** which determine what goods and services are produced in a free market; costs and benefits falling on others are likely to be disregarded. The price of the product may not therefore reflect the full cost (or benefit) of providing that product, and, as a consequence, too much (or too little) of the product may be produced. When there is a divergence between the private costs and the **social costs** of any activity, there is said to be an **externality**, the social cost of an activity being the private cost plus any externality or spill over.

Consider, for example, a firm that uses a production process which pollutes the environment by discharging chemicals and black smoke into the atmosphere. The firm will calculate the costs of production by reference to the costs falling on the firm itself. It will not, however, include the costs incurred by the local community as a result of the pollution, such as poor health or dirty washing. The market mechanism fails to take into account these external costs, as decisions are made on the basis of private costs only. We can represent this situation in a diagram. In Figure 7.4, if the firm were to meet the full

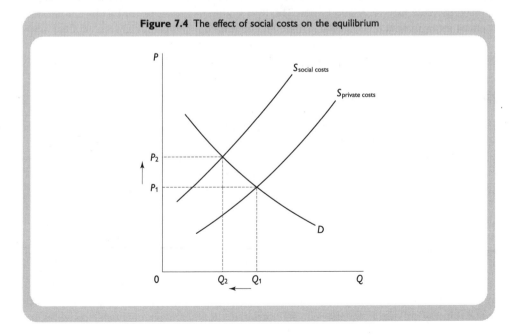

Figure 7.4 The effect of social costs on the equilibrium

costs of production, including the costs of pollution, its supply curve would shift to the left as a result of the increase in costs. Consequently, the level of output would be less than is the case at present (Q_2 instead of Q_1), and the equilibrium price higher (P_2 instead of P_1). But because the external costs are not included, more is produced, representing a misallocation of resources.

Health and education are examples of products which yield external benefits. Aside from the benefits to the individual, the economy and society as a whole benefit from having a healthy and educated workforce. In the case of health, society as a whole benefits if individuals are vaccinated against infectious and contagious diseases, while an educated workforce should have a positive effect on economic growth.

Exercise

Identify (a) the private costs, (b) the private benefits, (c) the external costs, and (d) the external benefits of each of the following:

1. The building of a by-pass around a busy town centre.
2. The decision by a firm to install labour-saving automated machinery.

To a certain extent the problems of externalities can be dealt with through the market mechanism. If consumers become increasingly aware of environmental issues, those firms who develop and promote a 'green' image may find that they have a competitive edge over rival firms, while those firms who have little regard for the environment may find that they lose customers and will either be forced to change their approach or go out of business. In this case, the market mechanism itself may result in firms introducing pollution controls, or environmentally friendly products such as 'dolphin friendly tuna', or packaging made from recycled paper. The firm is able to capitalise on this by publicising itself as environmentally friendly. However, leaving the price mechanism to deal with externalities is not usually a satisfactory solution, and in the next unit we shall consider measures which the government may adopt to tackle the problem.

Information failure

The market system assumes that consumers have perfect knowledge and act rationally. In some circumstances, however, consumers have imperfect information and are not always sufficiently informed to make rational decisions as to what products will benefit them most. Consumers are unlikely to have complete information on the full range of products and prices at all outlets, and this may lead to consumers making poor purchasing decisions. They cannot be expected to understand the complex technical details about many of the products they buy or be sure of the quality of the product. Sometimes, the market provides the information, through organisations such as the Consumers' Association and magazines such as *What Car?* which publish reports and features on quality, safety and prices of products, but they do not always provide complete and reliable information. Persuasive advertising may also distort consumer choice and lead to consumers buying products that do not maximise their satisfaction. The extract at the start of this unit, on the sale of warranties for electrical products, provides an example of information failure. The labour market is also subject to information failure, where unemployment may persist because unemployed workers are unaware of job vacancies.

Immobility of resources

According to the price mechanism, resources will be shifted out of those industries which experience a decline in demand, and shifted into those industries experiencing a rise in demand. In reality, however, resources do not always transfer from one use to another so easily in response to a change in demand. The workforce, in particular, is far from perfectly mobile, either from an occupational or geographical point of view. If there is a decline in the demand for coal, a miner cannot simply transfer into another occupation, since he may not have the necessary skills or qualifications. Likewise, he cannot easily transfer to a job in another part of the country, due to factors such as the housing shortage and family and social ties. This might therefore give rise to *regional unemployment*. Similarly, firms cannot easily switch production from one type of good to another, because resources cannot always be transferred from one use to another. There are also often barriers preventing firms from entering into an industry, such as lack of finance or technical expertise. (**Barriers to entry** are discussed more fully in Unit 9.)

Unemployment

We have described above how information failure or the immobility of resources may lead to **unemployment**, but, in addition, the free-market economy is subject to fluctuations in the level of economic activity. The uncoordinated decisions of thousands of individual producers means that, at times, resources will stand idle or be underutilised. The market system does not ensure the continuous full employment of all the resources in the economy, and this results in periods of heavy unemployment.

Volatile prices/unstable equilibrium

Markets tend to be constantly fluctuating. While price changes can have beneficial effects, acting as signals to producers, frequent price changes can be harmful, creating uncertainty and making it difficult for firms to plan for the future. Where supply is inelastic it takes a long time for supply to adjust in response to changes in price. This is often the case in the market for agricultural goods where there is a considerable time-lag between the decision to change the level of production and the eventual change in output. Prices are often volatile and may not settle at an equilibrium level, but instead may fluctuate widely. It may take a year or more after planting a crop for the supply to respond to an increase in demand. As a result, prices will remain high, and farmers may continue planting the crop in anticipation of high profits. But when the increased supplies eventually come onto the market, this may cause the price of the product to fall sharply and many farmers may suffer losses. Farmers may then cut back on the planting of this crop, in view of its low price, only to create a shortage again in the future and a consequent rise in its price.

In the labour market too, it may prove very difficult for a stable equilibrium to be reached. For example, if there is a shortage of skilled workers in an industry leading to an increase in their wage, it may take time for potential entrants to the industry to notice

Table 7.1: UK household income distribution by quintile groups, 1995/96

Quintile group	Share of national income (%)
Bottom 20 per cent	3
Next 20 per cent	7
Middle 20 per cent	15
Next 20 per cent	25
Top 20 per cent	50

Source: Economic Trends, March 1997.

the higher wage. It will take even longer for them to become qualified, and hence the shortage of a particular skill may persist for some time. Here too there may then be a problem of too many people entering the industry, so that eventually supply exceeds demand, leading in turn to a drop in wage levels.

Inequalities

The market system tends to produce wide inequalities in income and wealth that many find socially unacceptable. The distribution of income also has implications on how resources are allocated. We have seen that through the price mechanism, resources are allocated in response to the demand of consumers. But in order for demand to be effective, it needs to be backed by the ability to pay for the product: that is, it has to be backed by money. But as money is not equally shared out among the population, those people with a high income have more say in what gets produced than those on a low income. The price mechanism responds to those who have the greatest spending power. Thus some people are able to demand and obtain a wide range of goods and services, while others may have to go without basic necessities. Resources are used to produce what some people might regard as frivolous luxuries for the rich, while the poor have to forgo essentials. Table 7.1 illustrates that in 1995/96, the richest 20 per cent of households in the UK earned 50 per cent of national income and therefore had the greatest influence on how resources are utilised, while the remaining 80 per cent of households shared the other half of national income between them.

Summary

The market mechanism allocates resources through the interplay of demand and supply. The concept of consumer sovereignty ensures that resources are used to produce those goods and services which are in demand. Competition and the profit motive ensure that firms operate efficiently, providing a wide range of products at low prices and of a high quality. The system responds quickly to changing circumstances and requires no government bureaucracy to administer it.

However, in some circumstances, markets fail to produce an efficient allocation of resources. Market failure arises due to the inability of the market to ▷

provide public goods, the underprovision of merit goods, and the market's failure to consider external costs and benefits. The concentration of producer power may restrict competition, leading to inefficiency and restriction of consumer choice. Sometimes, markets are volatile and fail to settle at an equilibrium, and unemployment of resources is common. Markets may also fail due to information deficiencies.

Review questions

1. In what sense can it be said that, in a market economy, consumers determine the allocation of resources?
2. Explain what is meant by 'market failure'.
3. What are the main causes of market failure?
4. What is a public good? Give examples.
5. Why is the free-market system an ineffective means of supplying people with public goods?
6. What is a merit good? Give examples.
7. Are the reasons for the state provision of health and education the same as for the state provision of defence and street-lights?
8. Explain the reasons why governments vigorously promote the vaccination of children against infectious diseases such as polio and measles.
9. Are roads a public good or could some roads be provided by the market? What would be the advantages and disadvantages of having some roads provided by the market?
10. What is an externality? Give examples.
11. Provide examples of how the market mechanism might not provide adequate protection of the environment.
12. What are the main obstacles to the mobility of labour?
13. Provide examples where prices might only adjust slowly to changes in the conditions of demand and supply.

Essay questions

1. Explain how the price mechanism allocates resources. Outline the advantages and discuss the limitations of the market approach to resource allocation.
2. (a) Compare the main features of a market economy with those of a planned economy.
   (b) What problems might countries experience as they move from a planned economy towards a market economy?

Reading 7.1

The mid-1990s saw the appearance of a new kind of alcoholic drink, alcoholic lemonade. This was soon followed by a vast range of alcoholic fruit drinks and colas. Within two years, there were over 90 different brands of 'alcopop' in the UK, with sales believed to be worth around £300 million a year. The alcohol content of most of the brands is between 4 per cent and 5 per cent, stronger than many beers and lagers, and some are as potent as 9 per cent.

That fact that alcopops tend to resemble soft drinks has caused much concern in the belief that these drinks may encourage under-age drinking. Brewers have been criticised for using cartoon images to promote the drinks, and campaign groups such as Alcohol Concern feel that the drinks are deliberately marketed in such a way as to appeal to younger age groups. MPs have warned that legislation might be necessary to curb alcopop advertising, while Chancellors of the Exchequer have responded by raising the tax on alcopops in recent budgets.

Brewers have insisted that the drinks are targeted at an adult audience, and believe that there is no evidence to suggest that alcoholic lemonades incite young people to drink alcohol. They claim that if alcopops were being drunk by children, then sales of soft drinks would have fallen, which has not occurred. Instead, it is the sales of beer and cider that have been damaged by the increased popularity of alcopops.

Questions

1. Why might 'alcopop' drinks be classified as a demerit good?

2. Do you consider that the introduction of alcopops to the market is an example of consumer sovereignty in action, or is it a case of 'producer sovereignty'? Give reasons for your answer.

3. What additional measures could the government introduce if they felt that the sale of alcopops was not in the interests of society?

Government intervention in markets

EU destroys mountains of fresh food

The policies of the European Union continue to result in large payments to farmers for fresh produce that is then destroyed. The scheme, which covers fourteen different fruit and vegetables, involves the European Union paying farmers for the food when there is a good harvest in order to stop prices falling. Despite promises from the European Commission that it would reduce the waste, more tomatoes, cauliflowers, apricots and pears have been destroyed than in previous years. The system has been criticised as it is claimed that it encourages farmers to deliberately grow surplus produce, which then has to be destroyed. Meanwhile, families on low incomes are unable to afford to buy fresh fruit and vegetables because the prices are kept artificially high.

Although EU rules permit the surplus to be distributed free to hospitals and children's homes, or to be given away as foreign aid, most of the surplus produce is destroyed. This then creates further problems; so much has been dumped that it has started to pollute the water table in some areas. The European Commission defends the system by claiming that without the official intervention, there would be huge price reductions whenever there was a good harvest and farmers would suffer a loss of income.

In Unit 6 we looked at how markets work, and in Unit 7 we looked not only at the efficiency of the market system, but also at why markets may on occasions fail to promote an efficient allocation of resources. It is because the price mechanism fails to perform efficiently at times that the government intervenes in the market. In this unit, we look now at the part that government can play in countering the cases of market failure and at measures that they can take to help make the market mechanism operate more efficiently. Government intervention can range from total replacement of the market mechanism, through planning output and providing products itself, to trying to modify or regulate the market through the use of taxes and subsidies, price controls, and rules and regulations.

One of the most important instances of market failure is the breakdown of competition between firms and the development of monopolies. The government approach to monopoly firms is a subject that warrants particular attention and is covered elsewhere in this book (see Unit 11).

Taxes and subsidies

Taxes and subsidies can be used to influence market prices and therefore can affect the pattern of consumption and production. We saw in the previous unit that one of the drawbacks of the market mechanism was the failure of producers and consumers to take externalities into account when making decisions. Their decisions are based on the private cost and the private benefit to the individual without reference to the external costs and external benefits of production or consumption. This will therefore result in a misallocation of resources as people are not taking the full costs of production into account. Taxes and subsidies can be used to provide incentives to individuals to change their pattern of consumption or production so that their decisions generate fewer external costs and more external benefits.

Taxes

By placing a tax on a firm which causes an external cost, the government is forcing the firm to face up to the full cost of its actions. The tax will increase the private costs of production. Faced with increased costs, the firm will consider either adopting alternative methods of production that do not result in external costs and therefore do not incur the tax, or even switching production to a different product. If the firm is able to pass the tax on to the consumer in the form of higher prices, consumers will switch their demand to other products and the price mechanism will thus ensure that firms switch production away from the product which generates the external cost.

The effect of the tax is illustrated in Figure 8.1. The imposition of the tax increases the costs of production and so shifts the supply curve to the left. This results in a higher equilibrium price and a lower output than would have existed without the tax. An example of this is the higher tax that is levied on leaded petrol in comparison to unleaded petrol. Lead was originally added to petrol in order to improve vehicle performance, but an external cost of this expedient was to increase the amount of lead being discharged into the atmosphere and a subsequent increased risk of lead poisoning, particularly among children. The government therefore decided to tax leaded fuel more heavily than unleaded fuel, giving consumers an incentive to switch to the unleaded variety, motor

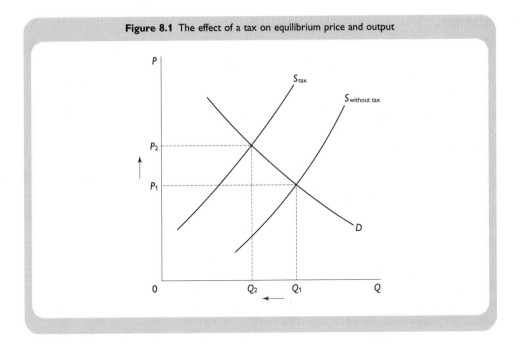

Figure 8.1 The effect of a tax on equilibrium price and output

manufacturers an incentive to switch to cars which run on unleaded fuel, and petrol companies an incentive to supply unleaded rather than leaded petrol.

The attraction of using taxes to counter the effects of external costs is that it is a move towards the 'polluter pays' principle. The polluter is having to pay for the costs and damage inflicted on others. Taxes provide incentives for firms to look for 'greener' methods of production, and also persuade consumers to switch to 'greener' products. The amount of pollution should therefore be reduced. In addition, it still involves using a market-based approach to the allocation of resources; the taxes merely amend market prices to reflect more accurately the true costs of production.

A problem that arises in the use of taxation to correct market failure is that its success depends on the price elasticity of demand for the product. If a product has a demand which is price inelastic, then there will not be a significant reduction in demand for the product following the imposition of a tax, and the switch to alternative products will not occur. A further difficulty with using taxation to deal with the problem of external costs is that it is not easy to impose a tax which exactly mirrors the effect of the costs to the environment. How, for example, can you accurately measure the costs of pollution? Costs cannot always be quantified, and hence to an extent it is a subjective valuation. It might be difficult to predict how long the effects of the pollution will last. Moreover, each firm produces a different level of pollution. It is therefore likely to be very difficult to identify and measure the amount of pollution generated by each firm and then to impose a tax that will accurately reflect the cost of that pollution. A government might also be reluctant to impose a pollution tax on firms as this will mean that their products will be less competitive in world trade if other countries do not impose equivalent taxes. On the other hand, it could be argued that, for example, lenient controls on car exhaust emissions in the EU have been to the disadvantage of European car manufacturers, since it has hampered the export of their cars to Japan and the USA.

Case study

Should there be a carbon tax?

Emissions of carbon dioxide from the use of fossil fuels are believed to be one of the chief causes of the 'greenhouse effect' and global warming. Most developed countries have agreed to reduce their emissions of carbon dioxide and other greenhouse gases. One proposal to help reduce carbon dioxide emissions has been to impose a carbon tax on the users of fossil fuels. Here we look at some of the issues associated with such a tax.

One advantage of the tax is that it will be the users of fossil fuels who have to pay for the damage associated with their use: the 'polluter pays' principle. Without such a tax, those who make use of fossil fuels do not bear the full cost of their actions. As a result of the higher prices, users of fossil fuels, both firms and consumers, are likely to reduce their emissions by switching to alternative fuel sources, thereby reducing the extent of the damage. The tax should also encourage research and development into alternative energy sources.

However, there are many arguments against such a tax. What should the level of the tax be? What is the extent of the damage caused through the greenhouse effect? The lack of a suitable alternative source of energy in many cases means that there is unlikely to be a switch away from the use of fossil fuels in the short run. The price elasticity of demand for energy is low, meaning that there would not be much reduction in carbon emissions as a result of the higher tax. Higher energy prices will have an impact on inflation, by pushing up prices. Increased costs of production might lead to lower rates of economic growth and higher unemployment, and would damage the international competitiveness of firms who have to pay higher energy costs than those firms in countries where there is no such tax. The tax would also be prejudicial to people on low incomes as they spend a higher proportion of their income on fuel and power than do the rich, although advocates of the tax argue that the revenue gained from the tax could be used to reduce other rates of taxation such as income tax and national insurance.

Subsidies

While taxes can be used in situations where there is an external cost to society, the government can also use **subsidies** in those cases where there is an external benefit. Subsidies provide firms and consumers with an incentive to switch to environmentally friendly production methods and products. Consider the case of a firm which spends time and money training its workers to a high level of skill and competence. It is not only the firm which benefits from the trained workers, but society as well. The government might therefore consider subsidising the training costs a firm faces in order to encourage it to train more people. Likewise, society as a whole and not just the firm itself benefits from any research and development carried out by a firm. The government might therefore decide to subsidise research activity. Firms can also be given subsidies to help pay for equipment and filters which reduce the level of pollution.

Consumer goods and services which are environmentally friendly can also be subsidised, lowering their price and making them more attractive to consumers. An example here would be the case of motorists who drive their cars into city centres, causing congestion and pollution that imposes costs on others. The local authorities could provide a free or subsidised 'park and ride' scheme, where motorists could leave their cars in a free car park on the edge of the city and use a subsidised bus service to gain access to the city centre. This would then reduce the congestion and pollution in the city centre.

The effectiveness of such a scheme, however, depends on the cross-elasticity of demand between bus transport and travel by private car, and on the price elasticity of demand of private car travel. If the cross-elasticity of demand between bus travel and travel by private car is low, then motorists will be unwilling to switch to the 'park and ride' scheme, despite the fact that it is subsidised and offered at a low price or even free of charge. The local authority might try to reinforce the scheme by imposing high charges for parking in the city centre. But if the demand to travel by private car is price inelastic, motorists will still drive into the city centre despite the high parking charges, and the overall result of the measures will have little effect on the problems of pollution and congestion.

Subsidies are also used in those cases where there is underprovision of a product by the market. In the case of merit goods such as health and education, some individuals may choose not to consume them or may not be able to afford to consume them if they were provided only at free market prices. One option for the government is to provide a subsidy to the private suppliers of these services, so that the user does not have to pay the full cost of the service, as is the case in dental treatment or assisted school places.

Regulations

Rather than use taxes and subsidies to try to influence the behaviour of firms and individuals, the government often takes a much more direct approach by imposing rules and regulations on the market in an attempt to correct market failure. The use of regulation is wide and varied, including, for example, regulations governing the design and construction of products to ensure safety standards, planning regulations to protect green fields and limit building developments, and regulations regarding monopolies, mergers and anti-competitive practices.

Regulations are often used to overcome the problem of information deficiencies. We saw in the previous unit that imperfect information is a cause of market failure. The government therefore has a role to play in improving the knowledge of consumers, workers and producers, thus helping them to make more informed decisions. Legislation exists to ensure the quality and safety of products such as cars and electrical goods. Doctors and dentists have to be registered and have recognised qualifications before they can practise. The ingredients have to be listed on a can of food or drink. In its attempts to introduce elements of the market system into health and education, the government has tried to improve the information available to those who consume these services by publishing tables showing the lengths of waiting lists at hospitals and school exam results.

The government might use legislation to deal with the problem of external costs. They might impose maximum levels on the amount of pollution that is allowed or they might prohibit the discharge of harmful effluents into the environment entirely. Any breaches of the regulations mean that the polluter is fined. Legislation, rather than the use of taxes and subsidies, is particularly likely to be used where the external costs to society are very great or life-threatening. For example, there are strict regulations regarding the conduct of nuclear power stations. Simply imposing a tax on the power stations that allow radiation leaks would not be very satisfactory.

The problem with using legislation to counter the effects of external costs is that an agency has to be set up to monitor, measure and supervise the polluters and enforce the legislation. Inspections might be few and far between, with the result that many firms will continue to impose external costs on society, since the chances of being caught are slim. The regulatory body will cost money to run and maintain. The implementation of regulation is costly and the situation may arise where the cost of regulation may be more than the external costs that it is designed to eliminate. What level of pollution should be permitted? There is no definitive answer. Zero pollution is not necessarily desirable as this might only be achieved through zero output. In addition, the problem of measuring the pollution and identifying the polluter still remains. Some externalities extend beyond national boundaries, for example pollution caused by British power stations causing acid rain and deforestation in Scandinavia. In circumstances such as this, action by national governments may not be sufficient, and there may be a need for international cooperation to deal with such a problem.

Although governments are having increasingly to respond to citizens' greater environmental awareness, the increased costs and regulations that firms are facing as a result of measures designed to change their behaviour may put them at a disadvantage when competing with international competitors. Strict environmental rules and regulations may also conflict with the government's desire to attract multinational investment into the country. Multinationals are likely to locate where there are least rules and regulations and production costs are lowest.

Government provision of goods and services

The most extreme form of government intervention in the market is for the government to provide the goods and services itself. Sometimes these services may still be sold through the market, as is the case with postal services, but government provision is also necessary in order to provide public goods, which the market mechanism is unable to provide. Thus services such as defence are provided by central government and street-lighting by local government. Merit goods, which the market mechanism is likely to undersupply, are also provided by the state or its agencies. Thus there is state provision of education and health, libraries and playing fields.

The nationalisation of an industry may be desirable where there are widespread external costs and benefits arising from production, since the government is more likely to take these into account when making production decisions. The government may, for example, decide to keep open an unprofitable coal-mine on the grounds that it is providing employment in an unemployment blackspot; a privately run firm would close the mine if it were unprofitable, regardless of the social costs of closure. Nationalisation should enable an industry to take advantage of the economies of large-scale production without incurring the problems associated with a privately owned monopoly. The assumption here is that state ownership of the industry means that it is more likely to be run in the public interest and not just for high profit. This argument applies particularly to natural monopolies, where the product can most efficiently be supplied by just one firm (e.g. water supply). Nationalisation and its problems are covered in more detail in Unit 12.

Equity

The free-market system results in inequalities in income and wealth, with the result that not everyone has an equal influence on how resources are used. Thus the poor have to go without basic necessities, while resources are used to provide luxuries for the rich. The government can try to make the distribution of income fairer through the use of progressive income taxes, where the rich pay a higher proportion of their income in tax than the poor, and through welfare payments such as unemployment benefit and retirement pensions. This will then lead to less demand for luxury products but more demand for, and therefore more resources devoted to, basic necessities.

Those opposed to the redistribution of income in this way argue that it destroys incentives. High tax rates, it is argued, may discourage people from working, while welfare payments might discourage effort.

An alternative way in which the government can overcome some of the problems of inequalities in income is to lower the market equilibrium prices of some products through the use of subsidies or price controls if it feels that those prices are too high.

Price controls

The government may feel that the equilibrium price which the market mechanism determines is too high or too low. It may therefore decide to impose a maximum or a minimum **price control** on the market.

Maximum price control

The government may decide to set a maximum price (a price ceiling) if it feels that the free market equilibrium price is too high. A maximum price control is most likely to be applied to a necessity product, where, perhaps because of a shortage in supply, the price has risen beyond the reach of many people. Such price controls are very common in less developed countries where the prices of basic foodstuffs are often controlled. In wartime, the supply of many essential products is interrupted, leading to huge increases in price. On the basis of fairness, the government might set a maximum price so that poorer people can still afford to buy the products. Maximum price controls have also been applied to the housing market where, because of a shortage of rented property, rents in some parts of the country rose to very high levels, which meant that some people were unable to afford housing.

However, the imposition of a maximum price control can lead to further problems. Consider Figure 8.2 which represents the demand and supply for a product. The market is in equilibrium, with the price at P_e and output at Q_e, but the government feels that the price is too high and out of the reach of the poorer members of the community. It therefore decides to impose a maximum price of P_{max} which is intended to help the poor, as they are able to afford this price. However, the price of P_{max} means that the market is in disequilibrium. Demand for the product has risen to Q_2 as a result of the lower price, while supply has fallen to Q_1, since many suppliers who were willing to supply the product at a price of P_e are no longer willing to supply it at the lower price of P_{max}. There is now an excess demand represented by distance Q_1Q_2. In a free market, the price mechanism would deal with the excess demand through an increase of price back to P_e,

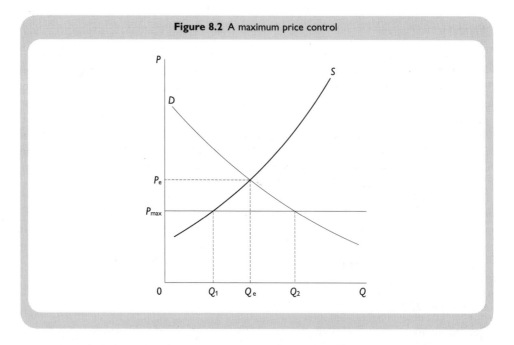

Figure 8.2 A maximum price control

where demand equals supply. However, the government has made it illegal to sell the product above the price of P_{max}, so the excess demand persists.

The shortage that persists will mean that queues are likely to develop for the product, as often happened in Eastern European countries where the governments frequently kept prices at a low level. Shopkeepers might start discriminating and only sell the product to selected customers. The government might have to introduce a rationing scheme, as was

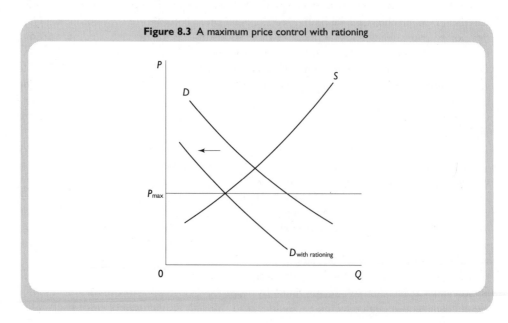

Figure 8.3 A maximum price control with rationing

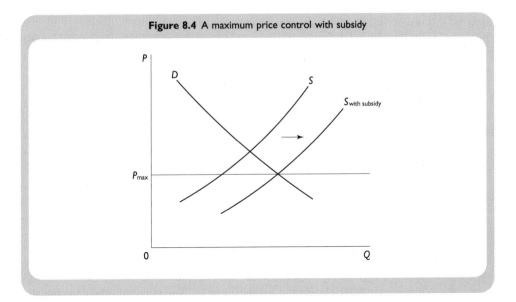

Figure 8.4 A maximum price control with subsidy

done in the UK in the Second World War, to ensure fair shares for all. The effect of rationing would be to limit demand, shifting the demand to the left (see Figure 8.3).

A maximum price is also likely to lead to a **black market** developing, where the product is sold illegally at a much higher price. An alternative approach which the government could adopt in conjunction with the maximum price control is one of subsidising production to encourage firms to produce more of the product. This would have the effect of shifting the supply curve to the right (see Figure 8.4). So although the government policy of a maximum price control was well intentioned, it has created additional problems. A rationing scheme needs financing and administering, as does a scheme of providing subsidies to producers, representing an increased cost to society. The maximum price control may encourage people to evade the law, by charging black market prices, and the poor, who were the ones the government was aiming to help, are unable to afford these prices. Maximum prices may also lead to a decline in the quality of products, as, due to the excess demand, producers know that they will have no problem in selling their output, even if it is not of the best quality.

Exercise

Melchester Rovers have been drawn against Newtown Athletic in the semi-final of the FA Cup. Demand for tickets to see the match is high, but the ground where the tie is to be played has a fixed capacity of 40,000 seats. In order to ensure that the average football fan can afford to buy a ticket, the football authorities have set the price of tickets at £15 each, even though demand far exceeds supply at this price.

1. Depict this situation on a supply and demand diagram, showing clearly on the diagram the total demand for tickets at £15 each, the amount of tickets that will actually be sold, and the excess demand that exists.

2. What is likely to occur as a result of the decision to fix seat prices at £15 each?

Minimum price control

The government might impose a minimum price control (price floor) if it feels that the equilibrium price determined by the market is too low. The reason for setting a minimum price control is usually to protect and maintain the income of producers, or, in the case of a minimum wage control, to ensure that workers receive a reasonable wage.

Consider Figure 8.5 which represents the demand and supply of an agricultural product. The government may feel that, given the current state of the market, the income that farmers get from the sale of this product is not sufficient to provide them with a reasonable standard of living. They therefore impose a minimum price of P_{min} in order that the farmers may sell their produce for a higher price. However, at the price of P_{min}, the quantity demanded has fallen to Q_1 as a result of the higher price, while the quantity supplied has risen to Q_2, as more farmers are now willing to supply the product, given that they can sell it for a higher price. There is therefore an excess supply, or a surplus, represented by the distance Q_1Q_2. In a free market the price would fall back to P_e where demand equals supply. If the government wishes to maintain a price of P_{min}, it must take certain measures to stop the price falling. One option is for the government to buy up the surplus, creating an artificial demand for the product. The effect of this is to shift the demand curve to the right, as shown in Figure 8.6. The government might then store this surplus, destroy it, or sell it in foreign markets, but it must not release it on to the domestic market, otherwise the increased supply will undermine the minimum price. Alternatively, it could restrict the amount that is supplied at the price of P_{min}, by placing quotas on the output of farmers, only allowing them to produce a limited quantity. This has the effect of shifting the supply curve to the left as shown in Figure 8.7.

The drawbacks of a minimum price control are that, as producers are guaranteed a price above the market equilibrium, they will consistently overproduce if their output is

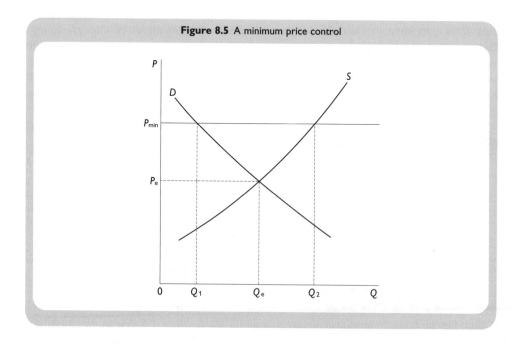

Figure 8.5 A minimum price control

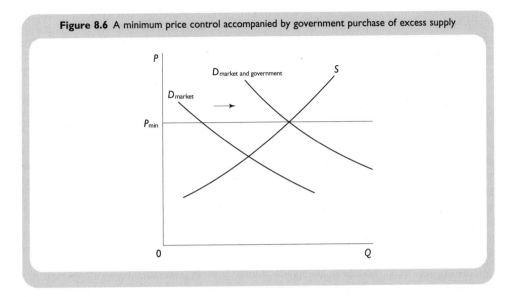

Figure 8.6 A minimum price control accompanied by government purchase of excess supply

not restricted by quotas. If the government decides to buy up the excess supply, this represents a cost to the taxpayer. It also means that resources are being directed towards producing those products that are not in demand, and away from other goods that might be in demand. This is the situation which exists under the European Union's **Common Agricultural Policy** (**CAP**), and which is referred to in the news item at the start of this unit. As a result of excess production, the authorities accumulated very large stocks of products. Land which previously was not used for production was farmed, resulting in

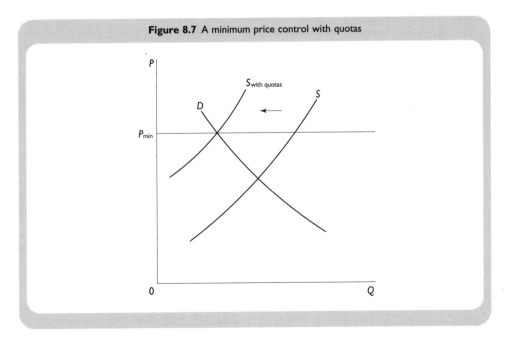

Figure 8.7 A minimum price control with quotas

overproduction in every year and the government having to buy up the surpluses, which eventually had to be destroyed. The Common Agricultural Policy of the European Union is covered in more detail in Unit 26.

Minimum wage

The government might decide to introduce a minimum wage to prevent workers from being paid low wages. The effect of this can be illustrated in Figure 8.8. The equilibrium wage is W_1, but the government has decided to impose a minimum wage of W_2. At this wage, however, the demand from firms for workers falls from Q_1 to Q_2. Some workers who were previously employed lose their jobs as a result of the higher wage. This is because some firms may go out of business and others may reduce output as a result of the increased costs of production. Other firms might decide to substitute machinery for workers, as a direct result of the increased wage costs. Not only does the demand for workers fall, but also at the same time more people are willing to offer their services at this higher wage, so the quantity of people willing and able to work is now Q_3. Therefore, at the wage of W_2, there is an excess supply of labour represented by the distance Q_2Q_3.

The extent to which a minimum wage creates unemployment depends on the elasticity of demand for labour. If the demand for labour is inelastic, as shown in Figure 8.9, the reduction in employment is much less than if the demand for labour is elastic (see Figure 8.10). This may be because the workers cannot easily be replaced by machines, or because labour costs represent only a tiny proportion of total costs of production and the increase in wage costs can easily be absorbed. It might also be because the products that the workers are producing have themselves an inelastic demand, and firms are thus able

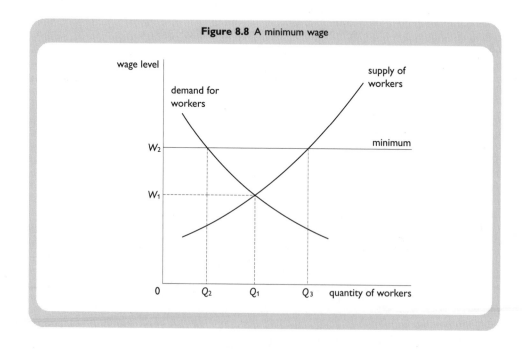

Figure 8.8 A minimum wage

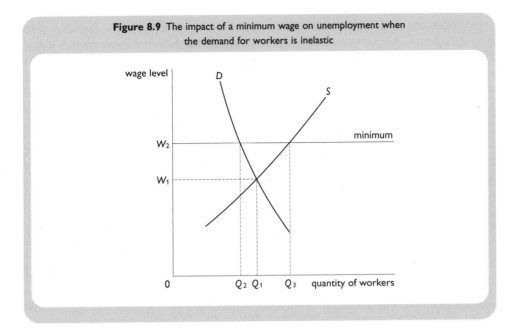

Figure 8.9 The impact of a minimum wage on unemployment when the demand for workers is inelastic

to pass on the higher wage costs to consumers without a significant fall in the demand for the product.

The imposition of a minimum wage may also lead to other problems. It is not only the wages of those who were previously earning less than the minimum wage that are likely to rise. Other workers who may have been earning an amount above the minimum wage may still demand a pay increase in order to maintain their wage differentials. If these increased wage costs are passed on to the consumer in the form of higher prices, this will have inflationary pressures on the economy. The resulting inflation will reduce the real

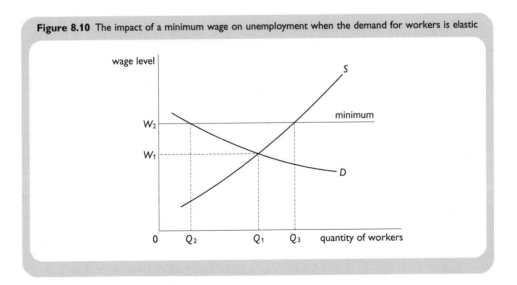

Figure 8.10 The impact of a minimum wage on unemployment when the demand for workers is elastic

wage of workers, meaning that those on low pay may, in real terms, be no better off than they were before the minimum wage was introduced. The effect of a minimum wage is discussed further in Unit 15.

Stabilisation of prices

One of the problems of the market mechanism is that prices may be volatile and not settle at a stable equilibrium. This is particularly true of agricultural produce, and the reasons for this were outlined in Unit 7. The government may therefore intervene in order to stabilise price. This might help to ensure that farmers' income remained stable from one year to another, which is preferable to having fluctuating incomes, with the attendant risk of very low incomes in some years and farmers being driven out of business. Price stabilisation will also prevent the consumer from having to pay very high prices in some years. Stable prices also provide certainty, giving the farming community the confidence to make long-term investment plans.

The use of maximum and minimum price controls, examined earlier in this unit, is one approach to the problem of fluctuating prices. An extension of this strategy, and a scheme which is often used as a method of stabilising agricultural prices, is for the government to operate a *buffer stock* scheme. In a free market, a good harvest leads to an increase in supply and a drop in the price of the product, whereas a bad harvest leads to a fall in supply and a rise in price. Under a buffer stock scheme, the government would buy up some of the output in a good year, thus reducing the supply released to the market and preventing price falling too far. In Figure 8.11, a good harvest results in output rising from Q_1 to Q_2. In an uncontrolled market, the price would fall to P_2. However if the government intervenes and buys up the quantity Q_1Q_2, withdrawing it from the market, the price will remain at P_1. The government can then put this output into storage, and

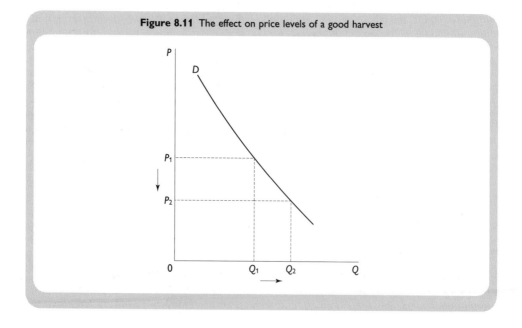

Figure 8.11 The effect on price levels of a good harvest

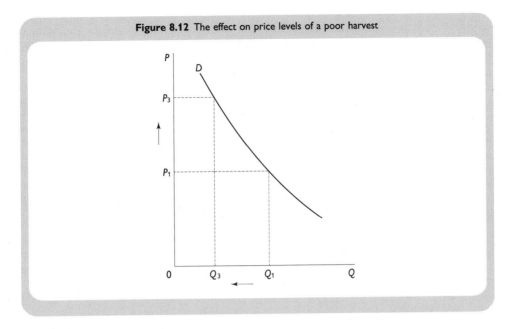

Figure 8.12 The effect on price levels of a poor harvest

release it on to the market in a bad year. Thus in a bad year (see Figure 8.12), the poor harvest would result in price rising to P_3 in an uncontrolled market. But under a buffer stock scheme, the government can release stocks onto the market, making up the shortfall between Q_3 and Q_1 and stabilising price around P_1.

One problem with a scheme such as this is that, although it stabilises price, it does not stabilise farmers' income. During a bad year, output is low, yet price remains stable, as the shortfall in supply is made up by the government releasing stocks on to the market. Farmers' incomes will therefore be very low during those years when there is a poor harvest. However, farmers will realise that it is in their interests to produce as much as they can each year, because no matter how great their output, they can always find a buyer at a guaranteed price – the government buys up any output that is not sold through the market. Thus a similar problem to that which occurred under a minimum price control is created: that is, the government accumulates very large stocks of products. The overproduction by farmers means that every year becomes a 'good' year, with the government having to buy up the surpluses and having little foreseeable opportunity of releasing these surpluses on to the market as there are no longer any years in which there is a shortage.

Buffer stock schemes also lead to the problems and cost of storage. Agricultural products tend to perish and cannot be stored easily. The cost of administering the scheme has to be met by the taxpayer.

Regional policy

The free-market system would appear to result in regional inequalities because factors are not mobile. Although those who support the free market believe that eventually the regional disparities should disappear, they have nevertheless remained for much of the twentieth century. Regional disparities lead to an inefficient use of the economy's resources, with underutilisation of resources in the depressed regions and congestion elsewhere. It is therefore possible to claim that government intervention is required to reduce the level of regional inequality.

The government could adopt a market-based approach to the problem, by introducing measures to make the market operate more efficiently and to remove those factors which hamper the efficient operation of the price mechanism. It could, for example, remove barriers to mobility in the labour market by providing information about employment opportunities elsewhere, or by retraining unemployed workers. It might try to ensure that wages more accurately reflect regional economic conditions, rather than national conditions.

Alternatively they could adopt a much more interventionist approach, by influencing the location of firms. This more interventionist approach has been adopted by the UK government for much of the second half of the twentieth century; it is also the approach favoured by the European Union which makes funds available to national governments to spend on regional policy. However, these policies might inhibit the expansion of firms in congested areas. Firms might decide not to expand at all rather than be forced to move to an area which they have no desire to move to. The firm might be handicapped by having to set up in what is not its optimum area, resulting in higher costs than might otherwise have been the case. Regional policy is also costly in terms of jobs created. It also faces the problem of giving aid to firms who might have moved to the area in any case without the government assistance.

As well as producing regional disparities, the market economy is also subject to fluctuations in the overall level of economic activity. At times the level of demand in the economy will be high, which might result in inflationary pressures, while at other times the level of demand might be low resulting in unused resources and unemployment. There is therefore a strong argument for the government intervening to try to influence the level of economic activity and thus exert some control over the level of unemployment and the rate of inflation. This argument will be looked at in detail in Module G of this book.

Government failure

Just as there are imperfections in the market mechanism, so there may also be problems arising from government intervention. Government intervention is costly and makes use of scarce resources. Therefore it is not worth intervening to correct every incidence of market failure. The skills and abilities of government are limited. Market conditions can change rapidly. Government rules and regulations may not change quickly enough to accommodate changing market conditions due to the bureaucratic nature of the regulatory bodies. The government itself may suffer from a lack of information. If it bases its decisions on poor information, it may not implement the optimal policies. Many argue that government intervention involves a loss of freedom for the individual. The market mechanism works by providing incentives and giving rewards. Too much government regulation may remove these incentives. The role of the government as a monopolist and the limitations of public ownership have resulted in many economies transferring the provision of goods and services back to the private sector. Political considerations affect government policy. Politicians are keen to retain political power and they might use policies to win votes in an election, rather than for economic reasons. And finally, there is no point in having government intervention in the market to remove market inefficiencies if the drawbacks and inefficiencies of the government intervention are greater than the original market inefficiencies it was intending to eliminate, resulting in **government failure**.

Summary

There are many different ways in which the government intervenes in the market in order to counter the effects of market failure. The use of taxes and subsidies is a market-based approach and provides incentives for people to change their behaviour to reflect more accurately the true costs of production and consumption. The government may intervene to make the market work more effectively by providing information where there is information failure. In some circumstances, however, a market-based approach is not adequate and a more direct interventionist approach is required, through the use of regulations. Government intervention into the market is not without its problems and drawbacks. Measures such as price controls can lead to shortages or surpluses. Government intervention involves administrative costs, and some argue that it involves a loss of freedom for the individual and removes incentives.

Review questions

1. Consider the alternative policies that a government could adopt in order to reduce the amount of air pollution from motor vehicles.

2. Explain what is meant by the 'polluter pays' principle.

3. Explain why the effectiveness of a tax placed on a product to discourage its consumption depends on the price elasticity of demand for the product.

4. Why might it be difficult to impose a tax on polluters that exactly mirrors the external costs of that pollution?

5. Why might legislation rather then taxation be regarded as a better method of dealing with external costs?

6. Figure 8.13 shows the supply and demand diagram for an agricultural product.
   (a) What is the equilibrium price?
   (b) If the government offered the farmers a guaranteed price of P_3, what would be the market surplus?
   (c) Which area represents the government expenditure required to purchase the surplus stock?
   (d) What other costs might be associated with such a scheme?

Figure 8.13 Supply and demand for an agricultural product

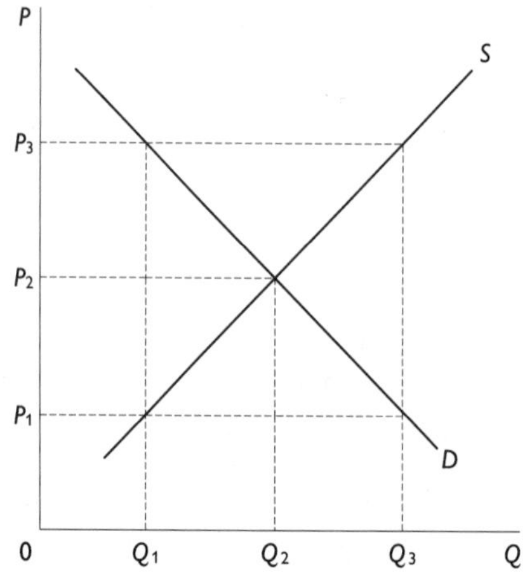

7. Outline the problems that might result from the imposition of a minimum legal wage.

8. Why might a buffer stock scheme or a minimum price control result in an excess supply of a product?

9. How might different pollution standards between countries act as a barrier to international trade?

Essay questions

1. Examine and evaluate the various methods which the government could use to correct the distortions in resource allocation caused by social costs.

2. Governments may impose price controls on basic necessities with the object of assisting lower-paid workers. Analyse the consequences of such a policy.

Reading 8.1

Smog adds £4bn to health bill

A report has claimed that air pollution in urban areas adds £3.9bn to the health bill. The main culprit is road transport, which accounts for 97 per cent of the pollution, while rail transport accounts for only 2 per cent and air travel 1 per cent. In addition to soiling and ▷

causing structural damage to buildings, air pollution increases the incidence of ill-health and even leads to premature death. It is the young, the old, and those who already have health problems who are most at risk: the increased incidence of asthma among young people in urban areas is a typical example. The government does not fully accept the findings. Although they are determined that transport users should pay for the full costs that they impose on society, they point out that it is difficult to calculate exactly what those costs are.

Questions

1. The Department of Transport wishes to ensure 'that transport users pay for the costs that they impose on society'. Explain this statement and identify what costs these might be.

2. What policies could be adopted in order to try to ensure that transport users pay for the costs they impose on society?

3. In view of the differing impacts of road transport and rail transport on the environment, what measures could the government take to encourage the use of rail as opposed to road transport?

4. Why might it be difficult to estimate the full costs of transport?

Industrial structure

After reading this module, you should be able to:

- explain how different market structures affect firm's pricing and output policies;

- compare the advantages and disadvantages of monopoly;

- understand why firms sometimes charge different prices for the same service;

- explain why firms engage in non-price competition;

- critically examine the government's competition policy;

- explain why the European Union has a competition policy, and how this affects firms;

- explain why some industries have been privatised;

- show how regulation can prevent exploitation in privatised utilities;

- show how competition has been introduced in privatised industries;

- understand why firms become multinationals; and

- assess the advantages and disadvantages of multinationals.

Monopoly and competition

Rich, richer, richest. That is Bill Gates, probably the world's richest man, whose assets are so many that even his computers cannot accurately count the dollars. His money comes from Microsoft the world's biggest software company whose products are used in most computers. And more computers means more money for Bill.

But even the rich have problems. Recently the US Justice Department, traditionally tough on monopolies, announced that it was starting an investigation into allegations that the firm had engaged in anti-competitive practices. Subsequently, the European Commission decided to investigate similar investigations.

Despite these threats, the likelihood is that Microsoft will continue to expand, and Bill Gates will become even richer.

Does monopoly matter?

Bill Gates built up his Microsoft empire from nothing. Among many computer innovations, his most successful product is *Windows*, the software that is used in almost every personal computer. To give just one example, the word-processing package called 'Word for Windows' must be run on a computer with *Windows*. Since this can only be bought from Microsoft, it follows that Bill Gates is in a very powerful position, and could potentially exploit this power, for example by charging high prices or by using his power to keep out competitors. Fortunately for Mr Gates, the investigations referred to at the beginning of the chapter ended in his favour, and Microsoft continued to go from strength to strength.

But the more general problem remains: sometimes firms can dominate a market and exploit consumers. This module explores this problem, and this unit sets the scene by setting out the *theoretical* analysis which is the basis of much policy. This is followed by Unit 10, which explores how firms actually behave. Unit 11 discusses the policies that attempt to reduce any exploitation, and Units 12 and 13 discuss two specific topics: privatised industries, and multinationals – two kinds of firm that have a profound effect on the economy as a whole and on everyone's life.

What is an industry?

Before we start our analysis, we need to discuss a basic question: What is an industry? In everyday life, we just talk about 'the motor industry' or 'the food industry', but as economists we need to be more precise. A firm may, for example, be a small enterprise in the food market as a whole, but may absolutely dominate the market for, say, kippers or asparagus. One factor to consider is *substitutability*: that is, can consumers buy something similar if they do not like the product on offer. This is a matter of individual choice. Personally, I don't mind whether I drink Coca-Cola or Pepsi, or indeed their supermarket equivalents, but some people do, and this enables such firms to charge a higher price for their product than the supermarket equivalent.

To aid us in defining an industry, we are helped by several rulings from case law, and also by agreements between statisticians. Thus, for example, the European Court of Justice solemnly declared that the market for meat cans was the same as the market for fish cans, since resources can easily be switched from one to the other.

More generally, there is an international standard classification of industries which groups together products that are related by a technical process or raw material. This classification is very detailed: it contains 17 sections, divided into 90 divisions, 900 groups and 9,900 subclasses. Table 9.1 gives a brief extract.

This classification system is useful and is used extensively by economists, but it can be misleading. For example, the system classifies the Channel tunnel as part of the rail industry, channel ferries as shipping, and cross channel-flights as aircraft. Yet all are alternative ways of crossing the Channel. Similarly, in the Standard Industrial Classification (SIC), plastic buckets are in one industry (processing of plastics), while metal buckets are in another (finished metal goods). In real life, as opposed to official classifications, these would both be in the 'bucket' industry, but the official classification tends to order industries according to the raw material they use.

Table 9.1: An extract from the UK Standard Industrial Classification	
Section A	Agriculture, hunting and forestry
01	Agriculture, hunting and related services
01.1	Growing of crops; market gardening; horticulture
01.11	Growing of cereals
01.12	Growing of vegetables
01.13	Growing of fruit, nuts and spices

Source: Standard Industrial Classification 1992, Central Statistical Office, London.

Structure, conduct and performance

There are a number of ways in which issues of monopoly and competition can be investigated. One of the most useful is called the structure, conduct and performance model, and this is illustrated in Figure 9.1.

This model suggests that the structure of an industry (e.g. the number of buyers, the number of sellers, the size of firms) will affect their conduct. By 'conduct' is meant the goals of the firm, their pricing and output, and also the amount they invest. In turn, their conduct will influence their performance: that is, their efficiency, profitability and growth. As an example, we will see later in this unit how it can be argued that industries with just one firm will tend to charge higher prices and have lower output than would firms in a competitive market.

Let us now develop this structure–conduct–performance model. A **market structure** can be defined as those organisational features of a market which have a significant influence on the nature of competition. These features include the following:

- **The number of sellers in a market** In some cases consumers will have little choice – we cannot choose which firm we buy our water from.

- **The number of buyers** For most consumer goods, there may be millions of buyers, but for some products (e.g. tanks, traffic lights, pit props), there may be only a few potential buyers, which gives the latter a strong position in any negotiations.

- **The size of firms in an industry** A firm may be, say, the only manufacturer of shrouds for coffins, but this monopoly position will not give it much market power, since other textile firms could easily produce shrouds if they thought it was profitable.

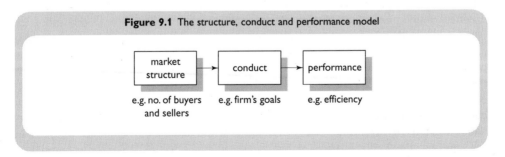

Figure 9.1 The structure, conduct and performance model

market structure → conduct → performance

e.g. no. of buyers and sellers   e.g. firm's goals   e.g. efficiency

- **Product differentiation** This occurs when a manufacturer makes many varieties of the basic product. This can be demonstrated at any supermarket, where one manufacturer will be seen to supply many varieties of crisps, while another may provide several different shampoos.

- **Ease of entry** Is it easy to enter the business? Anyone can start up as a hairdresser, so entry is easy, particularly as the equipment needed is relatively cheap. At the other extreme, to manufacture airplanes or set up a nuclear power station is very difficult, and so the barriers to entry are huge.

Market structure is important because it affects the firm's conduct. At one extreme there may be an industry with only one seller but making many products, with many buyers, and with large barriers to entry. Such a firm can be expected to be able to charge high prices and to make big profits without much need to spend on investment. At the other extreme, a small firm facing lots of competitors and only a few buyers will be in a weak position.

In turn, the firm's conduct will affect its performance. With little competition, a firm may be relatively inefficient but still be very profitable. A firm in a very competitive industry will often be forced to keep its prices down, thus becoming very efficient, but making only low profits.

So much for the underlying model. It is now time to explain the theoretical model which economists use to explain firms' behaviour. This concentrates on the number of *sellers* in a market as the crucial feature.

Perfect competition

In order to build up this model of how different market structures work, we will start at one extreme, when competition is at its fiercest. This is called **perfect competition**, and it exists when the following conditions are met:

- many firms selling an identical product;
- many buyers;
- no restrictions on entry into the industry; and
- buyers and sellers are perfectly informed about prices.

Let us examine these conditions in more detail.

Many buyers and many sellers means that no one person or firm can have any influence on the price of the product. If you buy a hundred loaves of bread, it would have no effect on the price of bread. Similarly, a small farmer growing wheat cannot influence the price, since there are thousands of farmers in many countries all growing wheat. Even if a farmer produced twice as much – or half as much – it would have no effect on the price. Consequently, when we have these conditions a firm is said to be a **price taker**: that is, it has to take the price as given, though it can decide how much to produce. Another example of a price taker is an individual operator in the world market for currencies. Such an operator buying or selling, say, US dollars is operating in a market with thousands of buyers and sellers all over the world, and cannot influence the price in the same way that Kelloggs, for example, can decide the price it charges for its cornflakes.

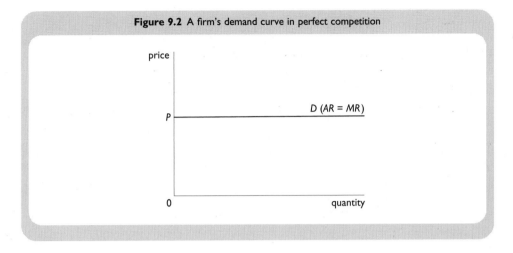

Figure 9.2 A firm's demand curve in perfect competition

When a firm is a price taker, its demand curve is horizontal, showing that it can sell all it wants at the going price. This is illustrated in Figure 9.2. This horizontal line shows that the firm's **average revenue (AR)** (i.e. total revenue divided by quantity) equals its **marginal revenue (MR)** (i.e. the additional revenue obtained by selling one more item). In other words, the firm does not have to cut its price if it wishes to sell more.

This price is determined by demand and supply in the industry as a whole as shown in Figure 9.3(a). The *industry* demand curve slopes down in the usual way and equilibrium is reached at the price where this intersects the supply curve. The individual *firm* takes this price as given. If it tries to charge more, it would have zero sales (since its product is identical to those produced by other firms, and since everybody knows about prices, no rational person would buy from the firm). Figure 9.3(b) shows how this translates into the firm's price.

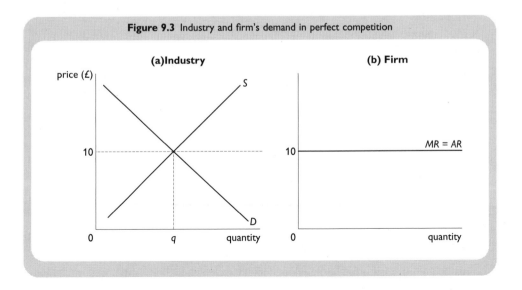

Figure 9.3 Industry and firm's demand in perfect competition

Table 9.2: Marginal revenue and cost for a firm in perfect competition

Quantity (per day)	Marginal revenue (£)	Marginal cost (£)
100	10	6
101	10	4
102	10	6
103	10	8
104	10	10
105	10	12
106	10	14
107	10	18

Despite not being able to choose the price it charges for its goods, the firm in a perfectly competitive market is not completely powerless: it can decide its output. It will do this by producing the output which gives it the greatest profit (or least loss). We can show this by considering an imaginary firm. Table 9.2 shows the marginal revenue and costs of this firm, and the figures are illustrated in Figure 9.4.

The marginal revenue in this case is always the same, since the firm can sell all it wants at the going price of £10. The marginal cost falls at first, reflecting increasing and then diminishing marginal returns as discussed in Unit 3 p. 29.

Now, at what level of output will the firm maximise its profits? The rule is that a firm will maximise its profits if it expands output until marginal revenue equals marginal cost. For example, if the firm's revenue exceeds the cost of producing, say, the ninth item, the firm will increase its profits if it produces this item. However, if the costs of producing the tenth item exceeds the revenue obtained by selling it, a profit maximising firm will not

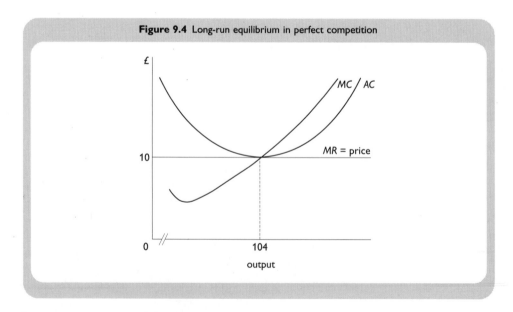

Figure 9.4 Long-run equilibrium in perfect competition

expand production to this level. Applying the rule that the firm will maximise profits when it produces the quantity where marginal revenue equals marginal cost, in this case the firm will produce an output of 104 items per day.

Several points arise from this analysis. First, you might ask why will the firm produce 104 items when the revenue obtained from producing this particular item only just equals the costs of producing it. The answer is that it is worthwhile for this firm to continue in business. That is because the economist's notion of costs differs from that of the accountant since economists include in their definition of cost a return on investment just sufficient to keep the firm in business. This is called **normal profit**. If the firm was not making this normal profit, it would be rational to sell the business and invest the money in, say, a building society to receive interest. Since, in this case, the firm is covering its costs – including this 'normal profit', it will continue to trade. Since normal profit is included in costs, the firm will produce where average cost equals average revenue.

Note that in analysing firms in this way, economists are not implying that directors of firms use words such as marginal cost or marginal revenue. But what does happen is that marketing and production managers will be asked: 'What will happen to costs if we increase output?' If the answer is that revenue increases faster than costs, it is rational to increase output.

The results of this analysis are as follows:

1. It suggests that perfect competition is efficient in the sense that the firm produces at minimum cost per unit: that is, at the bottom of the average cost curve. That is a strong argument in favour of competition.

2. The price is very low – any lower and the firm would go bankrupt. That is another strong argument in favour of competition.

3. Output is as high as possible, consistent with firms still remaining in the industry.

4. The typical firm in perfect competition is only just covering its costs. If the typical firm was doing more than covering its costs, new firms would move into the industry, since by definition it is easy to enter. The increased supply produced by these new firms would then force down the price, so that the eventual outcome would be as illustrated in Figure 9.4.

These four reasons provide a strong argument in favour of perfect competition, but, as we shall see, the argument rests crucially on the assumptions. Critics claim that these assumptions are not found in the real world, so that the conclusion does not necessarily follow. This argument underlies the competition policies discussed in Unit 11.

Exercise

Software prices fall

Compare the price and quality of a 1998 computer with one produced a few years earlier. The result is obvious: prices are down, quality is up.

What is less obvious is that software packages are following the same process. Manufacturers of word processors, databases and spreadsheets find that ▷

they have to run hard to stand still. They have to continue to invest to improve the quality of their product, but, at the same time, the market forces them to cut their prices. The result is a fall in profits. Thus in 1993 Borland's profit margin fell to only 2.6 per cent of their sales. Lotus did better, its profit margins falling, but only to 7.6 per cent.

1. To what extent do you think that the market for computer software satisfies the assumptions underlying perfect competition?

2. Why do you think that prices in this market have fallen? Illustrate your answer with a diagram.

Monopoly

Monopoly is the exact opposite to perfect competition. In economic theory, monopoly is defined as a market where there is only one seller of a particular good or service. This means that the firm *is* the industry. Thus the Post Office has a monopoly of the delivery of letters, while the water companies are examples of regional monopolies.

How monopoly arises

Monopolies can only continue to exist where there are barriers which prevent new firms entering the market. These barriers can take several forms:

Mergers and acquisitions

Firms can become monopolies by taking over other firms in the market. Mergers do not necessarily lead to higher barriers to entry, but they can do so. Over a century ago Karl Marx commented that 'one capitalist always kills many' so that there are a 'constantly diminishing number of the magnates of capital who usurp and monopolise all the advantages of the process of transformation (what we would now call production)' (*Capital*, vol. i, p. 836). Marx did not mean 'kill' literally; he was suggesting that big capitalists take over small ones so that power is concentrated in fewer hands. There are many examples of this; in recent years, Stagecoach has taken over a number of local bus services.

Legal barriers ·

These occur when a law or patent restricts competition. As we have seen, the Post Office by law has the exclusive right to deliver letters. Similarly, the law controls entry into occupations such as the law, accountancy and medicine. Patents are also a barrier to entry, since they give inventors the exclusive right to a product or process for a period of time; in the UK, this period is 16 years. The argument for patents is that they stimulate invention by rewarding inventors, but they also prevent competition. An example is Polaroid whose innovation is protected by patents which give it a monopoly of instant photographs. In the late 1970s, Kodak produced its own instant camera. Polaroid challenged Kodak in the courts, and Kodak was forced to recall all its instant cameras and to compensate Polaroid and the people who had bought its cameras.

Natural monopolies

A **natural monopoly** exists when the minimum efficient scale is sufficiently large so that there is room for only one producer in the industry. An example is the distribution of water, gas and electricity. The start up costs in these industries are so large – just imagine the costs of connecting every house to a pipe – that it is impossible for a competitor to enter the market. Even where there is no pure natural monopoly, in some industries (e.g. electricity generation or car assembly), the costs of entering a business can be so high that it is very difficult for new firms to enter.

Firms' behaviour

Firms can take action to increase the barriers to entry. These are discussed in the next unit, but one example concerns advertising. Where advertising is extensive, potential entrants face high costs if they wish to sell their goods.

Product differentiation serves the same function. A potential entrant to the crisp market would find it difficult because the supermarket shelves are already crowded by a wide range of potato snacks. A new entrant would find it difficult to persuade supermarkets to carry an extra brand – and even if they agreed, the new product would probably only capture a tiny part of the market.

Pure monopoly

Just as we analysed the effects of perfect competition, we can use the same methods to analyse the effects of **pure monopoly**. Our assumption here is that there is only one seller of a product in the market and that there are sufficient barriers to entry to prevent new firms entering the market.

In this case, the monopolist is a **price maker**. The firm has to decide what price to charge for its goods, and just like any other industry, its sales will fall as it puts up its prices: that is, its demand curve will slope down.

The revenue side of a hypothetical firm is outlined in Table 9.3. In this simplified example, as the firm cuts its price, its sales rise. For example, as the price falls from £8 to £7, sales rise from 2 to 3, and total revenue also rises from £16 to £21. Hence the marginal revenue received from selling the third item is £21 − £16 = £5. The relationship between the demand (i.e. average revenue) curve and the marginal revenue curve is shown in Figure 9.5. As you can see, both slope down, but the marginal curve falls more steeply because the firm will have to keep cutting its price to sell more.

So much for the monopolist's revenue. What about its costs? We assume that the monopolists costs will be the usual shape, with **marginal cost** falling and then rising as shown in Figure 9.6. This fall in marginal cost will pull down **average costs**, but then pull them up as it rises above average cost. (The relationship between average and marginal was discussed in Unit 3.)

If we now put costs and revenue together we have Figure 9.7, perhaps the most difficult diagram in the whole book, so let us examine it point by point:

1. The firm – like all firms – will maximise profits if it produces where $MR = MC$. This is at point X, and the quantity of goods produced will be q_1.

Table 9.3: A monopolist's total and marginal revenue

Price (£)	Quantity (per day)	Total revenue (£)	Marginal revenue (£)
10	0	0	
			9
9	1	9	
			7
8	2	16	
			5
7	3	21	
			3
6	4	24	
			1
5	5	25	
			−1
4	6	24	

2. Note that this level of output is not at the point where average costs are lowest. It can therefore be argued that monopoly is inefficient. (If the firm expanded output until average costs were lowest, it would lose money since it would have to cut its prices by a large amount to sell this higher level of output.)

3. Since this quantity of output is smaller than could be produced at lower cost, it can be argued that it is *allocatively* inefficient: that is, that consumers are disadvantaged since the best level of output is not being produced. Put another way, monopolies are characterised by excess capacity. More technically, one indication of allocative

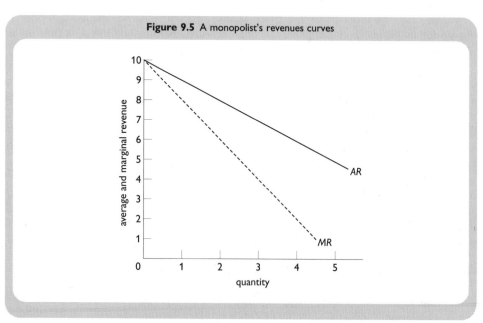

Figure 9.5 A monopolist's revenues curves

Figure 9.6 Average and marginal cost

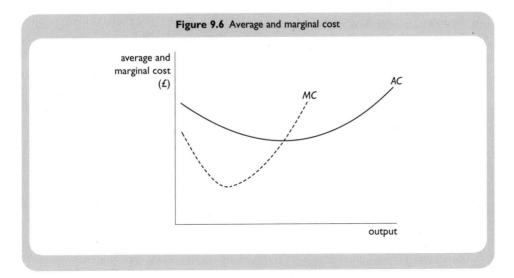

efficiency is that price equals marginal cost, so that the money paid for the last good produced just equals the cost of the resources used to produce it. In monopoly, price exceeds marginal cost.

4. Note that at this level of output, price ($0A$) is above average cost. This means that it can be argued that the customer is being exploited, though this conclusion depends on one's point of view. In economics, this is often called a 'normative' argument since it depends on a person's values.

Figure 9.7 Equilibrium in a monopoly

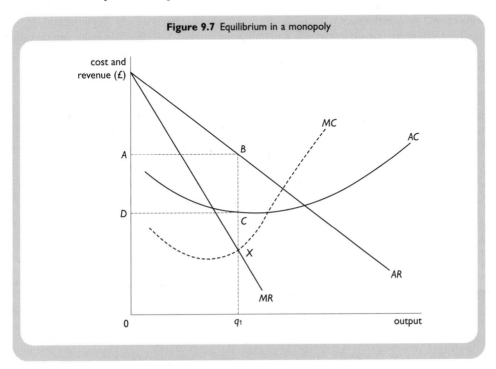

5. Profit can be defined as:

(Average revenue − Average cost) × Quantity

For example, a firm a selling a million ball pens at an average price of 10p and which had cost 9p to make would be making a profit of 1 million × 1p. The monopolist's profit is shown by the rectangle $ABCD$: that is, at output q_1, average revenue is $0A$ and average cost $0D$. This is much more than the normal profit found in perfect competition, and is usually called **monopoly profit**, though sometimes the terms 'supernormal' or 'abnormal' are used.

This theoretical analysis gives a formidable critique of monopoly. But, as with the analysis of perfect competition, the conclusion rests on the assumptions. For example, if the firm does not attempt to maximise profits (see the discussion of the firm's objectives in Unit 1), then none of these conclusions will hold.

Moreover, it can be argued that this is a *static* analysis, and that in a real dynamic economy, monopolists can only maintain their barriers to entry if they are more efficient than potential competitors. For example, Polaroid will only be able to maintain its monopoly of instant cameras if it continues to innovate and to protect these innovations with patents. Customers will therefore benefit from these improvements. These arguments in favour of monopoly are developed in Unit 11, where we discuss competition policy.

Oligopoly

Oligopoly can be defined as a market where a small number of producers compete with each other. This means that in making decisions each firm has to be aware of the possible response of its competitors.

Oligopoly is perhaps the most important type of market. For example, in the market for oil a few names such as Shell, BP, Texaco and Esso dominate the market. In British banking a few firms such as NatWest, Barclays, Midland and Lloyds dominate. In the retail food trade, Sainsburys, Marks & Spencer, Safeway, Tesco and ASDA have powerful positions. In the market for tampons two firms, Tampax and Lillets, dominate the market, which is a special form of oligopoly called a **duopoly**. In these markets, and many more, firms do not make decisions such as changing prices without considering what their competitors will do; if firm X cuts its price, will Y and Z do the same? If so, it might be better to keep prices constant.

Economists measure the extent to which a few firms dominate a particular market by using a concept called the five-firm **concentration ratio**. This measures the proportion of total output produced by the five largest firms in a particular market. Table 9.4 gives the proportion of sales by motor vehicle manufacturers in the European car market. What is the five-firm concentration ratio? In this case the five-firm concentration ratio is 13.3 + 12.5 + 11.8 + 11.4 + 10.1 = 59.1%. Note that in this example, the market is the *European* market; national markets would give a very different picture. Five-firm concentration ratios for a selection of UK industries are illustrated in Figure 9.8.

These figures can give a good picture of the extent to which large firms dominate a market, but they can also be misleading. Should the market be the UK as here, or, given the that the European Union is supposed to be a single market, should it be the EU as a whole? And, as we have seen (p. 142) exactly, what is the industry?

Table 9.4: New car registrations in EU countries

Firm	Market share (%)
PSA (Peugeot, Citroen)	13.3
General Motors	12.5
Ford	11.8
Renault	11.4
Volkswagen	10.1
Fiat	8.6
Rover	3.5
Others	28.8
Total	100.0

Source: Society of Motor Manufacturers and Traders (1995) *Motor Industry of Great Britain, World Automotive Statistics,* London.

Despite their limitations, five-firm concentration ratios give a good indication of the extent to which a few firms dominate a market. This has policy implications since if a few firms do dominate a market, they may combine to exploit the consumer.

How oligopolies operate

Oligopolies only remain oligopolies if they can maintain barriers to entry, making it difficult for new firms to enter the market. They maintain these barriers in much the same way as monopolies, though the particular barriers will vary according to the particular

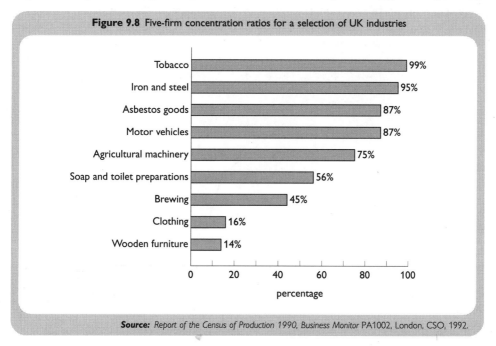

Figure 9.8 Five-firm concentration ratios for a selection of UK industries

Industry	Percentage
Tobacco	99%
Iron and steel	95%
Asbestos goods	87%
Motor vehicles	87%
Agricultural machinery	75%
Soap and toilet preparations	56%
Brewing	45%
Clothing	16%
Wooden furniture	14%

Source: Report of the Census of Production 1990, Business Monitor PA1002, London, CSO, 1992.

circumstances. In some cases, for example, there are economies of scale: for instance, it is difficult for a new firm to move into the aerospace business since it requires enormous capital and expertise. Sometimes oligopolies build barriers by product differentiation: thus the shampoo market is an example where there are so many varieties that it is difficult for a potential entrant to compete. Product differentiation is often buttressed by advertising: in this case, Bloggs washing powder would not be able to compete with Persil.

The kinked demand curve

One of the most influential models of oligopoly was developed by an American Marxist called Paul Sweezy. He wanted to explain why prices did not fall more sharply during the Great Depression of the 1930s. He noted that prices in oligopolistic industries tended to be fairly static – they did not seem to respond much to changes in demand.

He argued that the essential feature of oligopoly was that firms had to take into consideration the likely response of competitors when they changed their prices. He suggested that firms would reason as follows:

- If I put up my price, our competitors will not, so I will lose a lot of sales.
- If I cut prices, competitors will follow suit, so we will all be worse off.

The theory behind this line of argument is that of the **kinked demand curve**: namely, that the demand curve for an oligopolist's product is kinked. In Figure 9.9 at prices above price p, the demand curve is elastic, so revenue will fall if prices are raised. On the other hand, the demand curve is inelastic at prices below price p, so that revenue will fall if prices are cut. Hence the reluctance of oligopolistic firms to change prices if they can avoid it.

Sweezy's theory of oligopoly pricing has been criticised. In the first place, it does not explain how the price is determined originally. Moreover, oligopoly prices do change,

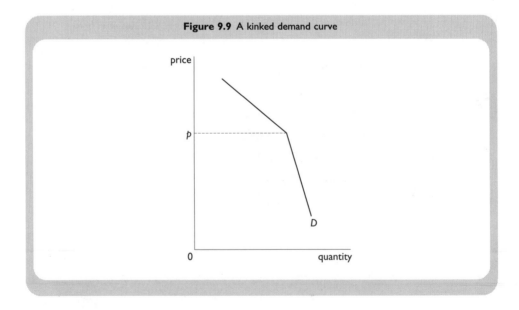

Figure 9.9 A kinked demand curve

perhaps as frequently as prices in the rest of the economy, and Sweezy's model does not explain how and when prices change.

Collusion

Oligopolists are price makers, and they have to decide the price that they charge for their products. From the oligopolists' point of view, the best strategy is to form a **cartel**. A cartel is an agreement of producers who agree to limit output and fix prices. This will allow them to maximise joint profits: in other words, to act as if they were a monopoly. Under a cartel, each firm is given a production limit and also agrees to sell at a particular price. Cartels are illegal in almost all countries, and firms attempting to profit from them ... s discussed in Unit 11.

The most successful cartels are those which ... re formed with the agreement of governments: the best example is the Organisation of Petroleum Exporting Countries (OPEC). In 1973, OPEC succ... doubling ...es – then doubled them again. The result was much higher income for the countr... nvolved, but also higher prices and ...ecession... world. OPEC's pow... subsequently declined, partly because ...producers such as the UK and Norway did not join OPEC, and partly because some member... of OPEC saw that it was in their interest to sell more than the agreed limit. (So long as all other countries keep to the limit, this strategy pays off.) The resultant increase in supply pushed down the price.

Although cartels are rare, similar results can som...ies be obtained in other ways. Firms have been known to agree a strategy for price and output, even though no *formal* agreement is made. Again, this is illegal, but it ...difficult to prove. If petrol prices – or ...use of collusion or because they are all affected by...rise in the price of crude oil or an increase in world interest...

An alternative way of gaining the benefits of a cartel without having to set up a formal ...eement occurs when there is a dominant firm in the industry. This firm puts up its ...ess...follow, knowing that it is ...eir best interests. There is no formal ...ment but everyone knows the informal rules ...so prices are raised, firms benefit, and

A p... of analysis called game theory has been developed to analyse ...olig... Game th... is a method of analysing the strategic behaviour of a small ...it.

As its name implies, monopolistic competition has some characteristics of monopoly, some of competition.

It resembles competition in that there is relatively easy entry to the industry. Someone who wanted to set up in business as a hairdresser, roof repairer or car mechanic, could do so with relatively little effort or capital. There are many other examples where barriers to entry are relatively low: picture framer, minicab firm or secretarial services, to name just three. This characteristic of easy entry means that if firms in these industries are making

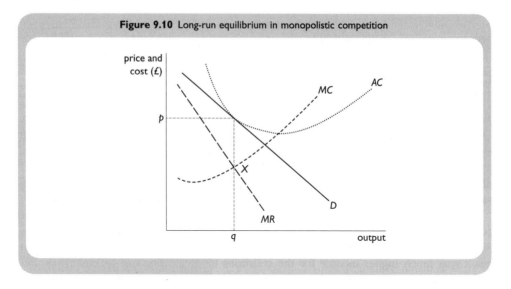

Figure 9.10 Long-run equilibrium in monopolistic competition

monopoly profits, then other firms will move in to the industry. This increase in supply will force down the price until only normal profits are made.

Monopolistic competition resembles monopoly in that there is product differentiation: for instance, one pub is different to another; no two hairdressers give an identical service. This ability to differentiate a product means that some firms in the industry will make monopoly profits from their innovation – at least, until other firms imitate their actions. A similar result can be obtained by advertising.

The result of these two tendencies is shown in Figure 9.10. The firm will maximise profits if it produces where $MR = MC$; this point is shown as X in the figure. Output will be q and price p. The result is excess capacity and inefficiency, as the firm is not producing at the bottom of the average cost curve. In these characteristics, it resembles monopoly. However, it differs from monopoly in that at this level of output it is producing where the demand curve touches the average cost curve. This means that it is only just covering its costs and making normal profit. In this, it resembles perfect competition.

Note that this is a long-run position. In the short run, the demand curve might lie to the right of the long-run position, for example if the firm has successfully differentiated its product. In this case, the average revenue/demand curve will be above the average cost curve and the firm will make monopoly profits, at least until new firms move into the market.

Summary

The relationship between the four types of market structure is shown in Figure 9.11. The analysis in this unit seems to suggest that competition is more beneficial to society than monopoly. But this conclusion depends on the assumptions underlying it: for example, that firms try to maximise profits. In the real world, the way that firms actually behave will determine the benefits and costs of particular forms of market structure, and this is the subject of the next unit.

Figure 9.11 Market structure

	Perfect competition	Monopolistic competition	Oligopoly	Monopoly
Numbers of firms in industry	many	many	few	one
Products	identical	differentiated	differentiated or identical	no good substitutes
Entry	easy	easy	significant barriers	high barriers
Firms control over price	price taker	some	considerable	considerable
Examples	wheat? stockbrokers?	retail sales soft drinks	airlines cars	water distribution instant cameras

Review questions

1. Summarise the structure, conduct and performance model.
2. What problems arise when trying to define an industry? Why does this matter?
3. Look up the SIC in the library and list the groups.
4. What are the features which influence the structure of a market?
5. What are the assumptions underlying the model of perfect competition? Are these assumptions ever fulfilled?
6. Draw a diagram to show long-run equilibrium in a perfectly competitive industry.
7. What are the results of perfect competition on prices, output and efficiency?
8. How does monopoly arise?
9. Draw a diagram to show long-run equilibrium of a monopoly.
10. What does this diagram suggest are the consequences of monopoly? Why might these consequences not arise in the real world?
11. Define, and give examples (not from the text) of oligopoly.
12. Summarise the kinked demand curve argument. Do you think that it gives a good explanation of oligopolistic markets?
13. What is meant by 'monopolistic competition'? What effect would you expect to find that this form of market structure had on output, efficiency and profits?

1. Compare the models of perfect competition and monopoly. Do you think that the assumptions underlying these models makes them irrelevant?
2. Why is market structure important?

Reading 9.1

The UK market for soluble coffee

The UK supply of soluble coffee is as follows:

Company	Market share (%)
Nestlé (Nescafé, Gold Blend)	56
GFL* (Maxwell House, Kenko, Cafe Hag, Mellow Birds)	25
Lyons Tetley	8
Brook Bond (Red Mountain)	6
Other suppliers	5
Total	100

Note: * GFL produces own-label coffees for others.

The average price charged by Nestlé was £1.46 for a hundred grams; GFL product prices varied considerably, but averaged £1.22; Lyons Tetley's price was only £0.80; and Brook Bond charged £1.24.

The Monopolies and Mergers Commission was concerned to find out if Nestlé was using its dominant position to the detriment of the consumers. They concluded that there was no exploitation – Nescafé was seen to be of a high quality for which consumers were made to pay more.

Source: Summarised from Monopolies and Mergers Commission, *Soluble Coffee* (1991), Cm. 1459, HMSO.

Questions

1. Why do you think that the five-firm concentration ratio is so high in this industry? Can this be explained by barriers to entry?
2. Why do you think that firms such as GFL make own brands for supermarkets which sell at lower prices than their own advertised brands?
3. Why can Nestlé charge higher prices than other firms?

Reading 9.2

The proposed merger of Allied-Lyons PLC and Carlsberg A/S*

In 1991, Allied-Lyons and Carlsberg agreed to merge their brewing and wholesale activities by forming a new company called Carlsberg Tetley Brewing Ltd. Under this agreement, Allied would continue to own its own 4400 pubs and, for a period of seven years, would buy all its beer from the new company.

The Monopolies and Mergers Commission was asked to investigate the proposed merger. The questions the Commission asks in passing judgement on a proposed merger include:

- Does the merger maintain and promote competition?
- Does it promote the interest of consumers?
- Does it promote the development of new products?
- Does it lead to the reduction of costs?
- Does it promote competitive activity in overseas markets?

The following are extracts from the MMC's analysis of the UK beer market:

1. Shares of the UK beer market are as follows:

	Consumption (million barrels)	By type (%)	
		Ale	Lager
1960	27.6	99	1
1970	35.0	93	7
1980	40.7	69	31
1990	38.6	49	51
1991	37.2	49	52

2. Imports of beer have been increasing, but from a very low base. In 1991, imports were 3.3 million barrels. Almost half of this came from the Republic of Ireland, and included Irish brewed beer destined for Northern Ireland.

3. Estimated share of the UK market in 1991 is as follows:

	Total %	Ale %	Lager %
Allied-Lyons	12	12	13
Carlsberg	4	0	8
Bass	22	20	24
Courage/Grand Met	21	20	22
Whitbread	12	12	12
Scottish & Newcastle	11	13	9
Other	18	23	12

Note: * A/S is an abbreviation for 'aktiengesellschaft', the German word for a joint-stock company.

4. Allied-Lyons and Carlsberg's main brands are as follows:
   Allied:
   Lagers: Skol, Castlemain, Lowenbrau, Wrexham lager, Swan Light
   (NB Some of these are not owned by Allied, but are brewed under licence).
   Ales: Tetley Bitter, Ansells Bitter, Tetley Mild, John Bull, Burton.
   Carlsberg:
   Lagers: Carlsberg Pilsner, Carlsberg Export, Carlsberg Special Brew, Tuborg Green, Dansk LA, Tuborg Gold, Carlsberg Elephant.
   Ales: None.

5. In 1991, Allied-Lyons spent approximately £24m. on advertising; Carlsberg spent £20m.

Questions

1. Do you think the criteria used by the Commission were appropriate for this investigation?

2. Why do you think that these firms produce so many competing brands? Why do they spend so much on advertising?

3. Calculate the five-firm concentration ratio for both ales and lagers.

4. What do you think would be (a) the benefits, and (b) the disadvantages of the merger for the firms and for consumers?

Firms' strategies in different market structures

Sainsbury's profits fall

Whatever TESCO can do, Sainsbury can do better. That used to be the conventional wisdom, but it is no longer true. Evidence for this comes in the form of a statement from Sainsbury saying that its profits would fall because of strong competition from other retailers, notably TESCO.

TESCO overtook Sainsbury a couple of years ago as the UK's leading retailer as a result of a series of innovations, the most notable being the introduction of a loyalty card. At first, Sainsbury rejected the idea of following suit, but eventually it was forced to introduce its own Reward card in order to keep its customer base. The costs of introducing this card are one reason for the fall in profits, but competition from price-cutting retailers such as Aldi are also costing Sainsbury market share and profits. The end result might well be a price war between retailers.

Game theory

In the last unit, we analysed four market structures. The analysis tended to be both static – focusing on long-run equilibrium – and theoretical. The conclusion reached there was that competition was likely to lead to a more efficient allocation of resources, since profit-maximising monopolists would cut output and increase prices in order to raise profits.

However, we also saw that pure monopoly was rather rare in the real world, the dominant market structure in a modern economy being oligopoly. In addition to the examples given in Unit 9, oligopoly is characteristic of industries as diverse as disposable nappies, breakfast cereals, instant coffee, detergents and cigarettes, not to mention insurance and computer programmes. Hence, in this unit we will analyse oligopoly in more detail, making use of a technique called **game theory**.

Game theory analyses the range of best moves available in a situation of mutual interdependence where the participants lack full information. The theory assumes that participants are self-interested, which, in economic games, usually means that they try to maximise their benefits: that is, in the case of firms, their profits. Some games are one-off, while more complicated games can be repeated.

Although game theory is essentially a mathematical technique, it is possible to approach it using matrix diagrams. In the games in this unit, the pay-offs that are shown are illustrative and are not intended to show realistic values. We will start our analysis with the most famous game, called the prisoners' dilemma, which, at first sight, seems to have nothing to do with economics. However, as we will see, its lessons are very applicable to oligopoly.

The prisoners' dilemma

Imagine two prisoners locked up in separate cells and unable to communicate. There are three alternatives:

1. If both prisoners confess, they will both receive four years' imprisonment.
2. If both deny their guilt, they will both receive two years' imprisonment.
3. However, if one confesses and the other denies, then the confessing prisoner will only receive one year's imprisonment, but the other, denying guilt, will be sentenced to six years.

What is their best strategy?

In Figure 10.1, prisoner Smith's position is shown in the bottom left-hand triangle of each of the four cells of the matrix. If the other prisoner, Jones, confesses, then Smith should also confess, since the result will be four years rather than six. If Jones denies guilt, then Smith should again confess since the result will be one year. Hence we can conclude that the dominant strategy for Smith is to confess, whatever Jones does. We come to the same conclusion when we examine Jones's options. It is always in Jones's best interests to confess. If Smith confesses, then Jones would get four years instead of six. If Smith does not plead guilty, then Jones should confess since the result would be one year.

The result of this analysis is that both Smith and Jones will receive sentences of four years. This is not the optimum result; that would be for them both to deny guilt and each receive sentences of two years.

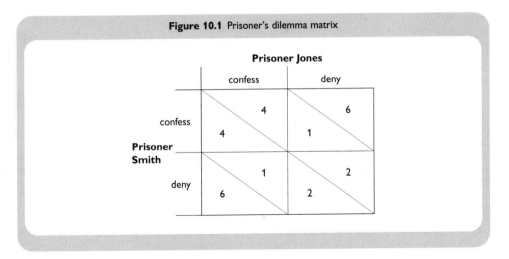

Figure 10.1 Prisoner's dilemma matrix

Now, what has this to do with the behaviour of firms? The answer is that it shows how independent decision making can lead to results that are inferior to those obtained from collective decisions. In the case of the prisoners, a collective decision was not possible, since they were prevented from collaborating. In the real world, however, collaboration between firms is usually possible.

Colluding oligopolies

We have seen that the central feature of oligopolies is that every firm must take into consideration the likely response of its competitors before making any decision – just as one prisoner had to take into consideration the likely response of the other.

This suggests that oligopolists will be able to improve their outcomes if they collude. Now, just as the prisoners were not able to collude, so in most countries collusion between firms is not possible, at least in theory, since it is illegal. However, in practice, collusion is difficult to detect, and there is no doubt that it occurs. Sometimes the collusion may be explicit, but more frequently it may be the result of large-firm dominance or unwritten understandings.

The simplest way to use game theory to examine business behaviour in oligopoly is to develop a duopoly game. A duopoly, you may remember, is an industry with just two firms, and in our imaginary industry we will call them Smith and Jones and assume that they have reached an agreement to collude to maximise profits, just as a monopolist would do.

But there is a difference. In duopoly, each firm may decide that it is in its best interest to cheat on the agreement. This is a reasonable assumption to make, since one weakness of a cartel trying to cut output and increase prices is that it is often difficult for its members to detect cheating.

Since each firm can either comply or cheat, there are four possible outcomes:

1. Both firms comply.
2. Both firms cheat.

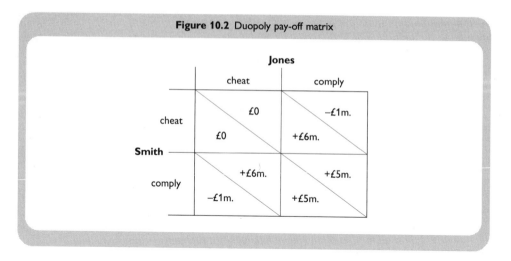

Figure 10.2 Duopoly pay-off matrix

3. Smith cheats but Jones complies
4. Jones cheats but Smith complies.

If both firms comply, then the best result (for the firms) is that they will make monopoly profits and that the proceeds will be shared equally between Smith and Jones. In Figure 10.2, the result is shown in the bottom right-hand corner of the matrix as a profit of £5m. for both firms.

In order to maximise profits, firms restrict output to the point where their joint marginal revenue curve equals their joint marginal cost curve. They will then be sharing monopoly profits. When this occurs, each firm realises that if it cheats on the agreement and increases output, more will be added to revenue than to cost, so that it will benefit, though the other firm will lose. There is, therefore, an incentive to cheat. (To understand why, look back at Figure 9.7. If both firms are each producing half the joint output of q_1, the individual firm's marginal revenue exceeds its marginal cost, so that expanding output will increase profits.)

One firm cheats   There are many ways for a firm to cheat; one of the most common is to cut prices to increase sales. If Smith does this while Jones continues to produce the agreed output, the result will be that Smith benefits from the additional sales: its profits rise to £6m. Jones, however, will then make a loss of £1m. (Note that total industry profits have also fallen, since the firms are no longer producing where industry marginal revenue equals industry marginal cost.) This result is shown in the top right-hand corner of the matrix. The result would be the same if Jones cheated and Smith complied, except that this time Jones would benefit.

Both firms cheat   What happens if both firms realise that they will benefit if they cheat so long as the other does not? The answer is that both Smith and Jones will cheat. They will both cut prices and increase output. Consumers will benefit from this, but both firms will lose. The result is shown in the top left-hand side of the matrix: both firms just make normal profits (i.e. profits of £0).

This analysis has used hypothetical figures to illustrate the conclusion – the same conclusion that was reached in the prisoners' dilemma – that independent decision making can lead to results that are inferior to those achieved through collective decisions.

We have also simplified the analysis in two other ways. First, we have analysed duopoly rather than several-firm oligopoly. That analysis can only be done using quite complex maths, but the result is the same.

The second simplification is that we have assumed a one-off game. In real life both Smith and Jones would learn from their experience and would continue to operate in the industry. In repeated games, one player always has the chance to penalise the other for earlier cheating. If Smith cheated last time, then Jones can refuse to collaborate this time. The results of a repeated game can vary. One possibility is that both firms will cheat, just as they did in the one-off game. The result will be the same – zero profits. The best result from the firms' point of view is for both firms eventually to conclude that, since they may be punished by the other for cheating, it is better to collude: that is, the threat of cheating may force the firms to cooperate. The result will then be maximum profits.

This analysis has been theoretical in that it has been concerned with hypothetical situations and illustrated with imaginary figures. So, how does it help us to understand the real world? The article about Sainsbury at the beginning of this unit shows how game theory can be used to illustrate real behaviour by firms. The best result for both firms might have been to keep prices and other activities as they were, but the actions of TESCO forced Sainsbury also to introduce its own loyalty card – the result as shown in the top left-hand corner of the Smith and Jones matrix, except, of course, that there was no cheating since there was no agreement. (Moreover, profits did not fall to zero!) The real world is also more complex in that the supermarket industry is not a duopoly, and both firms would have to consider the likely response of the other supermarkets.

Another example of how game analysis can be used to analyse real firm behaviour is to consider advertising. The detergent industry is dominated by two firms, Proctor & Gamble and Unilever. If one detergent firm decides to increase its advertising budget, the other will be forced to respond, otherwise it will lose sales. The best course of action for both would be to restrict advertising, since this probably does not increase total sales very much, but merely the distribution of those sales. However, detergent firms spend huge sums of money on advertising since they cannot collaborate. Here individual decision making again leads to a worse result than would a collective decision.

Life expectancy of collusion

Whether legal or not, firms sometimes do collude. The life expectancy of such collusion will depend on several factors:

- **The stability of demand** It is easier for firms to collude if demand is stable or rising, because then sales and profits are likely to increase. When demand is falling, then partners quarrel about who should cut production, and the collusion is likely to come to an end.

- **Price elasticity of demand** Collusion is easier when demand is inelastic, because if the firms want to cut output and raise prices, inelastic demand means that quite a large rise in price will only have a small effect on sales. This was the position when OPEC doubled the price of oil in the 1970s.

- **Recession** A recession leads to a fall in demand, and this is likely to cause disagreements among the colluders.

- **The ability to control most of the output** One reason for the weakness of OPEC was that new producers such as the UK and Norway entered the market. They were not members of OPEC, so OPEC's power to collaborate and raise prices was weakened.

The collapse of the international tin agreement in the mid-1980s illustrates the difficulties of maintaining a collusive agreement. The International Tin Council (ITC), was set up to try and stabilise the market, which was subject to considerable fluctuations in price. The idea was simple: a fund would be set up. This money would be used to buy tin when the price was low and sell it when the price was high. In this way, both producers and consumers would benefit from price stability.

The largest producer was Bolivia with 10 per cent of world output – a fatal weakness for the agreement since Bolivia was not a member. The next three largest producers with 45 per cent of the market (Malaysia, Indonesia and Thailand) were members.

In 1985 and 1986, demand for tin fell so that price also declined. The buffer stock manager intervened in the market to buy tin. In an attempt to force up the price he also entered into contracts to buy tin in the future. Eventually, he ran out of funds. The price then fell, one reason being the large buffer stocks that had been built up. The result was the collapse of the agreement.

This tin market example illustrates very well the difficulty of maintaining collusion when demand falls and when the cartel cannot control output.

Non-price competition

So far we have tended to concentrate on pricing as a crucial variable – as indeed it is. But both monopolistic competition and oligopoly are characterised by non-price competition. One reason for this in the case of oligopoly is that, as the kinked demand curve suggested, firms may be reluctant to make price changes. Hence the importance of competition in other areas.

One type of non-price competition is when firms try to improve their product, or to introduce new products. 'NEW!' 'IMPROVED!' are common labels on products, and show firms' awareness that product improvement can lead to increased profits. The car industry is an example of an oligopolistic industry which introduces frequent changes of models in order to attract customers.

Another, related kind of non-price competition is when firms try to improve the services which they provide. The car industry, again, provides many examples. Free insurance, free servicing and 'buy now, pay later' deals show that firms seek to compete in areas other than price. Similarly, supermarkets compete on price, but they also compete in other areas such as speedy check-outs or help with packing up purchases, as the article at the beginning of this unit illustrates.

However, the two main areas of non-price competition are in advertising and in product differentiation, and we will discuss each of these in turn.

Advertising

Advertising is an important industry in itself, and from our point of view it is particularly important because it has significant effects on other industries. Although there have been occasional troughs, spending on advertising in constant prices has grown in the UK from about a billion pounds just after the Second World War to over five billion now. Other countries have seen similar increases. The costs of a major campaign can be considerable – a full page spread in *The Times* costs about £17,000, a thirty-second advert on television at peak times will cost the advertiser about £100,000. In addition, there are the costs of preparing the copy. One of the largest campaigns in recent years was that of Microsoft, which in 1995 spent $150m. advertising *Windows 95*.

So, what effect does all this have? One obvious effect is that it increases firms' costs as shown in Figure 10.3. Average cost increases at all levels of output. A successful advertising campaign will also affect demand – the whole point of advertising. The effect is twofold, as shown in Figure 10.4. The whole demand curve will shift to the right from D_1 to D_2, meaning that more will be demanded at all prices. But there is another effect. A successful advertising campaign makes the consumer believe that the product is special, that it is different from its competitors. That means that the product has fewer competitors, so the demand curve becomes more inelastic. If people believe that Coca-Cola is different from any other cola, they will be willing to pay more for it than they would for any other cola. That is the implication of the inelastic demand curve.

Putting together Figures 10.3 and 10.4 gives us Figure 10.5. Original equilibrium is at the intersection of D_1 and AC_1, giving a price of p_1 and quantity q_1. The final result is a price of p_2 and quantity q_2. Hence the firm has benefited both from selling more goods and from the higher price, though as drawn here, the firm is only making normal profit. (Note, however, that if the firm was originally producing a much smaller quantity than q_1, the final result might be a fall in price, as the advertising campaign will

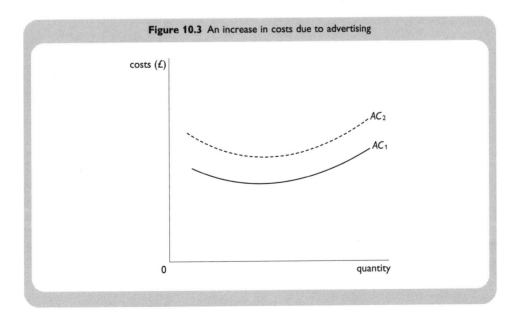

Figure 10.3 An increase in costs due to advertising

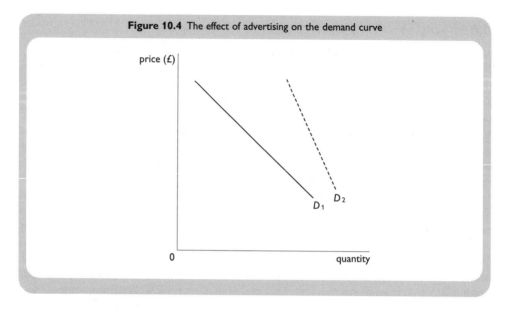

Figure 10.4 The effect of advertising on the demand curve

lead to a fall in average costs that outweighs the rise in price resulting from higher demand.)

Although the firm has benefited, the effects on the consumer are less certain. Advertising can be beneficial if it leads to greater consumer information, but it can be argued that it distorts consumer preferences – they spend more on highly advertised goods which are not necessarily the best, and they pay higher prices. Heavy advertising may also make it difficult for new firms to enter the industry. This has implications for competition policy, and is discussed further in the next unit.

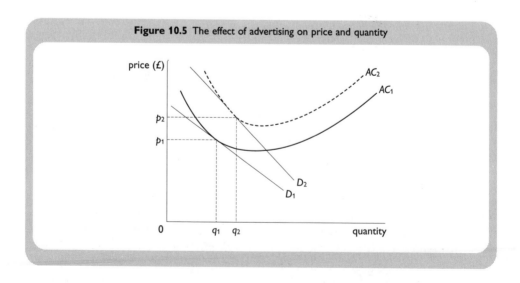

Figure 10.5 The effect of advertising on price and quantity

Exercise

Y and Z are firms in a duopoly making an identical product. Both firms are making profits of £2m. a year and neither is advertising. If Y advertises and Z does not, Y will increase its profits to £5m. while Z will make a loss of £3m. However, if Z advertises and Y does not, the positions will be reversed. And if both firms advertise, each will make zero profit.

1.   Construct a payoff matrix to illustrate this position.
2.   What is the probable outcome if the two firms (a) collaborate, and (b) cheat?

Product differentiation

In perfect competition there is no **product differentiation**: by definition, all firms have identical products. In pure monopoly, again by definition, the firm has a product that is different to any other. So it is in oligopoly and monopolistic competition that we find the clearest evidence of firms trying to make their product different from those of any competitors. The advantage of this for a firm is that its demand curve becomes downward sloping, making it a price maker, and, in the short run at least, enabling it to make monopoly profits.

One way in which firms can differentiate their product is by careful choice of name. In my local *Yellow Pages*, about 650 ladies hairdressing firms are advertised. This large number of firms is illustrative of the competitive element in monopolistic competition. The monopolistic element occurs because the products are not the same. The hairdressers include Talking Heads, Touch of Class, Warehouse Hair, Roots, Shear Magic and Blondes on Top – all clear evidence of attempts to portray a product that differs from other alternatives.

There are several other strategies which firms can adopt to make their product different:

● **Horizontal differentiation**
This refers to the choice of where to locate the business. This is particularly important in retail and service industries. The country has thousands of super-markets, but they are not all in competition with each other. If the two or three supermarkets in a particular town are more expensive than those in the next town, it may not pay consumers to travel because of the costs involved. Distance therefore serves to differentiate a product in the eyes of consumers, and that is why location is such an important decision for a shop.

● **Vertical differentiation**
This refers to differentiation on the basis of quality. Stereo equipment is one example: there is a wide range of quality available for every component of a stereo system, many made by the same firm, sometimes under different names. One reason for this is that consumers are differentiated by income: those with higher incomes may be willing to pay higher prices.

● **Varying product characteristics**

With many products it is possible to make the product look different from its competitors. Hence the importance of design in many markets. It is also possible to make the products differ in particular details. The car industry is a good example. When Henry Ford made his first cars he told his customers: 'You can have it in any colour you want so long as it is black.' All car manufacturers now offer a very wide range of cars, differentiated not only by colour, but also by engine size, and quality of accessories. The shampoo industry is another example: just look at the range available at the chemist or supermarket.

● **Advertising and sales promotion**

This has been discussed earlier. So far as product differentiation is concerned, firms hope that consumers substitute the advertising message for their own attempts to obtain information. If advertising makes people *believe* that a product is different from another, then the firm can benefit.

Product differentiation is a powerful weapon for firms. Brand names can lead to large profits. That is why, for example, Nestlé paid $4.5bn to buy Rowntree. But brand names are under attack from the growth of supermarket own brands. The recession in the early 1990s caused some consumers to seek cheaper products, and supermarkets responded by developing their own products to compete with well-advertised brand names. Own-label products are usually considerably cheaper than their branded equivalents, but so long as producers can make people believe that the branded product is different, its demand curve will be inelastic and its price higher than the supermarket equivalent.

Discriminating monopoly

So far in this unit we have been considering firms' strategies where there is some competition, as there is in monopolistic competition and oligopoly. However, there are some markets where a firm has considerable market power. In such cases, this may lead to **price discrimination**. Price discrimination occurs when a firm charges different customers different prices for the same good or service.

This is not the same as *price differences*, which occur when goods are sold for different prices because they have different costs. For example, suppose a firm supplies two customers with the same good, but one lives much further away, which involves higher costs. Thus the price to the more distant customer is an example of a price difference, but not of price discrimination.

Now look at Table 10.1. This shows the prices charged by Intercity for train journeys from Preston to London. Two questions arise from this table. First, is this is an example of price difference or price discrimination? The answer is not clear-cut, but in most cases it is price discrimination. However, the additional fare for First Class travel may be the result of higher costs, and therefore price difference.

The second, and more important question, is: 'Why are there so many different fares?', or, in other words, 'Why does price discrimination exist?' The short answer is that in certain circumstances it is profitable for firms to charge different prices for the same good. Figure 10.6 shows us the reason. For simplicity, we will just consider two fares, First Class and Standard (though this is not pure price discrimination since the good is not identical – for example, seats in First Class differ from those in Standard class). In both cases, the

Table 10.1: Return rail fares, Preston–London, 1997

Ticket type	Fare (£)
First Class	147
Standard	100
Apex First	58
Saver	50
Supersaver	39
APEX	29
SUPERAPEX	23

Note: In addition, Young Persons and Senior Citizen railcards give a third discount on most fares.

demand and marginal revenue curves slope down, showing that the firm has to cut its prices to sell more tickets. But there is one crucial difference: the demand curve for First Class tickets is much more inelastic. That is because people who travel First Class are usually better off than those who travel Standard, and, in any case, their tickets are often being paid for by their firm. Moreover, people buying Standard class tickets have a substitute available – to travel by bus. Also, in some cases, if the fare was higher, the Standard class travellers would not travel at all – they are probably travelling for pleasure, while many First Class travellers are going because they have to as part of their job. Their substitute might be air travel, but this alternative is also expensive.

The consequence of inelastic demand is that a firm can charge a higher price, which, as you will remember, was also one consequence of a successful advertising campaign. The firm will maximise revenue if it produces the output where $MR = MC$ in each market. For

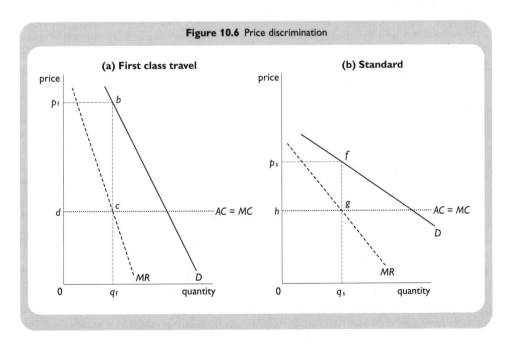

Figure 10.6 Price discrimination

simplicity, we assume that the marginal and average cost are the same for both groups. Thus the only difference is in the elasticity of the demand curves, and it is this which leads to the higher price – p_f compared to p_s. The total profit for the firm is given by the rectangle $p_f bcd$ in Figure 10.6(a) and by $p_s fgh$ in part (b). No single price can provide so large a profit, since these prices maximise profits in each market. Any other pricing strategy must sacrifice profits in at least one of the markets.

The conditions necessary for price discrimination

Why don't all firms price discriminate? The answer is that it is only possible if two conditions are met:

1. Firms must have some way of identifying their customers by their elasticity of demand. They can sometimes do this on the basis of some criterion such as age or income. Companies can ask for proof of age when issuing railcards, and empirical evidence can show differing elasticities. Magazines can offer discounts to first-time subscribers, since their records can confirm this. When such direct information is not available, firms can use indirect information. Rail companies cannot know the income of their customers, but they do know that many business people have to travel at very short notice, so they offer discounts to those who book several days in advance. But most firms cannot differentiate their customers in this way, and so they are unable to price discriminate.

2. Firms must be able to keep the different classes of customer separate so that they can divide their sales into different markets. If they cannot do this, then it would be profitable for someone to buy in the cheaper market and then sell on to someone in the more expensive market. It is for this reason that price discrimination is usually found in services rather than goods markets. A market stall selling tomatoes cannot practise price discrimination since (a) it cannot differentiate its customers by elasticity, and (b) it cannot prevent someone who bought at the lower price from selling on the goods. If people could do this, no one would buy at the higher price.

Other examples of price discrimination

There are many examples of price discrimination round most college and university campuses. Hairdressers are one example: many give student discounts, as do local nightclubs and restaurants. They can do this because they can satisfy the two conditions. They only offer the lower price on production of a student card, and they know that students, being poor, have very elastic demand. None of these shops offer discounts to lecturers, since they know that their demand is more inelastic (though they probably do not know the economic jargon).

Other examples are easy to find. Airlines and bus companies price discriminate for the same reasons as train companies. The telephone companies offer lower prices for evening and weekend calls (though it could be argued that these are not identical goods). Firms have to make calls in office hours, so demand is inelastic compared to most calls made in the evening and weekend. Similarly, electricity companies charge less at off-peak times (though here again, it may not be pure price discrimination, since firms' costs may be higher at peak times). Another example is the Post Office, which charges higher prices for first-class compared to second-class mail (though here again, the service is not identical, so it is not pure price discrimination).

Is price discrimination a good thing?

Price discrimination can obviously benefit firms, since it can lead to higher profits. Less easy to decide is whether or not price discrimination benefits consumers. It can be called inefficient, since firms will not be producing at the bottom of their average cost curve, but then neither do most firms that are not practising price discrimination. The biggest effect may be on equity, and here it can be argued that price discrimination can be beneficial, because the effect is to charge a lower price to customers with more elastic demand. Now these consumers usually have lower incomes than those with more inelastic demand: for example, lecturers have higher incomes and more inelastic demand than students. Hence lower income groups benefit from lower prices, while those with higher incomes may lose.

Summary

Unit 9 analysed firms using standard neoclassical analysis. The result showed that, given certain assumptions, competition was better than monopoly. In this unit we have taken a more dynamic approach and looked at the way firms actually behave in the modern world. In the next unit, we put these two approaches together, and consider the policy responses of governments who introduce policies to mitigate the less desirable effects of monopoly.

Review questions

1. What is 'game theory'? Why is it applicable to economics?
2. Summarise the prisoners' dilemma.
3. Develop your own one-off duopoly game, showing the consequences of firms cheating or complying.
4. What factors influence the likelihood of firms colluding?
5. Explain with your own examples, what is meant by non-price competition.
6. Use economic analysis to explain why firms advertise?
7. Why do firms practise product differentiation?
8. What is price discrimination? How does it benefit firms?
9. Under what circumstances can firms practise price discrimination?
10. Is price discrimination a good thing?

Essay questions

1. Explain with examples the benefits and disadvantages of price discrimination.
2. Explain what is meant by game theory and develop your own example to explain the behaviour of a duopoly.

Reading 10.1

Somerfield on song

Though no lives are lost, the retail trade more and more resembles a battle between giants. Decades ago, most little corner shops were forced out of business by competition from the supermarket chains. They fought back in various ways, most notably by opening for longer hours.

Now the supermarkets are also opening for longer hours and they are also engaged in a price war. This started with the advent of discount stores such as Aldi and Netto. In 1993 this caused Somerfield to cut many of its prices. Other supermarkets followed suit. Now Somerfield has launched another offensive by cutting prices on over 1000 items; in some cases, prices have been cut by half.

Predictably, the other supermarkets play down Somerfield's price cuts, arguing that they constantly offer low prices.

Questions

1. What form of market structure does this reading illustrate?
2. Use the kinked demand curve concept to analyse the effects of these price cuts.
3. Why should other supermarkets follow Somerfield's example of cutting prices?
4. Who gains/loses from a campaign such as the one described here?

Reading 10.2

Competition in the airline business

The international airline business is a curious mixture of intense competition and cosy cartel. The cartel arises because many fares are fixed by international agreement and because there is often only one airline flying between two particular destinations. The competition arises because many price-fixing agreements have ended, and where they have not, airlines compete for passengers by offering other inducements. ▷

Following moves by other airlines, in 1995 BA introduced a two-year £80m. plan to upgrade its in-flight entertainment systems. This will allow passengers to choose from over twenty film and entertainment channels from their seat. They will also be able to challenge other passengers at computer games. In 1997, BA intensified its attempts to attract customers by offering ticketless booking and check-in. Members of its Executive Club will be able to do all this by phone from their own home.

Questions

1. Which market structure is suggested by 'Following moves by other airlines...'?
2. Of which concept in the unit is the introduction of these facilities an example?
3. Who benefits and who might lose from this development?

UNIT 11

Competition policy

ECONOMICS IN THE NEWS

'People of the same trade seldom meet together, even for merriment and diversion, but the conversation ends in a conspiracy against the public, or in some contrivance to raise prices. It is indeed impossible to prevent such meetings, by any law which could be executed or which would be consistent with liberty and justice. But though the law cannot hinder people of the same trade from sometimes assembling together, it ought to do nothing to facilitate such assemblies, much less to render them necessary. ... The price of monopoly is upon every occasion the highest which can be got. The natural price, or the price of free competition, on the contrary, is the lowest which can be taken ... The one is upon every occasion the highest which can be squeezed out of buyers, or which, it is supposed, they will consent to give: the other is the lowest which the sellers can commonly afford to take, and at the same time continue their business.'

Source: Adam Smith *The Wealth of Nations*, 1776.

Do we need a competition policy?

The last two units have analysed the advantages and disadvantages of various forms of market structure, and shown that competition can have considerable advantages when compared to monopoly. In particular, competition can lead to:

● lower prices;

● a higher level of output;

● greater efficiency; and

● more consumer choice.

Despite this, some economists would argue that there is little need for governments to adopt policies to encourage competition. These economists, sometimes called 'Austrians' because the originators of many of these ideas originally came from Austria, argue that the market is a dynamic device leading to innovation that ultimately benefits consumers. For example, research and development agreements between firms may limit competition, but consumers may benefit because this speeds up technical progress. Thus even though it can be shown that firms which dominate an industry have high profits, this is not necessarily because they are exploiting the customer, but rather that the profits may arise because the firms are efficient. If this is true, monopoly profits will only arise so long as the firms making them are more efficient than potential competitors.

The crucial element in this argument is the extent to which new firms can enter the market. If this is difficult, then existing firms can indeed exploit the customer. However, if they are faced by the threat of competing firms, then any exploitation will be short lived; high profits will draw in new firms and the customer will benefit from competition without the need for any government action.

The idea of **contestable markets** suggests that what is important is not the structure of the market – for example, whether there are few or many firms in the market – but how easy it is to enter. This view emphasises the importance of **barriers to entry**: high barriers will lead to exploitation. The most formidable barriers are those imposed by the state. Examples of these legal barriers to entry include restrictions imposed by the Bank of England on entry into the banking industry, licensing laws which restrict entry into the market for public houses, and barriers created by the requirements for the licensing of casinos or taxis.

There is an alternative argument which also leads to the conclusion that an active competition policy is undesirable, namely, that competition policy can weaken domestic firms. A firm which is a national monopoly may face international competition and may need to be large to reap the benefits of economies of scale necessary to compete in the world market.

Despite these arguments, most economists would maintain that there is a need for competition policy, if only to stop firms increasing these barriers to entry.

Exercise

The Austrian school

In recent years, the attack on the structure–conduct–performance paradigm has been joined by a resurgence in 'Austrian' approaches to competition. ▷

Austrians have always been associated with a robustly free-market stance, and perhaps even more strongly, with an abhorrence of government intervention in the economy. They therefore tend to play down the need for government intervention to prevent market concentration.

Neo-Austrians are sceptical of the existence of long-run market power. They believe that if there are no legal barriers to entry, a high level of concentration in a particular market merely reflects underlying cost conditions.

According to Austrian thinking, persistent examples of the abuse of market power only tend to arise when enterprises are prevented from competition by the state – for example, nationalised industries. In a free market, supernormal profits will attract new entrants. These may not be producers of identical products, but rather products in a related fields. Word processors compete with typewriters, spicy corn chips with potato crisps, video games with board games, computer-based home shopping with department stores.

Source: Adapted from J.R. Shackleton, 'Market structure, competition and contestability' *Economics and Business Education*, vol. 11, part 2 (1995), p. 65.

Questions

1. What is the 'structure–conduct–performance' paradigm?
2. Explain with examples how the law can prevent competition.
3. Can you think of other examples of high profits attracting competition in the form of related products?

How the current system works

Competition policy in the UK is slow, complex and, so critics claim, ineffective. Three main bodies are responsible: the Office of Fair Trading (OFT), the Monopolies and Mergers Commission (MMC), and the Department of Trade and Industry (DTI), which is headed by the President of the Board of Trade. Each of these bodies has different responsibilities.

The OFT identifies a particular problem – perhaps because it receives complaints. It then does a preliminary investigation, and if this suggests that there is indeed a problem, it refers the problem to the MMC.

The issues referred to the MMC can be very varied; for example:

- **Market share** A company with more than 25 per cent of the market, which may give it the power to exploit customers.

- **Restrictive trade practices** Refusing, for instance, to supply a product which is scarce unless the customer also buys a product that is easily and more cheaply available elsewhere.

- **Price agreements** Where companies get together and agree to put up prices, for example.

● **Mergers** If two companies propose to merge, this may lead to a dominant firm, able to exploit its power. In the case of mergers, the OFT advises the President of the Board of Trade, who then decides whether or not to refer the matter to the MMC.

Once it receives a request to carry out an investigation, the MMC, a relatively small organisation, approaches the firm or firms involved to obtain information. It may also approach other people involved such as customers or consumers' associations. Very often competing firms who feel that they are being treated unfairly will also give evidence.

As a result of its investigations, the MMC then makes recommendations to the OFT. The final word rests with the President of the Board of Trade who can reject or alter the MMC proposals, perhaps as a result of political pressure rather than an impartial assessment of the evidence.

This process can take many months. Indeed, the investigation into the brewing industry lasted three years, from 1986 to 1989. This process then led to a long period of lobbying, the net result of which was that the Beer Orders – the legal documents implementing the decisions – took another three years to put into effect.

The legal framework

The legal framework of competition policy is contained in a series of laws. The **Restrictive Trade Practices Act** 1956 set up a Monopolies Commission (now the Monopolies and Mergers Commission) to examine monopolies (and also mergers from 1965) and a separate Restrictive Practices Court to deal with this aspect of the problem.

This Act was amended by the Restrictive Trade Practices Act 1976, which remains the basis for most current practice. As a result of this Act it became a legal requirement for agreements between companies to be registered with the Director General of Fair Trading. The Act covers a wide range of agreements including prices, quantities, processes and also geographical areas supplied. The basic assumption behind the legislation is that all agreements are assumed to be against the public interest unless the firm can show that the agreement passes through a 'gateway' as shown in Table 11.1. And even if the agreement manages to pass through one of the gateways, the firms must also show that the agreement must not cause any substantial detriment to the public.

The normal assumption under UK law is that people are innocent until proven guilty. Here, however, the assumption is the other way round – firms have to prove that any

---

Table 11.1: Some of the gateways through the Restrictive Practices Court

These gateways must illustrate that the agreement:

● confers specific and substantial benefit to the public;

● protects the public against injury;

● prevents a reduction in exports or in employment; and

● counteracts other restrictive agreements or is not likely to discourage competition.

agreement is in the public interest. In the early years the Court was very tough and allowed few exceptions, which has discouraged other firms from applying for their agreements to be allowed through the gateways.

The Fair Trading Act 1973 is the legislation that deals with monopoly and mergers. In this case, monopoly is defined not as one seller – as in economic theory – but occurs when a firm or two firms acting together supply 25 per cent of a good or service in a particular market.

One difficulty is deciding what constitutes a 'market'. As we have seen, the narrower the definition, the more likely it is for a particular firm to have a quarter share; no firm will have 25 per cent of the market for food, but it is quite possible for a firm to have more than a quarter of the market for a particular item, say, broad beans or sardines. Similarly, is the appropriate market the market for soft drinks as a whole, or the market for cola? A firm may dominate the latter, but is less likely to dominate the whole soft drinks market.

The problem of defining what is a market is increasing in complexity because in recent years there has been a growing tendency for markets to segment. For example, the market for snack foods can be divided up into several segments, as a visit to the crisp section of any supermarket will show. Moreover, in the Act, the relevant market can be defined not only in terms of product, but also as a specific geographical area, thus bringing local monopolies within its scope.

The Fair Trading Act is also the basis of merger policy, though there have been some minor changes since 1973. Mergers can be referred to the Monopolies and Mergers Commission (MMC) if either they create a 25 per cent market share, or the combined assets of the firms proposing to merge exceed £30m. The MMC then has to decide whether or not the merger is likely to operate 'against the public interest'. Whatever the MMC decides, the last word rests with the President of the Board of Trade, who can allow the merger even if the MMC advises against it.

One difficulty with this legislation is how to decide what is in the public interest. An attempt is made to define this in the Act, which mentions such factors as promoting competition and the interests of consumers, reducing costs, and encouraging the development of new techniques or products. However, in practice, it is often difficult to determine what is 'the public interest'. For example, consumers may benefit from lower prices, but if this drives some firms out of business, is price cutting in the public interest?

One final piece of legislation should be mentioned, the Resale Prices Act 1964. Until this Act was passed, manufacturers could control the price at which their product sold in the shops, which meant that a particular product was usually sold at the same price whatever the shop. Hence there was very little price competition in the retail trade. The 1964 Act stopped firms from deciding the price at which their product could sell – with two exceptions – pharmaceuticals and books.

In the case of books, it was argued that the abolition of price maintenance would allow supermarkets and similar shops to sell the most popular books at a discount. This, in turn, would adversely affect sales in specialist bookshops, so that some booksellers would go out of business, thus reducing consumer choice because less popular books would then become unavailable. The Net Book Agreement, as it was called, lasted for over thirty years, until it fell apart under pressure from price cutting shops in 1995. On another front, the agreement allowing pharmaceutical prices ot be fixed still continues, though it is under threat from some supermarkets. Again, the case for the agreement is that it gives consumers more choice by keeping open small chemists who depend on the profits made by selling these products.

All in all, though, the Resale Prices Act has had a significant effect on shopping in the UK. Certainly it is a main cause of the rapid growth in the number of competing supermarkets.

In 1992 a government Green Paper suggested changes to the present system of competition policy by moving towards the system used by the European Union, and this aspect is discussed later in this unit.

Monopoly

The MMC investigates a very wide range of firms, which, in recent years, has included industries as diverse as concrete roofing tiles, tampons, roadside advertising services, films, artificial lower limbs, soluble coffee, new motor cars, pest control services and many others. As we have seen, monopolies can abuse their power if there are substantial barriers to entry, so a useful way to investigate monopoly policy is to examine how firms try to maintain these barriers.

Perhaps the main way in which firms maintain monopoly power is by their pricing policy. In some cases, firms will cut their prices if buyers can produce evidence of a lower price offered by a competitor. At first sight, this may seem to benefit the customer – and so it does in the short run. But in the long run it means that it is difficult for new firms to compete because existing firms will always cut prices, thus making it impossible for new firms to sell profitably.

Monopolies can also make use of price discrimination. They can do this in several ways: by charging lower prices in areas where competition is greatest, for example, or by giving loyalty bonuses so that customers will continue to buy their products, both practices making it difficult for new firms to enter the market.

Another strategy is **commodity bundling**, the term used when a firm offers a bundle of goods at a lower price than the sum of prices for the components of the bundle. Commodity bundling can build barriers to entry because it prevents competition from suppliers of individual goods within the bundle. This was an accusation made against IBM which sells a wide variety of computing products.

Not all barriers concern pricing policy, however. Firms can use vertical restraints to keep out competitors. One example of this is 'full line forcing', the term applied when a firm refuses to sell a product in short supply unless the customer also buys goods which are cheaply and easily available elsewhere. A particularly strong kind of vertical restraint occurs when there is vertical integration, the best example of which is the supply of beer. A MMC investigation found that about 75 per cent of public houses were owned by brewers, making it very difficult for small brewers who did not own pubs to sell their beer.

Another barrier arises when a firm insists on long-term contracts with customers: the longer the contract, the more difficult it is for new firms to sell their products. Again, in the short run buyers benefit, but in the long run the exclusion of competition means that lower prices might not be forthcoming. The MMC found that long-term contracts were a significant feature of the market for salt, which was dominated by two large firms, British Salt and ICI.

Advertising can also form a barrier to entry. Brand image can help to ensure customer loyalty, thus making it costly for new firms to enter the market because they would have to spend large sums of money on advertising before they could sell their product. For example, the MMC found in its investigations into liquid petroleum gas (i.e. Calor Gas) and contraceptive sheaths (i.e. Durex) that the dominant firms had brand names which were identified by consumers with the actual product names. However, competition has since reduced this barrier, certainly in the market for contraceptives, perhaps giving support to the Austrian argument that an active competition policy is not necessary.

In recent years the work of the MMC has been criticised for giving more emphasis to the interests of producers and not enough to those of consumers. For example, the MMC investigated the perfume industry, partly because of the very high profit margins found there. They concluded that there was indeed a complex monopoly, but concluded that this was not against the public interest because people wanted exclusivity, rather then value for money. Consequently, the perfume manufacturers were allowed to continue as before, and potential price cutters such as Superdrug found it difficult to obtain supplies.

Sometimes it is difficult to suggest how consumers might be helped. In the wrapped ice-cream industry, for instance, the large manufacturers such as Mars and Birds Eye Walls control 90 per cent of the market. They restrict competition since they own the freezers in many retailers' shops. Because retailers do not have space for more than one freezer, the owner of the freezer can prevent the sale of other manufacturers' products. The MMC investigated this industry, but the report did not suggest any change. Indeed, it is hard to think of solutions which would benefit the consumer in this case. It is not really practicable to suggest that freezer owners should be forced to stock competitors' products.

Mergers

The British approach to mergers is that they should be forbidden if they operate against, or can be expected to operate against, the public interest. In practice, this has usually been interpreted to mean, 'Will the merger significantly reduce competition?' Thus in 1990, the MMC rejected a proposed merger between Kingfisher (which owns the Comet chain) and Dixons because it would clearly reduce competition in the market for domestic electrical appliances.

The 1990 Companies Act modified merger policy by simplifying the procedures. The Act allows companies to complete and submit a questionnaire on a proposed merger. If no reference is made to the MMC within twenty days of submission of the questionnaire, the merger can go ahead. Moreover, this Act makes it possible for a company to agree to sell off some of their assets in order to reduce the market share they would gain as a result of the merger. An example of this approach occurred when Guinness, at the time of its bid for Distillers, agreed to sell off some of the whisky brands it had earlier obtained through its acquisition of Bells.

Merger policy only affects a small number of proposed mergers. In 1989, for example, the Director General of Fair Trading scrutinised 427 mergers and recommended that only 14 should be referred to the MMC. Of these, two were abandoned after the reference and only two rejected. This may suggest that merger policy is unimportant. On the other hand, it could just as easily be argued that the very existence of a merger policy prevents some possible mergers that would otherwise take place, but which are never even suggested because it is clear they would never pass the public interest test.

Examples of mergers which have been allowed include British Motor Corporation (now Rover) and Pressed Steel (which made steel sheeting for cars), Thorn and Radio Rentals, and Unilever and Allied Breweries.

On a number of occasions the Minister has overruled the advice from the OFT or the MMC. In 1994, the latter body recommended that a proposed merger between the *Daily Mail* group and a firm called T. Bailey Forman should not be allowed. These two firms owned regional newspapers in the Midlands, and the MMC argued that this would give the new merged firm a dominant position, thus posing a threat to editorial freedom. However, the Minister allowed the bid to go ahead because the papers involved only overlap in a small area. Conversely, in 1990 the OFT considered that a bid by Ransomes (which makes grass-cutting machinery) for Westwood (makers of garden tractors) need not be referred to the MMC for investigation. The Minister decided to the contrary on the grounds that the merged company would have too great a share of the 'ride on' lawnmower market. After its investigation, however, the MMC recommended that the merger should be allowed to go ahead, and this recommendation was accepted.

Restrictive practices

Restrictive practices occur when firms make an agreement which is against the interest of the consumer. Examples are shown in Table 11.2, although the list is not comprehensive. The law is intended to remove agreements which have the effect of 'preventing, restricting or distorting competition', whether or not this is intentional.

The strongest form of restrictive practice is the cartel. This occurs when firms form some sort of central organisation to set price and output. The Organisation of Petrol Exporting Countries (OPEC) is a cartel which meets regularly to try to fix the price of oil and to allocate production quotas for member countries. Since this is an international organisation, though, it falls outside national legislation concerning restrictive practices. In the UK, the Cement Makers Federation met regularly until 1987 to discuss prices, deliveries and market shares. They calculated a common price based on a formula which averaged the costs of various producers.

Table 11.2: Unacceptable restrictive practices

- Fixing prices or giving discounts or credit terms which affect the real economic price paid for the commodity.
- Practices which could lead to the fixing of prices such as recommending fees.
- **Collusive tendering**: (e.g. when firms agree in advance what their tenders for a job will be).
- Sharing or allocating markets, customers or raw materials.
- Any other anti-competitive behaviour.

Although formal cartels are rare, tacit unwritten agreements are much more common. These can take various forms, such as the following:

● **Dominant firm leadership**
  Here the leading firm decides its price and then smaller firms follow suit. In 1990 companies who bought fleet cars accused the big car manufacturers of following the lead of Ford, which in this case seemed to be the dominant firm.

● **Collusive price leadership**
  This is an informal form of cartel where prices change almost simultaneously. This often seems to occur in the market for petrol: when one firms changes its price, others follow quickly. However, the firms involved would say that this occurs because firms are responding quickly to changed circumstances such as a change in the world price of crude oil.

Because the powers of the OFT are limited, and because the potential rewards of price fixing are so high, restrictive agreements may still be common, though few are brought to court. An example of one prosecution occurred in 1991 when three leading manufacturers of steel roofing supports were found to have operated a cartel to fix prices and to share out the market between them.

At the same time, while many practices are illegal, there are successful agreements which pass through the gateways mentioned earlier. For example:

1. The Distant Waters Vessels Association fixed minimum prices for fish caught in distant waters. At first sight, this is a clear breach of the regulations, but the Association argued that the demand for fish at auction was relatively inelastic, so that the price would fluctuate considerably if there was no price fixing. Moreover, without the fixed minimum price some fishermen would go out of business, the result of which would be fewer fish and ultimately higher prices.

2. In the case of cement, the court accepted that the existence of a fixed price agreement resulted in a lower price level than would otherwise have been the case. The fixed price made it cheaper to raise capital for new investment, which brought down the price.

3. In the investigation into Permanent Magnets, the court accepted the argument that the absence of price competition encouraged technical cooperation between firms, and this then gave purchasers the benefit of lower prices.

The European Union's approach to competition policy

In recent years, the EU has taken a much more active role in competition policy than it used to do, and its activities are having a significant effect on the running of large firms throughout the Union. One reason for this is the success of European integration, which has led more and more firms to engage in cross-border activities. This means that an EU approach is needed to enforce competition policy since firms doing business in several countries may adopt anti-competitive policies that cross national boundaries.

The EU's policy derives from the 1957 Treaty of Rome which set up the European Community, and the two clauses in the Treaty that give the Commission authority to take action in this area are summarised in Table 11.3.

Table 11.3: Articles 85 and 86 of the Treaty of Rome

Article 85 prohibits 'as incompatible with the common market all agreements ... which may affect trade between member states and which have as their objective or effect the prevention, restriction or distortion of competition within the common market'.

Article 86 states that 'any abuse by one or more undertakings of a dominant position within the common market or in a substantial part of it shall be prohibited as incompatible with the common market insofar as it may affect trade between member states'.

Restrictive practices and the EU

As Table 11.3 shows, Article 85 is concerned with restrictive practices. In fact, it complements national policies since it is concerned with practices that distort competition within the EU, which means, in practice, that the EU focuses on infringements which affect more than one country. Most of the decisions concern manufacturing rather than services, but in recent years decisions concerning services have grown to about 20 per cent of the total. Because of the size of the EU there is a danger that there could be so many cases that the system could clog up. Hence a system of block exemptions to the general rule of competition has developed. The most notable exception concerns research and development. Agreements in this area have been allowed because these activities can be seen as benefiting the consumer, by, for example, bringing new products on to the market.

A specific example of an exemption which illustrates the Commission's approach is the *Concordato Incendio* case. This was an agreement between Italian insurance companies to fix the premiums on fire-risk insurance. The Commission decided to give a ten-year exemption to the companies because it accepted the argument that, since there was market failure in the face of imperfect information among purchasers, the agreement actually improved efficiency. The Commission also accepted the argument that the agreement did not eliminate competition.

Dominant firms in the EU

The Treaty does not prohibit the *existence* of a dominant position; it is the *abuse* of such a position which is forbidden. In deciding whether or not a dominant position exists, the EU apply a number of criteria, particularly market share. The Commission has to find a substantial reduction of competition, however, in order to prove abuse of a dominat position. In practice, there has been relatively little EU activity under this Article, as Table 11.4 shows. One reason is that it is difficult to define the market. A firm may have a large market share within the Union, but this may be necessary due to economies of scale.

Sometimes the EU has not opposed large firms growing bigger through acquisitions, even though other firms object. Thus in 1997 the Commission approved a £1.2bn sale of Cadbury-Schweppes' bottling operations to a Coca-Cola subsidiary, even though rival

Table 11.4: Commission decisions relating to Articles 85 and 86

	Manufacturing			Services		
	1964–69	*1970–79*	*1980–90*	*1964–69*	*1970–79*	*1980–90*
Article 85	25	108	120	2	1	28
Article 86	0	6	10	0	0	5

Source: 'European Competition Policy in Manufacturing and Services', *Oxford Review of Economic Policy*, vol. 9, no. 2, 1993, by permission of Oxford University Press.

companies such as Virgin objected on the grounds that it would give Coca-Cola too much control of the market.

Nevertheless, when the Commission has acted, the fines have often been very large. In 1991, for instance, TetraPak was fined 75 million ecu (=£50m.). TetraPak is the largest manufacturer of cartons for liquid foodstuffs in the Union and it took over Liquipak, a producer of milk-packing machines. Liquipak had obtained an exclusive licence for a new sterilising technology, and TetraPak used its new acquisition to prevent its rival Elopak from using this new technology. The Commission felt that this was an abuse of a dominant position, hence the large fine.

Mergers in the EU

In the late 1980s, there was a great surge in the number of mergers in the EU. This led to concern about the danger of firms acquiring dominant positions across the Union. The result was a new regulation which came into force in 1990. It applies to mergers where the turnover is 5 billion ecu and the EU turnover of each firm is 250 million ecu. In other words, the intention is for the EU to focus on large, international mergers, leaving national ones to national legislation. The regulation has had relatively little effect, though. Of the sixty-five cases decided in 1990/91, only five raised serious doubts, and only one led to a prohibited merger. The latter case was a proposed merger between three aircraft manufacturers, de Havilland, Alenia and Aerospatiale. Opponents of the merger claimed that this would give the three merged companies too large a share of the market for commuter aircraft.

Summary

Competition policy is controversial. Some economists would argue that there is little need for such a policy as long as the state does not introduce regulations that limit competition, since the market will quickly remove any temporary abuses. However, both national and EU legislation assumes that monopolies can exploit their position and that some system is needed to prevent this. Moreover, restrictive practices between firms can also disadvantage consumers, and such practices therefore require attention. (Note that a particularly important form of competition policy, relating to privatised utilities, is discussed at length in the next unit.)

Review questions

1. Summarise the arguments suggesting that an active competition policy is not really necessary.
2. Why do most governments have a competition policy?
3. Outline the current system of competition policy in the UK. What criticisms could be made of this system?
4. Summarise the legal framework of competition policy in the UK.
5. What methods do firms use to maintain monopoly power?
6. How does the UK government control mergers?
7. Give four examples of unacceptable restrictive practices.
8. What forms of unwritten agreements do companies adopt?
9. Give examples of agreements which have passed through the restrictive practices gateways.
10. Outline the EU's approach to competition policy and give some recent examples of this policy.

Essay questions

1. Why do governments need competition policies? Critically evaluate the UK government's policy towards competition.
2. 'The price of monopoly is upon every occasion the highest price which can be got . . . the price of free competition, on the contrary, is the lowest which can be taken' (Adam Smith). Discuss.

Reading 11.1

Cement cartel fined

Today the EU Commission showed its determination to attack monopolistic practices in the EU. They fined 38 cement companies a total of £194m. for setting up a cartel in 1984 to divide up the EU cement market. The companies included several UK companies, among which are Rugby, Castle Cement and Blue Circle Industries.

According to the Commission, the firms agreed not to sell in other EU countries, and they facilitated this objective by exchanging price information. This enabled them to reduce price differences between countries and so cut any temptation to export.

The biggest fine, of £26m. was imposed on Italcement, but Blue Circle's fine was £12m., Castle's £6m. and Rugby's £4m. The difference between the fines reflected the extent to which they had taken part in the cartel. Several of the companies said that they would appeal. ▷

Questions

1. Explain what is meant by a cartel.
2. How much is an ecu worth in pounds sterling?
3. Under which EU authority does the Commission have the right to prosecute such cases?
4. **(a)** How would customers suffer from the activities of the cement companies?
   (b) How would the companies benefit?
5. If the companies appealed, what arguments do you think that they could use to justify their actions?

Reading 11.2

The market for white salt

White salt is obtained by the evaporation of brine, which is pumped to the surface from rock salt deposits that have been dissolved naturally by underground streams or artificially by water pumped from the surface. White salt is used to produce table salt, and it is also used in the production of caustic soda and chlorine and in water softening, as well as in food manufacture.

The MMC found that the market structure was duopolistic: ICI had a 45 per cent market share, and British Salt (BS) had a 50 per cent market share. The remaining 5 per cent was accounted for by two small producers and imports. The MMC also discovered that there was informal coordination of price increases and that prices were in excess of the competitive level since they were based on the costs of the higher cost producer (ICI). This meant that BS was particularly profitable.

The two firms were able to maintain high prices because of the existence of various barriers to entry, as follows:

1. In markets with two firms, potential entrants are aware that existing firms will cut prices to prevent new entrants. In this case, this factor would make the salt market unprofitable to new firms entering the industry.
2. The salt industry has excess capacity. In 1984, capacity utilisation for BS was only 69 per cent and for ICI only 64 per cent. Hence there was no unfulfilled demand waiting to be met.
3. Both BS and ICI had long-term contracts with major buyers. This would make it difficult for new entrants to win customers.
4. ICI might have been able to deny potential entrants access to brine because the only technique for extraction was one developed by ICI. Also, the mineral rights to the most suitable brinefields were owned by BS and ICI.
5. Government regulations might form a barrier to entry. There are unexploited salt reserves, but to utilise these would require planning permission, which might not be forthcoming.

Source: Adapted from G. Myers, 'Barriers to entry', *Economics and Business Education*, vol. 1, part 1 (1993), pp. 124–30.

Questions

1. Explain what is meant by 'barriers to entry'. Why are these important?

2. Do you think that these barriers would deter potential entrants? What strategies could a potential entrant adopt to overcome them?

3. What do you think the government can do to encourage competition in the market for white salt?

Privatisation

The truth about privatisation

'Beauty lies in the eyes of the beholder' claimed the poet; the same can often be said about truth.

Hansard records that on the 7 March 1995, John Major, then Prime Minister, claimed that: 'Opposition members may still relish the day when it cost the taxpayer £50 million a week to subsidise utilities so that Ministers could run them inefficiently. These days, those utilities are yielding about the same amount of money each day to the taxpayer.'

The opposition members concerned would no doubt have contested this 'truth', claiming that the utilities had previously contributed millions to the Exchequer. For example, in the ten years prior to privatisation the nationalised electricity industry made profits of over £8 billion, and since the industry was in the public sector this money belonged to the government.

So where does the truth lie?

Nationalisation

Imagine, if you can, the world in 1945. The Second World War had just ended. Britain was victorious, but a high price had been paid. So far as industry was concerned, one consequence was that there had been little or no investment in basic industries such as coal or rail for many years, and huge sums of money were now needed to bring them up to standard.

So, what was to be done? The answer seemed clear. In the war, the power of the state had shown that it could achieve great things: landing and equipping hundreds of thousand of troops on the Normandy beaches, building thousands of planes, and developing new weapons, to name but three. Now it was time to use the power of the state to reinvigorate industry.

One reason for public ownership was that some industries needed large amounts of investment. Private capital might not have been forthcoming, hence the need for state intervention.

There was also a political argument. According to its constitution, the Labour Party was committed to 'the public ownership of the means of production, distribution and exchange', and this meant taking into public ownership the most important industries in order to run them for the benefit of the people as a whole, rather than in the interests of private shareholders. This move would also give the government power over the commanding heights of the economy, enabling it to plan – or at least strongly influence – economic activity in a way that would ensure the achievements of goals such as full employment. In addition, socialists argued that while private sector firms aimed only for high profits at the expense of both workers and consumers, serving the public would be the chief objective of publicly owned industries.

In fact, public ownership was not really much of a party political issue. A few industries, such as the Post Office, had been in public ownership for many years, and the Liberal government of 1912 had passed the Act setting up the Port of London Authority. Moreover, Conservative governments had set up the British Broadcasting Corporation, British Overseas Airways Corporation (later British Airways) and the Central Electricity Generating Board. However, the Labour government after 1945 nationalised not only coal and rail, but also the Bank of England, steel and a large part of road haulage. The gas and electricity industries were also nationalised. Subsequently, companies such as British Leyland (now called Rover) and Rolls-Royce were taken into the public sector at short notice after they had encountered financial difficulties: these companies were considered too important to be allowed to go out of business.

For many years, both the Labour and Conservative governments accepted public ownership of most of these industries, though the Labour Party was more enthusiastic. Public ownership of basic industries was also common across Europe.

Nevertheless, there were problems and criticisms. Principally, the **nationalised industries** were often attacked for being inefficient. The central argument on this point was that since they could not become bankrupt or be taken over – that is, they were not really subject to competition and the discipline of the market – these industries had few incentives to be efficient.

This criticism is difficult to evaluate. In a perfectly competitive industry, the level of profits is a good measure of a firm's efficiency, but in a nationalised industry, profits largely reflect the prices that the government allows the industry to charge. Most economists would tend to the view that prices should reflect marginal costs, since these costs reflect the cost of producing an additional unit of output. But this causes problems in industries which have very high fixed costs and low marginal costs. If, for example, a water company just charges the cost of supplying an additional litre of water, the charge would not be high enough to cover all its fixed costs, so the company would make a loss. Hence nationalised industries were usually required to adopt some rule, such as making a return of, say, 5 per cent on their investment. This rule may have been reasonable – it would not have been appropriate for nationalised industries to attempt to maximise profits, since they were often monopolies, but it did mean that the level of profits was no guide to their efficiency. Moreover, the nationalised industries often had social obligations, such as the delivery of services to rural areas, which were inevitably not profitable. And since the nationalised firms were often the only ones in their particular industry, it was not possible to make direct comparisons between nationalised and privately owned firms. Thus evaluations of the efficiency of nationalised industries usually reflected political prejudice, rather than cool economic assessment.

State intervention in industry can take a number of forms, but the most typical method is for the government to nationalise an industry. This usually involves the government buying all the shares in that industry and setting up a public corporation. In a public corporation, the firm is run by directors, appointed by the government, who are responsible for the day-to-day running of the business along government-imposed guidelines. This is the method used to run the Post Office, and similar methods are employed for other publicly owned bodies, such as the BBC, London Transport, and the British Waterways Board, which are still in the public sector.

The meaning of privatisation

Privatisation can have several meanings. First, it can mean the liberalisation of entry into areas previously controlled by the state. Examples are telecommunications and bus services before they were sold to the private sector. In these industries, licensing regulations were changed to allow private operators to compete with public monopolies. This implies a movement from public to private provision of services.

A second definition refers to private provision rather than public provision. A good example here is refuse collection, which was traditionally undertaken by local authorities themselves. Legislation was then introduced which allowed this service to be contracted out to private operators. Similarly, hospital cleaning is now undertaken by privately owned firms.

A third meaning of privatisation – and the one on which we shall focus in this unit – is the sale of publicly owned assets.

Reasons for privatisation

There was little challenge to the idea of nationalised industries until the end of the 1970s when the idea of privatisation became popular. There were several reasons for this development:

- The first reason was political. Mrs Thatcher was elected as Prime Minister in 1979 with a radical economic programme. Yet privatisation was originally not part of that programme. Indeed, privatisation was a policy that came about initially almost by accident, though it did fit in well with her ideas about reducing the power of the state and an increased emphasis on supply-side measures such as reducing the power of the trade unions.

- One argument put forward for privatisation is implied by the long-standing criticism of nationalised industries, namely, that private ownership would lead to greater efficiency. The case is made that nationalised industries were overstaffed and complacent, while private ownership would give the stimulus of profits to improve efficiency. It was also said that nationalised industries were too closely linked to government, and that their managers were not free to innovate and were restricted by government intervention, which forced them to continue to provide unprofitable services and keep down prices.

- Another reason given for privatisation is to improve competition by allowing several firms to compete in markets previously the monopoly of a nationalised industry. Privatised firms may also increase allocative efficiency since they are more likely to be in tune with the need to respond to market forces.

- Privatisation also benefits the government's finances because the receipts of the sale can be used to reduce taxation.

- A related benefit is that privatisation widens share ownership. As we saw in Unit 2, private individuals currently own only 10 per cent of shares in the UK. While in office, the Conservatives wished to increase this figure for several reasons: the more people who owned shares, the less easy it would be for a later government to reverse the process of privatisation; share owners seemed more likely to vote Conservative; and there was also the social argument that people who own any form of property are more likely to contribute to a stable society. This last reason also influenced the Conservatives' policy of selling off council houses to tenants.

- Finally, nationalised industries were often accused of being too soft on the unions. The belief was that privatisation would discipline the unions and increase productivity.

These claims for privatisation will be evaluated later in the unit.

The extent of privatisation

The claims made for it led to a great surge in privatisation in the UK, as Table 12.1 shows. This is a very long list and it demonstrates what a complete turnround there was in economic policy after about 1980. Privatisation arguably became the most innovative aspect of British economic policy, and it was one which was copied in many other parts of the world. Almost all the countries in Western Europe have moved towards privatising their state-owned enterprises. In some countries such as Italy and France, the change has been relatively small. In Italy, this is because of recurring political crises combined with the great importance of state holding companies in the economy. In France, as in some other countries, a strong role for the state is considered important. Thus when Jacques Chirac was elected Prime Minister in 1986 he announced that the government intended to

Table 12.1: Major privatisations in the UK

Organisation	Date	Industry
British Petroleum	Various 1979–1987	Oil
National Enterprise Board	Various 1980–1986	Various
British Aerospace	1981, 1984	Aerospace
Cable and Wireless	1981, 1983, 1985	Telecommunications
Amersham International	1982	Scientific products
National Freight Corporation	1982	Road transport
Britoil	1982, 1985	Oil
British Rail Hotels	1983	Hotels
Associated British Ports	1983, 1984	Ports
British Leyland (Rover)	1984–1988	Cars
BT	1984, 1991, 1993	Telecommunications
Enterprise Oil	1984	Oil
Sealink	1984	Sea transport
British Shipbuilders	1985 onwards	Shipbuilding
National Bus Company	1986 onwards	Transport
British Gas	1986	Gas
Rolls-Royce	1987	Aero engines
British Airports Authority	1987	Airports
British Airways	1987	Airlines
Royal Ordinance	1987	Armaments
British Steel	1988, 1989	Steel
Water	1989, 1990	Water
Electricity distribution	1990	Electricity
Electricity generation	1991	Electricity
Trust Ports	1992	Ports
British Rail	1994 onwards	Transport
British Coal	1995 onwards	Coal
HMSO	1996	Stationary

Source: D. Parker, 'Has privatisation improved performance', in Brian Atkinson (ed.), *Developments in Economics*, vol. 11, Causeway Press, 1994.

privatise a large part of the public sector, but that there was no intention to privatise the public services.

In Eastern Europe, privatisation has progressed quickly in those countries which were not part of the Soviet Union. In the Czech republic, Hungary and Poland, most state-owned industries have been privatised. Progress has been slower in the countries which made up the former Soviet Union, though even here, small-scale enterprises such as restaurants have been privatised. Large-scale privatisation has been less conspicuous. One reason is that there is still a strong belief in the merits of state-owned enterprise. Furthermore, many of the state-owned enterprises are very large (in order to capture economies of scale). They are also considerably overstaffed, so that a transition to private ownership would involve many redundancies and a large rise in un-employment.

Methods of privatisation

In the UK the methods used to privatise varies with the industry. The most common method has been to offer shares for sale to the public. The government consults with merchant banks and others, and then fixes a price for shares. Since the government wants to dispose of all the shares it has on offer, it has tended to sell them at a low price to ensure that they are all taken up. This has led some people to 'stag': that is, to buy the shares with the intention of selling them straight away and pocketing the profit.

Critics have claimed that because the shares are sold at low prices, purchasers have benefited at the expense of the public as a whole who have lost ownership of valuable assets. The examples in Figure 12.1 suggest that there is some evidence to support this claim. In almost all cases, the price of shares has risen significantly after privatisation, allowing those who have bought shares to make large profits. Another criticism of this method of privatising state industries is that it is expensive. For example, the legal and administrative costs of privatising British Telecom amounted to £262m.; British Gas cost £360m.

A second method of privatisation is to sell by tender, whereby purchasers indicate how many shares they are willing to buy at different prices. The sale price is then decided, ensuring that all those who have offered to buy shares at that price can do so. Direct sale is a third method used in a few cases: for example, in the sale of Royal Ordnance Factories to British Aerospace. This is the preferred method when the privatisation is relatively small and other methods would therefore be too expensive. It is also used when industrial logic suggests that a particular company is interested in buying the firm.

In the case of bus transport and the National Freight Corporation, management buyouts have been the preferred method. It is claimed that buyouts lead to highly motivated workforces. When managers – and other workers – are allowed to buy the company they work for, this gives them an incentive to make the firm successful. However, management buyouts have not been widely used, largely because managers find it hard to raise the finance needed to buy large firms.

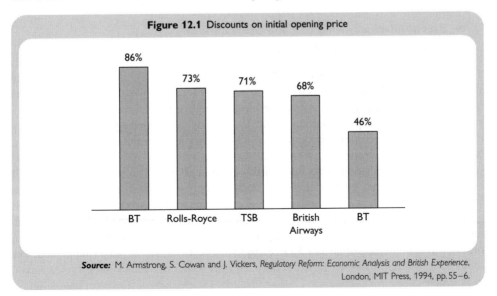

Figure 12.1 Discounts on initial opening price

Source: M. Armstrong, S. Cowan and J. Vickers, *Regulatory Reform: Economic Analysis and British Experience*, London, MIT Press, 1994, pp. 55–6.

The problem of natural monopoly

One of the reasons for nationalisation, and one of the difficulties of privatisation, is that some of the most important industries in the public sector were **natural monopolies**. In industries such as gas, electricity and water, it would be extremely inefficient to have two or more firms laying pipes to every door so that consumers could choose which supplier they would patronise. Industries like these have very high fixed costs and very low marginal costs: the cost of supplying an additional litre of water to a house is almost zero, but the cost of building a reservoir and then connecting this to a house is very high. Consequently, it is difficult to have competition in these industries.

There is a considerable likelihood that monopoly firms in these industries will be in a position to exploit consumers and make very high monopoly profits. The problem is exacerbated because supplies of water, gas and electricity are essential for most families. In fact, exploitation does not occur when such industries are in the public sector because the government can decide on a pricing structure that is considered to be fair. However, how can private sector monopolies be prevented from charging very high prices for products that we all need?

Two approaches have been tried to overcome this threat, and we shall discuss each in turn. The first method is to regulate the industry, while the second is to try to introduce competition, even though this may be difficult.

Regulation

Regulation of an industry is intended to act as a kind of imitation competition. It has the following aims:

- To enable an industry to produce on a large scale in order to obtain economies of scale.
- To prevent abuse (e.g. high prices and restricted output) that might occur with a monopoly.
- To encourage efficiency (e.g. low operating costs).
- To minimise the costs of regulation.

The USA has had many years' experience of regulating monopolies in the private sector. The method used there is to appoint a regulatory body which establishes the rate of return obtained by a company as the basis of regulation. This restricts a company's profits to a defined proportion of its capital. In this way it is hoped a regulator can ensure that a company's prices are reasonable and that consumers are not exploited. However, the method has disadvantages.

First, since a company knows that it will only be able to make profits of, say, 10 per cent on its assets, it has every incentive to build up more assets than it needs. The process is therefore characterised by excessive capital expenditure. The American system attempts to overcome this problem by differentiating between allowable and non-allowable capital expenditure, but this has led to many expensive law suits as companies try to increase the profits which the regulator allows. Hence this method only really achieves the objective of preventing monopoly abuse; the other objectives are either not achieved or only achieved in part.

Another second criticism is that there is no incentive to cut costs, since if a company does so, the regulator will force it to cut prices to match. Hence the managers have every inducement to dissipate resources on managerial perks, higher wages and generous staffing. The regulator has then to investigate these costs to judge whether they are justifiable. The result is a form of game in which the firm first asks for a much bigger price increase than it expects, the regulator knows this will happen and refuses to accept the firm's proposal, and the firm eventually agrees to a price rise that is half the figure it initially asked for.

Price cap regulation

The alternative method of regulation is called **price cap**, and this is the system used in the UK. Here, the privatised utilities are usually given a licence: BT, for example, has a licence for 25 years, and this period can be extended. The licence sets out various terms and conditions: again taking BT as an example, the company must continue to supply rural areas, provide call boxes and operate 999 calls. A regulatory body is appointed to ensure that each company carries out the conditions of its licence and this body also fixes prices. These regulatory bodies are given names appropriate to the industry such as OFTEL (telecommunications), OFGAS (gas), OFWAT (water) and OFR (rail). Each of the offices is headed by a Director General appointed by the government on a fixed-term but renewable contract. The Director General then appoints staff: OFWAT, for instance, has 150 full-time employees. The regulating body is entitled to information from the company, which can include accounting information, investment plans, and costs. If there is a dispute between the regulator and the industry, either side can appeal to the Monopolies and Mergers Commission. Thus, in 1992 British Gas requested an MMC enquiry after a dispute with the regulator about profits in the industry. Eventually, this enquiry led to a restructuring of the gas industry to facilitate greater competition.

In this system, prices are fixed using a formula such as $RPI - X$, where RPI is a measure of inflation such as the retail price index, and X is determined by the regulator. This was the formula first used in the case of BT, and subsequently used as a model for other privatisations. For BT, X was given the value of 3 per cent, so that if the rate of inflation was 4 per cent BT could raise its prices by $4 - 3 = 1$ per cent; if inflation was only 2 per cent then BT would have to cut its prices by 1 per cent. The reason there was a minus sign in the equation was because it was expected that the telecommunications industry was one where technological innovation was likely to occur on a large scale, making it possible to cut prices. Not all BT's prices are controlled by the regulator: for example, mobile services are not included.

The regulator fixes the value of X for a particular period, and for BT, the regime has toughened over the years, so that between 1993 and 1997, X was fixed at 7.5 per cent. The basic formula applied to BT was used in other privatisations, but the details varied, as shown in Table 12.2. In some industries, prices are allowed to rise by more than the rate of inflation for special reasons. Thus in the water industry, companies have to meet EU directives on water quality and other environmental objectives.

Factors which influence the level of the price cap include:

- the cost of capital to the firm;
- the firm's investment programme;
- expected future changes in productivity;

Table 12.2: UK price regulation

Organisation	Main features	Excluded from regulation
BT	RPI − 7.5%	Mobile services, apparatus supply
British Gas	RPI − 4%	Supply to large users
British Airports Authority	RPI − 4%	Retail, parking
Water supply*	RPI + 5.4%	Some services other than water and sewage
Electricity transmission (NSC)	RPI − 3%	–
Electricity distribution	Varies between RPI − 0% and RPI − 2.5%	–

Note: * The actual formula for water is RPI + K, with K varying according to the water company, and reflecting capital costs (e.g. of new sewage works), although 5.4% is the average.
Source: M. Armstrong, S. Cowan and J. Vaqueros, *Regulatory Reform: Economic Analysis and British Experience*, London, MIT Press, 1994, p. 177.

- the value of the firm's assets; and
- estimates of future demand.

Several advantages are claimed for the price cap system, the main one being that it encourages firms to improve their productive efficiency by cutting costs: for example, if BT is able to cut its costs by more than the X of the price cap, it can keep the benefits and so increase dividends to shareholders. Advocates of the system therefore argue that it benefits both producers, by allowing them to increase profits if they are efficient, and consumers, by ensuring that prices are not too high.

However, there are difficulties with the system, as follows:

- If firms seem to be making profits that are too high, then the next time that the X factor is fixed, it may be lowered to remove these excess profits. As a result, though firms may have an incentive to cut costs in the period just after the price cap has been fixed, this incentive will diminish as the next review approaches. Indeed, firms may seek to increase costs (e.g. by increasing investment) and reduce their profits in order to receive a more favourable review. If this occurs, then the end position will not be very different from those obtained by the rate-of-return approach discussed earlier.

- In order to make their proposals, regulators require detailed information about costs and profits. This requirement has resulted in detailed monitoring and more and more regulation. Since one of the arguments for privatisation was that it would remove firms from government control and let them get on with running the business, this is a serious criticism. Firms may be making decisions, not on the grounds that it will improve efficiency, but in order to satisfy the regulator. Moreover, the whole process involves considerable time and effort on the part of both regulators and firms.

● It is also possible that the efficiency factor (i.e. X) may be fixed at the wrong level. An example of this occurred in 1995 when the regional electricity companies reported large profits and caused the Director General of OFFER to intervene only a year after he had completed a price review.

A further criticism of regulation that certainly applies in the USA and may apply to other countries is **regulatory capture**. In theory, regulatory bodies are set up to protect the public, but they may end up by being 'captured' by the firms that they are supposed to regulate, since firms try to use their influence with government to have someone appointed as regulator who is sympathetic to them. Furthermore, regulators interact so frequently with firms that they may become sympathetic to their problems. This factor is reinforced by the firm's superior technical knowledge on which the regulatory agency comes to depend. An example of regulatory capture in the UK (albeit in another context) occurred in 1995 when the lottery regulator was found to have accepted free flights in the USA from one of the owners of the lottery company.

Another stricture often aimed at the system of regulation is that firms are allowed to pass on some costs to the consumer. This is called **cost pass through**, and is designed to protect firms from increases in costs that are outside their control; for example, if, after the regulator fixed the price which a utility could charge, prices of its raw materials rose significantly, that utility could be in deep trouble. Hence most utilities are allowed to pass on some prices: for instance, British Gas can pass on changes in its gas purchase costs; the British Airport Authority can pass on most of any changes in security costs; and the regional electricity companies can pass on increases in the price they pay electricity producers. Therefore, although there are strong reasons for allowing cost pass through, it does have one particular disadvantage, namely, if firms are allowed to pass on these costs, they have little incentive to try to keep them down. Consumers might then end up paying more than they should have to.

Regulating quality

One way in which a utility could increase its profits, even if its prices were fixed, would be to cut the quality of the services which it offered. For example, the water authorities could reduce the effort which they make in controlling pollution from sewerage works; the gas industry could cut the services it offers to inspect gas appliances or to offer advice on insulation; and BT could cut the number of phone boxes in rural areas.

In order to prevent the utilities from reducing the services in this way, the regulators have been given powers to specify services and standards which each industry must achieve. Table 12.3 shows some performance indicators for the water industry. As you can see, the figures suggest a significant improvement in the services offered by the water companies.

Introducing competition

Many state-owned firms have always faced considerable competition: for example, British Steel competed with overseas firms as well as with several privately owned British steel firms, and British Airways has always competed with overseas airlines. However, it is true that many of the firms in the public sector were essentially monopolies, and faced little competition. This was the case with the utilities.

Table 12.3: Some performance figures for the water industry in England and Wales

Activity	*1989/90*	*1993/94*
Drinking water quality:		
Compliance with standards	98.3%	99.4%
Sewage treatment works:		
Compliance with standards	85.0%	98.0%
Customer service:		
Loss of water from distribution system	187 million litres per day	135 million litres per day
% of properties at risk of sewer flooding	0.14%	0.10%
Billing queries:		
% dealt with in less than 2 days	45.0%	86.0%

Source: OFWAT.

Thus, though regulation is the main way in which these monopoly utilities are prevented from exploiting their customers, the other method is by the introduction of competition. Certainly, competition is generally thought of as desirable. This might not always be the case, however, and even if it is, it might not always be possible.

Figure 12.2 demonstrates the possibilities. In most industries, competition is both desirable and feasible, as shown in the top left-hand box of the figure. At the opposite extreme, in the bottom right-hand box, competition might be neither desirable nor feasible. It might not be desirable, for example, where there are large economies of scale, so that having several firms in an industry would be inefficient. In the third sector – the bottom left-hand box – it might not be possible to introduce competition. This is the case where supplying a service such as gas or water involves laying pipes to every house. Competition is thus desirable, but not possible, and here the regulator should act in a way which mimics the effect of competition. Finally, in the top right-hand box, there are circumstances where competition is possible, but not necessarily desirable, because incumbent firms adopt anti-competitive practices to prevent new firms entering the market. These practices can be very widespread. 'Cream-skimming' is one example,

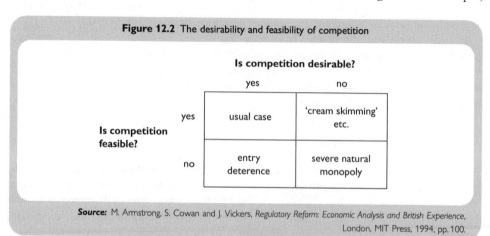

Figure 12.2 The desirability and feasibility of competition

Source: M. Armstrong, S. Cowan and J. Vickers, *Regulatory Reform: Economic Analysis and British Experience*, London, MIT Press, 1994, pp. 100.

which occurs when a firm takes the best customers and leaves the rest to others. For example, it would pay the Post Office to deliver letters to urban areas and to stop delivering to rural areas where the costs of delivering a letter are much higher; a privately owned firm might be tempted to do this unless prevented from doing so by the government. Similarly, a bus company might decide only to serve busy routes. In situations such as these, the regulator must act to maintain services.

There are several sectors of the economy in which privatised utilities undertake activities where competition is both possible and desirable. In the power industry, for instance, there can be competition in generating and supplying electricity if potential generators have access to the transmission system and if potential suppliers can use the monopoly distribution system to sell electricity to consumers. In communications, firms such as Mercury can make use of BT's lines, while gas producers can supply consumers if they are allowed to use British Gas's network of pipes.

Problems do occur, however. One concerns the social objectives which some utilities have to fulfil. The obligation of BT to run a free emergency call service is one example. If new entrants to the market did not have to do this, then BT would be at a disadvantage. Similarly, British Gas has to respond to gas leaks. The regulator therefore has to ensure that firms fulfilling social objectives are not disadvantaged, and one method is by charging new entrants an access fee which equates to the costs of the social objective.

On the other hand, the regulator must also ensure that existing dominant firms do not attempt to protect their monopoly by adopting anti-competitive devices such as **predatory pricing**.

Unrestricted competition may also be undesirable. Some industries require large investment and firms will only be willing to spend this money if they expect to receive a reasonable return on their investment. However, the threat of many new firms entering may deter such investment since their entry in to the market may force down the price. The regulator may therefore decide to limit the number of firms, in order that those who do enter can receive reasonable returns on their investment. Conversely, in 1991 OFTEL allowed other fixed line suppliers to compete with both BT and Mercury because it judged that by then Mercury was sufficiently well established to continue in business.

Another difficulty concerns **cross-subsidisation**. For example, when telecommunications was in the public sector, local telephone calls were subsidised by the profits made on long-distance and international calls. If cross-subsidisation is allowed, then a dominant firm can cut its prices in those areas of the business where there is competition and charge higher prices where there is little or no competition. In order to prevent this happening, regulators have forced suppliers to show the true costs of supplying particular services and have then tended towards forcing firms to charge the marginal cost of providing each service.

Despite the difficulties, competition can be introduced in many areas and in several ways, for example as follows:

1. By direct financial subsidy. The argument for this is that existing firms have the benefit of experience, while new entrants have to learn the most efficient way of doing the business. Hence an initial payment to new entrants can cover these learning costs and encourage them to enter.

2. At present, regulators lack powers to offer subsidies, but a variation of this approach would be to exempt new firms from some of the non-profitable obligations placed on existing firms. This could be regarded as a kind of subsidy.

3. By imposing restrictions on the existing firm's pricing. This can be done by preventing dominant firms from cross-subsidising services in areas which are subject to competition.

4. By raising barriers to entry to prevent too many firms entering the market. The argument here is that some competition is better than none, and unless potential entrants were given some guarantee that they would not face other entrants, they would not be willing to spend the large sums necessary to enter the utilities market. As we have seen, this was the argument used to restrict entry to the telecommunications market for a period in order to ensure that Mercury was a stable competitor to BT. One weakness of this argument is that if the second entry would make the first unprofitable, why would anyone expect the second firm to be able to make profits?

5. Ensuring that utilities make their distribution systems available on reasonable terms to new entrants: for example, BT has to allow Mercury to use its lines. In such cases, the regulator determines the terms.

Competition in the bus industry

The bus industry provides a good example of the problems and possibilities of privatisation. In this case it was relatively easy to introduce competition, since the industry is not a natural monopoly.

For many years, most bus services were provided by local authorities, which had a monopoly of services in their area. The arguments for this were that they could provide services in areas where it was not profitable, and they could also ensure an integrated service: that is, making sure that local bus services were coordinated with train timetables and with national bus services.

The Conservative government not only privatised the industry, but also allowed new entrants. The National Bus Company was broken up and market forces were allowed to determine the structure of the industry. Unprofitable but essential services could be subsidised by local authorities.

The effects varied in particular areas, but, in general, dominant firms saw off most new entrants, so that markets remained very concentrated and with little competition. One reason for this was that customers were familiar with the names of existing companies and new entrants therefore had to spend heavily on advertising their services. Moreover, existing firms were often willing to cut prices to deter or see off new entrants. In many other areas there was evidence of tacit collusion, so that firms matched fares, and there was considerable merger activity – indeed, there were six MMC reports into mergers in only two years, all but one of which concluded that the proposed merger was not in the public interest. Hence, even in areas where competition is possible, this example indicates that it is not always easy to ensure that the consumer benefits, since firms will act in their own interest, and that interest will usually lie in the reduction of competition.

Competition in other industries

While early privatisations did not take much notice of competition, it subsequently became a feature in several cases. Electricity privatisation reflected this growing emphasis. In England and Wales, the National Grid Company and twelve regional electricity companies were required to offer terms for the use of their distribution and transmission systems. The old Central Electricity Generating Board was split up into National Power,

PowerGen and Nuclear Electric (which remained in the public sector). Scotland had its own companies. New entrants were allowed to enter the generation market. In 1998 all customers were given the right to choose their electricity supplier.

We have already mentioned the competition between BT and Mercury. In recent years competition in the telecommunications industry has intensified, with cable companies offering lower prices in many areas, and also a rapid expansion of mobile phone services. One of the problems which arises is that BT makes a loss in providing local network services to users, and, in particular, in providing the last link in to a customer's house. BT covers this loss from profits made in other parts of the service. Since other companies such as Mercury make use of these local lines BT argues that they should pay some of these costs. The counterargument is that BT exaggerates the extent of these costs and that charging competitors might lead to less competition.

Similar problems arise in the gas industry. It is relatively easy for several firms to produce gas, but they must then make use of British Gas's pipelines to supply their customers, and arguments inevitably arise about the costs that they should pay to do this. In order to introduce competition into the market, large consumers were allowed to buy their gas from producers other than British Gas, and by 1995, British Gas's share of the industrial and commercial gas market had fallen from 100 per cent at the beginning of the decade to only 35 per cent. In 1993, the government decided to accelerate the introduction of competition for domestic consumers and in 1996 British Gas lost its monopoly on the supply of gas to small consumers.

Exercise

Competition in the gas industry

When the gas industry was privatised it was assumed that it would remain a monopoly supplier, with its prices controlled by the regulator. After all, it would be economic nonsense to build several pipelines into each house just in order to allow consumers to choose which gas to use.

Technology and time have changed all that. After British Gas's monopoly ended several new suppliers entered the market, including the trade unions who planned to form their own company. These competing companies will pay the privatised utility for the use of its pipelines. Another company, Amoco Western Europe Gas, claimed that it would be able to cut gas prices by 10 per cent.

Questions

1. Draw demand and supply diagrams to show why prices might be expected to fall if the new company achieves its plans.
2. What effect do you think such developments will have on British Gas's share price?
3. Will such developments make the regulator redundant? (Note: there will still only be a few firms in the industry, so what does oligopoly theory suggest might happen?)

Has privatisation been a good thing?

One of the reasons why privatisation has become such a popular policy with governments in many countries is that it provides them with revenue which can then be used to cut taxes and so gain political popularity. As Figure 12.3 shows, large amounts of money have been received in this way. These are huge sums: to give some indication of their importance, cutting the standard rate of income tax by a penny in the pound costs the government about £1.6bn.

A former Conservative Prime Minister, Harold Macmillan, called privatisation 'selling the family silver'. The chief criticism is that, although some nationalised industries made losses, overall they contributed substantial revenue to the Treasury. Once an industry has been privatised, this source of revenue is lost forever. However, the argument is rather more complicated, since the industries that are privatised will, if profitable, have to pay corporation tax and will therefore continue to contribute to the government's revenue, though probably at a significantly lower level than they did under public ownership.

A second claim made for privatisation is that it encourages a property-owning democracy by spreading share ownership. However, most shareholders only own shares in one or two companies and small shareholders have little real power in these industries, as we saw in Unit 2 (see p. 21). In addition, having a large number of small shareholders is costly for a company since they all have to be kept informed about the company's activities.

However, the main claim made for privatisation is that it would increase efficiency, and it is this claim which we shall now try to evaluate. There have been a number of

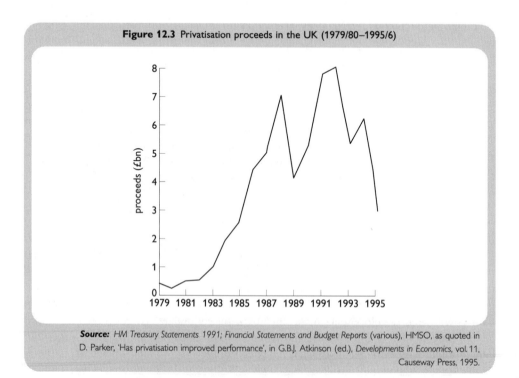

Figure 12.3 Privatisation proceeds in the UK (1979/80–1995/6)

proceeds (£bn)

Source: *HM Treasury Statements 1991; Financial Statements and Budget Reports* (various), HMSO, as quoted in D. Parker, 'Has privatisation improved performance', in G.B.J. Atkinson (ed.), *Developments in Economics*, vol. 11, Causeway Press, 1995.

Table 12.4: Labour productivity 1970 to 1990 (% increase)

Enterprise	1970/80	1980/90
British Airways	8.1	6.0
BAA	0.6	2.7
British Telecom	4.3	7.2
British Coal	(2.4)	8.1
Electricity supply	3.7	2.5
British Gas	4.9	4.9
Post Office	(0.1)	3.4
British Rail	(2.0)	3.2
British Steel	(1.7)	13.7

Source: M. Bishop and D. Thompson, 'Regulatory reform and productivity growth in the UK's public utilities', *Applied Economics*, vol. 24, Routledge, 1992, p. 1187.

investigations that have attempted to answer the question: 'Which is best – public or private ownership?' The evidence is mixed, but tends to suggest that privately owned firms tend to perform better in competitive markets, while state-owned firms outperform private ones in monopolistic markets. However, some state-owned firms do do well in competitive markets: Volkswagen, for example, was built up under state ownership and was very competitive.

The difficulty in coming to any firm conclusion is illustrated by Jonathan Aylen's research. He compared two steel firms: one in India had outdated plant, was overstaffed and bureaucratic, and had low productivity. The other, in South Korea, was entrepreneurial, up-to-date and efficient. Yet both firms were in the public sector. The difference was that India has a bureaucratic model of state ownership, while the South Korean management were given considerable autonomy. Thus, as this example suggests, it is not easy to come to any firm conclusion about the relative efficiency of state and private ownership, since results will vary according to the circumstances and environment in which firms operate.

There have been several studies of the performance of privatised firms, but again the results are inconclusive. Table 12.4 compares labour productivity in the 1970s (when the firms were all in the public sector) and the 1980s (when some were still state-owned and some were in the private sector). They found that in the 1980s productivity improved in both the private and the public sectors, which suggests that increases in productivity in the privatised industries may have been due to factors other than the change of ownership.

More recently, evidence has been accumulated to suggest that in some industries performance – as measured by such factors as profits, employment, relative wages and productivity – improved faster before privatisation than it did afterwards. This is true, certainly, for British Airways, British Gas and Rolls-Royce, the aero engine manufacturer. On the other hand, productivity rose faster after privatisation in BT.

The conclusion may be that *ownership* has less influence on productivity than other factors such as changes in technology, changes in demand, and exchange rates. Overall, privatisation does not *guarantee* performance gains.

Summary

The factors which influence the performance of an industry are not fully understood, but are certainly very complex. For many years after the Second World War, there was substantial agreement between the political parties that some industries should be in the public sector. This consensus ended with the election of Margaret Thatcher in 1979, and, in subsequent years, very many industries have been privatised.

In some cases, the firms were already in competitive industries, but in others privatising utilities meant that special arrangements had to be made to prevent consumers from being exploited. Regulators were appointed with powers to fix prices and to set quality standards, and in some industries competition was introduced.

The effects of these changes will continue for many years, but it is clear that the factors which affect a firm's performance are so complex so that it is not possible to conclude with any certainty whether or not privatisation has improved performance.

Review questions

1. Outline the reasons for nationalisation. Are these good arguments?
2. Critically assess the arguments put forward for privatisation.
3. List about ten privatisations.
4. What methods have been used to privatise industries?
5. What is a natural monopoly and what problems does it pose for privatisation?
6. Explain with examples what is meant by 'price cap regulation'.
7. What are (a) the advantages and (b) the disadvantages of the price cap method of regulation?
8. Why might competition be neither desirable nor possible in some industries?
9. How might a regulator encourage competition in some industries?
10. Critically assess the results of privatisation.

Essay questions

1. Critically evaluate the American and British methods of regulating utilities.
2. Has privatisation been successful?

Reading 12.1

Promoting entry into regulated industries

Statement by Sir Bryan Carlsberg, then Director General of OFTEL:

'All of you who have heard me speak before know about the importance I attach to promoting competition, know that I like to say that it is perhaps the most important thing that a regulator has to try to do. Often it is important, when you have a problem in regulation, to think first about the possibility that you can reduce the problem, or perhaps eliminate it altogether, by doing something in the area of assisting and promoting competition. I believe that we are on the track in the UK to achieving a really competitive environment in telecommunications ... In a few years time, we shall start to see the fruits of competition in a much more dramatic way than today.'

Source: M.E. Beesley (ed.) *Major Issues in Regulation*, Institute of Economic Affairs, London, 1993.

Questions

1. How can a regulator assist or promote competition? What difficulties might be faced in attempting to do this?

2. What are the 'fruits of competition'?

3. Do you think that the views of Austrian economists are similar to those expressed here? What criticisms could be made of these views?

Reading 12.2

UK v USA: the regulatory contest

How to regulate? That is the subject of an often fierce debate between British and American regulators.

Everyone agrees that there must be some regulation of utilities, otherwise as monopolies supplying essential services such as water, gas and electricity they could exploit their customers. But there is considerable disagreement about how this should be done.

In the American corner, there are large numbers of regulators – often lawyers – who impose restrictions on the rate of return that firms can make. British critics say that the system is expensive and that it gives firms incentives to pad out their costs – hence the need for hoards of regulators.

In the UK the system is different. Regulators limit the firms' price rises to a specified amount above or below changes in the retail prices index. The British regulators claim that this system is efficient because it encourages firms to cut costs. But – a heretical thought – is this system much different from the American? If British firms do cut costs and make huge profits, there is no doubt that next time round the regulator would toughen up the price control regime. The end result would then be very similar to that in America. ▷

Questions

1. Explain what is meant by 'privatisation' and give examples.

2. Why are utility industries largely monopolies?

3. Summarise the British and American methods of regulating utilities. What are the advantages and disadvantages of each method?

4. Can you think of any other method of reducing exploitation and encouraging efficiency?

Multinational enterprises

About BP

The British Petroleum Company plc is one of the world's largest oil and petrochemical groups.

Incorporated in 1909 to develop the first commercial oil discovery in the Middle East (in Iran), it has since grown to become a global group operating in about seventy countries. Today, BP directly employs about 60,000 people, approximately half of them in Europe and a further quarter in the USA.

BP shares are quoted on the stock exchanges in the UK, the USA, Japan, France, Germany and Switzerland.

BP consists of three core businesses: BP Exploration, BP Oil and BP Chemicals. It also has a network of national associate companies around the world that provide a local base for its business operations.

- BP Exploration is responsible for the company's upstream oil and gas activities which extend from exploitation ... to pipeline transportation and gas marketing. Most of its production comes from Alaska and the North Sea, but it is now focusing its exploration on 'new' areas such as Columbia, the Gulf of Mexico, waters to the west of Shetland, and offshore Vietnam.

- BP Oil manages the company's downstream oil activities covering the refining, marketing, shipping, distribution and trading of crude oil and petroleum products. It has a prominent position in many markets in Europe, the USA, Australasia and Africa, and is also focusing on the growth markets of Southeast Asia and Eastern Europe.

- BP Chemicals is an international manufacturer and marketer of petro-chemicals, intermediate products, and plastics. It has large-scale manufacturing and research facilities in Europe and the USA, and is increasing its presence in the Asia-Pacific region.

Research and technology play vital roles in securing the competitiveness and efficiency of BP's products and operations. They also support the group's aim of maintaining the highest health and safety practices and environmental standards.

Source: Adapted from the BP Diary, 1996.

What is a multinational?

Imagine you want to buy a car, a cola, or a computer. The chances are that the company that makes it is a multinational. **Multinationals (MNCs)** are sometimes also called **transnationals (TNCs)**. In this unit, we will use the terms interchangeably, though sometimes 'transnational' is used to describe a firm that operates in at least two countries, while 'multinational' suggests operations in many countries. Whatever the term used, they are a dominant feature of the modern world. They are not companies which produce a product in one country and then export it. The crucial feature of a multinational is that it *owns* and operates production or distribution facilities in two or more countries.

Some multinationals produce the same goods in several countries: a horizontal expansion, as shown in Figure 13.1. Examples of this are Marks & Spencer, which owns shops in several countries, or Ford, which makes cars in several countries. Others expand vertically: they produce resources or semi-finished products in one country and then send them to another part of the firm in another country to be finished. Car manufacturers do this, making parts such as gear boxes or engines in one country and then using these parts to assemble cars in another. The large oil companies are another example: they drill for oil in one country and then sell it in others. The commentary at the beginning of this unit shows the huge extent of the operations of a large multinational in this industry.

The three main characteristics of a multinational company are:

1. It controls economic activities in more than one country.

2. It can take advantage of differences between countries. Geographical and natural resource differences are examples.

3. It can move resources between different parts of the world within the company so that it does not have to use markets.

This last characteristic is illustrated in Figure 13.2, which contrasts (a) traditional trading between countries that takes place through markets, and (b) trade between different parts of the same firm that is determined by decisions taken within the firm and not by market forces. Hence the multinational company supplies inputs like technology, management and marketing skills and also controls their use. It is the parent company which decides

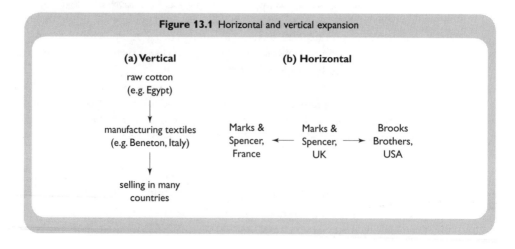

Figure 13.1 Horizontal and vertical expansion

(a) Vertical

raw cotton
(e.g. Egypt)

↓

manufacturing textiles
(e.g. Beneton, Italy)

↓

selling in many
countries

(b) Horizontal

Marks &
Spencer, ◄─── Marks &
France   Spencer, ───► Brooks
              UK   Brothers,
                            USA

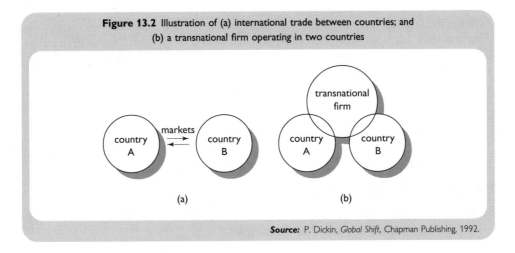

Figure 13.2 Illustration of (a) international trade between countries; and (b) a transnational firm operating in two countries

Source: P. Dickin, *Global Shift*, Chapman Publishing, 1992.

such things as the location and size of new investments, the location and size of R & D activities, and the prices which are charged on intra-firm activities.

The actual powers delegated to foreign subsidiaries will vary from company to company: in some they will be tightly controlled, while in others they will have considerable freedom to react to local conditions. McDonald's restaurants, for instance, are the same the world over; in other multinationals local managers might be able to decide investments within an agreed budget, and to vary marketing details. Whatever the powers of local management, they have to put the interest of the whole company before their own national interest.

Development of transnationals (TNCs)

The involvement of large organisations in international transactions goes back a long way in time. Companies such as the East India Company engaged in trade in several countries over hundreds of years, but these were not multinationals per se since they were engaged in international trade rather than in production in several countries. The real forerunners of the multinationals were the European-owned firms that exploited the raw materials to be found in Africa, Asia and South America at the end of the nineteenth century. These firms were mainly engaged in less developed countries and in plantations of tea and coffee, in cattle raising and meat processing, and in sugar and tobacco.

Much of this development in international trade was made possible by improved communications. The pattern was often one of *core* and *periphery*. In the nineteenth century, the core (and particularly Britain) imported raw materials (e.g. cotton), and then exported finished goods (e.g. textiles) to the periphery (i.e. the rest of the world).

By the beginning of the First World War, the United Kingdom was still the chief source of overseas investment, much of which was in the colonies. Then the emphasis switched as American-owned companies in the early twentieth century began manufacturing automobiles, chemicals, oil and aluminium in several countries. Other European countries also invested overseas, particularly in chemicals and electrical machinery. By the time of the Second World War, the USA was the principal source of international investment and the emphasis of MNCs had moved from raw materials to manufacturing.

Since then, MNCs have become more important in service industries, and companies from the USA, UK, and other European countries have been joined by many Japanese companies, and indeed, by companies from Asian countries such as South Korea and Taiwan. Although world trade has grown very rapidly since the Second World War, its growth has been slow compared to that of TNCs. Similarly, although national income has grown steadily over the years, in many contries foreign direct investment has grown four times faster than national incomes.

The importance of foreign direct investment

Foreign direct investment (**FDI**) comprises:

1. The acquisition of share or loan capital through mergers or joint ventures and also through starting new subsidiary companies.
2. The transfer of funds from parent companies to overseas subsidiaries.
3. The transfer of profits from overseas to the parent company.

It does not include what is called **portfolio investment**, which is investment in the shares of a company. Portfolio investment is usually undertaken by financial institutions such as insurance companies and merely transfers the ownership of a financial asset from one person or firm to another, whereas foreign direct investment is concerned with real productive assets such as factories.

The total *amount* of FDI is staggering. In recent years it has averaged about US$250,000 million a year. The *pattern* of this investment has changed over the years. As we have seen, it was originally associated with a centre–periphery pattern where a metropolitan country such as the UK invested in a less developed country. Now most FDI takes place between the developed countries. In the last decade or so, the industrialised countries have been responsible for over 90 per cent of outward FDI. As Figure 13.3

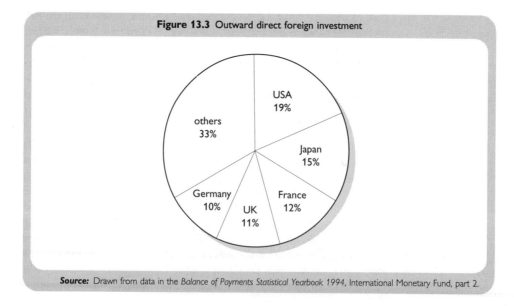

Figure 13.3 Outward direct foreign investment

USA 19%

others 33%

Japan 15%

Germany 10%

UK 11%

France 12%

Source: Drawn from data in the *Balance of Payments Statistical Yearbook 1994*, International Monetary Fund, part 2.

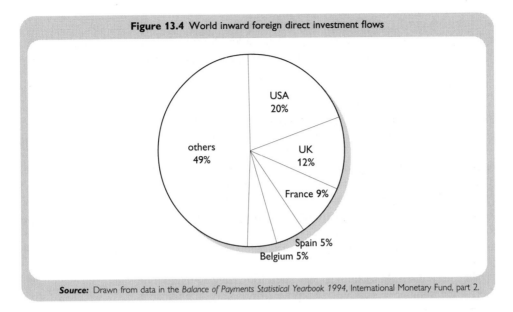

Figure 13.4 World inward foreign direct investment flows

Source: Drawn from data in the *Balance of Payments Statistical Yearbook 1994*, International Monetary Fund, part 2.

shows, the USA was the largest investor, accounting for about a fifth of the total, with Japan and France next in size. In fact, over the years, the American share has tended to fall and the Japanese share to rise. However, these three countries were responsible for almost half of all outward flows between 1989 and 1993.

The *inward* flows of investment are not primarily to the less developed countries, as we might expect, but to the richer industrialised countries, which receive two-thirds of all such flows. As Figure 13.4 shows, the USA is the prime recipient of funds, followed by the UK and France.

There are several reasons for the large amount of investment into the USA. The obvious one is that it is a huge and rich market. Moreover, it was reinforced for several years by a fall in the value of the dollar, which meant that American assets become relatively cheap. This has encouraged takeovers of American companies: for example, Marks & Spencer bought the American company Brooks Brothers, makers of high-quality clothes. The UK has also received a considerable amount of investment, mainly because it is an English-speaking gateway into the European Union, although a contributory reason might be that UK labour costs are relatively low compared to those in the rest of Europe.

Why do companies become multinationals?

If a company wishes to do business in another country it has several alternatives, of which foreign direct investment is only one.

The simplest way to do business is simply to export domestically produced goods. This is a relatively inexpensive way of selling abroad, and it also allows a firm to produce on a large scale and so benefit from economies of scale. It does have several disadvantages, however. First, foreign distributors may be inefficient: poor, for example, at marketing or servicing. Secondly, the exporting firm may find it difficult to keep in touch with conditions in many overseas markets if it trades through foreign distributors. Thirdly, foreign governments may impose import restrictions, or changes in exchange rates may make exports unprofitable.

An alternative method is for a firm to form a strategic alliance with a firm in another country. This can allow each firm to contribute particular skills to the enterprise. For example, the German car producer Volkswagen formed a joint venture with a Chinese company to produce cars in China: VW contributes its research and manufacturing skills, while the Chinese firm has local knowledge of labour relations, marketing and government. One disadvantage of strategic alliances is that the partner firm may not be reliable; disagreements between partners in alliances are by no means a rare occurrence.

Licensing offers yet another way into foreign markets. A firm can licence a foreign firm to produce its product, and in return receives royalties. Coca-Cola is an example. This method allows a firm to expand its overseas sales with relatively little risk, but the returns are entirely dependent on the foreign firm, which may or may not prove to be a suitable partner.

While there are alternatives to FDI, therefore, they all have disadvantages. In addition, there are a number of positive reasons for firms to become transnationals, which we shall now examine.

Cutting costs

Firms may undertake direct foreign investment because it enables them to cut costs. This is often associated with vertical integration where the later stages are located separately from the source of supply. The oil companies such as BP were early examples of this approach (as the commentary at the beginning of this unit states). BP developed an oil well in Iran as early as 1909. Other multinationals have also located overseas in order to obtain low-cost supplies. Another example is provided by companies locating abroad to take advantage of low wages.

Cutting transaction costs

Markets are often imperfect. As we have seen in Unit 7, markets sometimes fail because the parties to an agreement lack information. This may give one or other party an advantage, or it can make it difficult to negotiate a fair contract with a supplier. Where there is uncertainty, there is an incentive to *internalise* the market: that is, for the firm to control transactions by owning the supplier. In this instance, the bauxite market is a good example. This raw material, used to make aluminium, is heavy and of low value, so that it is not practicable to transport it long distances. However, a firm which owned only an aluminium refinery could be at the mercy of its bauxite supplier since alternative supplies would be difficult to obtain. Hence the owner of a refinery also frequently owns the bauxite mine, and then transports the aluminium to other countries for sale.

There are other transactions costs that can be cut by vertical integration. For example, the costs of finding both suppliers of inputs and distributors, and then negotiating with them, can be large; these costs can be cut by owning the supplier and/or distributor.

Improving marketing

Some multinationals are motivated by the promise of new markets. This is a horizontal expansion, and as we have seen, most FDI takes place between advanced industrial economies. In many cases, firms are often selling the same (or very similar) products in several markets. The car industry is a good example of this situation, since a basic model is sold in several countries, with perhaps some small variations to cater for local taste or because national regulations differ (e.g. cars made for the UK market have right-hand drive).

A variation on this theme occurs when firms want to maintain quality control. Here, the international hotel industry is a good example. It would be quite possible for a hotel company to license the use of its name by an overseas firm, but it might then find that the overseas firm was inefficient, providing such a poor service that the hotel company lost its good reputation. Hence, the company may decide instead to own hotels overseas.

Ownership-specific advantages

Successful FDI can only take place if the incoming firm has some advantage that domestic firms do not possess in order to overcome the benefit of local knowledge which the domestic firms have. Ownership-specific advantage may take several forms: for example, it may arise from the ownership of a patent or from experience of large-scale production.

Technology – which can include marketing and organisation as well as production – is a very important firm-specific advantage. However, a particular characteristic of much technology is that it is easily passed from one firm to another. A firm must therefore be most careful not to lose its technological advantage, for example through its appointed licensee gaining knowledge of the process as well as the right to use it. Thus in order to protect its technology, a firm may choose to produce overseas itself rather than to license its process.

Even if there is little danger of losing technological advantage to a rival, FDI often takes place because an incoming firm which possesses more advanced technology than its rivals has an advantage over local firms. An example of this is Japanese car manufacturers locating in the UK: these manufacturers are the most efficient in the world, and when they locate overseas they can compete most successfully against local rivals.

Some of these explanations can be combined using the concept of the **product life cycle**. Initially, a firm may be content with the domestic market, but at some stage this market may become saturated, and a firm may need to expand overseas if it wishes to continue to grow. Though it may start by exporting, eventually the disadvantages of this method may be felt, and the firm will then seek to gain greater control of its overseas sales. It may do this by buying an existing local firm or by starting a new company.

Figure 13.5 shows a possible sequence. In phase 1 the company produces in the USA and also exports to other countries. Then in phase 2 the company also starts production in Europe, perhaps to gain greater control of the market or to take advantage of lower wage costs. In phase 3 the firm's European factories begin exporting overseas, displacing some American exports. In phase 4, the firm's European plants export to the USA. Eventually the firm also begins production in less developed countries and, in phase 5, these LDCs then export to the USA.

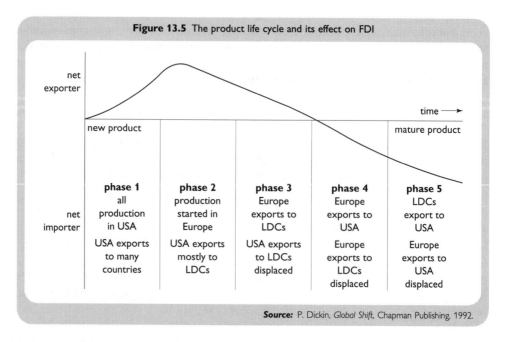

Figure 13.5 The product life cycle and its effect on FDI

Source: P. Dickin, *Global Shift*, Chapman Publishing, 1992.

What reasons do you think that these firms might have had for undertaking the developments described below?

1. In 1992 ICI opened a £150m. greenfield manufacturing plant for pure terephthalic acid in Taiwan.

2. In 1993, Jacobs Engineering (USA) acquired the UK-based engineering group Humphreys & Glasgow.

3. In 1993, Mercedes Benz announced that it was to build a greenfield manufacturing plant in the USA. Mercedes' decision followed that of BMW who likewise decided to shift production out of Germany to the USA.

4. In 1993, Coca-Cola acquired a 30 per cent stake in Femsa, Mexico's leading soft-drinks bottling concern.

5. Usinor Sacilor, the French steelmaker acquired ASD, the UK's largest independent steel stockholder, creating a vertically integrated concern.

6. In 1992 Grolsch, the lager brewer, acquired the UK real-ale brewer Ruddles, having earlier bought the German brewing group Wickuler.

Costs and benefits of transnational corporations

Transnationals are controversial. Some people extol their benefits and claim that they bring money and jobs; others say that they are too powerful and that they use their power to exploit local economies.

One difficulty in reaching any conclusion about the costs and benefits of TNCs is the number of factors involved. All multinationals are not alike, so it might be quite possible for some to exploit, while others bring benefits. For example, since a new factory creates jobs, it is more beneficial if a multinational builds a brand new factory than if it buys control of an existing firm. The nature of the host country also affects the way that multinationals operate. In less developed countries, the government may be relatively poor and weak, and so relatively powerless. This is much less likely to be the case if a multinational locates in another developed country.

Capital flows

One of the most important benefits of FDI is the movement of capital from the home of the parent firm to the host country. Such capital flows are particularly valuable to less developed countries, since one consequence of poverty is a lack of capital to finance investment.

They are also important to developed countries, as Table 13.1 makes clear. However, in these cases, the funds for investment may well have been obtained by borrowing from local sources (e.g. banks), so that there may be relatively little inflow of funds. Moreover, when the investment is productive, profits will flow out of the country, so that the net long-term effect on the flow of funds is uncertain.

There may also be a cost attached to obtaining the foreign investment. If firms are free to invest in several countries, then to attract overseas investment from these footloose firms, countries may have to offer inducements such as tax holidays or subsidised sites. Hence the undeniable benefits of extra funds brought into a country by multinationals may not always be without an offsetting cost.

Transfer pricing

Another possible cost to host nations arises from the possibility of **transfer pricing**. A multinational company may produce parts in several countries and then transfer them to other company plants. For example, a car manufacturer may build its gear boxes in country A and its engines in country B, while assembling cars in country C. Now if countries A and B have high tax rates, it will pay the firm to arrange its internal prices so

Table 13.1: Major foreign investments in the UK 1994–95

Organisation	(£m.)
Siemans	1100
Ford/Jaguar	840
Fujitsu	800
Samsung	500
Chunghwa Picture Tube	260
Toyota	200
Ocean Technical Glass	190
Montupet	140

that the subsidiaries in A and B charge low prices for the parts sent abroad for assembly, and, in so doing, make only low taxable profits. The assembly plant in country C will then benefit and make high profits which will only be taxed at a low rate. This strategem will enable the company to achieve global profit maximisation.

Thus transfer pricing offers companies the possibility of avoiding taxes, but there is little evidence available on the extent to which companies actually use this ploy to reduce the taxes they pay. Less developed countries often lack the means to monitor multi-nationals, so it may be that transfer pricing abuses are greatest in poor countries. However, there is some indirect evidence to suggest that the practice also occurs in more advanced countries. In the USA in 1992 it was alleged in Congress that the government was losing tax receipts of several million dollars because of the tax-avoidance tactics of foreign companies. Among the evidence produced to support this allegation was the fact that foreign-controlled enterprises earned only a 0.51 net return on their assets compared with a much larger return for US-owned enterprises.

Technology transfer

As well as transferring capital, multinationals also transfer technology, and this may be one of the greatest benefits of FDI. In this sense, 'technology' is a much wider concept than simply the transfer of machines.

One of its most important aspects is management skills, which are transferred along with capital. For example, when Nissan established a car assembly plant in the UK it insisted on much higher standards from its component suppliers than had been the usual practice. Nissan's engineers helped suppliers to achieve these standards, and this help included management practices. For example, one of the 'demonstration effects' of Japanese multinationals has been that host countries should adopt practices such as 'just in time' (where management of stocks is improved to the extent that supplies reach the plant just in time to be used on the production line, thus entailing far lower stock levels).

Certainly, the potential for technology transfer is very high, but the extent to which it actually takes place is probably limited. Companies often locate their R&D facilities in their home country, so that foreign subsidiaries may be little more than 'screwdriver' plants, where relatively unskilled workers assemble complex products made in other countries. Similarly, when, for example, Japanese firms locate in other countries such as the UK, they are often followed by other Japanese firms which supply their components, so that there is relatively little transfer of technology to domestic firms.

Balance of payments

Transnationals *may* improve a country's trade. On the other hand, as we have seen, TNCs often take their profits out of a host country, so weakening its **balance of payments**. On the other hand, this may be offset by exports – or import substitution – from the factories built by overseas companies, which will help the country's **balance of trade**. Indeed, a prime motive for a TNC to locate overseas might be to use the country as a base for exports. There is no doubt, for instance, that one reason for Japanese firms locating in the UK is to facilitate their exports to the rest of Europe.

The extent to which a transnational improves a country's balance of payments depends on several factors. Does the TNC import its raw materials and parts or does it use local suppliers? Japanese car firms locating in the EU have to buy most of their parts in the EU, so helping to reduce imports and increase exports. Hence the importance of TNCs can be illustrated by the fact that just over a quarter of the UK's exports are accounted for by foreign-controlled firms.

Employment

Foreign firms employ local people – though the takeover of an existing firm may actually lead to fewer jobs if the new owners seek to improve productivity by reducing the number of people employed. However, the establishment of a greenfield site leads to increased output and employment. When a greenfield development is undertaken, there will also usually be secondary (multiplier) effects on the economy, as the new firm buys parts from local firms and because people who now have jobs spend their earnings with local firms.

One concern is that jobs created by TNCs may not be permanent. These firms are constantly seeking to improve worldwide profits, which may involve closing down plants and transferring the work elsewhere. Two examples illustrate this point. In 1990 Ford transferred the production of Sierras from its Dagenham plant in the UK to its plant in Gent in Belgium, and in 1997 it announced plans to transfer production of the new Escort from Halewood to other European countries. Similarly, in 1993, CPC (UK), the subsidiary of a US company, transferred the production of its Knorr brand of soups and cubes from Scotland to newer plants in Italy and France, with a loss of 350 UK jobs.

Overall, however, the evidence suggests that TNCs are employment creating.

Conclusion

Whatever their potential disadvantages, the vital importance of TNCs is shown by their crucial position in the UK economy. In 1993, foreign-controlled enterprises, accounting for about 1 per cent of the total number of manufacturing firms, employed 16 per cent of the labour force and accounted for 22 per cent of total UK output and 27 per cent of total investment.

Multinationals and governments

We have seen that it is not easy to evaluate the effects of multinationals on a country, and one reason is that these effects will vary according to the characteristics of the particular firm and also of the country in which it is located.

Although foreign firms can benefit their host countries, there is a widespread feeling that their arrival leads to some loss of autonomy: that is, countries lose control over some aspects of their economy, because the private interest of the TNC may not be the same as the public interest of the host country. Some examples can illustrate this point:

- Firms may use transfer pricing to reduce the taxes they pay to the host country.
- They may cause countries to compete with each other to attract foreign firms. For example, in 1995 Ford announced that it was to invest £400m. to develop a new Jaguar car in the UK, rather than in the USA – but this was only after it had been promised £80m. in aid from the UK government.

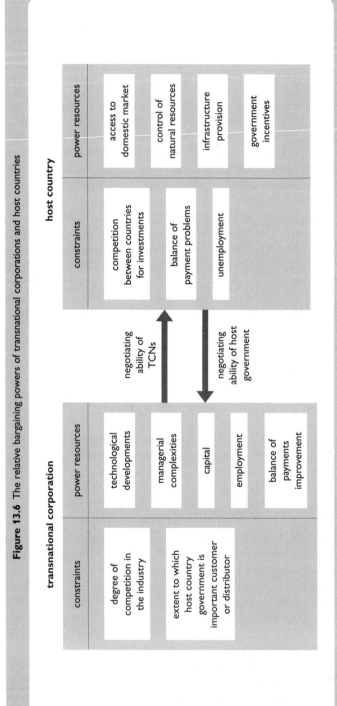

Figure 13.6 The relative bargaining powers of transnational corporations and host countries

Source: P. Dickin, *Global Shift,* Chapman Publishing, 1992.

- TNCs may send home profits, so weakening a country's balance of payments.
- The TNC may say to the government: 'If you pass this law (or don't pass that law) we will transfer all our operations to another country.' Thus Fiat rejected directives from the Italian government to develop the poorer southern part of Italy (the Mezzogiorno) and, instead, expanded production in Brazil. Similarly, Michelin responded to French indicative planning regulations by building plants outside France in a three-to-one ratio to those inside.

Constraints and power resources

In the final analysis, the relationship between TNCs and host countries depends on their relative bargaining powers. Some of the main considerations are illustrated in Figure 13.6.

Transnationals

Transnational firms are faced by two main constraints. First, there may be considerable competition in the industry, so reducing the power of any one company. Secondly, the host country may be particularly important to the firm, either as a customer or as a source of scarce resources. Both these factors will limit the power of a TNC in any negotiations.

However, the multinational has several power resources. These include the benefits which they can bring – or take away – from a country, as we have already discussed. The capital, technology and jobs which a TNC can offer give them considerable negotiating power.

Host country

The host country, too, has considerable power, to counterbalance the strengths of TNCs. At the extreme, it can refuse entry to the domestic market and it can control access to essential natural resources. In addition, it can offer substantial incentives, not only in the form of grants, but also by providing suitable infrastructure such as roads and telecommunications, and by offering to train labour.

However, the host country also faces constraints. Other countries may well be seeking to attract foreign firms. Even in developed countries there may be high unemployment and considerable poverty, exposing their governments to internal pressures to attract foreign firms. Factors such as these may weaken a government in any negotiations with footloose foreign firms.

Overall, therefore, it is probably safe to conclude that whether the arrival of a foreign firm creates net costs or net benefits will depend very much on the specific context: that is, on the relative strengths and weaknesses of the firm and the government.

Summary

Most of the well-known companies in Britain – BP, Shell, Unilever, Ford, Kelloggs – are multinationals. Companies sometimes become multinationals to secure markets, or to exploit natural resources or cheap labour. By producing in several countries they can reduce transactions costs, and by using transfer pricing, they can reduce the amount that they pay in taxes. ▷

Many of these companies are so large, and operate so widely that it becomes almost meaningless to think of 'British companies' or 'American companies'. This sometimes gives rise to feelings that these firms are too powerful, and using their economic muscle to exploit host countries. Despite these criticisms, there is no doubt that in favourable circumstances they can benefit host countries enormously, often bringing jobs, entrepreneurship, new technology and exports to host countries.

Review questions

1. What are the three main characteristics of a multinational?
2. Outline, and give reasons for, the changing development of TNCs.
3. Using your own examples, distinguish between FDI and portfolio investment.
4. Comment on the flow of funds illustrated in Figures 13.3 and 13.4.
5. Summarise the advantages and disadvantages of the alternatives to FDI for a company wishing to do business overseas.
6. Why do firms become multinationals?
7. Summarise (a) the costs and (b) the benefits of multinationals.
8. What factors determine the relative powers of governments and TNCs?

Essay questions

1. Discuss the importance of MNCs in the world economy.
2. Critically assess the advantages and disadvantages of multinational corporations to a country.

Reading 13.1

Hail Chungwa!

Chungwa? What's Chungwa?

The answer will soon be clear to the 3000 engineers and technicians who get jobs in the firm's new factory in Lanarkshire. The multiplier effect will also become familiar to 1000 other workers who will get jobs in firms supplying parts to Chungwa.

For those not in the know, Chungwa is one of Taiwan's largest firms. Its representative today said that the Scottish factory will cost £260m. and would eventually produce 10 million tubes annually.

▷

What was not announced was the cost to British taxpayers in grants to Chungwa which were needed to beat off foreign offers to the firm.

Questions

1. Why do you think that such a factory might act as a magnet for other Taiwanese firms?
2. What do you think is meant by the 'multiplier effect'?
3. Why should the British government pay foreign firms to come to the UK? Do you think that it is in the national interest to do this?

MODULE E

Labour

After completing this module, you should be able to:

- explain the factors which determine the demand and supply of labour in the economy;
- critically assess the competitive market approach to analysing the labour market;
- discuss the segmented labour market approach;
- understand why women, on average, earn less than men;
- explain the objectives of trade unions and the constraints they face in achieving them;
- show how a union is sometimes able to increase wages and employment;
- summarise the case for and against a national minimum wage;
- outline the human capital model and assess some of the criticisms made of it; and
- explain why the government might have a role in providing training.

Wages and employment

The rules of attraction

Does your physical appearance affect your earnings?

Men are forever moaning about the time and money that women spend slapping on make-up, dieting and shopping for clothes. Yet, according to two new studies by American economists, it is a worthwhile investment: looking good yields big financial returns. Susan Averett and Sanders Korenman have examined the link between pay differentials and weight for 23 to 31 year olds, after adjusting for differences in social class. The hourly wage of fat women is, on average, 20 per cent lower than the pay of a women of average weight. But slimmers be warned: underweight women also take home slimmer pay packets than average women do. However, skinny women make up for this in the marriage market: they marry men with the highest earnings. ... Underweight men take home by far the lowest earnings, while slightly overweight men enjoy the fattest pay packets – 26 per cent more than their underweight colleagues.

A second study by Daniel Hamermesh and Jeff Biddle considers how workers' earnings are affected by their overall looks, rather than just their weight. They found that the job market clearly rewards beauty. Very attractive men and women enjoy hourly earnings about 5 per cent higher than those with average looks. Plain women earn 5 per cent less than average lookers, plain men 10 per cent less.

Source: Adapted from *The Economist*, December 1993.

The labour market is important to all of us. Most students have had part-time or temporary work, and hope for interesting, well-paid work when they graduate. And employers want to recruit adaptable, well-qualified workers. But what factors determine the number of people in work? And what decides the level of wages?

It will come as no surprise to find that there are no universally agreed answers to these very complex questions. A good starting point, however, is to consider the market for labour as if it were similar to other markets, with the forces of supply and demand determining, or at least strongly influencing, both the quantity of labour employed, and also the wages of those in work.

The supply of labour

Why do we work?

The short answer to that question is that we work for money. Of course, it all depends on what is meant by 'work'. We all do household jobs at home without pay, and many people also help neighbours or charities without pay. In this unit, however, by 'work' we mean paid employment. Even here, though, people do not work just for money. Many people find their work enjoyable because it gives them a feeling of fulfilment. Others like work because they find friendship and companionship there.

Despite all this, as in the market for goods and services, price is the main determinant of supply. Thus in the labour market the wage is the main determinant of the quantity of labour that is supplied. This can easily be illustrated by a simple hypothetical example. If someone offered you a job for £1 a week, you would not take it, but if someone offered £1000 a week, you would take the job. So we can begin our analysis by assuming that the supply curve of labour is upward sloping, just like the supply curve for goods.

Nevertheless, there is a difference: people are not machines – they can make decisions. They can (to some extent) choose between working and not working. Though the hours of work of many people are fixed by their terms of employment, many do have a choice, and we can simplify the analysis by assuming that all workers can choose. This means that individuals and households have to decide between work and leisure. As incomes rise, there may come a point when people decide not to work longer hours because their income is high enough, and they choose leisure instead.

We can now separate out the two effects. The **substitution effect** suggests that the higher the wage rate, the more people will substitute work for non-market activities (such as leisure and other household activities). This gives us the familiar upward sloping supply curve. However, there will also be an **income effect**. Generally, this refers to the effect that a change in income has on consumption: in this case, that means the consumption of leisure. Leisure has a high income elasticity of demand, so as income rises, many people will choose to consume more leisure and cut the amount of time that they spend working.

These two effects are shown in Figure 14.1. At first, the substitution effect predominates and the supply curve slopes upward, but at wage W_1 the income effect takes over and the supply curve becomes backward sloping.

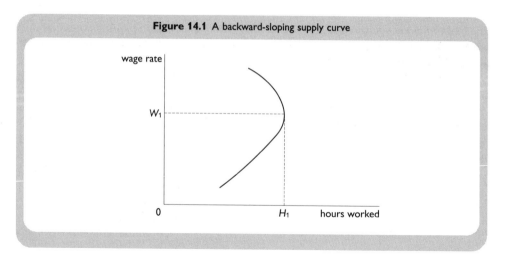

Figure 14.1 A backward-sloping supply curve

The overall supply of labour

So far we have discussed the supply curve of individuals, but we also have to consider the supply curve of labour for the economy as a whole.

The main determinant of the supply of labour in a country is the size of the population. Figure 14.2 shows that the population in the UK has risen in recent years, and is expected to continue to rise, primarily because the birth rate is higher than the death rate. Migration has only a tiny effect. For most of this century emigration has exceeded immigration, though in recent years there has been a small net inflow of people.

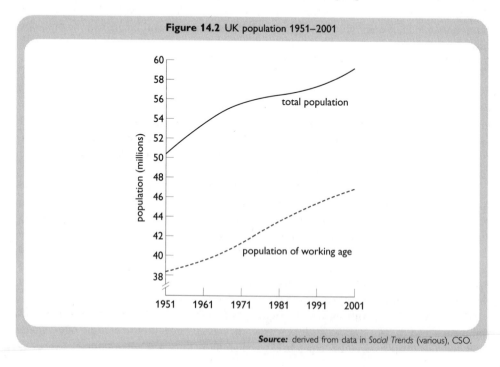

Figure 14.2 UK population 1951–2001

Source: derived from data in *Social Trends* (various), CSO.

However, the size of the population is only a crude determinant of the supply of labour. By law, those under the age of 16 cannot be in full-time employment, so this reduces the size of the potential workforce as shown in this figure.

Another reduction in the potential labour force occurs because many people are considered to be economically inactive. One large group is those who have retired; principally those men over 65 and women over the age of 60, though many men now retire before the age of 65 and some women continue to work after the age of 60. The number of elderly people will continue to rise right into the next century, so reducing the potential labour force.

A further qualification of the supply curve of labour is that not all potential workers do actually work. The labour supply depends not only on the size of the potential labour force, but also on the proportion of the population of working age which chooses to join the labour force. The statistical measure of labour supply activity within the population is called the labour force participation ratio, which can be calculated using the following formula:

$$\text{Labour force participation ratio for men} = \frac{\text{male labour force}}{\text{male population}}$$

In recent years there has been a steady fall in the male participation rate from about 80 per cent in 1971 to under 75 per cent in the mid-1990s.

However, much more dramatic have been the changes in the position of women. According to data in the *Employment Gazette* (historical supplement, 1993), in 1931 only 34.2 per cent of women participated in the labour force; by 1991 the figure was 53.1 per cent. For married women the change was even greater showing a rise from 10.0 per cent to 59 per cent in the same period.

The main reason for the huge rise in the number of married women working is that there has been a change in attitude. Though there were exceptions such as the cotton industry, before the Second World War it was generally considered that women's place was in the home. Once married, most women did not think about the possibility of taking a job, and indeed, in many industries, they were automatically discharged on marriage.

One reason for this change was the decline in the number of children per family, and this still remains the most important determinant of whether or not a woman works. For example, in 1994, 66 per cent of women with four or more dependent children were economically inactive compared with only 32 per cent of women with only one child.

Economic activity rates are relatively high in the UK. In the EU, only Denmark has higher rates (see Table 14.1), which reflects the fact that in Denmark mothers have a legal right to return to work for three years and are therefore counted as **economically active** during this period.

The number of hours worked is yet another determinant of the overall supply of labour. As you can see in Figure 14.3, the hours worked by both men and women have increased in recent years.

This is not the whole story, however. One of the most notable characteristics of the supply of labour is the growth of part-time employment, particularly among women. In the decade following 1984, the number of women in part-time employment rose from 4.3 million to nearly 5.3 million. On the supply side, the main reason why women choose to

Table 14.1: Economic activity rates by gender (%)

	Males	*Females*	*All persons*
Denmark	74.5	62.7	68.5
UK	74.0	52.8	63.0
Portugal	71.9	50.2	60.3
Germany	71.5	48.4	59.4
Netherlands	71.1	46.5	58.6
France	65.7	48.0	56.4
Irish Republic	70.6	37.7	53.9
Luxembourg	69.7	39.5	54.2
Italy	65.4	34.9	49.5
Belgium	62.1	39.5	50.4
Spain	65.6	34.1	49.4
Greece	65.5	34.8	49.4

Source: *Social Trends*, vol. 25 (1995), table 4.7.

work part-time is that they have young children and it is often convenient for them to fit in paid part-time work while still being able to look after their children. There are also demand-side factors. Many employers like to employ part-time workers because they can then take on extra workers for short periods: a good example is the increased number of people employed at supermarket check-outs on Friday evenings and Saturdays. Moreover, firms that employ part-time workers can sometimes cut non-wage labour costs such as holiday pay, sick pay and pension contributions.

The growth of part-time working shows how the interaction of demand- and supply-side factors can influence the labour market, and we now turn to examine the demand side in more detail.

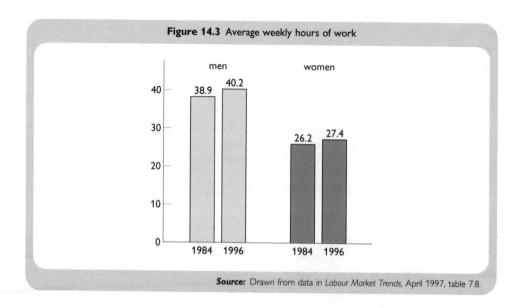

Figure 14.3 Average weekly hours of work

Source: Drawn from data in *Labour Market Trends*, April 1997, table 7.8.

The demand for labour

It is useful when analysing the demand for labour to begin by assuming a perfectly **competitive labour market**. This involves many of the same assumptions of the perfectly competitive market for goods. For example, that:

- Buyers and sellers of labour are price takers in both the labour market and in the market for goods and services. They cannot individually alter wages or the price of the goods they sell.

- Everyone in the market is perfectly informed, so that everyone knows the going wage rates and job opportunities.

- Workers can move freely in to and out of work and can choose how many hours to work.

- Firms aim to maximise profits.

- There is no government intervention in the labour market.

However, the labour market differs from other markets in several respects. In particular, the demand for labour is a *derived* demand. We want ice-cream because we feel like eating ice-cream, but firms demand labour not for its own sake, but because of the profits labour can bring. This means that labour will only be employed if it is profitable for the firm.

In the long run, firms can increase profits by varying the quantity of *all* the factors of production that they employ. In the short run, though, the quantity of land and capital is fixed; firms cannot suddenly build a new factory. But they can vary the quantity of labour.

This brings into action the **law of diminishing returns**, which states that when all the factors of production except one are fixed, an increase in the variable factor will eventually bring about **diminishing returns**. This law was discussed in Unit 3 and is illustrated here by a hypothetical example in Table 14.2. As extra workers are employed, total output increases. However, **marginal physical product (MPP)** – the physical quantity of output produced – starts to decline after the employment of the second worker. So diminishing returns set in when the third worker is employed.

Since we have assumed perfect competition, the firm can sell all that it produces at the same price, and here we assume for simplicity that each item sells for £10. **Marginal revenue product (MRP)** is calculated by multiplying the marginal physical product by

Table 14.2: The demand for labour

Number of workers	Total output	Marginal physical product	Marginal revenue product (£)
1	20	20	200
2	44	24	240
3	62	18	180
4	76	14	140
5	86	10	100

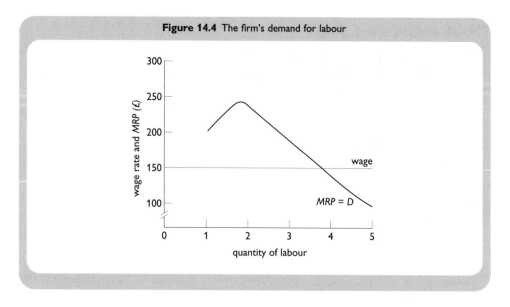

Figure 14.4 The firm's demand for labour

the **marginal revenue** produced by the additional worker. In this example, marginal revenue equals price since we have assumed perfect competition, and here MRP declines with the employment of the third worker.

We are now in a position to calculate how many workers the firm will employ. If we assume a wage of £150 a week, employing the first worker will produce a profit of £200 − £150 = £50. The second worker will produce additional profits of £240 − £150 = £90, and the third worker will also produce a profit. However, employing a fourth person would lead to a loss, since the wage of £150 exceeds the revenue brought in by this employee. Hence, a rational profit-maximising firm will employ three workers. This result is illustrated in Figure 14.4 where the horizontal line shows the wage rate and the downward-sloping marginal revenue product curve also indicates the firm's demand for labour. Note that the firm's marginal revenue product curve is also its demand for labour curve because we are assuming that the firm employs the profit-maximising quantity of labour.

If the cost of employing an additional worker is less than the additional revenue the worker brings in, the firm will employ one more worker. On the other hand, if the revenue brought in by an additional worker is less than the cost of employing the worker, the firm will not employ that worker. So the firm will continue to employ additional workers until the cost of employing an additional person equals the revenue brought in by that person. This occurs when the wage rate equals the marginal revenue product and the quantity of labour demanded by the firm is such that the wage rate equals the marginal revenue product of labour. (Note that this is a specific example of the general rule that a profit-maximising firm will expand output until marginal revenue (MR) = marginal cost (MC).)

Table 14.2 and Figure 14.4 can be used to make predictions. What will be the result if the wage rate is increased to £190 a week? In this case, it will not be profitable to employ the third worker. On the other hand, if the wage rate is cut to £100 a week the firm will expand until it employs five workers.

So this analysis leads to the conclusion that a cut in wages will lead to an increase in employment, while a rise in wages will lead to a fall in employment. This is an important conclusion which, as we will see in Unit 23, has implications for employment policy. However, it is important to remember that the conclusion rests on the assumptions of perfect competition; if these assumptions do not apply, then the conclusion does not follow.

Shifts in the firm's demand for labour curve

Just as an ordinary demand curve for goods shifts, so does the firm's demand for labour. The three factors which cause this are: the price of the firm's output; the price of other inputs; and technology:

1. Other things being equal, the higher the price of the firm's output, the higher will be the quantity of labour demanded by the firm. That is because a higher price increases the marginal revenue product: in terms of Figure 14.4, it shifts the MRP curve to the right. Similarly, a fall in the price of the firm's output will lead to a fall in its demand for labour.

2. The prices of other inputs have their main effects in the long run when the firm can vary all its inputs. For example, if there is an increase in the price of labour relative to capital, firms will tend to substitute capital for labour. This is why advanced industrial countries, characterised by high wages, employ more capital than do poorer countries where labour is cheap. In practice, however, it is often difficult to substitute capital for labour. Thus if wages of Post Office workers rise, it will be impossible to replace the workers with machines that deliver mail.

3. The third factor which leads to a shift in the firm's demand curve for labour is a change in technology. For example, the development of computers led to a fall in the demand by banks for bank clerks since financial records could be kept much more cheaply by computer. At the same time, the introduction of computers led to an increase in demand for electronic engineers.

Competitive equilibrium in the labour market

As with the market for goods, in a competitive market quantity and price – in this case, wages – are determined by the interaction of supply and demand. We can illustrate this by looking at two contrasting examples:

1. Figure 14.5 illustrates the market for a type of labour which is in short supply and where demand is high (e.g. successful footballers and pop singers). Here, the supply curve is close to the vertical axis and is inelastic, since an increase in wages would not lead to much of an increase in supply. The result is equilibrium at a high wage and low quantity.

2. Figure 14.6 shows a contrasting position. The supply of labour is large because little skill is needed (e.g. cleaners and workers in fast-food restaurants are examples). Equilibrium is thus achieved at a low wage, with a relatively large number of people employed.

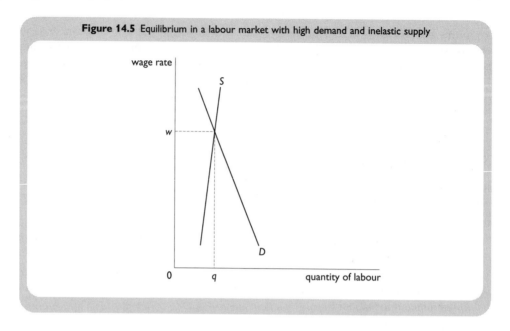

Figure 14.5 Equilibrium in a labour market with high demand and inelastic supply

In both cases, an increase in the demand for labour – for example because of an increase in the demand for the product – would lead to a rise in wages and in the quantity of labour employed. However, there is a difference. In Figure 14.5 the result is a relatively large increase in wages and only a small increase in the number of people employed. One example of this occurred in the early 1990s. For many years, BBC and ITV had paid relatively small sums of money for the right to televise football. The advent of Sky TV, willing to pay large sums to clubs, increased their demand for star players and hence players' earnings. In contrast, an increase in the demand for, say, hamburgers would lead to only a small rise in wages in the fast-food industry, though there would be a relatively large increase in the number of people employed.

Market clearing and the competitive model

As we have seen when discussing the market for goods and services, a market which works efficiently will produce an equilibrium, so that the market clears. In the case of the labour market, this means that everyone who wants a job at the going wage rate can find

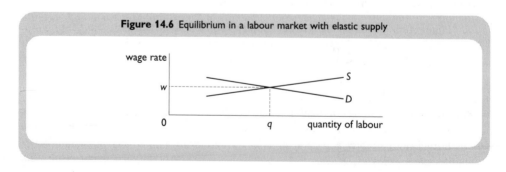

Figure 14.6 Equilibrium in a labour market with elastic supply

employment, and firms will be able to satisfy their demand for labour. Any disequilibrium will be eliminated by changes in the wage rate. Moreover, efficient labour markets will produce an optimum allocation of resources across different occupations and also in different areas of the country. Workers will receive wages which equal the value of the goods that they produce (i.e. their marginal revenue product).

However, all this depends on the assumptions underlying the model being satisfied. If that does not happen, then these conclusions will not result. So, are the conditions satisfied?

Few, if any, of these conditions are likely to be satisfied in full. In the first place, many firms will have some monopoly power in the market for goods. This means that firms can choose not only the level of output, but also the prices which they charge. The quantity of labour employed will also depend on the price which the firm chooses to charge for its goods, rather than on the impersonal working of the market. In addition, some firms will be **monopsonists** (i.e. they will be the only or dominant buyer of some particular type of labour). For example, most teachers and soldiers work directly or indirectly for the government; train drivers and police officers too have little choice of employer. This means that such employers have power in the market to influence wages. On the supply side, trade unions may be able to force up wages, and this is discussed in the next unit.

Secondly, few employers or workers will have complete information about the labour market as a whole, or even about all the jobs in their area or occupation. Employers, for example, may not know the true quality of the workers who they employ. This means that the wage offered may be greater or smaller than the marginal revenue product. Even once people are employed, it is still very difficult for employers to discover the marginal revenue product of each worker. Similarly, few workers will be aware of all the job opportunities open to them.

Thirdly, neither workers nor employers can easily vary the number of hours that are worked. And, as we have seen in Unit 2, employers may choose to make satisfactory profits rather than aim at profit maximisation. Hence they may employ more or less workers than would result from profit maximisation.

Fourthly, there is significant government intervention in the labour market. Government requires firms to obey health and safety legislation, for instance, and outlaws race and sex discrimination.

Finally, there are several reasons why labour markets differ from the market for goods. The most obvious difference is that people can think. Workers form a personal relationship with their colleagues and employers, and so personal feelings will sometimes be stronger than financial considerations. A cabbage has no say in the market, and presumably no feelings – workers and employers do. Social considerations have therefore to be taken into account. For example, one reason why the researchers quoted in the opening commentary to this unit found that physical appearance affected earnings may be that employers prefer to appoint attractive people.

In summary, therefore, the conclusions resulting from the assumptions may not apply, and there may well be a case for governments to intervene in the labour market in order to make it work more efficiently. If monopsonists use their power to exploit workers, then governments – or trade unions – may be needed to ensure a more equitable distribution of the rewards of work.

Some of these issues will be discussed in the next unit. Here, we shall focus on one particular issue – discrimination.

Discrimination in the labour market

Let us begin by looking at some facts. Figure 14.7 compares the earnings of men and women in recent years. Two features stand out. First, earnings of both men and women have risen over the years. In part this reflects higher real incomes, but the main reason is that wages rise because of inflation. Secondly, on average, men earn more than women. Why is this? That is a simple question to ask, but a difficult one to answer. Indeed, in order to do so we need to explore the reasons why some people earn more than others irrespective of gender.

Our earlier hypothesis of supply and demand offers some explanation of wage differences. People whose skills are in short supply and for which there is considerable demand will earn more than those whose position is reversed. Someone who is brilliant at football will earn more than someone who is good at netball because there is more demand for football players. And people who work in occupations where supply is limited – steeplejacks, airline pilots, doctors – will earn more than those in occupations where supply is large – cleaners, drivers, care assistants.

But that explanation gives far from a complete picture. A more specific proposition is called *human capital theory*.

Human capital theory

The essence of the **human capital** approach is that it compares investment in human beings with investment in machinery. Before investing in a new factory or machine, a profit-maximising firm will compare the costs and the benefits of the investment; only if

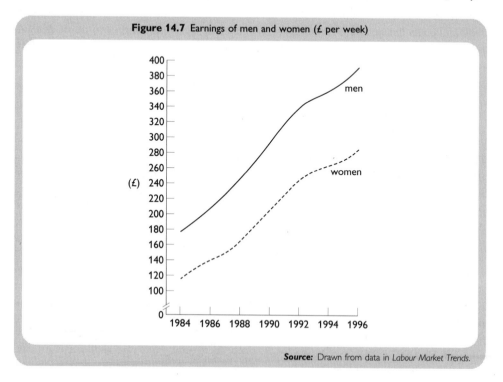

Figure 14.7 Earnings of men and women (£ per week)

Source: Drawn from data in *Labour Market Trends*.

Exercise

When any expensive machine is erected, the extraordinary work to be performed by it before it is worn out, it must be expected, will replace the capital laid out upon it, with at least the ordinary profits. A man educated at the expense of much labour and time to any of those employments which require extraordinary dexterity and skill, may be compared to one of those expensive machines. The work which he learns to perform ... over and above the usual wages of common labour will replace to him the whole expense of his education, with at least the profits of an equally valuable capital. It must do this too in a reasonable time.

Source: Adam Smith, *The Wealth of Nations* (1776), book 1, chapter 10.

Questions

1. What rewards do you expect from your education?

2. Do you think that it is justifiable to compare investment in education with investment in machinery?

the benefits – that is, the profits – exceed the costs, will the firm proceed with the investment.

Equally, it is possible to analyse decision making in education in this way. People go to university for many reasons, one reason being that they think it will help them to get a better job. In other words, the time spent studying will eventually pay off in terms of higher income later in life. This approach is also taken by governments. Many people have analysed the reasons for the relatively poor performance of the British economy since the Second World War, and one reason often given is that our workforce is less well educated than that of our competitors. The implication here is that education pays off in terms of higher productivity.

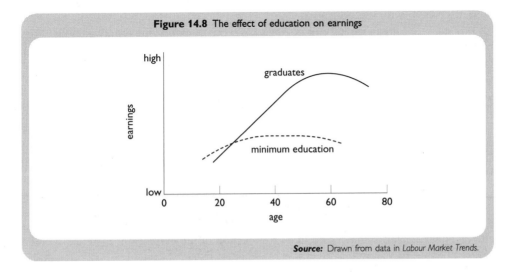

Figure 14.8 The effect of education on earnings

Source: Drawn from data in *Labour Market Trends*.

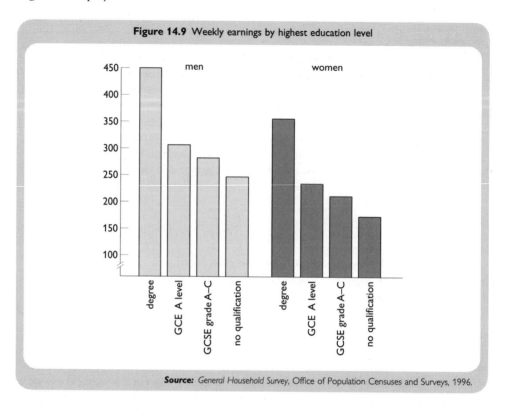

Figure 14.9 Weekly earnings by highest education level

Source: General Household Survey, Office of Population Censuses and Surveys, 1996.

Although some highly educated people earn very little, and some less well educated people earn large sums, on average the statistics tend to confirm the predictions of human capital theory: highly educated people do, on average, earn more than those who are less well educated. This is illustrated in the typical age–earnings profiles shown in Figure 14.8. Specific figures comparing earnings by education and gender are given in Figure 14.9, and these clearly indicate that typically, for both men and women, educated workers earn more than those with less education.

This study of human capital can be linked into our demand-and-supply analysis. Thus highly educated people earn more than those who are less well educated because the supply of highly educated people is less than the supply of those with poor education.

Difference in earnings between men and women

Returning now to discrimination, how do these findings on human capital relate to the earnings of men and women? The first point to note is that men's higher earnings are of long standing and also geographically widespread. In the Bible, we read: 'The Lord said to Moses, Speak to the Israelites and tell them: when anyone fulfils a vow of offering one or more persons to the Lord, who are to be ransomed for a fixed some of money, for persons between the ages of twenty and sixty, the fixed sum shall be ... fifty silver shekels for a man and thirty shekels for a woman' (Leviticus 27:1–4). Rather surprisingly, this biblical ratio is rather similar to that found in a cross-section of the earnings of men and women today, as Table 14.3 shows.

Table 14.3: Female/male earnings ratios corrected for hours (all workers)

Country	Rate
Germany	0.688
UK	0.634
USA	0.685
Austria	0.726
Switzerland	0.617
Sweden	0.767
Norway	0.731
Australia	0.749

Source: F.D. Blau and L.M. Kahn, 'The gender earnings gap: learning from international comparisons', *American Economic Review*, vol. 82, no. 2 (1992), pp. 533–8.

There are three primary explanations for women's lower earnings. The first builds on the model of competitive labour markets that we have developed earlier. One possible cause is that women may have a lower supply curve than men, due to the difference in women's work preferences: for example, they may not be willing to work overtime. Another reason may be that women have less human capital: that is, there is a smaller supply of skilled women than of trained men. This may be due to discrimination: for example, women may have less opportunity to participate in training programmes if employers are reluctant to pay for the training of part-time workers, who are mainly women.

The second explanation is that women's lower pay may stem from a lower demand for their services. In many instances, women are perceived as having a lower marginal revenue product than men, for three reasons:

1. They have less physical strength than men, but this is only relevant in a few jobs.

2. More generally, it could be because they are considered to have less education and training than men, though this is an incorrect assumption. It may have been true in the past, but in recent years, women entering the labour market are often better qualified educationally than their male counterparts.

3. Some women are more likely to take time off work to look after their children, which makes them less productive in the workplace.

A third point is that lower earnings among women may be the result of discrimination. In the long run, discrimination is difficult to explain using the competitive model. If labour markets are competitive, then employers will pay workers their marginal revenue product. Firms that discriminate will be acting against their own interest since they will be giving up the opportunity of employing efficient women.

In the short run, there may be discrimination. Employers may discriminate because, according to the Nobel prize-winning economist Gary Becker, they 'have a taste' for it. They may dislike employing women because they believe that women are less productive, or because they believe that men will not like working under a female boss. In these instances, they are also likely to pay women less than men.

However, in this competitive model, discrimination cannot survive. Prejudiced employers, who employ more males than their more egalitarian rivals, will put up their own wage bill and eventually they will be unable to compete. The pressures of the market, therefore, will put them out of business or force them to change. Discrimination can only exist in the long run if competition is limited, for example if there are imperfections such as oligopoly.

The big weakness of this competitive assumption is that it fails to explain why lower wage rates for women are so persistent over time and across many countries. This weakness has led to a group of theories built round the assumption that labour markets are segmented.

The segmented labour market approach

The essence of this approach is to look at the labour market, not as a single competitive entity, but instead to view it as divided into a series of constituent parts.

There are several variations of the **segmented labour market** approach. One, sometimes called the job-crowding hypothesis, suggests that women earn less than men because they are 'crowded' into a few occupations. The main reason for this concentration is social: that is, certain occupations appeal more to women. For example, if young girls are asked what they want to be when they grow up, they tend to reply 'nurses'. Hence women are 'crowded' into caring occupations such as nursing, teaching young children, secretarial and cleaning. Very few find work as airline pilots, chief executives, or even engine drivers.

This segregation can lead to lower wages. Certainly, if there is a huge supply of women to particular jobs, then this will force down the wage rate. Yet while job crowding has a degree of impact on women's wages, empirical evidence casts some doubt on the legitimacy of this argument. For example, in occupations such as teaching, where there are large numbers of both men and women, and where both have very similar qualifications, men on average still earn more than women in both primary and secondary schools.

A more recent variation of the segmented labour market approach is called the dual labour market hypothesis. This splits the labour market into two divisions; primary and secondary. In the primary labour market, workers have high wages, stable employment and chances of promotion. In the secondary labour market there are low wages, poor fringe benefits and working conditions, high labour turnover, and little chance of advancement.

In order for this hypothesis to be convincing, there has to be a barrier that prevents workers moving from the secondary market to the more desirable primary market. One such barrier is education and training; another is socialisation, which can restrict certain groups such as women from even applying for certain jobs. Geography also plays a part: some jobs require a labour mobility that may be difficult for women, especially those who are married with children. Finally, discrimination again can form a barrier. Thus in this approach, the labour market is an active generator of economic inequality since it prevents people who could do the work from entering the primary sector and taking good jobs.

In determining which labour markets are primary and secondary, the crucial feature is the stability of the product market. Where demand is relatively stable (e.g. in the professions), there will be primary sector employment. Where demand for the product is unstable (e.g. the fast-food industry), there will be mainly secondary sector employment.

Exercise

Men and women tend to do different jobs. When we think of a doctor, an airline pilot or a dustman, we think of a man. And secretaries, nurses and cleaners tend to be women.

However, research suggests that this different pattern of employment is not the main reason why women, on average, earn less than men. If women had the same kind of jobs as men but still earned the women's rate, their earnings would hardly change.

To earn the same as men it is not enough to do the same kind of jobs as men – they need to earn the same pay rates as men.

Questions

1. Why are women and men likely to be concentrated in different occupations?
2. How do you think that this research finding relates to the job-crowding hypothesis?

Anti-discrimination legislation

Despite disagreements about the causes, all the economic theories of discrimination agree that it leads to welfare losses, not only for the individuals discriminated against, but also for society as a whole since it prevents an optimum allocation of resources. This has caused laws to be passed in several countries aimed at outlawing discrimination.

In the UK, an Equal Pay Act was passed in 1970 and phased in until full enforcement occurred in 1975, the same year in which the Sex Discrimination Act was passed that set up the Equal Opportunities Commission. The ratio of female to male earnings in the UK rose from 0.61 in 1970 to 0.79 in 1980, which seems to suggest that these Acts had a significant effect. Certainly, the equal pay legislation provided a legal basis that enabled negotiators to push for rises. Hence one factor that contributed largely to this rise in women's earnings was that in the 1970s most women's wages were determined by collective agreements between unions and employers.

There were problems, however. The 1970 legislation did not affect women doing different jobs from men, and, as we have seen, women and men are often concentrated in different occupations. In 1984 the position changed. In that year a European Court ruling gave women a right to claim equal pay if their work was 'of equal value' to that of men. This enabled women who worked, for example, as cooks to claim equal pay with men working as, say, fitters, providing they could prove that their work was of equal value. This did help some women, but the procedures involved in proving 'equal value'

Table 14.4: Average hourly pay of ethnic minority groups as a percentage of that of the white population

	All (%)	Men (%)	Women (%)
All ethnic minorities	92	89	99
Black	93	88	106
Indian	90	91	90
Pakistani/Bangladeshi	72	68	81
Mixed/other origins	103	106	106

Source: Employment Gazette, June 1995, table 8.

through the courts are long and complex, and the ratio of women's wages to men's has hardly changed as a result of the ruling.

Racial discrimination

In the United Kingdom about 6 per cent of the population describe themselves as being from an ethnic minority (*Employment Gazette*, June 1995, pp. 251–60). They tend to be less economically active than the white population. In 1994, participation was highest for black men and women (73 per cent) and those of Indian origin (71 per cent), compared with 79 per cent for the white population. Moreover, the unemployment rate for ethnic minorities was more than twice that of white people, and rose as high as 51 per cent for young black males.

The incomes of ethnic minority members who were in work varied considerably, as Table 14.4 shows, and this conceals wider differences: former Ugandan Asians, for example, tend to have high educational qualifications and earnings. Nevertheless, the general position is clear: people from ethnic minorities tend to earn less than white people.

The methods of analysis, and the conclusions reached in explaining these figures, are very similar to those which applied when sex discrimination was analysed. On the one hand, economists who believe that labour markets are competitive focus on the demand and supply of labour. They suggest, for example, that overall, those from ethnic minorities have lower educational qualifications than the white population and would therefore be expected to have lower marginal revenue product. Supporters of the segmented labour market approach, on the other hand, suggest that people from ethnic minorities are concentrated in the secondary labour market and that racial discrimination is one reason why they find it difficult to move to the better paid primary labour market.

Summary

Labour markets can be analysed using the same concepts used to analyse the markets for goods and services. Some economists believe that labour markets are competitive so that the marginal revenue curve and the supply of labour determine the level of employment and the wage rate. Others suggest that labour markets are segmented so that workers find it difficult to move from one sector to another. ▷

These differences in approach also characterise explanations of the lower earnings of women and ethnic minorities. Advocates of the competitive market approach suggest that these lower earnings represent lower marginal revenue product; others who support the segmented market approach say that there is persistent discrimination.

Review questions

1. Explain the income and substitution effects as they relate to work.
2. What factors determine the supply of labour in an economy?
3. Summarise the law of diminishing returns.
4. Assuming perfect competition in the labour market, show how wages and the quantity of labour to be employed will be determined.
5. To what extent are the assumptions underlying the competitive model satisfied in the UK economy?
6. Outline the human capital theory.
7. Use the competitive labour market model to explain discrimination against women in the labour market.
8. How does the segmented labour market model explain women's lower wages?
9. Has anti-discrimination legislation succeeded?

Essay questions

1. What factors determine the level of wages?
2. Why, on average, do men earn more than women?

Reading 14.1

The part-time labour market

It's growing. Employers love it. So do some workers. But it costs the taxpayer. What is it? Answer: the part-time labour market. Employers love it because it saves them money. In many cases they don't have to pay national insurance contributions. In the last decade, the number of women workers not paying national insurance contributions trebled. Part-time work also means that firms can avoid paying for other benefits such as sick pay and maternity benefits. One example of an employer benefiting from this development occurred when the Burton Group introduced 'zero hours' contracts in 1993. These require workers to be on standby without any guarantee of work. There are no minimum or maximum hours of work, ▷

so the employer can employ workers as needed. The introduction of these measures allowed Burton to cut its costs by making 2000 full-time workers redundant.

Nevertheless, some workers like part-time work since it can fit in with other obligations such as child care.

But the benefits to the employer cost the taxpayer, since the government has to pay benefits to those workers earning low pay.

Questions

1. Outline the advantages and disadvantages of part-time work for (a) the employer and (b) the employee.
2. What theories can be used to explain (a) the low pay of part-time workers, and (b) why they are mainly women?
3. Do you think the state should intervene to protect the interests of part-time workers?

Reading 14.2

Earning differentials

(a) The National Lottery caused large smiles yesterday – but not among the punters. This time it was the operators who were smiling. Chief executive Tim Holley's pay package rose by 53 per cent to nearly £600,000 a year, while the Director of Communications, David Rigg's pay rose by over 90 per cent, from £175,000 to £333,000.

(b) The Low Pay Unit has many stories of workers earning pathetic rates of pay. One example is a warehouse worker hired by a Leeds firm, ASC Staffing. The man worked a 47-hour, five-night week loading goods destined for Sainsbury's.

The worker claimed that he told the agency which hired him that he had arranged to attend his pub soccer team's Christmas party. When he did not report for work the agency pointed out a clause in his contract which said: 'Should you fail to turn up for any assignment without giving reasonable notice ... your renumeration will be reduced to £1 a day for any work carried out previously.'

Questions

1. Which explanation of wages do you think best explains these two extracts?
2. Do you think that there is a need for government intervention in the labour market to reduce earnings differentials?

Intervention in the labour market

For Rosa Maria Mendoza, 1995 was a year of struggle. For the first eight months, she struggled to sew 4800 buttons a day on designer shirts at the Formosa Textiles factory in an industrial park east of San Salvador.

She struggled to survive on a £60 a month wage. She struggled against illnesses brought on by drinking water from the plant's cockroach-infested cistern.

In August Ms Mendoza embarked on a different struggle. Along with 86 colleagues she joined a union.

In October they were sacked. When they tried to force their way into the factory to demand severance pay, all of the plants 400 workers were locked out.

In El Salvador, as in many of the countries where contractors make branded goods for sale in the USA, many employers consider forming a union a sackable offence, resulting in mass lay-offs and probably the closure of the factory.

Source: Adapted from the *Guardian*, 5 January 1996, p. 15

Why intervene?

In the last unit we examined how wages were determined, first assuming perfect competition in the labour market, and then assuming segmented markets. The logic of competitive markets is that no intervention is needed since such markets will result in a desirable allocation of resources, just as it does in the market for goods and services.

However, the assumption that the labour market is segmented leads to the conclusion that resources may not be allocated satisfactorily. This may lead to under- or over-employment of labour and to wages which are too low – or sometimes too high. There is a need for government action to prevent such distortions.

In this unit we shall examine two interventions. We shall look first at the intervention of workers as they combine in **trade unions** to remedy what they see as the unsatisfactory results of market forces, compounded by the manipulations of powerful employers. Finally, we shall move on to intervention by governments, focusing on the pros and cons of a legal minimum wage.

Organisation of trade unions

Trade unions originated as a response to capitalism. For employers, workers are a cost; for the workers, a well-paid secure job is a paramount objective, and unions were formed in order to secure this. An individual worker has little power compared to that of an employer, but the combined strengths of many workers can give them power.

A trade union can be defined as: 'An association of wage earners formed in order to maintain or improve the conditions of their working lives.' The legal definition is very similar. The Trade Union and Labour Relations (Consolidation) Act of 1982 emphasises that unions may be temporary or permanent and consist wholly or mainly of workers, and stresses that their principle purpose is the regulation of relations between workers and employers.

The basic unit of organisation of a union is the branch. Sometimes this is geographically based, but often it is composed of the workers in a particular factory or firm. The members of a branch elect local representatives to negotiate for them; they also elect regional and national representatives. A National Executive Committee is usually responsible for running the union, though a national conference of members is the supreme decision-making body. Full-time officials such as the general secretary and president also have considerable influence.

Almost all the unions in Britain are members of the TUC. This is the official face of the union movement and it speaks on behalf of the unions nationally and internationally, though it has little or no power over individual unions. The TUC has a congress which meets annually and a General Council which carries out policy between congresses.

Membership

There has been a decline in recent years in the number of unions. This has occurred primarily because unions have merged, often for the same reasons that firms merge. There can be considerable economies of scale in merging unions: for example, they can have one set of accountants, one membership department and one union newspaper. Thus in

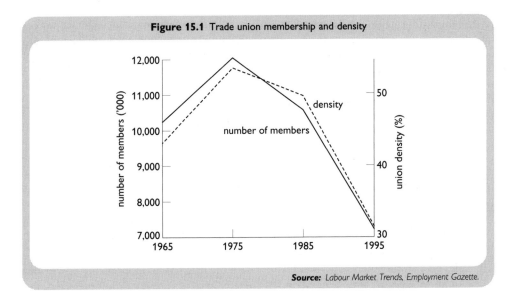

Figure 15.1 Trade union membership and density

Source: *Labour Market Trends, Employment Gazette.*

1993 a new union was formed called UNISON. It was formed by merging the National and Local Government Officers Association, the National Union of Public Employees and the Confederation of Health Service Employees. On its formation it became the largest union with 1,400,000 members, and one of the few large unions with more women members than men. The next largest unions are the Transport and General Workers Union (T&G) with 940,000 members and the Amalgamated Engineering and Electrical Union (AEU) with 830,000.

In recent years both union membership and density (i.e. the proportion of workers that belong to a union) have declined, as Figure 15.1 shows. In part, this is because of the decline in industries such as coal mining and shipbuilding where unions were very strong. Government policy has also contributed to the decline, as unions found their powers curtailed by legislation to a degree that potential members decided there was little advantage to be had in joining. This legislation was reinforced by tougher management; some firms refused to recognise unions. The commentary at the beginning of this unit, though not from Europe, reflects the spirit that influenced many managers. The decline in membership has meant that unions have become weaker. Nevertheless, a union which represents nearly all the workers in a firm will have a much stronger bargaining position than one which only represents a few workers.

Union objectives and constraints

Trade unions have a number of objectives, some of which may conflict, but it is possible to devise four categories:

1. *Improving workers' compensation* Members' compensation is primarily concerned with the level of wages of their members. This is perhaps the prime objective so far as union members are concerned, and we will examine this in more detail later in the unit.

2. *Improving working conditions* Trade unions put much effort into improving the working conditions of their members. In some industries, there is considerable emphasis on health and safety measures. This is so in the coal mines where the National Union of Mineworkers has been very active in negotiating safety measures. It is also true in engineering where dangerous machinery is in use. Unions also seek improvements in other conditions of service such as the number of hours worked. A frequent demand of unions in negotiations is a reduction in the length of the working week and an increase in holiday entitlement. Finally, they are concerned with other issues in this area such as the right of workers to such things as maternity leave, and here they seek to make use of the European Union which has taken several initiatives in this area: for example, in the last unit we discussed its impact on equal pay.

3. *Expanding employment opportunities* A prime aim of unions is to maximise the employment opportunities of their members, which may well conflict with the desire to increase wages since an increase in wages could lead to a fall in the level of employment. This will be the case if the firm has no monopsony power and if all workers are union members. (If some employees are not union members, the union may try to ensure that any redundancies occur among non-union workers.) There are several ways in which unions can attempt to improve employment opportunities for their members. One way is to cut the supply of labour (see p. 250). They can also try to increase the demand for their members' labour, sometimes by campaigning against imports of competing goods (e.g. the textile unions' campaign against imports of cotton goods), or more positively, by encouraging higher investment so that their members' marginal revenue product is increased.

4. *Providing services* The fourth union objective is to provide various services to its members. These can include cheap insurance and mortgages, discounts at various firms, and legal advice and representation, for example at industrial tribunals. Thus, in 1995, unions won £304 million for individuals who were injured at work.

The unions' ability to achieve these objectives depends almost entirely on the power of collective action. A union with a large and enthusiastic membership can be very powerful because it can impose significant costs on employers. The ultimate union weapon is the strike. If successful, this means that firms' income disappears because they are not producing any goods. This effect may last for a long time if customers go elsewhere. However, strikes are also costly to the workers because they will not be paid for as long as the strike lasts, and indeed they may face dismissal. Employers sometimes reduce the power of the strike by recruiting new workers. An example of this occurred in 1995 when workers at Liverpool docks went on strike over redundancies and the employers responded by sacking strikers and taking on new workers.

Because of the high costs involved, strikes are relatively rare, and in recent years government anti-union legislation has reduced them further. Unions often take other measures. These depend to a large extent on the industry, but include: refusing to work overtime; 'working to rule', which means that workers take a long time following the precise rules (e.g. checking all equipment before beginning work) on jobs that are usually done quickly; and refusing to initiate improvements.

Union power is constrained by various factors. We have already mentioned the fall in union membership that has considerably reduced their influence. In addition, union power has been reduced in recent years by a series of laws that have weakened their legal position. For example, the 1980 Employment Act reduced employees' rights under the unfair dismissal provisions; the 1984 Trade Union Act insisted that secret ballots had to be held before industrial action could be taken; the 1990 Employment Act imposed restrictions on unofficial action (i.e. action not sanctioned by unions) and employers were given greater freedom to dismiss any employee taking unofficial action; and the 1993 Trade Union Reform and Employment Rights Act forced unions to give employers seven days notice of official action and insisted on postal ballots before any strike (previously many votes had been taken at branch meetings).

A further limitation on union power is that employers are better organised than in earlier years.

Employers' associations

Employers' associations are usually organised on an industry basis. Thus one of the largest employers' associations is the Engineering Employers Federation which has about 4500 members. (The National Farmers Union is larger with a hundred thousand members, but these usually employ only a few workers, and some members have no employees.) Membership of employers' organisations has fallen in recent years, largely because most negotiations are now done at company level rather than on an industry basis. For example, car manufacturers such as Ford prefer to negotiate with the unions directly, rather than combining with other employers and producing an industrywide agreement.

The work of the employers' associations parallels that of the unions. They sometimes negotiate with unions on an industry basis, they give advice to their members on employment law and personnel matters, and they set up procedures for making agreements and resolving problems.

The employers' equivalent of the TUC is the Confederation of British Industry (CBI) which represents 12,000 companies employing about ten million people. The CBI represents the interests of employers, for example in discussions with the government and in the EU. Its policy is determined by a council of 330 members, but most work is done by its permanent employees. As with the TUC, it has no power over the actions of its individual members.

How do employers respond to unions?

One approach is for employers to try to minimise union influence. This tactic became more popular in the 1980s, in part because it was encouraged by the government and aided by anti-union legislation. Employers sometimes ceased to 'recognise' unions: that is, they ignored them and refused to negotiate. Since unions were declining in both members and influence, and so had limited ability to retaliate, this ploy often succeeded in reducing union power.

A variation of this approach was taken by employers who disliked unions but who believed that employees' views needed a voice. This was the line taken by some Japanese companies who allowed workers to join unions, but who also set up works councils and other forms of worker representation so that employees could have a say in the future of the firm. The rights of employees to be consulted is encouraged by the Social Chapter of the Maastricht Treaty (1992). This led to regulations which forced large firms employing over 150 workers in at least two EU countries to set up works councils, where workers could discuss the future of their companies. This legislation did not apply to the United Kingdom since we opted out of this part of the Maastricht Treaty. Nevertheless, many British firms have followed its recommendations and in 1997 the new Labour government announced that Britain would join the Social Chapter.

A different employer approach to the unions is to work with them, seeking a rational and reasonable form of union involvement with the firm. One reason for this more positive approach is that existing forms of union representation seem to work well, for example in dealing with day-to-day grievances. Sometimes these seem trivial – but are nonetheless important – such as the cleanliness of the toilets or the menu at the firm's canteen. Sometimes the topics discussed will include discussion of health and safety measures or the firm's disciplinary procedures. Constructive union involvement in such topics and issues can certainly help the smooth running of the firm. Thus in many cases, managers and union representatives are developing an amicable relationship, and are finding that they can work well together to solve problems.

Collective bargaining

The outcome of **collective bargaining** will depend, in part, on the relative strengths of employers and unions, but the nature of the market is also important, and here we will discuss three possibilities; unions in a competitive labour market; the position where the employer is a monopsonist; and the situation where both the union and firm have some monopoly power.

Unions in a competitive labour market

What happens when a union seeks to increase wages in a labour market where there are many firms and many workers, all acting independently?

A union may try to increase wages by restricting the supply of labour or by threatening to take industrial action. In either case it will try to obtain a wage increase while minimising any fall in employment that might result. Figure 15.2 illustrates a competitive labour market. The intersection of the demand for labour curve and the supply of labour curve gives an equilibrium where q_1 units of labour will be employed at a wage of w_1.

Now suppose that a union is formed and negotiates with employers' representatives for a wage increase by threatening to restrict the supply of labour. (This would be difficult in a competitive labour market, but in non-competitive labour markets it can be done, for example by insisting that new entrants have specific qualifications (e.g. accountancy). The result would be a new supply curve of S_2 and a new equilibrium at a higher wage rate w_2, but employment falls to q_2.

A more realistic analysis would occur if we assume that the union does not try to cut the supply of labour in the way suggested – in our example, by insisting on qualifications – but, instead, threatened strike action. As before, original equilibrium occurs where the demand and supply curves intersect, so that the wage rate is w_1 and the quantity of labour employed is q_1. The effect of the strike threat is that no labour will be supplied below a wage rate of w_2. There is therefore a new supply curve at this level which is horizontal

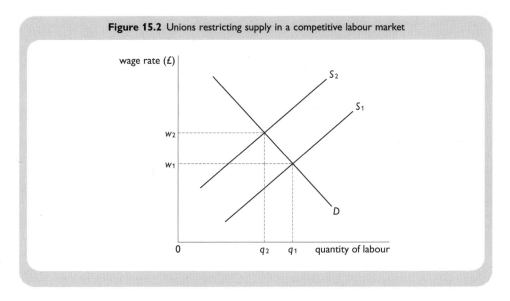

Figure 15.2 Unions restricting supply in a competitive labour market

until it meets the old supply curve. It then slopes upward, since workers will be willing to supply more labour at higher wages. If the union's demands are met, the new equilibrium will be at wage w_2 and q_2 of labour will be employed. If the union's demands are not met in full, but in part, the result would be a new supply curve somewhere between w_1 and w_2 and a new equilibrium between the original position and that which would have occurred if the union's demands had been met in full.

Monopsony

So far we have assumed competitive labour markets, but many markets are not competitive. Let us now examine the results of union action to secure higher wages in a labour market that is characterised by **monopsony**: that is, where there is just one large buyer. In the past this was quite common: for instance, in many areas a single employer such as a coal mine or steel works dominated local employment and so was substantially a monopsonist. This is much less likely now, since many workers have cars and can travel quite long distances to find work. However, it still occurs when workers want one form of employment, such as in the fire service or army. (Note that since these organisations are not seeking to maximise profits, the analysis which follows does not necessarily apply in their case.) However, a firm such as an airport may be the only employer offering certain kinds of jobs. In this instance, if workers possess imperfect information about job opportunities, a crucial feature of monopsony may apply: workers will not immediately leave a firm where wages are lower than are available elsewhere.

Figure 15.3 enables us to analyse the position. The *MRP* (= demand) curve shows how much total revenue increases from selling the output produced by the last unit of labour employed, and the supply curve, *S*, shows how much labour will be made available at each level of wages.

Now, because it is a monopsonist, the firm will have to pay a higher wage if it wants to employ more workers. The result is the marginal cost of labour curve, *MCL*. If you find this difficult to understand, think back to the relationship between the average revenue

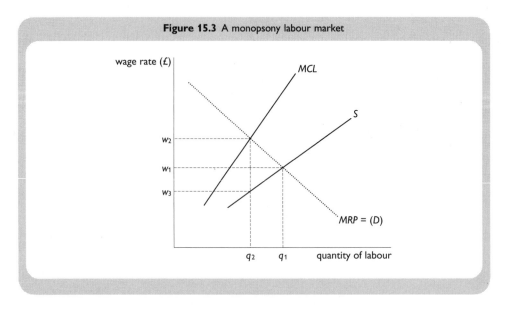

Figure 15.3 A monopsony labour market

curve and the marginal revenue curve. There, a firm wishing to sell more goods had to cut its price. This lower marginal revenue curve then pulled down the average revenue curve. In the present case, a firm wishing to employ an additional worker has to pay higher wages, and this is shown in the new MCL curve.

The relationship between the MCL curve and the supply curve is similar to that between the average and marginal cost curves that was discussed in Unit 3. The supply curve is like the average cost curve. Hiring an additional worker costs extra money and so pulls up the supply curve, which shows the average cost of attracting extra labour.

Equilibrium in this market will not be at the competitive level at wage w_1 and quantity q_1, but at the point where the marginal cost of labour curve intersects with the marginal revenue product curve. If the firm employed fewer workers than q_2 it would pay the firm to take on more workers because the revenue they brought in would exceed the cost of employing them. Similarly, if the firm was employing more workers than q_2, it would benefit by cutting back since the cost of these extra workers exceeds the revenue that they bring in.

Equilibrium will therefore be at the point where the marginal cost of labour to the firm is wage w_2 and the firm will hire quantity q_2 of labour. However, the firm can hire this quantity of labour at wage w_3, considerably below that which would result in a competitive labour market wage. Hence workers can be exploited in a monopsonic labour market, unless the union can prevent this.

Bilateral monopoly

One way to analyse the effects of a union is to treat it as if it was a monopoly seller, in this case of labour. Hence we have a monopsonist buyer of labour faced with a monopoly seller of labour. What will be the result?

Figure 15.4 follows on from Figure 15.3. You will recall that without a union, the firm would employ quantity q_2 of labour at a wage of w_3. Now suppose that the union steps in

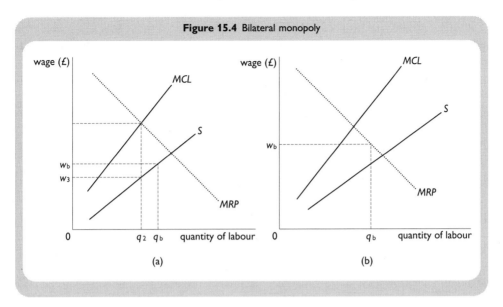

Figure 15.4 Bilateral monopoly

and bargains with employers so that a wage is agreed of w_b, and that this is below the competitive equilibrium. The result is as shown in Figure 15.4(a). No labour will be supplied at wages below this level, so the supply of labour is horizontal at this wage. Wages therefore rise, and so does employment to q_b. The monopsonist has been forced to forgo some of the high profits, and the workers benefit accordingly.

What happens, though, if the union negotiates a wage that is above the competitive level? The result is shown in Figure 15.4(b). No labour will be supplied at wages below this level, so this becomes the new supply of labour curve, and the end result in this case is a higher wage. Employment, however, is below that which would occur in a competitive labour market, but still higher than that which would be the case if the monopsonist was not faced by a union.

These theoretical analyses show that unions can have a significant effect on the labour market. Note, however, our assumptions that firms are seeking to maximise profits, and that labour markets come to an equilibrium. In Unit 1 we discussed the likelihood of firms having objectives other than profit maximisation. Should this be the case here, then the analysis does not necessarily apply. Moreover, it may be that labour markets do not come to an equilibrium. This may occur for several reasons: for example, because labour is not very mobile geographically or between occupations, so that adjustments take place very slowly. Hence the factors that cause the demand and supply curves to move may change before the labour market has completed its response, and in this situation also, the results we have predicted may not apply.

Empirical evidence concerning the effects of trade unions

If theoretical analysis cannot provide conclusive evidence about the effects of trade unions, we need to look at the results of empirical investigations. However, the results of such investigations should be treated with some caution for two reasons.

First, methodologically it is very difficult to compare what actually happened with what would have happened if there had been no unions, particularly since other factors such as changes in the economy as a whole can also have significant effects on pay levels and employment. Many investigations try to estimate union strength in order to make comparisons, but there is no satisfactory way of doing this. Membership is one way, but it is quite possible for a union to have a large membership which is unenthusiastic and therefore weak.

Second, this is a topic in which people's feelings and values are heavily engaged. It is not surprising, therefore, that economists who dislike unions come up with results which suggest that unions are undesirable, while pro-union economists decide that their effects are beneficial.

The effects that unions have on pay have been widely studied, and there is fairly general agreement that unions do achieve higher pay for their members. There is some argument about the precise size of this union–non-union differential, but a typical figure is that unions succeed in raising the wages of their members by about 8 per cent, with rather larger effects for semi-skilled workers and a lower figure for skilled workers. In addition, the degree of wage dispersion is less in unionised firms than it is in non-unionised ones: that is, unions seem to reduce pay inequalities between their members within a given establishment.

The effect of unions on employment is more controversial. We will examine this issue again in Unit 23 when we analyse unemployment, but here we can consider micro-economic evidence. Some researchers find that unions reduce employment. For example, research by Blanchflower and others in 1991 (published in the *Economic Journal*) found that employment grew more quickly in non-unionised establishments by about 3 per cent a year. However, this result has been criticised on methodological grounds, and in 1991 Machin and Wadhwani (also in the *Economic Journal*) found that the effect of unions varied over time. In some periods, employment in firms with 100 per cent unionised membership grew at a faster rate than in non-union firms, while in other periods it grew more slowly.

In addition to employment and pay, we can also examine the effect that unions have on other aspects of the economy. For instance, the conventional view is that unions have a negative effect on output. They are seen as pushing up firm's costs and slowing down innovations because these may threaten their members' jobs. Hence it is argued that they lead to lower productivity and output.

On the other hand, there are reasons to suggest that unions have positive economic effects:

● Without a union, unhappy individual workers may have little choice but to leave the firm or to remain unhappy and uncooperative. A union can reduce grievances and so improve morale.

● If this reduces labour turnover, it will also cut the costs which employers incur when recruiting and training new workers.

● Unions working with management can suggest ways to improve efficiency, and if they succeed in pushing up wages, they may also stimulate management into increasing investment.

Indeed, it is sometimes suggested that one reason for the UK's relatively poor economic performance is that unions are too weak. This means that wages remain low, so that management has little incentive to innovate. Instead of being a high wage, high productivity economy, the UK is turning into a low wage, low productivity economy.

There is a good deal of research evidence to support claims for the positive effect of unions on productivity. Thus Nickell *et al.* found that productivity growth in unionised firms rose on average 2.9 per cent faster than in their non-unionised counterparts in the period 1980–4; this was also the case in the preceding period, though by a smaller amount.

Government intervention and minimum wages

We have examined one form of intervention in the labour market – the effect of trade unions – in some detail. Now we shall examine another kind of intervention, that of the government. This can take many forms. We have already seen that there is substantial government intervention in the form of laws which affect unions, and government legislation on health and safety also affects the workplace. Decisions of the government about the pay and conditions of its own workers are also influential. If the government decides to keep down pay rises for its own employees, this will give a signal to negotiators in the private sector that employers should be tough on any wage increases.

However, our discussion here will focus on government intervention in another form: the introduction of a national minimum wage.

Exercise

JobCentre jobs don't pay

Manchester's Low Pay Unit investigated all the jobs on offer in Greater Manchester. They found that nine out of ten jobs pay less then £200 a week.

A quarter of all the jobs paid below the National Insurance threshold of £58 a week, and more than 45 per cent paid less than £100 a week. On average, the hourly rate of pay was just £3.66 an hour, while 12 per cent of jobs paid less than £2.75 an hour.

Source: Jobwatch '95, Greater Manchester Low Pay Unit, 23 New Mount St, Manchester.

Questions

1. Elaborate the reasons why the figure of £58 a week is significant.

2. Go along to your local JobCentre. What is the average rate of pay? Do you think that the jobs advertised there are typical of all jobs? If not, why not?

3. Do you think that market forces should determine wages or should the government intervene to raise the wages of the low paid?

Government intervention to help the low paid is not new. In the early part of the century the government initiated Wages Councils, which had the power to fix wages in certain industries that were characterised by low pay and where unions were relatively weak. The most important examples are agriculture, catering, retailing, hairdressing and clothing manufacture (though there are many smaller cases, including that of coffin furniture makers). Employers and workers were both represented on these councils, and they could make proposals on pay, holidays and other conditions of employment. These proposals, if accepted by the government, then had legal status.

Wages Councils were criticised on two grounds. First, workers criticised these bodies because, despite their legal status, many employers ignored their recommendations, and workers were either unaware of their legal rights or were too frightened of losing their jobs to complain. Secondly, others argued that Wages Councils were an interference in the working of the labour market. Wages, they argued, should be determined by demand and supply and not by government bodies. They also argued that increasing wages above the market level would lead to unemployment.

This second line of argument gained popularity with the government in the 1980s, though as late as 1992 there were still 26 Wages Councils in existence, covering 2.3 million workers. Their demise came in 1993 when they were abolished by the Trade Union Reform and Employment Rights Act.

Would minimum wages cut jobs?

Since the abolition of the Wages Councils, pressure has been growing from the TUC for the government to introduce a national minimum wage. They argue that a national minimum wage is common in other parts of the world, and indeed, is in operation in every other EU country and in the USA. Moreover, a national minimum wage would be better than the old Wages Councils since everyone would know their rights, making the provision easy to enforce.

The number of people who would gain from a national minimum wage would depend on the level at which the wage was set. Table 15.1 shows that young people and women would be the main beneficiaries. However, opponents of a national minimum wage argue that many of the low paid are not really poor, since many of them are young people living at home or are women whose husbands are working, so that their household income is well above the poverty level.

Table 15.1: Percentage of workers who would benefit from a national minimum wage

	Hourly minimum wage	
Category	£3	£4
All workers	6.2	19.4
Males aged 18–19	19.2	36.0
Males aged 20–24	6.6	22.4
Females aged 18–19	13.4	35.4
Females aged 20–24	9.1	31.1

Source: H. Sutherland, 'Minimum wage benefits', *New Economy*, vol. 2, no. 4 (1995), p. 216.

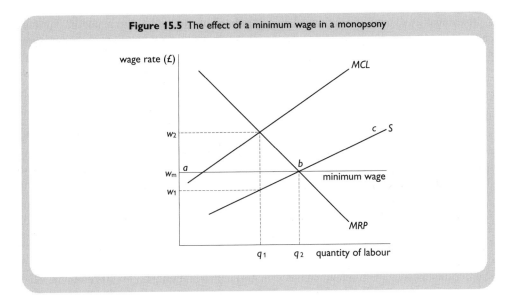

Figure 15.5 The effect of a minimum wage in a monopsony

As we have seen, the point is also made that a national minimum wage would distort the labour market and lead to a loss of jobs. Let us now examine this claim, first theoretically and then by examining some evidence.

If labour markets are competitive, there is no doubt that a legally enforced minimum wage that was above the equilibrium level would lead to fewer jobs, just as a price above the equilibrium level in the goods market would cause some goods not to be sold because their price was too high for the market to clear. In the case of the labour market, the higher wage would mean that demand for labour was less than the supply. Those people in work and receiving the higher wage would benefit, but at the expense of those who were now unemployed.

However, this conclusion depends on the assumption that labour markets are competitive, and as we have already seen (p. 234), there are several reasons to suggest that this might not be the case. On the other hand, if the labour market is characterised by monopsony, then the imposition of a minimum wage can lead to higher employment. Figure 15.5 allows us to develop the argument.

A profit-maximising monopsonist will employ labour up to the point where the marginal revenue product of labour equals its cost. That is at output q_1 when wages will be w_1 – the point where the supply of labour equals the quantity of labour demanded. Now, assume that the government fixes a minimum wage above this point but below w_2 at, say, w_m. There will now be no labour supplied below this level, so the labour supply curve becomes abc. The firm will now maximise profits if it employs labour up to the point where the new labour supply curve cuts the MRP curve, at b. The result is that the quantity of labour employed is now q_2 – an increase from the original equilibrium level of q_1. However, even in monopsonic markets, there is a limit to the extent to which a rise in the minimum wage leads to an increase in employment. If the minimum wage is set too high – in this case above w_2, then the result will be a fall in employment. So, theoretically, if labour markets are monopsonistic, then a minimum wage at the correct level can lead to an increase in employment.

Empirical investigation confirms that a minimum wage can lead to a rise in employment. Machin and Manning ('The effects of minimum wages', *Industrial and Labour Relations Review*, vol. 47, no. 29, 1994) examined the effects of a relative fall in the minimum wages recommended by Wages Councils in the 1980s. In competitive labour markets, this fall would be expected to lead to a rise in employment in these industries, but these researchers found that it had no effect on the level of employment in most cases. In the USA, two researchers, Card and Kreuger, analysed the effects of a large rise in the minimum wage in New Jersey (*Myth and Management: The new economics of the minimum wage*, Princeton University Press, 1995). Nearby states left their rates unchanged. Card and Kreuger collected data in 410 fast-food restaurants and found that in New Jersey wages rose – as expected – but that employment also rose in comparison to employment in eastern Pennsylvania where wages had not risen. This research has been criticised on a number of grounds. For example, other economists have pointed out that employment might have risen because, although more people were employed, they may have worked less hours. This research is therefore not conclusive.

The likely effect of a national minimum wage depends on several factors. As we have seen, in monopsony, it can lead to a rise in employment. However, a national minimum wage applies to all industries, and few economists would claim that all firms were monopsonists. Where firms faced competitive labour markets, the imposition of a national minimum wage would lead to a fall in employment.

The other critical factor to be considered is the level at which the minimum wage should be set. Too low, and it will have little effect; too high, and it might lead to unemployment. Of course, this might be acceptable if the rise in unemployment was very small and the relief of poverty was great.

The effect on government is also complex. Since many low-paid workers are employed by the government, a national minimum wage would increase government spending. On the other hand, it would cut government spending on income support and other social security benefits. To solve these dilemmas, the incoming Labour Government in 1997 set up a Low Pay Commission to make recommendations, chaired by George Bain, the Head of the London Business School.

Summary

Trade unions are a feature of all modern economies. They originated with the Industrial Revolution, and essentially they seek to use the combined strength of their members to gain benefits for them. In recent years, they have suffered from hostile legislation and declining membership, but they still play an important part in industrial relations.

The effect that they have on pay and employment depends largely on the nature of the labour market. In competitive markets, they would find it difficult to raise wages, and if they succeeded, it could be at the expense of employment (though possibly non-union members would suffer most job losses). However, where markets are monopsonistic, they can raise both wages and employment.

The likely effects of a national minimum wage are also controversial, reflecting political opinions as much as impartial analysis. Critics suggest that it will be ▷

at the expense of jobs, and that low pay is not necessarily associated with poverty because they are often second incomes. Supporters claim that many low-paid workers are the sole earners in many households, and that even where this is a second income, it is often needed because the other income is also low. Moreover, they suggest that a national minimum wage would not necessarily lead to a fall in employment.

Review questions

1. Outline the decline in union membership in recent years, and comment on its implications.
2. What do unions try to achieve for their members?
3. What constraints do they face in trying to achieve these objectives?
4. How do employers respond to unions?
5. Using a diagram, discuss the effects a union may have in trying to raise wages in a competitive labour market.
6. Show how a union in a monopsonistic labour market can raise wages and employment.
7. Summarise the empirical evidence on the effects of trade unions.
8. Outline the case for and against a national minimum wage. Which argument do you think is strongest?

Essay questions

1. Critically examine the ability of a trade union to raise the wages of its members.
2. Is a national minimum wage desirable?

Reading 15.1

Cezanne and the workers

The Cezanne Exhibition opened last week, and the Tate is hoping that it will be the most popular – and most profitable – exhibition that it has ever held. But they could be disappointed. The attendants are unhappy and there could be a strike.

The union concerned is one few people have ever heard of – the Public Services Tax and Commerce Union. That is because it was only formed a month ago, as a result of a merger between the National Union of Civil and Public Servants and the Inland Revenue Staff Federation.

▷

In the past, the salaries of Tate employees were based on those paid to civil servants. But now the gallery wants to set up a new system and to set up a works council with representatives from the union and also from non-union members. The workers, the men and women who patrol the exhibition rooms, don't like the change and see it as an attempt to weaken union power.

If the workers were to call a meeting during opening hours, then the gallery would have to close.

Questions

1. What reasons could explain why two unions should merge?
2. Explain why some workers should be 'non-unionised'.
3. What do you think are the strengths and weaknesses of the union in this case?

Reading 15.2

Liverpool workers fight for their jobs

For years, unions have been in retreat. Now some are fighting back.

Mersey dockers have been on strike since the end of September. The strike was provoked when an agency employing 80 workers sacked one of them for refusing to work overtime when his wife was coming home from hospital with a new baby. The other dockers protested, and they too were sacked.

The sacked dockers set up a picket line. When the other 500 dockers came to work the next day they refused to cross it. Their employers, the Mersey Docks and Harbour Company sacked them too. The dockers union, the Transport and General Union refused official backing, largely because it was afraid of the legal consequences. Despite this, the strikers set up permanent picket lines and they also mounted a vigorous campaign to gather support from other workers. They travelled to many countries to gain support and ships which have been loaded by strike breakers have been boycotted by foreign ports.

Questions

1. Why do you think that the union refused official backing?
2. What are the strengths and the weaknesses of (a) the workers and (b) the employers in this dispute?

Economics of personnel and training

Watch out Japan – here comes Tracy Logan

Tracy Logan is a typical British sixteen year old, leaving school this year. But to Japan, and to our other international competitors, she's a big threat ... that's because this year she'll be starting two years' paid skill training on the new YTS ... Tracy will be spending the next two years learning how to take trade away from them for a change.

Source: MSC advert for the new two-year YTS scheme in the *Guardian*, 28 January 1986.

What is training?

People are an important economic resource. We have already seen in Unit 14 that education has an impact on the level of wages, and in this unit we shall develop the ideas of **human capital** theory to assess the importance of training for the economy. The commentary at the beginning of this unit illustrates the exaggerated claims that are sometimes made for training, but it is not easy to decide how much training is needed in a country, or indeed, in a particular firm.

One of the difficulties is that there is no agreed definition of 'training'. One reason for this is that it covers many boundaries, overlapping with education and also covering both on- and off-the-job training, training for young people, and training for the unemployed. Sometimes it is paid for by the people undergoing training, sometimes by the firm, and sometimes by the government.

For the economist, skilled labour is an economic resource with important character-istics. First, it is an important input into the production process, but it can sometimes be substituted. For example, there is some evidence to suggest that in engineering, British firms use graduates where the Germans would use skilled technicians. In part, this reflects the high quality of German training systems. Another example is that because of the increased supply of graduates, they are now doing jobs that would once have been done by non-graduates. This may be desirable if their higher education makes them more efficient than the non-graduates used to be.

Secondly, particular skills can be produced in different ways. It is therefore possible to distinguish three main types of training:

1. An apprenticeship system, where entrants combine practical on-the-job training in firms with a theoretical input from colleges. The apprenticeship system has been in decline in the United Kingdom and has been replaced to some extent by other types of training for young people.

2. An alternative system where training is based on more formal off-the-job training in establishments such as schools or colleges.

3. Mixed systems where training is partly on-the-job and partly off it. This is typical in the UK. Intending teachers, for example, receive a theoretical element largely in universities or colleges, but this is combined with a practical element in schools.

Although skills can be substituted to some extent, some jobs and some industries will always be more skill intensive than others. Over the years, some jobs which used to require minimum amounts of physical capital have become more capital intensive. People used to sweep the street with just a brush and a wheelbarrow. As labour has become more expensive so these implements have been largely replaced by motor vehicles with sweeper attachments. Similarly, many jobs now require more skill: for instance, previously a typist just had to be able to type, but now requires mastery of word processing as well. Despite the general rise in skill requirements, it is likely that for the foreseeable future some industries will continue to require more skills than others: for example, building airplane engines will require more training than is needed in the cleaning industry.

The human capital model

The human capital model was introduced briefly in Unit 14 where it was used to explain why some people earn more than others, and evidence was given to show that educated people are the highest earners. We now need to develop this model, and also to criticise it.

The basic idea of the human capital approach is that investment in people can be analysed in the same way that we analyse investment in machinery, and one way to do this is by using a **production function**. This shows the relationship between outputs of goods and services and the inputs needed to produce them. The analysis can be done for particular factories, but here we are concerned with the economy as a whole.

The relationship can be shown by an equation:

$$Y = f(K, L, T, Q)$$

where Y is output, K represents physical capital, L the quantity of labour, T is technical progress, Q the quality of labour (or human capital) and f (for function) indicates the relationship between these inputs. This equation suggests that there are several ways in which a country can increase the output of goods and services. First, the country can increase the quantity of labour. Thus one reason for the increase in GNP in the UK since the Second World War has been the rise in the number of women workers. Secondly, output can be increased by adding to the stock of physical capital or by improving technology. Thirdly, the quality of human capital in the country can be improved, as the commentary at the start of this unit suggested.

One complication is that it is not enough simply to increase the quantities of these variables: the f in the equation means that relationships between the variables have to be considered too. It will be a waste of money to increase physical capital if the people who are supposed to use it cannot do so because they lack the necessary skills.

The human capital model has considerable explanatory power. For example, how do we explain the very rapid recovery of countries such as Japan and Germany after the terrible destruction of the Second World War when most of their physical capital was destroyed? The human capital approach would suggest that this was because the people who survived had previously received relatively high levels of education: that is, they had high levels of human capital.

Variations of this approach have been used by several economists to calculate the contribution which human capital makes to the growth in output. One of the most influential is that of Denison (*Accounting for United States Economic Growth*, Brookings Institution, 1974). His method was very complex, but essentially he analysed economic growth in the USA over a forty-year period by calculating the extent of educational inputs into the economy and relating this to labour's share of national income. His results suggested that advances in knowledge accounted for approximately a third of the growth in the American economy, while education, in the form of the average amount of education received by workers, accounted for a further 14 per cent. Other significant sources of economic growth were the increase in the size of the labour force and the use of more capital. Thus, though Denison's work is not conclusive, it does suggest that education and knowledge can make a substantial contribution to economic growth.

This conclusion is reinforced by the results of another approach. We have already said that the essential feature of the human capital approach is that it treats investment in human beings in the same way that a firm would analyse investment in physical capital. The techniques that firms use to do this is discussed in detail in Unit 19; here, it is sufficient to say that it involves calculating all the costs and all the benefits which would result from an investment.

In the case of education and training, a large amount of the cost is made up of such items as teachers' time and other labour costs (e.g. secretarial and technician time), together with expenditure on goods such as books, chemicals and other equipment. However, the largest cost is often that of students' time. It is often forgotten when looking at the costs of education that students' time is also valuable. The usual way in which this cost is calculated is to use the earnings forgone. In the case of university students on three-year degree courses, this would involve calculating the amount which students could have been expected to earn if they had been working instead, though allowance would have to be made for the possibility of unemployment.

These costs are then related to the benefits which result from education or training. For the individual, the benefits are usually the higher earnings which can be expected to flow from a better education. For society as a whole, the main benefit is the increased productivity which is presumed to result from higher standards of education.

To some extent this argument is plausible. Educated people can be assumed to be able to learn new ideas and techniques more quickly and to be more flexible and innovative: for example, by being able to analyse problems better and to suggest solutions. It is for this reason that employers are willing to pay graduates higher salaries: they are more productive, and their higher income is a measure of their higher productivity.

Criticisms of human capital theory

However, this line of argument has been criticised. Perhaps the higher earnings do not reflect higher productivity, but simply the fact that education acts like a *screen* which is used to separate graduates from others. So an employer, faced with twenty applicants for a post, of whom five were graduates, might well draw up a short list consisting of the five graduates, one of whom would then get the job. If this is so, the higher earnings of graduates are not the result of their higher productivity, but merely indicate that they are *more likely* to get the better jobs.

Again, there is probably some truth in this criticism of the human capital approach. Nonetheless, supporters of the education–higher productivity link would respond that employers are not fools, and that many internal promotions go to graduates who would not be promoted if they were not more productive.

Critics add another point. Perhaps graduates are indeed more productive, but the source of this higher productivity may be simply that graduates are more intelligent than non-graduates anyway, and so would produce more goods irrespective of how much education they had received. If this contention is true, then the case for high public expenditure on education and training is gravely weakened, since they do not directly contribute much to higher productivity. In fact, some credence can be given to this suggestion, and researchers in this area often adjust their results to account for it. For example, their investigations may lead to the initial conclusion that graduates do earn double the wages of non-graduates, primarily because of their higher productivity, but they then go on to reduce this differential to account for the screening and intelligence arguments.

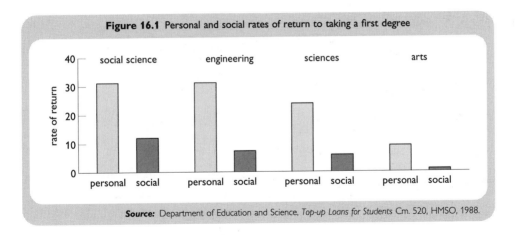

Figure 16.1 Personal and social rates of return to taking a first degree

Source: Department of Education and Science, *Top-up Loans for Students* Cm. 520, HMSO, 1988.

Empirical evidence

The results which follow from this kind of research suggest that education is indeed a good investment, both for the individual and for society as a whole. Individuals benefit from higher earnings, and society from higher output. Figure 16.1 gives one estimate. This figure shows the rates of return which arise from investing in a three-year degree course. The methods used are discussed in detail in Unit 18. Here, we can say that just as putting money in a building society will give a return which can be expressed as a percentage return, so will investing time and money in education. The higher the return, the better the investment.

There are a number of points which arise from this figure. First, as you can see, the return to the individual student is much larger than that to society as a whole. That is largely because individual students do not normally pay the full tuition cost of their education; these costs have to be paid by society as a whole (i.e. by the government). Second, this analysis was completed in the 1980s, and was used to support the argument that student grants should be cut and a system of loans instituted because individual students were clearly benefiting from their education. Finally, the results show considerable differences between subjects. In part, these differences arise because some courses such as engineering are more expensive than others, but it is also true that the rewards accruing to particular subjects do vary. If these results were accepted by the government they would suggest an expansion of social science education, while received wisdom suggests that the UK is short of scientists and engineers. We will examine this argument next.

Is Britain undereducated?

The case that the United Kingdom is undereducated – or at least undertrained – can be put quite briefly. Table 16.1 shows that Britain lags far behind competing countries in the proportion of young people receiving full-time training, and even if part-time training (which might mean only evening classes) is included, the level is still considerably below that found in other countries. This low level of qualification is repeated in the workforce. Two-thirds of British workers have no vocational or professional qualification compared with only a quarter in Germany. The position is particularly serious in engineering where

Table 16.1: Percentage of 16–18 year olds participating in education and training

	Full-time (%)	Part-time (%)	All (%)
Belgium	82	4	87
Denmark	73	6	79
France	69	8	77
Germany	49	43	92
Italy	47	18	65
Japan	77	3	79
Netherlands	77	9	86
Sweden	76	2	76
UK	36	33	70

Source: Employment Department Group, *Training Statistics* (1993), p. 125.

countries such as France and Germany have been producing roughly twice as many qualified people as the UK.

Nevertheless, while there is a good deal of evidence to suggest that Britain is falling behind its competitors, that evidence is not entirely conclusive. In the first place, international comparisons of educational standards are always tricky since a year of education or training in one country may be at a much higher or lower standard than a year in another. Similarly, a degree in one country may be of a higher or lower quality that elsewhere. Moreover, Britain does quite well in some aspects of education and training. In nationally recognised qualifications, for example, 10 per cent of the UK workforce have university degrees compared with 11 per cent in Germany and only 7 per cent in the Netherlands and 5 per cent in France.

It is also not possible to prove that countries with high levels of qualifications are necessarily on the right track – too much can be invested in education and training as easily as too little. This line of reasoning would be supported by those who emphasise market forces. They would argue that if there is a demand for skilled manpower, then salaries of educated people will rise and so encourage people to undertake education. The same theory would suggest that if there is a shortage of particular skills such as engineers, then their salaries will also rise, so encouraging people to train as engineers.

Despite this counterargument, however, the weight of opinion holds that the UK is undertrained, and that something must be done to correct this situation if we are to compete in the future against countries where the workforce is currently better trained.

The supply of skilled workers

The supply of skilled workers depends largely on decisions by three groups of people: individuals, firms, and the government. We shall examine the factors which influence decisions by each of these groups in turn.

The individual and training

As we have seen, economists tend to favour the human capital model, which suggests that the main factor influencing the decision of individuals on whether or not to train is the economic benefit that would result compared with the cost of training. The returns to training include higher incomes, better working conditions and more interesting work. The costs to the individual include the earnings lost while undergoing training.

This proposition is supported by the evidence. The very large rise in the number of young people staying on at school or college in the late 1980s and early 1990s was in part due to the rise in unemployment. This reduced the opportunity cost of education. If it is easy for 16 or 18 year olds to obtain jobs, many of them will do so. However, if youth unemployment is high the potential earnings lost by continuing in full-time education will be doubtful, and so many will stay on. Cost-benefit analysis also explains why the UK has tended to have relatively low numbers of young people in education and training. Youth wages in the UK are comparatively higher than those in other countries, which would encourage young people to leave education.

Human capital theory has helped explain why in the past young women were less likely to go to university: the probable benefits were relatively low because they expected to leave the labour force after a few years to have children, so bringing down the expected returns from extra education. Since women are now less likely to leave the labour force, the rewards from education are higher, and so more women will go to university.

There are also strong sociological factors which influence people. Thus children of highly educated parents are much more likely to continue their education than the offspring of unskilled parents. Furthermore, attitudes learned at home may continue into working life so that those who are encouraged by their home and school background will tend to volunteer for training once they have started work.

The firm and training

Firms are one of the chief sources of training. Indeed, some economists would argue that the government should only be involved in correcting market failures and that the responsibility for training should lie in the interaction of individuals and firms. Individuals will undertake training if it pays them; and firms will also organise training for their workers if they think it will be profitable.

General and specific training

Two concepts are useful in enabling us to analyse firms' approaches to the provision of training. Some training can be categorised as general, other training as specific.

General training refers to processes that increase workers' performance irrespective of the firm which employs them: that is, the productivity of the worker improves by the same amount in the firm which provides the training as it would in other firms. In contrast pure specific training only improves productivity in the firm which provides the training. For example, a firm which trains its workers in general computer skills such as word processing is providing general training; one which teaches its employees its own computer systems is providing specific training.

The distinction is often blurred in practice, but it is nevertheless important because profit-maximising firms will have little interest in general training. A firm which provides general training will bear the cost of it, only to find that the employees it has trained then leave for better-paid jobs with firms which incur few or no training costs. For example, the NHS trains health workers, who might then be snapped up by private sector employers; the BBC also has a good record for training, but often finds its workers moving to other employers such as Sky. Hence general training is usually provided or paid for by

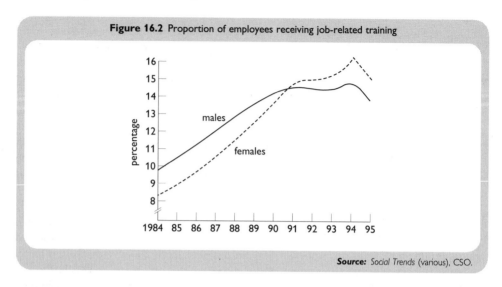

Figure 16.2 Proportion of employees receiving job-related training

Source: Social Trends (various), CSO.

Exercise

Consider Figure 16.2, and answer the following questions.

Questions

1. Comment on the changing pattern of male and female training.
2. What factors do you think explain the changes you see in the table?

individuals seeking to maximise future incomes or by governments who believe that general training is necessary for future economic growth. Firms may indeed provide general training if they feel that it generates other benefits such as higher morale. They may also provide general training if their workers are relatively immobile, or have imperfect information about other job opportunities, and will therefore stay with the firm after training, even though higher wages are available elsewhere.

Specific training is a more complicated subject. Much depends on who bears the costs and who benefits from workers' higher productivity in the future. Figure 16.3 can help the analysis.

The straight line W_c shows the competitive wage (which is also the worker's marginal product). This would be paid throughout the worker's productive life if there is no specific training. If some training is provided, then this will reduce the marginal product while the training takes place (since the worker cannot produce and train at the same time). This is shown as W_{t1} in the figure. However, after training, the worker's marginal product will rise to W_{t2}. The difference between W_c and W_{t1} shows the costs of training, while the difference between W_c and W_{t2} represents the higher productivity resulting from the training.

If the worker were to bear all the costs, wages would be W_{t1} during training and W_{t2} after it. But this would be risky. Even if the potential benefits exceeded the costs, the

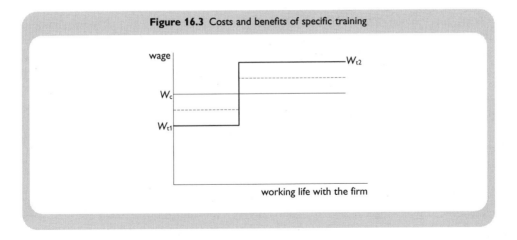

Figure 16.3 Costs and benefits of specific training

worker may be fired, the firm go out of business or a change in technology make the training obsolete. Hence rational workers will not undertake firm specific training if they have to bear all the costs. Similarly, there are risks for the firm: the worker may leave before the firm has recouped its training costs. Hence we can expect the costs and benefits to be shared between the worker and the firm. In the diagram, these benefits are shared equally between worker and firm, as shown by the dotted line, but in real life the proportions may differ.

This analysis explains various patterns we find in labour markets. First, industries which employ workers with general education and skills have higher employee leaving rates than other industries. Second, workers who receive specific training tend to receive higher wages than those without such training. Third, many firms have a policy of 'first in, last out': that is, when redundancies have to be made, firms often make newcomers redundant first. This is logical because workers who have been with the firm longer have probably received a greater degree of specific training.

The outcome of this analysis is that firms may be expected to provide specific training, but that general training needs to be provided by others. Workers might be expected to pay for their own general training if labour markets were perfect, but in the real world there are many imperfections: for example, they may lack knowledge of what training is available and also of the benefits which might accrue to them in the future from training. In addition, they may not be able to pay for the general training, or to stand the loss of wages during training. While they can sometimes borrow to cover these costs (as many students do during their degree courses), money markets are reluctant to lend full costs because the investment is risky. Students, say, can offer little collateral, so banks' lending is limited. Hence the need for government intervention.

Government and training

Though there is some overlap, it is convenient to categorise three types of government activity in the training area.

The first category is concerned with school leavers. In effect, the removal of social security benefits from young people aged between 16 and 18 means that they are coerced into either continuing with full-time education or else joining a government-sponsored training programme. The economic reasoning behind this move is that young people have imperfect knowledge of the labour market and so need an incentive to undertake training. There are also externalities insofar as training young people benefits others. This benefit may take the form of greater productivity, so that society benefits, and, in addition, such training may reduce teenage crime if it keeps young people busy and gives them an objective to aim for. Politically, such training benefits the government because it brings down the level of unemployment.

Whatever the rationale, over 170,000 young people undertook such training each year in the mid-1990s, but whether this training is cost effective is open to argument. Cynics say that the training is poor and does little to add to future output; supporters claim that it does increase employment skills.

Youth training overlaps with the second category of government activity, training schemes for the unemployed. Here again, however, it is difficult to evaluate the costs and benefits. Many people do obtain jobs on completing their training, but it may be that these are mainly the people who would have found employment in any case.

The third area of government intervention is to encourage training for those currently in work. Most of this activity is coordinated through Training and Enterprise Councils (TECs). These are local employer-led, government-funded organisations that aim to identify skill needs and then to ensure that training is provided to meet these needs. However, since they have little or no power over individuals or firms, they have often concentrated on training the unemployed rather than adding to the skills of those already in employment.

Human resource planning

The interaction of demand and supply in the labour market may not lead to the supply of skilled workers that employers – or the economy – needs. This means that there is a case for government intervention to ensure an adequate supply of skilled workers. This approach is sometimes called **human resource planning** (it used to be called man-power planning, but this term has now been largely abandoned because of its sexist connotations). Human resource planning involves government intervention in the labour market in order to ensure that the supply of labour matches the demand.

Now one reason why markets may fail is that there are long time lags involved in supplying labour. In the first place, individuals – or the government – have to realise that a potential shortage of suitably skilled workers looms. Training centres then have to be built, or existing centres enlarged. Finally, it takes many years to train people to enter some occupations (e.g. medicine or engineering). Therefore the initial stage of any plan for human resource development is to produce a forward estimate of the country's human resource need for some years ahead.

There are several ways in which this estimate can be prepared – none of them, unfortunately, very precise. One is to extrapolate from the present position: for example, to note that the number of jobs for, say, accountants has increased by x per cent in recent years and to assume that this will continue. This is very imprecise – if there is one thing that is known about the future, it is that it will be different from the past. It also leaves out of the calculation the growth of new occupations: for example, the need for computer programmers which arose after the development of computers.

An alternative approach is to look at more advanced countries: to say, in effect, that countries such as Germany and Japan have more engineers than us, therefore we need to train more engineers. There is some merit to this approach, but its weakness is that advanced countries follow different patterns. Thus a country which decided to follow the American example would train many more lawyers, while one following the Japanese model would seek to train more engineers.

A third way to predict future needs is to ask employers about shortages, but again, this approach presents difficulties. Employers' forecasts of the future may well be inaccurate. They also have an incentive to exaggerate shortages, since if the government responds by increasing the supply of skilled labour, wages of this group of workers will fall, so benefiting employers.

Nonetheless, despite the problems outlined, human resource forecasts are needed. The only alternative is to put complete faith in the market to produce the appropriate numbers of skilled workers, which is not wholly feasible.

Once the required forecasts have been made, the next step is to compare the anticipated future needs with the present position and then to make appropriate plans. Thus, if there is an anticipated shortage of dentists, the government can arrange the expansion of dental schools. A further dilemma arises at this point, however. The government can plan the expansion of places, but it cannot force people to take them up. That is what has occurred in engineering: the government believes that the country will need more engineers in the future, but individual students currently prefer in the main to take other subjects.

Overall, the British position is that market forces have primary place in supplying future human resource needs, but that market forces need to be influenced by government intervention, for example by increasing the supply of training places in areas of short supply. Planning future needs is certainly undertaken extensively in education, which requires large numbers of teachers. Here the government is the largest employer, so it must have a fairly clear idea of future needs and the ability to ensure that these are met.

Summary

People are important. The causes of economic growth are complex and not fully understood, but there is no doubt that the quality of the labour force can play an important part in determining future levels of output.

Human capital theory provides one important way of analysing the relationship between education and economic growth. Essentially, it suggests that investment in education and training can be analysed in the same way that firms analyse possible investment in machinery, by asking, 'Does it pay?' The answer in many cases seems to be 'Yes'. Investment in the education and training of people brings benefits that exceed the costs.

Market forces can play a part. People will be willing to train for jobs if they think that these will be well paid. And firms will be willing to train workers if they believe that this will lead to higher productivity.

However, market forces may not be enough. Consequently, governments intervene in the market by providing or financing training and by forecasting what skills will be needed in the future.

Review questions

1. Outline the important characteristics of skilled labour for the economist.
2. What is a production function? Write a production function for the production of graduates in a university.
3. Outline the human capital model and assess some of the criticisms made against it.
4. Is Britain undereducated?
5. What factors influence the supply of skilled workers?
6. Why is the distinction between general and specific training important?
7. What role does the government play in ensuring a supply of skilled labour?
8. How is human resource planning undertaken? Why is it not accurate?

Essay questions

1. Critically assess the human capital approach to investment in education.
2. Should governments intervene in the labour market to ensure an adequate supply of skilled labour? If so, how should they do this?

Reading 16.1

Educated guesses are wide of mark

Education and training are like apple pie and motherhood. After all, the better trained and educated the workforce, the better the performance of the economy and the more just the society.

Although such protestations are self-evidently true, they fall short of providing a robust guide to just how much a government can rely on eduction and training to deliver the growth process. A well-educated and trained workforce may be a necessary condition for growth, but plainly it is not sufficient. So, what is to be done?

Recent research is sobering about how much education and training can achieve by themselves. The necessary expenditure to close income inequality, raise skill levels and lower unemployment is vast; the pay-offs are slow, and unless education and training are embedded in a wider array of policies, notably raising levels of investment and expectations of future demand, the results are likely to be variable at best.

The international evidence on training is particularly disappointing. Sometimes training hits the jackpot, but Swedish experience suggests that sometimes it actually increases unemployment by increasing workers' expectations of higher wages. And American research suggests that to improve the educational attainment of the bottom half of the US population to take income inequality back to 1970 levels would cost $3 trillion. Research also suggests ▷

that the crucial determinant of productivity is not skills but management capacity and strategy. Well-organised, long-termist firms are the key to success; not training itself.

Source: Adapted from Will Hutton in the *Guardian*, 8 January 1996, p. 15.

Questions

1. Outline the arguments to support the proposition that 'the better trained and educated the workforce, the better the performance of the economy'.
2. How do you think that education can lead to 'a more just society'?
3. Use the notion of a production function to elaborate why 'an educated and trained workforce may be a necessary condition for growth, but plainly it is not sufficient'.

Reading 16.2

Down with training!

Politicians and public alike express the importance of training. This seems reasonable. The case for public support for training is strong: skilled workers are more likely to be employed, and highly trained workers are likely to be more productive. And though there are exceptions – the Spice Girls and Gazza are examples – the educated earn more than those less educated.

However, the evidence is not conclusive. The OECD investigated the effects of several training programmes for unemployed adults. It concluded that there is only meagre support for the effectiveness of such programmes. Similarly, almost a quarter of a million people joined the UK Youth Training programme. Investigation showed that almost half of those who joined dropped out before the schemes ended, while those who completed the course had higher unemployment rates than the age group as a whole. The Training and Enterprise Councils put on schemes that cost one and a half billion pounds, but the House of Commons Select Committee on Employment found that only 27 per cent of adults on TEC courses had work, and even the best courses had a success rate of less than half.

Despite this kind of evidence, Britain's new Labour government in 1997 made training for young unemployed a central policy of its first year in office.

Questions

1. Summarise the reasons why there is a strong case for public support for training.
2. Use the concepts of general and specific training to explain why firms might not be willing to train workers.
3. Why do you think that training programmes seem to be unsatisfactory? What could be done to make them more effective?

MODULE F

Money

After reading this module you should be able to:

- discuss the functions of money;

- understand how banks create money and how the government attempts to control the money supply;

- show how the government can influence interest rates;

- understand how firms can raise finance;

- summarise the factors which influence a firm's decision to invest;

- explain the net present value and internal rate of return methods of investment appraisal; and

- appreciate how the public sector can use cost-benefit analysis to evaluate investment decisions.

Money creation and control

Money is a singular thing. It ranks with love as man's greatest source of joy. And with death, as its greatest source of anxiety. Money differs from an automobile, a mistress or cancer in being equally important to those who have it and those who do not.

Source: J.K. Galbraith, *The Age of Uncertainty*, Broadcast version, 6th programme, BBC

What is money?

Everybody knows what **money** is: it is what we spend when we go shopping. Yet it is really very difficult to be precise about what is or is not money. So, let us start with a definition: '**Money** is anything which is generally accepted as a means of payment.'

There are two points to note about this simple definition:

1. The emphasis is on 'generally accepted'. If I go into a British shop with a ten-franc French coin, that would not normally be accepted as a way of paying for my shopping. Therefore, this coin is not money in the UK.

2. Credit cards and cheques are not money. In the first place, they are not generally acceptable – just try buying a box of matches with a credit card. Second, a cheque is simply a written instruction to a bank to transfer money from one person to another. Similarly, a credit card is a form of identification which allows you to borrow money in order to buy now and pay later.

The functions of money

Imagine a world without any money. You need a new pair of shoes. What do you do? The answer is that you need to find someone who has a pair of shoes that would fit you and who also wants something that you have which is of equal value. This is very difficult to do. Barter – the way goods are exchanged without money – requires this double coincidence of wants. You not only have to find someone who has what you want, but the same person has to want what you have to offer.

The functions of money are therefore as follows:

1. *To act as a medium of exchange.* Money ensures that there is always a double coincidence of wants, because, by definition, money is generally acceptable. Without money, economies cannot develop beyond a very low level because they have to depend on barter.

2. *To act as a unit of account.* This allows us to compare prices – for instance, whether a pair of shoes costs more or less than a shirt. This function of money also allows us to keep accounts and draw up balance sheets.

3. *To act as a store of value.* We can put money aside and know that we can use it in the future. This function of money is weakened when there is **inflation**, because money then loses some of its value. *Expectations* of inflation in the future will also make people unwilling to hold money.

4. *To act as a standard of deferred payment.* Again, this function of money is weakened if there is inflation, but in general, money makes it possible for people to save up in order to buy something in the future. This function of money also makes it possible to borrow and pay back the debt later – an important feature of modern economies.

Types of money

The oldest kind of money is called **commodity money**, because it can be used as a commodity in its own right. Commodity money needs certain characteristics:

- It must be durable – ice-cream would be useless as money because it would simply melt away.

- It must be scarce – sand would be useless as money in the Sahara because everyone would have as much as they wanted and would not accept it as a medium of exchange.

- It must be divisible, so that small things can be bought – elephants are scarce and durable, but not much use if you want to buy a box of matches.

In the past, many commodities have satisfied these characteristics. Gold and silver coins are the most widespread, but commodities as diverse as tobacco leaves, cowrie shells and dogs' teeth have been used, and even today, cigarettes are often used as a medium of exchange in prisons.

The big advantage of commodity money is that it is generally acceptable because the commodity itself is valuable. However, it has disadvantages. For example, coins can be debased – people used to chip bits off coins, and governments cut back the amount of gold they contained.

The supply of gold was limited, too, and as trade increased there were not enough gold coins to finance this expansion. Additional money was therefore required. At first, this took the form of convertible paper money. Goldsmiths issued receipts for the gold that they had in their safes, and this became acceptable in place of the gold coins. A relic of this time still appears on notes in the UK, which contain a promise 'to pay the bearer on demand the sum of £x'.

In fact, this promise is meaningless, because in the twentieth century the Bank of England started to issue **fiat money**, which is notes and coins that are not backed by gold, but are issued by the Bank to facilitate trade. If shops and banks complain that there is a shortage of, say, £10 notes, the Bank of England will issue more. As long as this is not done to excess and people accept the notes, this facilitates trade and has no harmful effects.

In a modern economy, only a small proportion of the total money supply is in the form of notes and coins. To see that this is so, consider the case of a monthly paid worker. At the end of the month she has earned a certain amount of money. However, before she receives it, some goes to the Inland Revenue as income tax and other money goes to pay for National Insurance and superannuation. Then the remainder is paid into her bank account where money is taken out to pay her mortgage and various insurances, perhaps plus direct debits to pay gas and electricity bills. Now, in all these transactions, not a note or coin has changed hands. All that has moved has been figures in various accounts.

Where has this money come from, then, if it does not have a physical existence in the sense that you can touch it? In order to answer that question we need to look in detail at how banks and building societies create money.

The supply of money

The basic idea is simple. Suppose that Mr A goes to the bank and deposits £100. This means that its assets are £100 – it has Mr A's money – and its liabilities are also £100 –

Table 17.1: Money creation

	Bank	
Step	Assets (£)	Liabilities (£)
1. A deposits £100	100 cash	100 owed to A
2. Bank keeps 10%, lends 90%	10 cash 90 loan	100 owed to A
3. B deposits £90	100 cash (10 + 90) 90 loan	190 owed to A and B
4. Bank keeps 10%, lends 90%	19 cash 171 loans (90 + 81)	190 deposits
5. C deposits £81	100 cash 171 loans (90 + 81)	271 deposits
This process will continue until	100 cash 900 loans	1000 deposits

it owes Mr A this amount. However, the bank does not keep that money in a special place, separated from all its other money. Instead, it keeps some of the money, and lends out the rest in order to receive interest on it – that is how banks make their profits. Now how much the bank keeps, and how much it lends depends on a trade-off between the need for security, which would incline the bank to keep a high proportion of each deposit, and the need for profit, which would be an incentive to keep only a small proportion and to lend the rest.

For simplicity, let us assume that in this case the bank keeps 10 per cent of the money deposited by Mr A and lends out 90 per cent. The person who borrows this will use it to buy some good or service and the seller (Mrs B) will then deposit the £90 in the bank. This is shown in Table 17.1 as steps 1, 2 and 3.

Similarly, when the bank receives the £90 it keeps 10 per cent for security and lends out 90 per cent (£81) to Mr C. This is shown in the table as step 4. Its assets are now £190 (made up of £10 plus £9 cash) and £171 loans (made up of £90 lent to Mrs B and £81 to Mr C). So the money supply – the amount of money in circulation – has increased from our original £100 to £190.

At step 5 Mr C uses his loan of £81 to buy goods, and this money is then deposited in the bank by the seller. This increases the bank's assets to £271. Again the bank keeps 10 per cent and lends out 90 per cent of this new deposit of £81.

This process will continue until eventually the total money supply reaches £1000, made up of the original £100 cash and £900 created by the bank through its loans.

Obviously, this is a simplified account of what happens in reality, but the basic description is accurate. We have described a system with only one bank; a description with several banks would be more complex, but would go through the same steps and come to the same result.

The amount of money which the banks can create varies inversely with the amount that they keep in reserve. In the example above, if they kept 10 per cent, the eventual amount of money they created would rise tenfold. If they had to keep 25 per cent in reserve, their ability to create money would be only four times the original deposit. The formula for calculating the rise in money supply is:

$$\text{Initial deposit} \times \frac{1}{\text{Reserve ratio}}$$

We have assumed, of course, that every time a bank lends out money it is immediately deposited with another bank. In fact, to complicate matters, some money will be kept in circulation without being deposited in a bank, and this will reduce the ability of the banks to create money.

Money in the UK today

Because money is so diverse, it is not surprising that there are several ways in which the money supply can be measured. We shall discuss just two of these methods.

M0 consists of notes and coins in circulation (including banks' till money), plus banks balances with the Bank of England. This measure of money is closely linked to the function of money as a medium of exchange. For example, people spend more just before Christmas, and therefore they need more notes at that time of year. Because it is so closely linked to money's role as a medium of exchange, changes in M0 can give an indication of the extent to which consumer spending is rising. As Figure 17.1 shows, M0 rose by approximately 70 per cent in the decade after 1985.

M4 is much larger, and has three main components:

1. Notes and coins held by the private sector.
2. Private sector sterling deposits at the banks.
3. Sterling deposits at building societies.

M4 is the official measure of money supply in the UK today. Because it is so broad, it is a good measure of money fulfilling several functions.

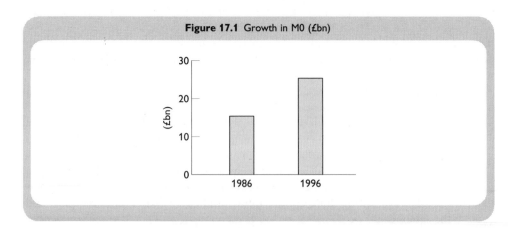

Figure 17.1 Growth in M0 (£bn)

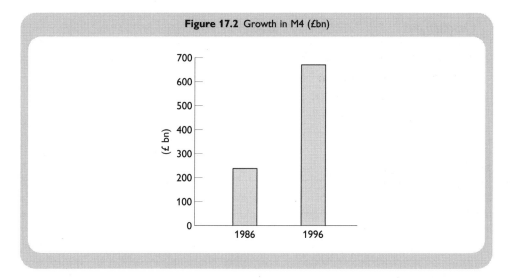

Figure 17.2 Growth in M4 (£bn)

Figure 17.2 shows the growth in M4 over a decade. It makes clear that M4 is much larger than M0 (note that the scale on the two figures is different), and also that it has grown more quickly, in this case by about 180 per cent over the decade.

In addition to these two measures of money, several others can be used: for example, there is M5 which, as well as the components of M4, includes such things as Treasury and some other bills (these are discussed later in this unit) and some national savings instruments, which are sometimes called 'near money' as they can be converted into money quite quickly. All these components give a huge total for money supply, but as it is not closely related to money's function as a medium of exchange, M5 is not often used.

In this section we have seen that most money in a modern economy is not in the form of notes and coin (i.e. cash), but is actually created by the banks. The banks' ability to do this is constrained largely by their need for security and, as we will see, by the actions of the monetary authorities acting through the Bank of England. In order to see how this operates, we need to examine the financial institutions in a modern economy.

Exercise

Are bras money?

What do you do if there is a fall in the demand for the machine tools that you make?

The enterprising managers of a factory in Vorunezh in Russia arranged a swop. The found a firm in China which would pay for their tools in Chinese-made bras. So far, so good. But they couldn't sell all the bras, so they had to pay their workers in bras.

I wonder if the tax authorities would accept payment in bras?

Questions

1. Are bras money?
2. Outline the disadvantages of this form of payment.
3. Why do you think that UK factories do not use this method of payment when they are in financial difficulties?

Financial institutions

The financial industry is one of the largest in any modern industrial society, and its functions are also complex. Figure 17.3 gives a simplified outline of some of the institutions and markets that are involved.

At the apex is the central bank; in the UK, this is the Bank of England. The Bank gives advice to the government on economic matters but, more importantly, it has control over monetary policy. This power was obtained in 1997 when a committee of the Bank was set up with a mandate to control inflation by using monetary policy. Previously, the Bank only had power to advise the government on monetary matters.

The Bank of England also acts as the government's agent in its dealings with other banks – for example, in implementing monetary policy as described below – and as banker both to the government – keeping the government's accounts and arranging to borrow money for the government when necessary – and to the other banks. All the other banks keep accounts with the Bank of England, and it is lender of last resort, making money available to other banks when funds are scarce.

The next group of institutions are called the bank financial intermediaries. They are called intermediaries because they are part of the mechanism by which the savings of individuals and firms are passed on to borrowers at home and overseas. The best known of these bank financial intermediaries are the commercial banks such as Barclays, NatWest

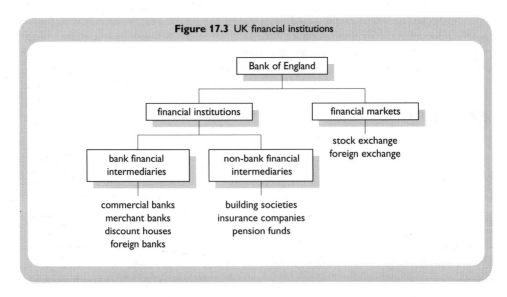

Figure 17.3 UK financial institutions

Table 17.2: The balance sheet of all the banks in the United Kingdom, 1996 (£bn)

Assets			Liabilities		
Sterling assets:	*£bn*	*£bn*	*Sterling liabilities:*	*£bn*	*£bn*
Notes and coin	4		Notes issued	2	
Balances at Bank of England	2		Sight deposits	248	
Loans to discount houses	9		Time deposits	350	
Loans to other financial intermediaries	187		Other liabilities	200	
Bills	20				
Other securities	28				
Other advances	452				
Other assets	104				
Total sterling assets		806	*Total sterling liabilities*		800
Other currency assets			*Other currency liabilities*		
Loans and investments overseas	713		**Sight** and **time deposits**	830	
Other assets	365		Other liabilities	254	
Total other currency assets		1078	*Total other currency liabilities*		1084
Total assets		1884	**Total liabilities**		1884

Source: Bank of England Quarterly Bulletin.

Note: **Sight deposits** are deposits that can be withdrawn 'on sight' (i.e. immediately). Current accounts at banks are an example. Money in **time deposits** can only be withdrawn after giving a period of notice.

and Lloyds. These banks are also **clearing banks**, so called because they have a central mechanism for clearing cheques. These banks are retail organisations offering services to millions of customers. An examination of these banks' assets can give us a good picture of the way that they operate.

Thus Table 17.2 shows the balance sheet of all banks in the UK. Several things need to be explained in this table. First, note that total assets equal total liabilities. That is because, as we have seen when discussing money creation, every time a bank receives a deposit it also creates a debt for the bank. Second, note the international aspects of the table: British banks have large amounts of assets overseas. Third, note the relatively small amount of notes and coin as a proportion of total assets. In order to maintain their **liquidity** the banks also keep some money at the Bank of England, just as you might keep some money in a commercial bank. The cash held by the banks plus the money deposited at the Bank of England make up its reserves. These are needed in case many customers want their money back at the same time. If all – or even most – of a bank's customers wanted their money back at the same time, the banks would not be able to repay them. The system works on confidence. If this goes, banks collapse.

The banks use some of their resources to lend to other financial intermediaries, one group of which are called discount houses. These are very important but little-known institutions which form a link between the Bank of England and the commercial banks. Discount houses borrow from the banks on a short-term basis and use this money to buy **Treasury bills** from the Bank of England and other organisations (bills are a kind of short-term IOU). These loans, plus loans to other financial intermediaries, are very liquid: that is, they can be recalled very quickly should the lending bank need money.

The largest amount of the banks' assets are advances in the form of bank loans and overdrafts, which occur when the bank lends money, for example to a firm. Since it charges borrowers higher rates of interest than it pays to lenders, this is an important source of profit. These assets are not very liquid. If a bank lends money to a firm, it cannot ask for it back in the next day or so.

The other kind of bank to note are the merchant banks. If banks such as Barclays can be described as retail, then merchant banks operate in the wholesale market. They accept bills of exchange, advise firms on mergers, manage pension funds, and underwrite (i.e. guarantee) new capital issues. Their role is discussed in more detail in the next unit.

The most important non-bank financial intermediaries in Figure 17.3 are the building societies. Building societies differ from banks in a number of ways. First, they are regulated by the Building Societies Act 1986 rather than by the Bank of England. Secondly, they have a ceiling on the wholesale funds that they can raise, they only rarely offer overdrafts, and they are not significant lenders to industry. A third major difference is that building societies are mutual institutions: that is, they are owned by their members, the people who lend them money or who borrow from them, whereas banks are profit-orientated institutions.

Despite these differences, the distinction between banks and building societies is diminishing: for example, they now both issue cheque books and lend money for house purchase. Some former building societies, such as Abbey National and the Halifax, have given up their mutual status and become banks, owned by shareholders. They believe that this gives them greater flexibility in the money market.

Controlling the money supply

Why should the government want to control the money supply? This question will be answered in some detail in Unit 22 which deals with inflation, but the short answer is that there is undoubtedly a close link between the quantity of money and the level of inflation. Imagine, if you can, a government wishing to court popularity printing large quantities of money, and giving thousands of pounds to everyone in the country. Such a gesture would not make people richer – it would not produce any more goods and services – but it would cause prices to rise drastically. Hence governments have to take care that the banks do not create too much money.

There are several methods which the government can use to control the money supply; different governments place more or less emphasis on one or another. In the past, governments placed direct limits on the amount of money a bank could create. It did this by issuing directives ordering the banks to reduce their lending. If this seemed too draconian, the Bank could simply suggest strongly to the banks that they should restrict their lending. Such methods are no longer used. Instead, there are three principal methods. All are quite complex, so what follows is slightly simplified.

Controlling reserve assets

The first method is to work on the banks' asset requirements. In the example we gave above showing how banks could create money, we assumed for simplicity that the banks kept 10 per cent of any deposit as security and then lent out 90 per cent. If they were forced to keep more than this in reserve, their ability to create money would be restricted.

In the UK at present, the banks' only legal requirement is to deposit at the Bank of England 0.35 per cent of its 'eligible liabilities'. These are their total liabilities minus certain deductions such as certificates of deposit (these are large deposits which are not very liquid, but which pay relatively high rates of interest). If the Bank of England increased this percentage, it would leave the banks with less deposits, so they would be unable to create as much money. Controlling the quantity of reserve assets has not been used recently to control the money supply. One reason for this is that deposits at the Bank of England comprise such a small part of the banks' total assets that they often keep more than 0.35 per cent of their assets with the Bank as a prudential measure. In these circumstances, increasing the legal requirement would have little effect.

Open market operations

Another way in which the Bank of England can influence the money supply is by undertaking open market operations. It does this by buying or selling **bonds**. These are issued by the government when it wishes to borrow money. Bonds issued by the government pay a fixed rate of interest. Their value therefore changes as interest rates change. The financial pages of the quality newspapers show the current prices of these government bonds; they are sometimes called 'gilts', which is short for 'gilt edged securities', implying that because they are issued by the government they are safer than loans to commercial companies.

If the government wishes to borrow money, it offers bonds for sale. These will be bought by individuals (you can do this through the Post Office) or by companies. The buyers write cheques payable to the Bank of England. The money then leaves the commercial banks where they have their accounts and passes into the Bank of England. This ensures that the commercial banks have less deposits, and thus their ability to create money is reduced. Conversely, if the government wishes to increase the money supply, it redeems some of its bonds. The money then passes from the Bank of England to the commercial banks, so increasing their deposits and their ability to create money. In summary, when the government sells bonds to the public it will reduce the money supply; when it buys from the public, the money supply will rise. (Note that the effect differs when the central bank sells bonds directly to the commercial banks. Since this increases the latter's assets it can allow them to create more money.)

The constitution of the **European Central Bank**, which will be charged with operating European monetary policy, makes it clear that **open market operations** will be its method of controlling money supply.

Raising interest rates

An alternative approach to controlling the quantity of money is to work on the demand side. This can be done by raising interest rates. Just as an increase in price reduces demand for goods, so an increase in the interest rate will reduce the amount of money which people wish to borrow from banks. Hence, even if the banks should wish to lend more, they will find it difficult, and this will restrict the growth in the money supply. The role of interest rates is discussed in more detail below.

The demand for money

So far we have looked at the role that banks, building societies and the government play in creating and controlling the money supply. Now we shall move on to look at the demand side.

The term **demand for money** is an odd one. We would all like more money, so the notion of discussing the factors which influence the demand for money strikes us as inappropriate. Yet this is an important concept. A good way to analyse money is to think of it as if it were any other commodity. We have discussed the factors which determine the demand for goods in some detail. Thus when economists talk about the demand for money they are not asking if you would like to be richer, but rather they are seeking to discover what factors determine whether people choose to hold their assets in the form of money rather than as, say, shares, buildings or bonds.

In his book *The General Theory of Employment, Interest and Money* (1936), Keynes suggested that there were three main reasons why people chose to hold money rather than other assets. There was a transactions demand, a precautionary demand and for speculation. We will discuss each of these in turn.

Transactions demand

People want money because they want to buy things. If you wanted to buy a newspaper it would be most inconvenient if you first had to sell some other asset to get the money you needed to buy the paper. There would be a large opportunity cost in terms of your time. More generally, people need to hold money for transactions because their receipts of income and their expenditure do not coincide. Many people receive their income monthly, but many bills have to be paid every week. Hence they need to hold some money to pay these bills.

The amount of money which people choose to hold to pay for transactions will depend on two factors. In the first place, it will depend on how much they intend to spend, and this, in turn, will depend largely on their income. A millionaire will expect to spend much more than a student and so will choose to hold more money to pay for these transactions. The second factor is uncertainty about the general level of prices. If prices are rising very quickly, or are expected to rise in the future, then people will choose to hold more money to pay for the expected price rises. Putting together these two factors – income and price rises – we can say that demand for money to pay for transactions depends on expected real expenditure: that is, expenditure adjusted to take account of inflation.

Precautionary demand

The precautionary demand for money arises because we cannot forecast the future precisely. For a household, this might arise because the car needs repair or the washing machine breaks down. For a firm, the reason might be that a debtor goes out of business, so that expected income is not received.

Again, the main determinant of the amount of money that people keep for precautions is their level of income. A rich person will be able to afford to keep more money at hand than a poor one.

The speculative motive

The third reason for holding money is called the speculative motive, and is rather more difficult for students to understand, not least because few students have enough assets to speculate, for example, on the stock market. Let us assume, however, that in 1987 you were relatively rich, had money invested in shares, and were good at guessing the future. In that position, you would sell all your shares early in the year because subsequently there was a great crash and shares lost much of their value. You would therefore move your assets out of shares and instead hold money. When you thought that the stock market was due to rise again, you would choose to hold less money and, instead, buy shares.

Thus some people's demand for money is influenced by the speculative motive. But, what determines the amount of money that they will hold for this purpose? There are two approaches to answering this question, both leading to similar results.

Opportunity cost

The first is relatively straightforward. There is an **opportunity cost** to holding money: that is, the interest that is lost. Thus if interest rates are very high, then holding money in cash or in a bank account which pays little or no interest will be costly because considerable interest will be lost. Hence when interest rates are high we would expect there to be a fall in the demand for money. Conversely, when interest rates are low only a little interest will be lost when holding money, so demand for money will be relatively high.

Money or bonds

The second approach is to assume, as Keynes did, that people can choose between holding money or bonds. (Keynes used bonds to represent a wide variety of illiquid assets such as land or buildings.) Now, as we have said, bonds pay a fixed rate of interest: let us assume that this is 5 per cent. If, therefore, interest rates generally are also 5 per cent, then a bond with a face value of £100 will be worth £100. However, if interest rates rise to 10 per cent, no one would be willing to pay £100 for this bond because they would only receive £5 interest, while £10 is available elsewhere. So the price of the bond would fall to £50 ensuring that someone with £100 to invest could buy two bonds and receive the going rate of £10 interest. Thus we can conclude that when interest rates are high the price of bonds falls, and when interest rates fall the price of bonds will be expected to rise. Consequently, speculators will buy bonds when interest rates are high and expected to fall. This means that they will have a low demand for money at high interest rates. Conversely, when interest rates are low and expected to rise, people will not buy bonds (because bond prices will fall), so instead they will choose to hold money.

We can show this relationship between the quantity of money demanded and the rate of interest in Figure 17.4. This resembles a traditional demand curve. Indeed, it is a demand curve except that we have labelled the curve L (for liquidity) rather than the traditional D. The curve slopes down showing that at low rates of interest there will be a higher demand for money. Note that the curve does not touch the vertical axis. That is because the distance between the vertical axis and the curve is influenced by the other factor influencing the demand for money – the level of income. The higher the level of income, the further from the axis will be the demand for money curve.

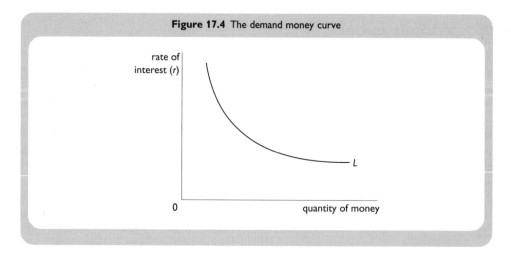

Figure 17.4 The demand money curve

The rate of interest

So far we have discussed the supply of money and the demand for money. Now it is time to bring these two factors together. This is done in Figure 17.5.

In the figure the supply of money is shown as a vertical line. That is because the supply of money is fixed at any one time and does not normally vary with the interest rate. The demand for money curve is determined in the way illustrated in Figure 17.4. Equilibrium occurs at the intersection of these demand and supply curves.

How does this equilibrium come about?

Imagine that the interest rate is 10 per cent, but that at this rate of interest the supply of money exceeds the demand. Consequently, people are holding more money than they want. They will use this excess money to buy goods or securities such as bonds. However,

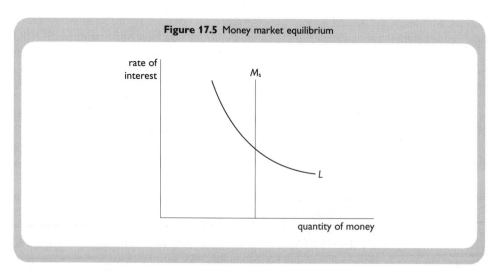

Figure 17.5 Money market equilibrium

if many people are trying to buy securities their price will rise. As we have seen, there is an inverse relationship between the rate of interest and the price of securities. If the price of securities rises, therefore, the rate of interest will fall. This process will continue until the demand for money equals the supply. Conversely, if the demand for money is more than the supply, people will sell bonds, so pushing up the interest rate until equilibrium is reached. Thus the rate of interest moves to bring about equilibrium in the money market.

In Unit 8 we discussed government intervention in markets for goods and services. For very similar reasons, governments intervene in the money markets. The first reason is to combat inflation. This is discussed in detail in Unit 22, but basically a rise in interest rates will dampen down economic activity and inflationary pressures. For example, high interest rates will make borrowing more expensive, and people will therefore be less likely to borrow in order to buy consumer goods. On the other hand, if the government feels that a recession is looming, a cut in interest rates will help to stimulate the economy.

A second reason for government intervention in the money markets is to influence exchange rates. These are the rates at which one currency exchanges for another: for example, one pound sterling might buy 2.50 German marks. Now it is easy for firms to buy and sell currencies, so if interest rates in Germany rise, then some people will sell pounds and buy marks to benefit from this higher interest. Selling sterling will force down the value of the pound. If the British government does not want this to happen, it might well respond by putting up interest rates to match the rise in Germany.

Thus, for various reasons, governments often intervene to change the rate of interest. There are several ways in which they can do this. The first follows from Figure 17.5. If the government increases the supply of money the M_s curve will shift to the right and the rate of interest will fall, just as an increase in the supply of a good will cause its price to fall. Similarly, the government can increase the rate of interest by cutting the money supply. Note that this assumes no change in the demand for money. If demand does change – for example, because people expect changes in interest rates – the government's action on the supply side might be nullified by a shift in the demand curve for money (L in the diagram).

The Bank of England can also influence interest rates more directly. One way is for the Bank to change the rate at which it makes money available to the other banks. Suppose that the Bank wishes to increase the interest rate. The banks' deposits at the Bank of England may be relatively small, perhaps because the Bank has sold Treasury bills, so reducing the banks' liquidity. In this case, the banks restore their liquidity by selling assets such as commercial bills to the discount houses. In turn, the discount houses find the money by borrowing from the Bank or by selling the bills to the Bank. If the Bank wants to raise interest rates it will increase the interest rate it charges the discount houses, and this rate will be passed on to the banks and will set a base from which other interest rates are calculated.

The Bank can also influence interest rates by changing expectations. If the Bank makes it clear that it expects interest rates either to rise or fall, this will change expectations and market forces will then move rates in the way desired by the authorities.

Despite the weapons at their disposal, the authorities cannot *control* interest rates. If inflation threatens, strong forces will push up rates, and if rates are rising internationally, national authorities find it very difficult to resist the trend.

One final point should be made about money creation and control. In future, the European Central Bank will be responsible for controlling the money supply of those countries that join the single currency, and this will also have an effect on the policies of those countries that do not join. These issues are discussed in Unit 26.

Summary

Money is important, not only to the individual, but also to the nation. Money supply affects prices, and interest rates affect both consumer spending and firms' investment. Hence governments intervene in the money market. They do this by limiting banks' ability to create money and by influencing the rate of interest.

Review questions

1. What is money, and what functions does it perform in a modern economy?
2. Show how banks can create money.
3. How does the trade-off between profitability and security influence banks' attitude to lending?
4. What is the difference between M0 and M4?
5. What functions does the Bank of England perform?
6. How can the government control the money supply?
7. What factors influence the demand for money?
8. Draw a diagram and show how the demand and supply of money determine the rate of interest.
9. To what extent can the Bank of England influence the level of interest rates?

Essay questions

1. How do banks create money? What factors constrain their ability to do this?
2. Describe how the government intervenes in the money market.

Reading 17.1

The Bank of England

The Bank of England is the central bank of the UK. Most countries have a central bank: for example, the Federal Reserve System in the United States; the Deutsche Bundesbank in Germany; the Banque de France and the Bank of Japan. Each differs a little from the ▷

others in the range of its activities, in the powers and techniques it can use, and in the nature of its relationship with its government. However, they all serve as bank to both their country's government and to its banking system. It is through the interaction of these two roles that central banks come to play their key part in carrying out monetary policies in their respective countries, that is, policies affecting the cost and availability of money and credit.

Source: *The Bank of England,* Bank of England Fact Sheet, September 1994.

Questions

1. How does the Bank of England serve as bank to the government and to the banking system?
2. How does it carry out 'policies affecting the cost and availability of money and credit'?

Reading 17.2

Operations in the domestic money market

In a modern market economy the main instrument of monetary policy is the short-term interest rate. Central banks have a variety of techniques for influencing interest rates, but they are all designed, in one way or another, to affect the cost of money to the banking system. In general, this is done by keeping the banking system short of money, and then lending the banks the money they need at an interest rate which the central bank decides. In this country, such influence is exercised through the Bank of England's daily operations in the money markets.

Source: *Monetary Policy in the United Kingdom,* Bank of England Fact Sheet, May 1994.

Questions

1. How can the Bank of England keep the banking system short of money?
2. Why should the Bank of England intervene in the money markets?
3. Look up the prices of short- and long-term gilts in the newspaper. Why do different securities have different interest rates?

Finance for firms

ECONOMICS IN THE NEWS

Eric Cantona's shock decision to quit soccer in July 1997 caused shares in Manchester United to fall by £8.7 million on its £441 million stock market valuation.

All firms need finance. They need it in the short term, for example to buy raw materials, and they need it in the long run to finance expansion.

This unit describes how firms find funds (see Figure 18.1). It therefore forms a link between the last unit, which was concerned with the role of money in the economy, and the next unit, which describes how firms decide whether or not to invest in a particular project.

One of the ideas in the last unit was that the money markets do not always work in the way that governments would like and that governments therefore intervene, for example to influence the rate of interest. In a very similar way, if capital markets worked perfectly, this unit would not be required, because firms with profitable opportunities would be able to raise money to finance their activities, while firms seeking investments which were not profitable would be unable to raise money. Unfortunately, we do not live in a perfect world. Some firms with good ideas cannot raise money, while others find it easy to raise funds for projects which ultimately fail.

Critics of the system argue that the problem is worse in the UK than in other competing countries and that this is one reason for the UK's relatively poor economic performance. Thus one reason why British Aerospace sold Rover to BMW was that it required risk finance and longer lines of bank finance than British bankers would provide. The banks would not supply sufficient credit because they said that British Aerospace should not borrow more than a pound for every pound of capital assets it had. In contrast, Honda in Japan can borrow £4 for every pound of capital.

The problem is particularly acute for small firms, partly because they are riskier than large firms and also because they have fewer sources of finance. These failures in the system indicate that there is a case for government intervention to help firms find finance for investment.

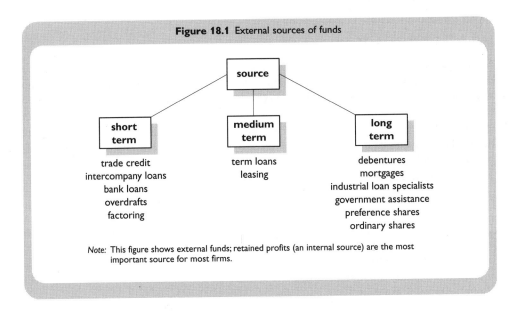

Figure 18.1 External sources of funds

```
                         source
            ┌───────────────┼───────────────┐
        short            medium            long
        term              term             term

     trade credit       term loans       debentures
   intercompany loans    leasing          mortgages
       bank loans                   industrial loan specialists
       overdrafts                    government assistance
        factoring                      preference shares
                                        ordinary shares
```

Note: This figure shows external funds; retained profits (an internal source) are the most important source for most firms.

Sources of short-term finance

In most economics, the phrase 'short term' does not refer to a specific time period, but instead indicates a period when certain constraints apply. For example, in the short term, firms can increase the amount of labour that they employ, but they cannot build a new factory. However, in the present context, we can indicate a time period. 'Short term' in the context of firms' finance usually suggests a period of about a year, but can be extended for up to two or three years. There are several ways in which firms can obtain finance for this length of time.

Trade credit

The basic idea behind **trade credit** is simple. Imagine a small furniture shop. If the shop has to pay on delivery for the furniture it has on display, and also pay on delivery for furniture ordered by its customers, then it will need considerable funds, not only to start up the business, but to continue, since it will always be paying out for goods before it receives any money. However, if the furniture suppliers offer it, say, two months' credit, then the firm can afford to have furniture on display and also to supply its customers before receiving payment. As a result, it will be able to order more furniture, and both supplier and retailer benefit.

Trade credit is the simplest way for a firm to finance its activities. It can provide benefits both to the firm which supplies credit and to the firm receiving it. These benefits, however, may be uneven, depending on the relative power of the two parties involved.

In some cases, the terms of credit are agreed between the two parties. Often, though, the stronger firm simply delays payment for goods received: for example, when a large firm buys goods from a relatively small supplier which is dependent on the buyer for continuing orders. The three factors which affect the relationship are:

1. The proportion of the firm's sales or purchases involved.
2. Monopolistic and monopsonistic power.
3. The strength of the firm's liquidity position.

A firm which is relatively strong in all three areas – possessing monopoly power, where the sales were only a small part of its total turnover, and whose liquidity position is strong – will be in a good position to exploit the other firm. Conversely, a firm with the opposite characteristics will be in a weak negotiating position. This is particularly important when credit is difficult to obtain or when interest rates are high. In these circumstances, large firms will often delay payments, and this is one reason why many small firms go out of business. Their debtors delay paying them, but their creditors insist on immediate payment, and firms which cannot pay are then made bankrupt.

Intercompany loans

Sometimes firms can obtain finance from other firms. This method originated in the USA before spreading to other countries, and by the early 1990s outstanding loans of this kind amounted to nearly £4 billion in the UK alone. These are short-term loans, usually of about six months' duration.

A firm seeking credit issues promissory notes to the public, in this case to other firms with surplus funds to invest for short periods. The ability of a firm to borrow in this way depends on its credit worthiness, and only a firm in a strong position would be able to obtain intercompany loans.

Bank loans and overdrafts

These are extremely important forms of finance for firms. In the last unit, we saw that bank advances were the largest source of bank assets and the interest they receive on these loans gives banks most of their profits.

Firms obtain money from banks in two main ways:

1. A loan can be obtained by a firm to provide working capital and is designed to last for a specific period. The money is credited to the firm's account and must be repaid by a certain date. The bank may charge a fee for arranging the loan and in addition charge interest. The interest rate will vary according to the credit worthiness of the borrower, so that a financially strong firm will be able to obtain loans at lower rates of interest than a new firm or one which is in some financial difficulties.

2. The other kind of short-term finance from banks is an **overdraft**. This gives the borrower the right to borrow from the bank up to a limited amount, but the period is not specified. It is therefore very useful for firms which have to borrow regularly, for example because their receipts are often delayed. A good example is a small building firm, wanting to build a few houses for sale, which will have to buy land, raw materials such as bricks, and also pay its workers, while its receipts will be delayed until the houses are built and sold. Hence the firm needs to borrow, though it may be able to start repaying some of the overdraft when the first house is sold.

Interest rates on overdrafts are not fixed, but fluctuate over time; they also vary according to the firm's financial strength. Because they fluctuate over time a firm can be lucky and benefit from falling rates, but the converse also applies and many firms have gone out of business because the interest charged by their bank has risen so high that they cannot pay that interest.

One advantage of an overdraft from the borrower's point of view is that the firm may not need to borrow all the money allowed by the bank, and so would only pay interest on the amount actually borrowed. Thus if its cash flow proves to be better than expected, a firm with an agreed overdraft limit of £100,000 may need to use only £80,000 of this, and so will only pay interest on £80,000. The main disadvantage of an overdraft is that it can be called in by the bank at any time. This may happen if the bank thinks that its loan is no longer secure, and decides to recover its money if possible before the firm sinks to a position where it cannot repay the loan.

Factoring

Factoring involves a variety of services provided by one firm to another. These services centre on the provision of sales accounting and debt collection services and protection against bad debts in conjunction with a credit facility. This can be helpful to a firm which is running short of current funds principally because it is owed money which it is finding difficult to collect. A factor will take on this responsibility and make funds available immediately.

The firm benefits from factoring in two ways. The first is that the factor pays the client firm the full value of debts at an agreed date less a service fee which may amount to 3 per cent of turnover. The second benefit is that the factor provides a financial facility which is very similar to an overdraft provided by a bank. Indeed, factoring can be regarded as one form of borrowing against a firm's assets, in this case debts. The similarity to banking is not surprising because most of the factoring firms are bank subsidiaries.

In addition to these financial services, factoring organisations provide other services, such as sales ledger management, that can be useful to firms which do not feel competent on this side of their business.

Factoring services are found in many countries. They are particularly popular in Italy and the USA, with the United Kingdom third in the list of countries using this system.

Exercise

Factoring service

If you sell goods or services to other businesses, you may experience cash-flow problems. Lombard NatWest offer a factoring service to help successful small businesses in this situation. You can receive up to 80 per cent of all approved invoices straight away, less Lombard NatWest's charges. You receive the rest as soon as your customers pay.

Lombard NatWest usually reduces the length of time that your customers take to pay. They will also run your sales ledger for you and keep you up to date at all times. The service charge is usually between 1.5 per cent and 3 per cent of the total value of your invoices. There is also a finance charge under the 'prepayment' arrangements at rates similar to our rates of interest for overdrafts. You can apply for the factoring service if your business sells at least £75,000 worth of goods and services to trade customers each year.

Source: National Westminster Bank, 1996.

Questions

1. Why do you think this service is not offered (a) to firms with a turnover of less than £75,000, and (b) firms trading with the public?

2. What advantages and disadvantages does the service offer to eligible firms?

Medium-term finance

If 'short term' in this context is one year stretching up to two or three, then 'medium term' can be regarded as a period of time which may be as short as eighteen months or as long as five or six years. There are two main forms of finance for industry which are useful in this period. The first is the bank, which may be willing to provide a term loan. The second involves leasing of equipment rather than the actual lending of money, and this can provide tax advantages.

Term loans

A **term loan** is a business loan which is provided for a specific period of time (hence the 'term'), usually more than a year, and which is not repayable on demand by the bank unless the borrower has broken the conditions of the loan. Most loans of this type are for one to five years. The loans may be made in sterling, but the development of the European Union has encouraged the granting of loans in other currencies – a facility which is useful to borrowers who intend to buy equipment from another country.

Term loans may be repayable in a lump sum at the end of the loan, or they may be repayable in part at specific periods leading up to the end of the loan. The second method may be useful to a firm which intends to use the money to buy equipment at set times in the near future and where returns on those investments will accrue before the final repayment: in other words, to correspond to the firm's expected cash flow.

Because interest rates in recent years have fluctuated so much, banks are now reluctant to make term loans at fixed rates of interest. As we have noted earlier, flexible rates can benefit borrowers when interest rates fall, but they can have devastating effects when they rise and firms cannot make the unexpected increased repayments. The actual rate of interest will depend in part on the bank's estimate of the risk involved, though it will usually be higher than that charged for a short-term loan in order to compensate the bank for the loss of liquidity and also the greater risk which arises when lending for relatively long periods.

Term loans offer a number of advantages to the borrower. Most importantly, the firm knows for sure that the money is available for a specific period of time, and that this will often be long enough for the firm to recover its investment expenditure. Furthermore, although the rate of interest is higher than that on short-term loans, the borrowing costs are lower than might be involved in raising money in other ways, such as the issue of shares.

Leasing

In leasing, the borrower enters into an agreement with an intermediary who provides equipment and, in return, the firm over time pays back enough to cover both the capital value of the equipment and also a notional interest on the capital. In essence, it is really very similar to a term loan except that the firm receives equipment rather than money.

Leasing can take a number of forms. A very common one is contract hire, when, for example, a firm leases motor vehicles for a fixed period. At the end of this period, say three years, the vehicles revert to the owner. The advantage of this type of scheme to the borrower is that is does not require any capital outlay and the lender is often responsible for repairs.

Longer-term finance

The difference between medium and long term in this context is very vague, but long term can be regarded as over four or five years.

Retained earnings

We have just said that the meaning of long term is not very precise, and here we immediately move away from the notion of a fixed period to a more permanent position.

The most important source of finance for most firms is retained profits, which is the way in which most firms finance their short-term needs for raw materials and equipment. Retained earnings also provide a foundation that can be used as a base for borrowing money for future developments.

When a firm makes a profit, some of this profit will be taken in the form of **corporation tax**, and then the firm will have to decide what to do with the rest. Part of the surplus will be paid to shareholders as dividends, and part retained by the firm to pay for expansion or replacement of obsolete machinery.

Retained profits have many advantages as a source of finance. The firm has total control. There are no banks or leasing firms to persuade, and no rate of interest to negotiate.

External loan capital

There are several ways in which a company can borrow money for relatively long periods.

Debentures

Debentures are loan documents issued by a company which pay a fixed rate of interest. They are secured on the assets of the company, and hence a company with assets of £1 million could not issue debentures for £2 million. The holder of a debenture is a creditor of the company, not an owner. The firm promises to pay interest on the loan each year and to repay the principal on an agreed date. By law, these sums must be repaid whether or not the company makes a profit, and debenture holders have first call on the assets of a company if it is unable to pay its way.

Firms choose to raise capital through debentures because this method gives them a fixed sum of money, ensures certainty about the rate of interest, and does not dilute the ownership of the company. The lenders may be general investors, institutional investors, or the loan may be arranged through the stock exchange. As in the case with short- and medium-term loans, the rate of interest will depend primarily on the general rate of interest in the economy, but the perceived creditworthiness of the company will also influence the rate. Risky companies will have to pay higher interest rates.

Mortgages

Just as an individual can borrow money for a long period of time to buy a house, so can firms mortgage their assets to borrow money for long periods. The firm's fixed assets such as buildings and land are the security offered to lenders, who may be banks or other financial institutions.

Industrial loan specialists

There are a number of firms, sometimes linked to merchant banks, which specialise in lending money to firms for long periods. One example is called 'Investors in Industry', which specialises in providing loan capital for medium-sized and larger businesses.

Government assistance

Central and local government both provide help for industries. Sometimes this is done as an aspect of regional policy to attract firms to areas of high unemployment, and sometimes it is focused on smaller firms which may have difficulty raising capital. The rationale for government assistance is that there are market failures in this area, so intervention is needed. The role of government is discussed in more detail later in this unit.

Preference shares

Preference shares can be regarded as a halfway house between debentures, discussed above, and ordinary shares which are discussed in the next section. Preference shares differ from debentures in that their owners are shareholders in the company, although, unlike ordinary shareholders, they have no say in the management of the company. Instead, they have preference when dividends are paid, so that if a company is not doing very well they are more likely to receive dividends than ordinary shareholders. This additional security makes these shares attractive to some investors and, because they are slightly riskier, they usually offer a higher rate of return than debentures.

From the company's point of view, preference shares can be attractive because they provide an additional source of capital without the need to allow the shareholder to participate in company decision making. Moreover, whereas interest on mortgages and debentures has to be paid whether or not the company is making a profit, preference shareholders do not need to be paid if the firm is making losses.

Equity finance

The stock market is such an important source of long-term funds that it needs a separate section. Its importance is made clear in Figure 18.2, which shows the comparative size of methods of raising **equity finance**. Total capital issues of UK industrial and commercial companies amounted to £13,114 million in 1996, of which ordinary shares accounted for 58 per cent.

The basic method of obtaining funds in this way is to issue **ordinary shares** – called 'ordinary' to distinguish them from preference shares. The owners of ordinary shares are

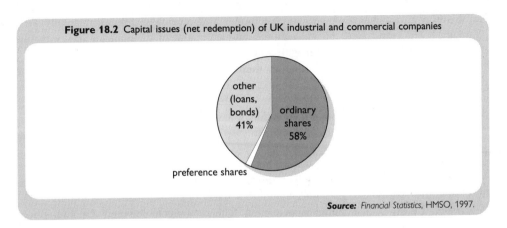

Figure 18.2 Capital issues (net redemption) of UK industrial and commercial companies

other (loans, bonds) 41%

ordinary shares 58%

preference shares

Source: *Financial Statistics, HMSO, 1997.*

the owners of the company (though to keep control of the company a few companies issue non-voting shares). They have the right to attend shareholders' meetings and to elect directors. They can benefit financially in two ways: by receiving dividends, and from a rise in the value of their shares. An increase in share value happens when the demand for shares exceeds the supply, which, in turn, will occur when investors expect the company's earnings to be higher in future.

In Unit 7 we saw that one reason for market failure was information failure. In the case of the stock market, if it is to work efficiently, any information relevant to the firm must be reflected in its share price. Hence the flow of information is crucial to the efficient working of the market. For this reason governments ban **insider trading**: that is, when an insider (e.g. someone who works for the firm) buys or sells shares using knowledge not available to the general public.

In the context of the stock market three forms of efficiency have been differentiated:

1. The weak form of efficiency occurs when historical information about prices or yields is fully reflected in share prices.

2. Semi-strong efficiency occurs when all publicly available information (e.g. company annual reports and newspaper reports) is reflected in the share price.

3. The strong form of efficiency asserts that any information, whether public or not, is accurately reflected in the share price. This would mean that there was no need to legislate against insider trading and that announcements about possible takeovers would have no effect on the share price since the information would already have changed the share price.

The British stock market satisfies the weak form of efficiency, and also perhaps the semi-strong form, though not everyone makes use of available information. There is little evidence to support the notion that the strong form is characteristic of the UK – or any other – stock market.

Bringing a new company to the stock market

Because large sums of money are involved, without detailed regulation there would be considerable opportunity for people to make huge profits by cheating. Hence the procedures for bringing a new company to the stockmarket are carefully regulated. It can therefore be an expensive way to raise money and is only suitable for relatively large companies. The firm has to provide an accurate statement of its financial affairs and its past trading performance, together with an estimate of its prospects.

In addition to this financial information, there are legal barriers to be crossed, and firms have to appoint advisers to handle the process. These advisers are called issuing houses and are usually merchant banks. They advise the firm on the terms and methods of going public, and also on a share price which they consider will ensure that all the shares on offer are sold. To assist in this objective, the issuing house may guarantee to buy any shares not sold.

The precise method can vary, but the most common method used in the UK is called *offer for sale*. Here, the company sells shares at a fixed price to an issuing house, who, in turn, sells the shares to the public, again at a fixed price and with a minimum value guaranteed by an underwriting arrangement. The difference between the two prices represents the issuing house's profit. The underwriters are usually pension funds or insurance companies, who buy their shares at a discount as a reward for guaranteeing a purchase in advance.

Because the procedure is complex, it is also costly. The company has to hire advisers, print and distribute a prospectus, advertise, and pay underwriting and registrar's fees. These costs tend not to vary much with the size of the issue. They can therefore be regarded as a fixed cost, and this acts to deter relatively small companies from using this method of raising finance.

Rights issues

It is not only new firms that offer shares on the stock market. Firms which already have a listing on the exchange can find it a useful way to raise additional capital. Thus in 1991 ASDA issued additional shares to reduce the £900 million debt it had incurred when it bought 60 Gateway stores. Other companies issue shares to finance new developments such as a new factory or an expansion overseas.

When an existing firm issues new shares, these are called **rights issues**. The stock exchange insists that these shares must be offered first to existing shareholders in proportion to their existing holdings, so that an investor who held 10 per cent of the company's shares would be offered 10 per cent of the new issue. This stipulation is to ensure that ownership need not be diluted; existing owners can keep control if they so wish. In addition, existing shareholders benefit because these shares are offered at a discount on the price of existing shares.

Raising capital by existing firms is easier and cheaper than it is for new firms, primarily because existing firms already have a listing on the exchange. Thus the value of the company's assets is already known, and the current share price gives a good indication of the likely value of the additional shares which are on offer.

The price of the new shares will depend largely on how prospective investors see the company. Since the price of shares can fall as well as rise – the resignation of Eric Cantona discussed in the opening commentary to this unit is an example – prospective investors are often cautious. If they believe that the firm needs additional capital because it is in financial difficulties, then the shares will be offered at a substantial discount. However, if they are convinced that the additional money will be used to finance profitable developments, then the price of the new shares will be relatively high. In both cases, the shares will probably have to be sold at a lower price than existing shares: they represent an additional supply, and, as you will remember, an increase in supply, whether of shares or goods, leads to a fall in price.

Small firms

Small firms were discussed in Unit 4. Figure 18.3 reminds us of their importance in creating employment. Their importance, in fact, varies greatly by industry. There are not many small firms building jet engines, but they are prominent in industries as diverse as agriculture and hairdressing: that is, in those industries where there are relatively few economies of scale. Whatever the industry, small firms face similar problems in the financial aspects of their activities.

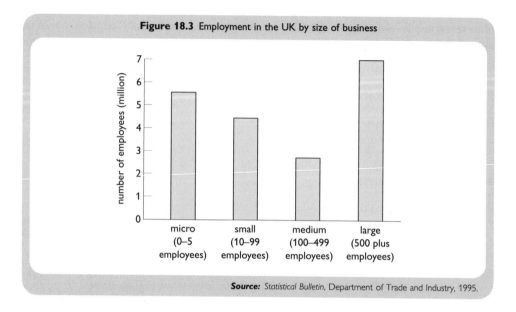

Figure 18.3 Employment in the UK by size of business

Source: Statistical Bulletin, Department of Trade and Industry, 1995.

The financial difficulties of small firms

The difficulties faced by small firms in raising finance is a long-standing problem. As long ago as 1931 the Macmillan Report said that small and medium-sized firms reported difficulty in raising finance. The same conclusion was reached by the Radcliffe Report in 1959, which stated that 'the growth of small firms may be impeded because they lack some of the facilities open to larger companies for obtaining capital'.

So, what are these difficulties?

● First, smaller companies tend to have more variable profits. A large firm may produce several goods, so that when one does badly the others may provide stability. A small firm does not have this stability; in a good year profits may be very high, but in a bad year the firm may go out of business. Hence there is often a need for short-term finance to carry the business into the next recovery.

● Small firms are riskier than large ones. This makes financial institutions reluctant to lend, and if they do, it is at higher rates of interest than large firms would pay. According to Midland Bank testimony to the House of Commons, typical margins were 1.5 per cent above base rate for companies with turnover exceeding £10 million, but rose to 3 per cent above base rate when turnover was less than £1 million. Small firms employing less than 30 people were charged 3 to 5 per cent above base rate, and this was doubled if the firm breached its overdraft limit even briefly.

● Large concerns have more sources of finance than small ones. They can make use of all the sources discussed above, while some, such as the issue of shares on the stock market, are not available to small firms.

● Large firms sometimes exploit their power by delaying payments to their smaller suppliers. This causes cash-flow problems for the small firm.

Despite these difficulties, both the banks and the government work hard to make funds available. The banks offer a variety of services. The NatWest Bank, for example, offers:

- business development loans;
- leasing contract hire;
- factoring;
- reserve accounts;
- business insurance service; and
- a variety of advisory leaflets such as *The Business Start-up Guide*, and the help of small firm business advisers.

Other banks offer similar services.

The role of government

The government becomes involved because markets fail. It is also involved because future economic growth depends in part on present investment, and if firms cannot raise finance on terms similar to those obtained by competing firms in other countries, then the country will fall behind.

The UK system of financing industry has some similarities with those in competing countries: for example, retained earnings are the main source of finance in most countries. However, there are differences:

- In the UK, there is a greater reliance on overdrafts. For example, overdrafts account for 56 per cent of small firm debt in the UK compared to 14 per cent in Germany. This is a disadvantage because overdrafts can be called in at any time, and they are therefore not conducive to long-term planning.
- Dividend payouts to shareholders are higher in the UK than in countries such as Germany and France. Thus, for a given level of profit, less is retained for investment.

Government is aware of the problems and has introduced a number of schemes to mitigate them. In 1981 the Small Firms Loan Guarantee Scheme was introduced. This scheme is designed to promote investment when conventional loans are not available due to lack of security or proven track record. Under this scheme, loans up to £250,000 can be guaranteed by the government. In return for the guarantee, borrowers pay a premium of $\frac{1}{2}$ to $1\frac{1}{2}$ per cent of the loan. In the period 1994/5, the number of loans guaranteed under this scheme rose from 3851 to 6207. Yet despite this rise in numbers, the sums involved are relatively small, amounting to only £94 million.

In 1992, the Bank of England began an initiative on the financing of small firms. This examined the problems of such firms. Its second report identified a number of areas for concern:

- Banks need to continue to make progress in developing and packaging loan products, and in increasing the transparency of decision making.
- The need to increase the ability of small firms to change banks more easily, so that they can take advantage of the different services provided.

- The financial skills of small firms must be improved.
- The problem of late payment of trade debt must be alleviated.
- Small firms should receive help to trade in overseas markets.
- Coordination of public policy in these areas.

Summary

Finance for industry is important. Future prosperity depends largely on present investment and this requires funds that cannot usually be generated inside the firm. Hence the need for external finance.

In most cases, short-term finance can be provided by the banks, but this is often at high rates of interest, and overdrafts can be recalled at any time, which makes them unsuitable for long-term projects.

The stock market is another source of funds. This does provide large sums of long-term finance, but this method is not available for small firms, and government schemes have not solved the problems facing this group of firms.

Review questions

1. In what circumstances might a firm use trade credit as a source of finance?
2. Compare and contrast bank loans and overdrafts as sources of short-term finance.
3. Outline the advantages and disadvantages of factoring to a firm.
4. When might a firm make use of a term loan?
5. Why are retained earnings important to a firm?
6. What is the difference between debentures and preference shares?
7. Outline the procedures needed to bring a firm to the stock market. Why is this not a suitable method of raising finance for small firms?
8. What difficulties do small firms face in raising external finance?
9. What part does government play in mitigating market failures in the capital market?

Essay questions

1. Outline the main sources of funds available to firms in the UK. What advantages and disadvantages attach to these methods?
2. Why do small firms face special problems in raising finance. What methods are open to them to solve this problem?

Reading 18.1

Business finance

Business Development Loan

There may be times when you need to borrow money to develop your business: for example, to invest in new equipment, to move to new premises, or to expand your market. If so, a NatWest Business Development Loan can be the answer.

With a Business Development Loan you can:

- benefit from a fixed interest rate and fixed term;
- borrow from £2000 to £250,000; and
- repay over a period from 1 to 20 years.

To ease repayments during the first two years you can arrange to pay only the interest in this period.

Other business loans

Although a fixed interest rate has many benefits, you may decide that a variable rate of interest would suit your needs better. If so, we can help by providing a variable rate loan. We also have a number of special lending schemes. For example, with the Small Firms Loan Guarantee Scheme, a guarantee from the Department of Trade and Industry enables us to provide loans to businesses which have a realistic business plan but lack security or a track record.

Overdraft

An overdraft is flexible and versatile, which makes it a convenient way to finance day-to-day spending. You control the amount you borrow within a sensible limit decided by us. The interest rate is variable and you are not charged interest for the overdraft when you do not use it.

Leasing

When you want to buy new plant or equipment we can help you to raise finance for amounts over £5000. We can offer leasing and contract hire facilities through our subsidiary company, Lombard Business Finance. Your business benefits from the assets without having to lay out a large amount.

Source: National Westminster Bank, 1996.

Questions

1. What is the difference between a fixed and a variable rate loan? What are the advantages and disadvantages of each?

2. How do the facilities for loans discussed here differ from those offered by banks to students?

3. If you were a small business and wanted to borrow up to £20,000 to finance new equipment and also raw materials to expand your business, which service would you choose? Why?

Reading 18.2

Finance for small firms

Banks continue to be the most significant source of external finance for small firms. All of the banks remain wholeheartedly committed to the small business market, recognising that the sector offers potential both in terms of growth and profits. Provisions against bad debts have continued their steep downward trend, reflecting the improvement in the quality of banks' loan books. This trend towards quality has been enhanced by the banks increasingly seeking to base lending decisions on business intentions and cash flow, with the availability of security a secondary (but still important) consideration. . . . as the number of small firms has continued to rise during the recovery, increasing competition and the inherent riskiness of the sector are likely to reassert their influence.

Source: Bank of England, *Finance for Small Firms*, 1996, p. 15.

Questions

1. What sources of finance other than banks are available to small firms?

2. What do you think is the significance of banks basing their lending criteria on 'business intentions and cash flow', rather than security?

3. Why is the sector inherently risky?

Investment appraisal

NOTICE IS HEREBY GIVEN,

THAT the TOLLS arising at the several Toll Gates or Bars hereunder-mentioned, erected upon and across the Turnpike road leading from GLOSSOP to MARPLE BRIDGE will be put up to be LET BY AUCTION to the best bidder for the term of One Year, at the house of Mr John Wagstaffe in Glossop on Thursday the 17th day of May at the hour of two in the afternoon.

The said Tolls were let the last year for the several undermentioned sums, and will be put up at those, or such other sums respectively, as shall be declared immediately the putting up; and at the same time whoever happens to be the best bidder must be prepared to give security to the satisfaction of the Trustees.

Rose Brow Bar	£105
Holehouse Bar	260
Glossop Mill Bar	100
Glossop Bar	90

MATTHEW ELLISON
Clerk to the said Trustees
Glossop Hall, April 16th, 1821

Source: *Manchester Guardian,* 5 May 1821, reprinted on 4 May 1996.

The entrepreneur

In Unit 1 we discussed why firms exist and also their objectives. Thus whether or not a firm's aim is to *maximise* profits, it is certainly essential for adequate profits to be made. Now profits do not appear by chance; they have to be planned, and the person or persons in a firm responsible for doing this is the **entrepreneur**. The term 'entrepreneur' was coined two hundred years ago by a French economist, Jean Baptist Say. He defined the job of the entrepreneur as reallocating resources to improve productivity and yield.

The characteristics of the entrepreneur vary according to the individual. Some of those characteristics are as follows:

- An ability to overturn – revolutionise – known ways of production.
- An opportunism and confidence to make changes.
- An alertness to the possibilities of making profit.
- A willingness to bear risk in order to make profits.

The entrepreneur is therefore an agent of change. Moreover, the characteristics listed above suggest that an entrepreneur will be someone with a particular personality. This is very true – someone who is cautious, uncertain and indecisive is unlikely to become a successful entrepreneur.

However, despite this emphasis on individualism, the emergence of successful entrepreneurs is often linked to social factors. A static society offers little opportunity for entrepreneurial talents to flourish, no matter what individuals' personal characteristics may be. Hence it is probable that change in society enables individuals to emerge who enhance that change.

Entrepreneurship also emerges in some immigrant groups, and religion may also play a part. Centuries ago, the Protestant Huguenots were expelled from France and were subsequently prominent in the development of the cotton industry in Lancashire. Similarly, Quakers and Jews have long traditions of entrepreneurship, and, more recently, Asian immigrants have been active in developing new businesses in the UK.

So far we have presented the entrepreneur as a successful individual. Yet modern firms are large and complex organisations, and the modern entrepreneur has often to work in such an organisation. Certainly, the growth of the large firm has caused some debate as to whether or not a manager in a firm can be regarded as an entrepreneur. Traditionally in economics, profit has been regarded as the reward of the entrepreneur, just as wages are the reward of the worker. Many managers will be prevented by their job description from taking decisions about the allocation of resources and will not receive profits directly. In this case, some economists would argue that managers are not entrepreneurs. In other instances, managers will be empowered to make innovative decisions and will receive rewards not only as bonuses, but also as some form of profit sharing. For our purposes, we can regard such managers as entrepreneurs.

The factors affecting private sector investment

Entrepreneurs operate within a capitalist society where profits are all important, and where standing still allows competitors sooner or later to produce new products or to find new ways of producing existing products. Hence the entrepreneur is constantly forced to

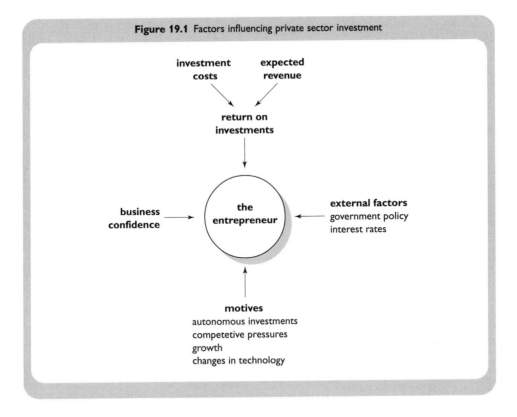

Figure 19.1 Factors influencing private sector investment

consider change, and change requires investment. Figure 19.1 lists some of the factors which influence the decision to invest.

Motives

- The fact that existing machinery is worn out may initiate investment. This is sometimes called *autonomous investment* and it is a recurring feature affecting all firms. A hairdresser may have to replace scissors, for example, while at the other end of the scale, a bank may have to replace its computer system, or a car manufacturer an obsolete production line.

- *Competitive pressures* provide another factor. If one firm is introducing new machinery, then others will have to follow. A generation ago a weaver in the cotton industry might be expected to work with four looms; in the course of a decade or so, competitive pressures increased the number to forty. This development was possible because the new machines required less attention and so cut labour costs.

- Firms may be motivated by a desire for *growth*. Some growth may be achieved by taking on more workers, but diminishing returns will soon set in unless they have machines to work with, and new machines require investment.

● Finally, *changes in technology* spur investment. If a new machine becomes available which does the job more quickly or at less cost, then firms will be forced to introduce it. For example, for many years banks recorded each transaction by hand in bank books. Computers made this unnecessary, and no bank could now operate without an extensive computer network.

Business confidence

The extent to which these motivational factors influence the decision to invest will depend in part on business confidence. Keynes called this 'animal spirits', and sometimes these will be high. Entrepreneurs filled with confidence as a result of a successful sale or good news in the papers will be more likely to invest than those who are pessimistic. This is one reason why future investment is difficult to predict. Furthermore, the effect of confidence – or the lack of it – can be cumulative. Thus, if a large firm is optimistic about the future it will place new orders; entrepreneurs in the firms receiving orders will be affected in turn and may well increase their own investment as a result. On the other hand, if a large firm cancels an order, the effects of this setback will also spread, and the resulting pessimism will lead to a fall in investment.

External factors

External factors are critical to investment decisions. For instance, a rise in interest rates will make it more expensive for firms to borrow money and, other things being equal, will tend to lead to a fall in investment. Changes in government policy will also affect decision making. Sometimes such changes will simply increase or decrease the level of optimism, sometimes they can have a more direct effect, for example when a government changes the method of company taxation, but either way, investment will be affected to some degree.

Costs and revenue

At the top of Figure 19.1 are the topics which form the heart of this unit. The decision on whether or not to invest will depend finally on a comparison of the expected costs of the investment and the revenue which the investment will produce. There are several methods of analysing the relationship between these costs and revenue, and each will be discussed in turn.

Project classification

To some extent, investment decisions will depend on the type of project. Some types of project will require detailed and expensive analysis. Others will be more routine, with the decision coming through established procedures. Projects can be classified as follows:

● *Replacement projects* consist of spending to replace worn-out or damaged equipment. This will be necessary if the firm is to continue in the line of business that needs this equipment. For example, a firm selling agricultural machinery over a wide area will have to provide its sales staff with cars, and these will need replacing regularly. Consequently, such firms will have a policy of replacing these cars, let us say, every two years because of the high mileage. The decision to replace will therefore be made without much discussion, perhaps focusing only on the type and expense of car to be provided. Similarly, a large organisation such as the Post Office will have a set procedure for replacing its huge fleet of vehicles.

● *Cost reduction projects* include investments to replace serviceable but obsolete equipment. Spending in this category is intended to cut spending elsewhere, for example on staffing or raw materials. A detailed analysis is usually required for projects in this category.

● *Mandatory investments* are those which are required by government legislation, for example to increase safety at work. They are usually non-revenue raising, and because they are compulsory, investigation is often limited to finding the cheapest way of fulfilling legal requirements.

● *Expansion projects* involve expenditure to increase output. This may require the building of a new factory or other expensive facility. It can also involve decisions to buy other firms, to develop new products, or to expand into overseas markets. Expansion projects usually require detailed forecasts of expected income and expenditure, and a complex and thorough investigation is therefore required. We will concentrate on this type of project for much of the remainder of this unit.

Capital markets in theory

We began our investigation into the market for goods with an examination of perfect competition. In the same way, we can examine capital markets by looking initially at the theory of perfect capital markets. This is an economic model based on a set of assumptions that helps to explain how firms make investment decisions. The assumptions underlying the model are as follows:

1. There are no transaction costs involved in raising money to finance investment.
2. Firms can borrow or lend as much money as they want at a common rate of interest which does not vary over time (you may notice the similarity here to the assumption underlying perfect competition, namely, that the firm is a price taker because there are so many buyers and sellers that no one can influence the price of goods).
3. There is no intervention by government, for example by imposing taxes.
4. Firms try to maximise profits.
5. Decision makers have perfect knowledge of relevant information.

These assumptions mean that the firm will make any profitable investment, since it will always be able to raise sufficient capital to finance the investment.

In a perfect capital market, entrepreneurs will undertake any investment that brings in a higher return than the market rate of interest. Table 19.1 gives a simplified example which assumes both an interest rate of 10 per cent and also that all money for the investment has to be borrowed. In this case, investment A would be selected; investment B would not, since the return on investment is less than the market rate of interest.

Table 19.1 Investment in a perfect capital market

Project	A	B
Investment required (£)	1000	1250
Amount to be borrowed (£)	1000	1250
Interest rate (%)	10.0	10.0
Total cost (capital + interest) (£)	1100	1375
Return from investment (£)	1150	1350
Percentage return (%)	15.0	8.0

In the real world, however, perfect capital markets do not exist. In particular, interest rates are not common or constant over time, and firms do not have access to unlimited funds. Consequently, we make use of the imperfect capital market theory which refines the perfect market theory in a number of ways.

First, this theory assumes that there is not a single rate of interest, but that interest rates vary between firms. Second, limitless funds are not available, so that entrepreneurs sometimes have to forego desirable projects which they believe will be profitable because they are unable to borrow to finance the investment. Instead, they have to decide which will be the most profitable projects: that is, they have to rank possible projects. Third, the timing of cash flows as well as total profits have to be estimated. Many companies go out of business in the expansion phase because the money does not come in as they had expected and they simply run out of funds.

Moreover, in an imperfect capital market decisions may be taken for non-financial reasons. For instance, in the days of apartheid, some companies were reluctant to invest in South Africa; today, the USA penalises companies which invest in Cuba. Hence political decisions may sometimes prevent profit maximisation.

Knowledge concerning possible investment opportunities may also be incomplete in an imperfect market. This problem may be due to lack of proper market research that could have identified potential markets. However, it may also be because forecasting the future is difficult. As a result, entrepreneurs' optimism or pessimism will affect investment decisions, with the inevitable corollary that some profitable opportunities will be missed, while some investments will turn out to be loss making.

Finally, the techniques used by the entrepreneur may be inadequate, and it is to these techniques that we now turn.

Discounting the future

Before analysing **discounting** techniques in detail, a general point needs to be made. Imagine that someone gives you a job in the vacation. At the end of the week you are offered a choice: 'Would you prefer your £100 wages now or in a year's time?' The answer is obvious: you would prefer your money now, and there are several reasons for this preference:

● In a year's time, £100 will buy less than it does now because inflation will cause prices to rise in the interim period.

- Your £100, if paid now, can be invested straightaway and start to bring in interest.

- If you have the money now you have the choice to spend it now or in a year's time. Delayed receipt denies you this choice.

- There is a risk in waiting a year for your money. The person who owes it to you may die, disappear, deny that the money is owed, or go bankrupt and so be unable to pay you.

These reasons mean that a pound now is worth more than a pound in the future. Put another way, future returns have to be *discounted* to find their present value.

People will have high discount rates for a variey of reasons: if inflation is high, if they need the money now, if interest rates are high, or if the payee's future seems uncertain or risky. Students have very high discount rates, for example, because they need money now.

To estimate your discount rate, answer the following questions:

1. *Would you prefer £100 now or £110 in a year?* Students inevitably choose the money now. This means that their discount rate is more than 10 per cent.

2. *Would you prefer £100 now or £120 in a year's time?* Again, most students would prefer the money now, so their discount rate is more than 20 per cent.

3. Continue increasing the amount offered in the future until you find it difficult to decide between the money offered now and that promised in the future. That is your discount rate. For example, if you find it difficult to decide between £100 now and £130 in a year's time, then your discount rate is about 30 per cent.

The formula for calculating the **present value** of a sum of money to be received in the future is:

$$PV = \frac{FV}{(1+r)^n}$$

where

PV = present value;
FV = future value;
r = rate of interest; and
n = number of years of the investment.

For example, if the sum of £100 was to be received in 3 years' time and the rate of interest was 10 per cent, its present value would be:

$$PV = \frac{£100}{(1+0.1)^3} = \frac{£100}{1.331} = £75.13$$

Table 19.2 shows the present value of a pound at different discount rates.

The implications of discounting are important. Investment receipts are in the future, and if these are discounted, their value diminishes. At a discount rate of 10 per cent, for example, a pound received in ten years' time will only be worth 39 pence now. At a discount rate of 20 per cent, it will only be worth 16 pence. Therefore, investments which give rise to a stream of income for a long time in the future will be less likely to receive the go-ahead than projects which give high returns for short periods of time. This helps to

Table 19.2 The present value of £1 at different discount rates

Year	10%	15%	20%
1	0.909	0.870	0.833
2	0.826	0.756	0.694
3	0.751	0.658	0.579
4	0.683	0.572	0.482
5	0.621	0.497	0.402
6	0.564	0.432	0.335
7	0.513	0.376	0.279
8	0.467	0.327	0.233
9	0.424	0.284	0.194
10	0.386	0.247	0.162

explain the phenomenon of 'short termism' which was discussed in the last unit. Firms in other countries may have lower discount rates and so be more willing to invest in long-term projects.

Payback period

The emphasis on short-term rewards explains why some firms use the **payback period** to determine whether or not a project should go ahead. The basic idea of the payback approach is that the entrepreneur measures the number of years it is expected to take to recover the initial investment. Sometimes this is done using discounting; sometimes expected returns in the future are not discounted and actual figures are used instead, which will make projects seem more attractive. Another way to view the payback period method is to think of it as a **breakeven period**. The shorter the payback period, the more desirable is the project; the longer the payback period, the less desirable is the project. The article at the beginning of this unit illustrates a situation where the payback period is only one year (because the right to collect tolls is only for one year), so that it is relatively easy to calculate its desirability, although there is some uncertainty as to the returns. For example, how many people will pass the toll bars? And what charges will maximise income?

Using the payback period to determine whether an investment should go ahead has two distinct advantages. In the first place, it is simple. A decision is made that projects with a payback period of less than four years will go ahead, while those with payback periods of more than four years will not. Alternatively, a firm which is considering which of two projects to finance may choose the one with the shortest payback period. In both cases, all that the firm has to do is to estimate the payback period. Second, it reduces risk. The near future is more certain than the distant future, so a method of evaluating investments which emphasises early returns will cut the risk of unforeseen future developments.

However, the payback period method also has disadvantages. For example, a number of excellent projects may have relatively long payback periods. Building a new factory, training the workers and obtaining new markets for the product will take much longer than merely buying a new machine, yet building the factory may be the best option for the firm in the long run. An example will illustrate this point. A firm has £40,000 to invest and has to choose between two projects, both costing this amount. The estimated returns for the projects are:

Year	A (£)	B (£)
1	15,000	5,000
2	14,000	6,000
3	8,000	10,000
4	4,000	15,000
5	0	20,000
6	0	25,000
7	0	30,000

Project A has a payback period of just under four years, while project B would be four months into the fifth year before it recouped its costs. Hence the payback period criterion would mean that A would go ahead and B would not. Yet it is clear that, in the long run, B is a better investment (though this advantage would diminish if future returns were discounted).

Projects which take a number of years to pay back their investment are characteristic of those which involve the development of new markets or new products – markets and products which the economy emphatically needs if it is to succeed in a competitive world environment. Hence there are suggestions that the payback method leads to short-termism – the weakness of the United Kingdom economy. Nevertheless, while this criticism has considerable strength, it is not true of the entire economy. The pharmaceutical industry is one of Britain's strongest, yet its products have a very long payback period. If that industry used the payback method of investment appraisal, then very few new medicines would be developed.

The benefits of the payback method, particularly its simplicity, means that it will continue to be used as a method of making investment decisions, and particularly the minor investment decisions which regularly confront a firm. But its serious inadequacies mean that large investments require more sophisticated methods of appraisal.

Net present value and internal rate of return

These two methods of investment appraisal are closely related. They both involve the same steps, and usually – though not always – give the same recommendation as to the desirability of a proposed investment.

Net present value

The basic rule using the **net present value** (**NPV**) method is to ask: 'Does the present value of the returns exceed the present value of the costs?' If the answer is yes, then the project should go ahead since it will increase profits.

There are several steps to be taken in order to answer this question. First, the firm has to estimate the costs. In some cases, this will be relatively easy: for instance, if the proposed investment is to buy a machine, then quotations can be obtained. In other cases, however, estimating the costs will be time-consuming and the results only approximate. This would be the case where the project involved developing a new market overseas. An example would be Marks & Spencer's decision to extend their operations to France, which required them to estimate not only the costs of buying property in France, but also other costs such as taxes, buying in services such as electricity, publicity and staff recruitment, training and wages. Costs such as these, some of which lie in the future, would be difficult to measure precisely.

The second step is to estimate future returns – and if estimating costs is imprecise, then forecasting future returns is much more so. Returning to our Marks & Spencer example, they would have had to try to forecast future sales – a very difficult task when they had no experience of the French market.

Third, both future costs and future benefits have to be discounted, so the firm has to decide its discount rate. Companies involved in risky operations (e.g. drilling for oil) will have higher discount rates than those involved in more mundane operations. Whatever the rate chosen, however, since returns are in the future and costs tend to bunch in the present, a high discount rate will reduce the likelihood of the present value of future returns exceeding present value of costs.

Table 19.3 gives a simplified example to illustrate the NPV method. In this example, we have assumed a project that requires an initial investment of £500 and has no future costs. The returns start in one year's time and continue for ten years. The discount rate chosen is 10 per cent so that £100 received in one year's time has a present value of £90.9; a receipt of £100 in two years' time has to be discounted twice and so has a present value of £82.6, and so on. In this case, the present value of costs is £500 (these do not have to be discounted since they occur in the current year) and the present value of returns is £614. Since the present value of returns is greater than the present value of costs, the project should go ahead. If the discount rate was higher, the project might be turned down. For example, if the chosen discount rate was 20 per cent, then the stream of returns would be

Table 19.3 Net present value at a discount rate of 10 per cent (£)

Year	Actual cost	Present value of costs	Actual returns	Present value of returns
0	500	500	0	0.0
1			100	90.9
2			100	82.6
3			100	75.1
4			100	68.3
5			100	62.1
6			100	56.4
7			100	51.3
8			100	46.7
9			100	42.4
10			100	38.6
Total	500	500	1000	614.4

£83, £69, £58, and after ten years, only £16, giving a total for discounted receipts of only £419. Since this is less than the cost, the project would be rejected.

The formula for calculating net present value is:

$$\text{NPV} = \frac{A_1}{1+r} + \frac{A_2}{(1+r)^2} + \frac{A_3}{(1+r)^3} + \cdots + \frac{A_n}{(1+r)^n} - I$$

where:

A = net amount of cash flow in a particular year
r = the firm's discount rate
n = the length of the project
I = the initial cost of the investment

Exercise

Does it pay to buy Shearer?

Entrepreneurs are in business to make money – but football may be different. Newcastle United bought Alan Shearer for £15 million, but if this is written down over 5 years (the period of his contract) and his wages are added in he could be costing the club £5 million a year. Since the reward for winning the Champions League is about £5 or £6 million, buying Shearer is uneconomic.

Questions

1. What method of investment appraisal is being used here?
2. Re-read Unit 1. What, if any, are Newcastle United's objectives?
3. What method of investment appraisal do you think would be appropriate for a professional football club? An amateur club?

Internal rate of return

This approach builds on the net present value approach. In this case, however, the method is to calculate that rate of discount which will make the present value of costs equal to the present value of benefits. This rate of discount is called the **internal rate of return (IRR)** and the rule governing investment is that a project should go ahead if the internal rate of return exceeds the firm's discount rate.

In the example of NPV given above, the investment would go ahead if the firm's discount rate was 10 per cent, but would be blocked if the discount rate was 20 per cent. It follows that at some point between 10 per cent and 20 per cent the future stream of costs would just equal the future stream of benefits. In this case it can be computed at just over 15 per cent. This is the internal rate of return.

Finding the IRR is a matter of trial and error. The easiest way is to use a computer programme which will do this for you, but Figure 19.2 shows how it can be done approximately. In this figure we assume that the relationship between discount rates

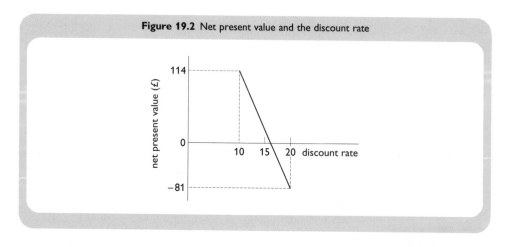

Figure 19.2 Net present value and the discount rate

and the IRR is linear. If discounting at 10 per cent gives a net present value of £114, i.e. (£614 – £500), and discounting at 20 per cent gives a net present value of –£81, i.e. (£419 – £500), then graphing these results will show approximately the point at which the IRR is zero.

Choosing between the NPV and IRR methods

The NPV method has several merits:

- It gives a clear quantitative result.
- It emphasises the time value of money, and this makes it superior to methods which do not involve discounting.
- It involves maximisation of present values of future cash flows and so facilitates profit maximisation.
- The discount rate reflects the rate of interest which firms would have to pay to borrow the money.

The IRR method also has some advantages:

- It is easier to understand a percentage return as opposed to a figure for NPV, and this is an advantage for decision makers in the firm who are familiar with the idea of rates of return (e.g. it is easier to understand a rate of return of 15 per cent as opposed to a net present value of £114).
- Managers do not need to chose a discount rate. Instead they can decide if a certain rate of return is acceptable.

The two methods usually give the same result. They differ when the cash flows are not smooth, for example when the stream of benefits moves from positive to negative and then back to positive.

Purists prefer the NPV method, principally because the alternative IRR method is a relative one: that is, it compares returns with the initial investment. The IRR method takes no account of the absolute magnitude of that initial investment, and it therefore does not distinguish between large investments with a good rate of return and small investments giving very good returns. This can be a serious limitation, since nearly all investments in practice will have different capital outlays and different streams of revenue. Despite this drawback the IRR method is prevalent, largely because it is easier to understand than the NPV method.

Risk

In several places in this unit we have pointed out that investment involves risk. Occasionally, one risk factor, such as a change in government taxation policy, will affect almost all firms. Sometimes unforeseen risk will hit just one industry. Thus in 1996 the possibility that 'mad cow disease' in the UK could spread to humans caused a huge fall in beef consumption throughout Europe and led to an EU decision to ban British exports of beef. In other instances, the risks will be more local. For example, a firm introducing a new product will often be unable to estimate future demand, or a promising new method of production may run into unforseen snags.

How, then, can entrepreneurs take account of risk and uncertainty? One way, which we have already discussed in Unit 5, concerns diversification. A firm which diversifies will face less risk because if one product fails the others produced by the company will allow the firm to continue in business. It is a method usually only available to large companies, however. Hence a small builder who puts houses on the market which don't sell may well go bankrupt, whereas a large building firm may be able to afford to sell the same houses at a loss and rely on other estates to carry the business.

Nevertheless, there are several ways in which all firms can reduce the adverse effects of risk. Most of these methods depend on assessing the *probability* of possible outcomes. In turn, this depends on the firm making accurate estimates of the likelihood of possible outcomes. Few firms will plan for the possibility of the Earth being hit by a meteorite from space, but most will be able to assess the likelihood of more probable risks such as a new competitor entering the market.

Game theory provides one way in which firms can reduce risk. For example, a firm planning to build a new factory in order to increase output will need to estimate the level of future demand: too large a factory and money will have been spent to no good purpose; too small a factory and the firm will still be faced by excess demand. One approach to this problem is for the firm to estimate the probability of several likely levels of demand and then undertake NPV analysis for each possibility. In this case, the factory should be built to the size that gives the highest NPV.

One alternative is to adopt a cautious approach, perhaps best suited to the pessimistic investor who asks, 'What will be the consequences if this goes wrong?' A strategy is then adopted which minimises the risks all round – and probably reduces the size of the profits too if the investment is successful. Conversely, an optimist might choose an approach which seems to offer the highest return, thus increasing the risk element considerably. However, a compromise approach is available: the firm should use a weighted average of the best and worst possible outcomes for each possible investment. The weighting will depend on the optimism/pessimism of the particular investor. One who is risk adverse might give a weighting of, say, 70 per cent to the minimum payoff and 30 per cent to the maximum payoff; an investor who is more optimistic could well reverse these weightings.

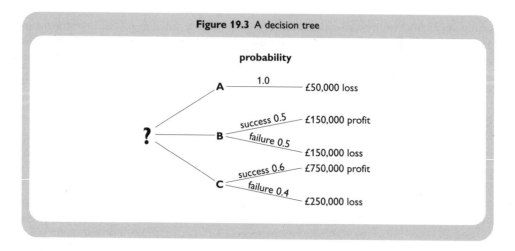

Figure 19.3 A decision tree

This compromise approach can be illustrated by the use of a *decision tree* such as the one shown in Figure 19.3. In this example, we assume that both the firm's existing product and its manufacturing methods are old. The firm is faced with three choices, each with different probabilities of success and failure and with different financial consequences.

1. Option A is to close down the operation. In this case, the probability is 100 per cent – no other result is possible. The payoff is a loss of £50,000 to cover redundancy and other closure costs.

2. Option B is to continue more or less as before, but to renovate some of the factory. In this case there is a 50 per cent chance that the investment will succeed in cutting costs and increasing output leading to a profit of £150,0000. There is an equal chance, however, that sales will not rise, resulting in a loss of £150,000.

3. Option C is to upgrade both the factory and the product, for example by redesigning it. In this case there is a 60 per cent chance that the investment will succeed and lead to a profit of £750,000, but there is also a 40 per cent chance that the investment will fail leaving the firm with a loss of £250,000.

The decision tree does not necessarily lead to a particular conclusion, but it does clarify the options. In this example, an optimist would choose option C, a pessimist option A, and a compromiser option B.

Yet another approach to risk reduction is the use of **sensitivity analysis**. This method involves finding out which variables in an investment appraisal are sensitive in the sense that any variation will have a substantial effect on the result. For example, a firm which is seeking to invest in a new market and has undertaken an IRR or NPV analysis can experiment by changing the variables one at a time. Thus, if the firm considers that wages might rise above its original estimate, then it can redo the analysis, keeping all the other variables unchanged but increasing wage costs. If the result is little different to the original analysis, then an increase in wages will not have a significant effect on the profitability of the investment. On the other hand, if the increase in wage costs leads to a very different result, then the firm must consider how likely wages are to increase to the new level or above, and either decide to pull out of the investment, or else make sure that wage control has a high profile in the way it runs its business. Other variables can be investigated in turn. Will a failure to reach sales targets be disastrous? Will an increase in interest rates lead to a loss? Thus sensitivity analysis can be used to explore all such possibilities and so reduce the risk of an investment.

Sensitivity analysis is a very useful technique, but it does have drawbacks. In particular, it assumes that only one variable is changing and all other variables are held constant. In practice, though, variables may interact. For example, an increase in the price of raw materials bought by the firm may be the result of inflation, which could lead to an increase in wages and perhaps a fall in sales if the firm is forced to put up prices. Sensitivity analysis cannot easily cope with multiple interactions such as this.

Exercise

Rover closes Bulgarian factory

Eastern Europe offers a tempting location for new investment. There is a large population, some of whom are newly rich. Workers are relatively highly skilled, yet wages are low. Hence the temptation to set up factories there.

Rover, a subsidiary of BMW, decided to locate a factory in the Bulgarian city of Varna on the Red Sea. The result was disastrous: only 10 per cent of the 2200 Maestros built were sold. Rover closed the plant. The firm blamed the Bulgarian government for failing to keep a promise to buy cars.

Question

What techniques could Rover have used to reduce the risks of this investment?

Public sector investment

In this unit we have concentrated thus far on private sector investment. But the public sector also invests on a large scale. How much should the government invest on higher education? Would it be a good idea to build a new motorway? Should the National Health Service build a new hospital? These are just a few examples of public sector investments which require some procedure to determine whether or not they should go ahead.

The techniques used for determining private sector investment can also be used in the public sector, but they do require some modification. One particular reason for this requirement is that the private sector invests to make a profit, whereas the public sector has different motives. Thus public sector investments should maximise social benefit minus social cost, and this may not involve *any* financial returns, let alone the maximisation of profits.

Many decisions in the public sector are taken for political rather than economic reasons, and so lie outside the scope of this book. There is, however, one technique which is used on a large scale in the public sector, namely, **cost-benefit analysis**. Essentially, cost-benefit analysis involves a comparison of *all* the costs and benefits of a proposed investment. This immediately distinguishes it from techniques used in the private sector since a profit-maximising firm will only be concerned with the costs and benefits which affect the firm and so will ignore externalities. In the public sector, externalities may be the largest element in the calculation.

The procedure is simple to describe, but is full of difficulties when put into operation. Let us take the example of a new motorway.

The first step is to calculate the costs. In the case of a proposed new motorway these will include the costs of buying the land and the costs of plant and labour needed to build the road. These costs are relatively easy to calculate. The difficulty arises when environmental costs are included. Building a motorway almost always involves cutting down trees, destroying grasslands that seem often to contain rare insects, and ruining attractive views. Environmental costs can only be estimated since they are not bought and sold in the market. Inevitably, therefore, they are treated very subjectively: the road lobby, for instance, would doubtless suggest much smaller costs than would Green activists.

Looking now at the benefits to be gained, one major benefit from the construction of a motorway is that it reduces journey time. Calculating the value of this benefit involves estimating the number of people who will use the road and the amount of time they will save – not an easy task. Then the value of this time saving has to be quantified. There are no market prices to help us, so **shadow prices** have to be used. Shadow prices are estimates of the value of costs and benefits. In this instance, the shadow price might be the average wage per hour, though a lower shadow price might be used for motorists using the road in leisure time.

Another benefit of a new road is that it will probably lead to a reduction in the number of accidents. Again, the value of this is difficult to calculate. One way to place a monetary value on a life is to estimate the opportunity cost: that is, the value of the output which the individual would have produced if he or she had lived. This method gives a figure which can be inserted into a computer, but it can be questioned on a moral basis. Is the life of a 20 year old (whose death would mean a large lost output) worth more than that of a 60 year old? And is the life of a high earner worth more than that of a housewife? Similar difficulties arise in estimating the benefits that arise from the prevention of accidents which do not lead to death but which would require expensive treatment and mean considerable pain for those involved as well as loss of output.

Motorways also give rise to environmental benefits (e.g. less congestion and pollution). Again, though, this leads to difficulties in estimating the monetary value of the benefit. One method of doing this is to ask people how much they would be willing to pay to obtain a particular benefit – for example, halving the amount of traffic on the street outside their house – and then multiply this sum by the number of people involved. Alternatively, traffic pollution may result in a fall in the value of house prices; the prices of similar houses in different areas can therefore be used as a measure of the deleterious effects of pollution in a particular area.

Once all the costs and all the benefits have been calculated, they can then be used in a calculation in the same way that private sector firms use NPV and IRR. One difference to note, however, is that, whereas a private sector firm may use the interest rate it has to pay to borrow money, the public sector can usually obtain finance more cheaply (since it will not become bankrupt). This factor has led some commentators to suggest that using the rate at which the government can borrow money will cause overinvestment by the public sector.

Table 19.4 Costs and benefits of an expansion of higher education

Costs	Benefits
Building costs	Higher productivity
Running costs	Consumption benefits
(e.g. lecturer and other salaries)	to students
Students' output forgone	Externalities

Education provides another example of how cost-benefit analysis can be used in the public sector. Table 19.4 summarises the types of costs and benefits to society of an investment in education such as an expansion of degree courses. The costs include building-related costs plus the costs of actually providing the education (e.g. the salaries of lecturers, librarians, and administrative and technical staff). Another cost that is often ignored is student time, which is a valuable resource. After all, if students were not at university or college, they could be producing goods and services that would benefit the community. A way of measuring this factor is to use the incomes of people who are working and who have similar qualifications to students, and to assume that this salary represents the value of the output the students would produce. This figure then has to be adjusted to allow for unemployment: some students would be unemployed if they were not studying, and no output would therefore be lost. All these costs now have to be calculated in terms of cost per student per year to give a flow of costs over time. For a typical degree course, these costs will be spread fairly evenly over three years.

The benefits that result from investment in higher education are often difficult to measure. The main reason why governments invest in education is because they believe that educated people are more productive. In educational cost-benefit analysis this increased productivity is usually measured by the higher wages earned by educated people, on the basis that if rational employers pay more money it is because such workers are more productive. (Other explanations for the higher wages earned by educated people are of course possible. For example, it can be argued that graduates are more intelligent than non-graduates and that their higher earnings are the result of their intelligence rather than their education.)

There are also consumption benefits stemming from education. For most students, university life is better than working, and the jobs which graduates get are, on the whole, more pleasant and more rewarding (in a non-financial way) than the jobs of non-graduates. These are consumption benefits which accrue to the educated, but they count as benefits to society because graduates are part of society.

Finally, there are considerable externalities in education. For example, the children of educated people benefit from their parents' education. Equally, society as a whole can benefit from others' education; thus Alexander Fleming's education enabled him to discover penicillin and so benefit many millions of people.

For a cost-benefit analysis, the problem hedging all these benefits is that they are difficult, if not impossible, to quantify. How much is student life worth to you? How much will your education benefit society? Such questions cannot be answered with any precision, and so, in many cost-benefit studies they are ignored, even though this gives a misleadingly low figure for the returns to education. Nevertheless, the cost-benefit

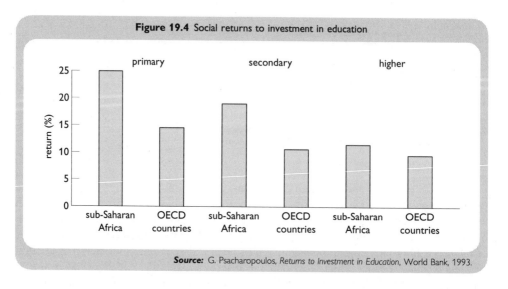

Figure 19.4 Social returns to investment in education

Source: G. Psacharopoulos, *Returns to Investment in Education*, World Bank, 1993.

studies that have been carried out do show a positive return to education. Figure 19.4 outlines a sample of such research. As you can see, in less developed countries, the research suggests very high returns to primary education. One reason for this is that the opportunity costs are very low: children attending primary school would have earned little or no money if they had not been at school. On the other hand, high opportunity costs are the reason why returns to higher education are relatively low: undergraduates would normally be expected to earn reasonable wages if they were not studying.

Cost-benefit analysis in the public sector does not provide definitive answers as to whether or not a particular investment should take place. There are too many unquantifiable variables for that, and political factors often take precedence. It does, however, provide a basis on which decisions can be made, and the technique is used quite extensively in deciding whether or not, for example, a new road should be built.

Summary

Entrepreneurs are the decision makers of the business world. Their decisions on investment are influenced by external factors such as government policy, and also by their own optimism/pessimism.

To help them make good decisions, a number of techniques are available. Simple procedures such as the payback period can give some indication about a particular investment, but the method has many drawbacks. More sophisticated techniques such as net present value (NPV) and internal rate of return (IRR) give more reliable results.

The same methods are also used in the public sector, but here, investment decisions are particularly difficult because of large unquantifiable externalities and also because political factors may take precedence.

Review questions

1. What is an entrepreneur?
2. Summarise the factors which influence the level of investment.
3. How might investment projects be classified?
4. What are the differences between perfect and imperfect capital markets?
5. Why should future income be discounted?
6. Show how the present value of a future sum of money can be discounted.
7. Outline the payback period method of investment appraisal. What are its advantages and disadvantages?
8. Explain the net present value method of investment appraisal.
9. Outline the internal rate of return method of investment appraisal.
10. How can firms reduce the risks involved in an investment?
11. How can the public sector decide whether or not a proposed investment is a good idea?

Essay question

How should entrepreneurs decide whether or not to proceed with an investment?

Reading 19.1

To build or not to build?

The Labour government is cutting back on many of the road schemes planned by its Conservative predecessor. The main reason is the need to reduce government spending.

The Private Finance Initiative (PFI) offers a way out of the dilemma. In the past, the main determinant of whether or not a road would be built was the rate of return on the investment. But new roads are expensive and even high returns require high initial investment. Under the PFI scheme contractors build, finance and run new roads. The government pays them back according to how many vehicles use the road.

Questions

1. What are the advantages and disadvantages of using rates of return to determine the road building programme?
2. What are the advantages and disadvantages of the PFI scheme to the government, contractors and the general public?

Reading 19.2

A fast-food takeaway is considering whether or not to start a home delivery service. The initial cost is estimated to be £5000, and the returns to be £2200 after a year, £3360 in year two and £1331 in year three. The firm's discount rate is 10 per cent.

Question

Should the firm go ahead with the delivery service?

Running the economy

After studying this module you should be able to:

- construct a simple model explaining the determination of national income;

- identify the main types of expenditure within the economy;

- understand why the levels of expenditure might change and the implications of these changes for the economy and for businesses;

- explain how the level of economic activity is measured;

- identify the primary macroeconomic objectives of governments;

- explain why and how governments might attempt to influence the level of economic activity;

- identify the causes of inflation and the measures the government may use to control inflation;

- understand the implications of inflation for the economy and for firms;

- identify the causes of unemployment and the measures the government can use to reduce unemployment; and

- understand the implications of unemployment for the economy and for firms.

The measurement and determination of national income

How should we measure success and progress? Are gross domestic product (GDP) statistics really a good guide to living standards and the quality of life in a particular country? We can probably deduce fairly confidently, from Figure 20.1, that the standard of living and quality of life is better in Switzerland than in Ethiopia, but GDP statistics do not provide a complete guide to living standards and progress. They do not take into account many of the costs that often

Figure 20.1 GDP per capita, 1995 (US$)

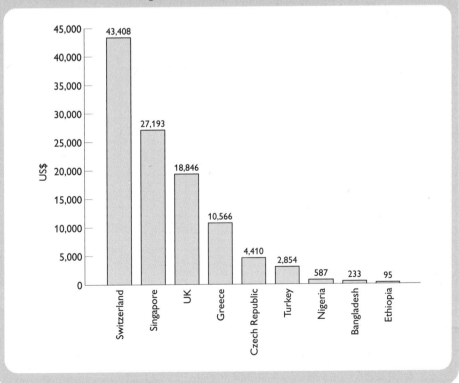

accompany a high and rising GDP. For example, though a country with a high GDP per head is likely to have a high level of car ownership, this could result in high levels of pollution, causing health problems such as increased asthma attacks.

Many economists believe that an alternative method should now be used as a guide to living standards – a measure that would take the external costs of production into account – as there is an increasing divergence between levels of income and the quality of life.

Macroeconomics looks at the behaviour of the economy as a whole. It is important that firms understand the macroenvironment in which they operate because changes in macroeconomic variables such as inflation and unemployment will have a considerable influence on the firm. In this unit we examine the factors which help to determine the level of economic activity, and the problems which arise in measuring the level of national income.

National income

National income refers to the sum of all the incomes obtained from the production of goods and services in a country throughout the year. It can in be measured in three ways. In addition to the sum of the incomes of the country (the 'incomes approach'), it can also be derived by adding the value of the output of the goods and services produced by the country (the 'output approach'), or by adding the total expenditure on goods and services within the economy (the 'expenditure approach').

This measurement can be demonstrated in Figure 20.2, which represents a simple economy comprising just firms and households. In this simple model of the economy, households provide firms with factor inputs (i.e. land, labour, capital and enterprise). In return, the households receive income for the provision of these inputs: wages as a payment for the provision of labour, rent as the payment for the supply of land, interest as the payment for the supply of capital, and profit as the reward for the entrepreneurs. These flows of factor inputs and income are shown on the left-hand side of the diagram. Firms use these factor inputs to produce goods and services which are then sold to the households. In this model, households spend all of their income on the goods and services produced by the firms. These two flows, the output and the expenditure of the economy, are shown on the right-hand side of the diagram. The value of the circular flow within the model is the same whether we measure the amount of income (A), the value of the goods and services produced (B) or the amount of spending (C). Thus:

National income = National expenditure = National output.

In order to make our model more realistic, we can introduce additional elements. So far, we have assumed a 'closed' economy: that is, there are only domestic firms and

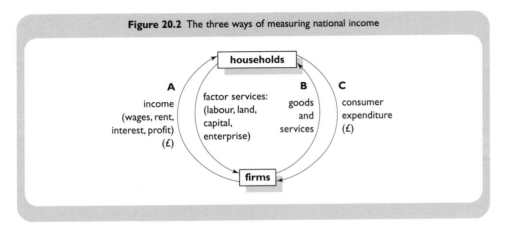

Figure 20.2 The three ways of measuring national income

households

A
income
(wages, rent,
interest, profit)
(£)

factor services:
(labour, land,
capital,
enterprise)

B
goods
and
services

C
consumer
expenditure
(£)

firms

households in our model, and the households spend all their income on the output produced by these firms. If, however, we open up our model to incorporate international trade, not all expenditure will be directed towards output produced by domestic firms. Households may decide to spend some of their income on imports. In this case, some of the income 'leaks out' of the circular flow of income and is not passed on to domestic firms. Likewise, households may decide to save some of their income rather than spend it. And if we introduce a government into our model, some of the household income and expenditure is likely to be taxed, leaving households with less to spend.

Savings, taxes and imports all represent **withdrawals**, or **leakages**, from the circular flow of income. Any leakage from the circular flow will cause the level of income circulating within the economy to decrease. For example, if households decide to spend part of their income on imported products domestic, firms will notice a fall in demand for their products. If this fall in demand persists, they will revise their production plans and cut back on output. They may make workers redundant, or reduce the hours of each worker. In either case, the output of domestic firms will fall, leading to a fall in the level of income earned by households.

Figure 20.3 illustrates a circular flow of income without any leakages. Household income is £100m. and it is assumed that they spend all their income on domestically produced products, which means that the circular flow is in equilibrium at a level of £100m. If, however, households decide to spend £10m. of their income on imports, as shown in Figure 20.4, expenditure on domestic goods and services initially falls to £90m., which means that the level of income earned by households, shown on the left-hand side of the diagram, will also fall initially to £90m.

We can also add elements to our model that will increase the size of the circular flow of income in the economy. Our assumption so far is that all expenditure originates from domestic households, but firms may sell some of their production to overseas customers, creating export earnings. In addition, it is not only consumers who purchase goods and services. Firms also purchase capital goods, such as machinery and equipment, from other firms. This is referred to as investment expenditure. And if we introduce the government into our model, they too are a major source of expenditure on, for example, health services, education, defence and road building, to name just a few sectors. Investment spending, government spending and exports are **injections** into the circular flow of

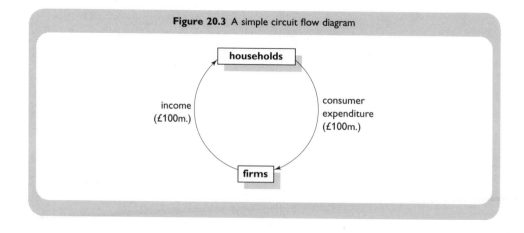

Figure 20.3 A simple circuit flow diagram

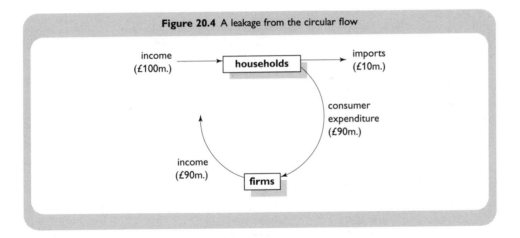

Figure 20.4 A leakage from the circular flow

income, and any injection into the circular flow of income will increase the size of the flow.

In Figure 20.3, the level of income and the level of consumer expenditure were both £100m. If, however, firms sell an additional £10m. of goods and services overseas, these exports will increase the value of income, which will initially rise to £110m. (see Figure 20.5).

Table 20.1 summarises the three withdrawals from and the three injections into the circular flow of income, while Figure 20.6 illustrates the model with all three withdrawals and injections. Note that this represents a simplified version of the circular flow, since – to give just one example – firms also pay taxes in addition to households. When total injections are equal to total withdrawals, the circular flow of income will remain stable and the level of national income will tend to remain constant, as shown in Figure 20.7 where both injections and withdrawals are equal. If total injections are greater than total withdrawals, then the size of the circular flow will increase, while if total withdrawals exceed total injections, the size of the circular flow will decrease.

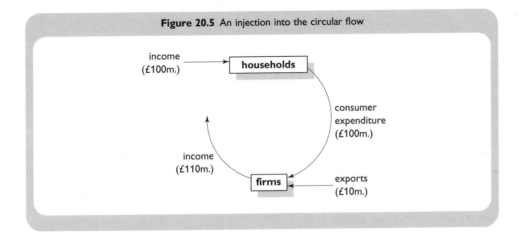

Figure 20.5 An injection into the circular flow

Table 20.1 Withdrawals and injections into the circular flow of income

Withdrawals	*Injections*
Savings	Investment
Taxes	Government expenditure
Imports	Exports
An increase in withdrawals leads to a fall in national income	An increase in injections leads to a rise in national income

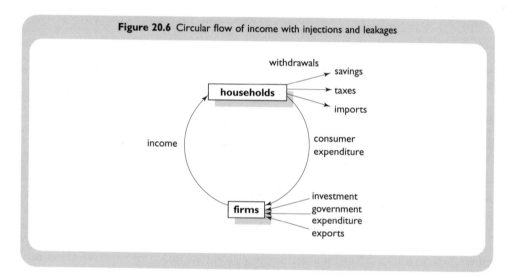

Figure 20.6 Circular flow of income with injections and leakages

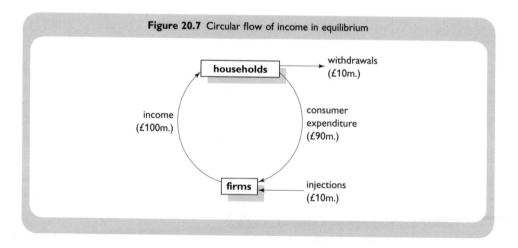

Figure 20.7 Circular flow of income in equilibrium

The multiplier process

An increase in withdrawals will lead to a fall in the level of national income, while an increase in injections will raise the level of national income. However, the multiplier process magnifies the effect of any additional injection into or withdrawal from the economy. If we consider an additional injection into the circular flow model, it means that the eventual increase in income and output will be greater than the additional injection. Likewise, if there is an additional leakage from the circular flow, the eventual fall in income and output will be greater than the amount of the leakage.

A simple example can be used to demonstrate the **multiplier effect**. Suppose the government decides to build more hospitals. This represents an additional injection into the circular flow model, as it is an increase in government expenditure. The construction firms which are to build the hospitals will have to take on more workers. The firms who supply the hospitals with equipment and materials will also have to expand their output and employment. However, the increase in employment and output does not stop here. Many of those who gain employment with the construction firms or the suppliers of hospital equipment might previously have been unemployed, and are therefore now receiving a greater income. This income will be spent on goods and services that would not otherwise have been purchased, thus leading to even more output and employment, not just for the firms producing these goods and services, but also, for example, in the retail and distribution industries. The recipients of these new jobs will then spend their extra income on yet more goods and services; the sequence continues so that the eventual increase in output, employment and income in the economy may be several times greater than the original injection of government expenditure.

The multiplier process also works in reverse. If the government closes a coal mine, it is not just the miners who suffer a loss of income. The reduced expenditure from those previously employed in the mine means that other businesses, particularly those in the immediate locality, will suffer a drop in trade and may need to make staff redundant, leading to further job losses and reductions in income. Thus the downwards spiral continues.

The size of the multiplier effect depends on the proportion of any additional income that is passed on within the circular flow. If, for example, those receiving an increase in income spent most of the increase on imported products, then the multiplier effect would be very small. In addition to imports, the other leakages – savings and taxation – will also reduce the size of the multiplier effect.

The proportion of any additional income that is passed on within the circular flow can be referred to as the **marginal propensity to consume (mpc)**. If, for example, the mpc = 0.8, this indicates that consumers spend 80 per cent of any additional income on domestically produced goods and services, while 20 per cent of the additional income 'leaks out' of the circular flow in the form of imports, taxes or savings. The higher the mpc, the greater is the multiplier effect. The size of the multiplier can be calculated by using the formula:

$$K = \frac{1}{1 - \text{mpc}}$$

where:

K = the symbol for the multiplier; and
mpc = the marginal propensity to consume.

Thus, if the marginal propensity to consume is 0.8, the size of the multiplier would be:

$$K = \frac{1}{1 - 0.8} = \frac{1}{0.2} = 5$$

If the government injected £100m. into the economy, therefore, the eventual increase in income would be:

$$5 \times £100m. = £500m.$$

This multiplier process is illustrated in Table 20.2, where the additional spending by one sector of the economy becomes additional income for others in the economy.

An alternative method of calculating the size of the multiplier effect is to use the formula:

$$\frac{1}{mpw}$$

where mpw represents the proportion of any additional income that is withdrawn from, or leaks out of the circular flow. Thus:

$$mpw = mps + mpt + mpm$$

where:

    mps = that proportion of any additional income that is saved
            (i.e. **marginal propensity to save**);
    mpt = that proportion of any extra income that is taxed
            (i.e. **marginal propensity to tax**); and
    mpm = that proportion of any income that is spent on imports
            (i.e. **marginal propensity to import**).

You should now realise that mpc + mps + mpt + mpm will always be equal to one.

Table 20.2 The multiplier process (£m.)

Change in income (£m.)		Change in consumption (mpc = 0.8) (£m.)
Initial injection =	+100.0	+80.0
Subsequent changes in income	+80.0	+64.0
	+64.0	+51.2
	+51.2	+40.96
	+40.96	+32.77
	.	.
	.	.
	.	.
	+500.0	+400.0

A government statistician estimates that of every additional £100 income received by consumers, £25 is taxed by the government, £5 is saved, and £10 is spent on imported goods.

Questions

1. (a) If there is an increase in private sector investment of £300m., calculate the change that should occur in national income, assuming the statistician's estimates are correct; and (b) if there is a reduction in government spending of £1000m., calculate the effect this would have on the level of national income.

2. How would your answers to 1(a) and 1(b) differ if the amount saved out of an additional £100 income rose to £15?

Although the model of the circular flow of income that we have used is rather simplistic, it can be useful for illustrating the effect of any changes in any of the withdrawals or injections, and, in particular, the effect of any government policy measures.

Aggregate demand

Aggregate demand (*AD*) is the total amount of money which people wish to spend within the domestic economy (see Figure 20.8). This includes not only **consumption expenditure** (*C*) by consumers, but also investment spending by firms (*I*), government expenditure (*G*) and, if we open the economy up to international trade, income from exports minus any of the domestic spending that is spent on imports $(X - M)$. Thus:

$$AD = C + I + G + (X - M)$$

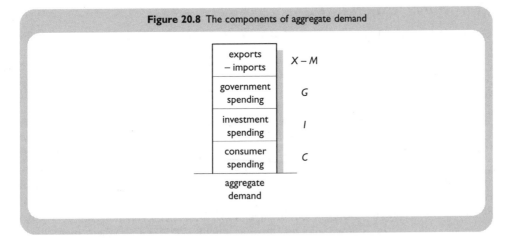

Figure 20.8 The components of aggregate demand

Table 20.3 Comparative shares of
aggregate demand in the UK, 1996 (%)

	(%)
Consumer expenditure	50
Investment	12
Government expenditure	16
Exports	23

Source: Economic Trends, May 1997, table 2.3.

This level of spending influences macroeconomic variables such as the level of employment. If there is an increase in the level of expenditure, this is likely to lead to an increase in the level of employment. But high levels of spending might also cause inflationary pressures or lead to more imports coming into the country. Governments therefore may wish to try to control the level of income and spending within the economy in order to influence the levels of unemployment, inflation and the balance of payments. We shall look at their attempts to do so in the following units in this module.

In addition, any change in the national economy can have a significant impact on business organisations. Firms need to be able to anticipate and respond to macroeconomic changes. A rising national income is likely to mean an increase in aggregate demand, and firms may therefore wish to plan for increases in output, particularly as it often takes time for a firm to step up production levels, perhaps due to the need to purchase new machinery, enlarge premises or to recruit new workers.

In order to try to assess what determines the level of national income, we need to analyse what affects the various components of aggregate demand (see Table 20.3). Factors influencing the amount of government spending and the level of exports are looked at elsewhere in this book. In this unit, we look at what determines the other two components of aggregate demand: consumption expenditure by households, and investment expenditure by firms.

Consumers' expenditure

Consumers' expenditure, as can be seen from Table 20.3, is the most important component of aggregate demand.

Income and consumption

The major factor determining the level of consumption expenditure is the level of income, or, to be more precise, the level of disposable income: that is, income after taxes have been deducted. The multiplier process depends on consumption responding to fluctuations in the level of income. The multiplier concept and this relationship between income and consumption is associated with the economist Keynes, who argued that the level of consumption depends on the level of current income. However, Keynes also argued that as income rises, the proportion of that income which is spent on consumption falls. Thus someone who is on a low level of income might spend all of their income on consumption (students are a good example!), while a person on a higher level of income is likely to save some of their income and only spend a proportion on consumption. Thus the marginal propensity to consume (mpc) falls as income rises. The mpc of someone on a low income is likely to be almost 1.0, while the mpc of a richer person might be 0.75.

It might seem fairly obvious that the level of consumption depends on the level of current income, and that as people earn more, so they spend more. However, other theories claim that consumption does not respond so readily to fluctuations in the current level of income.

The permanent income hypothesis, which is associated with the economist Milton Friedman, suggests that consumption spending is not so much related to current levels of income, but is dependent on the income that a person expects to receive over their lifetime. Therefore, in deciding how much to spend on consumption, a person takes into account not only their current level of income, but also the income that they expect to earn in the future. Thus students who are surviving on a grant might be on a low income, but they base their expenditure on the expectation that they will be receiving a much higher income once they have completed their studies. Their expenditure on consumption is in fact likely to be greater than their current income, made possible through the taking out of a student loan. On the other hand, a middle-aged person might be earning a relatively high income, but does not necessarily spend most of this on consumption as they anticipate a much lower level of income once they have retired, and will save some of their current income in anticipation of retirement. This theory therefore suggests that an individual averages out total expected lifetime income and bases current expenditure on this average figure. This would mean that a short-term fluctuation in the level of current income would not influence expenditure as it would have very little impact on the permanent lifetime income of the individual.

Other factors

Apart from income, there are a number of other factors which might influence the level of consumption.

The propensity to save

If a person saves a high proportion of their income, this implies that their level of consumption will be reduced. Social attitudes may influence the proportion of income that people save. If the general view of society is that saving is a virtue and that one should not spend beyond one's means, then the level of consumer spending is likely to be reduced. However, if consumers live in a very materialistic society where the possession of consumer goods is highly valued and people have a 'buy now, pay later' mentality, the level of consumer spending is likely to be much higher.

Price and availability of credit

If interest rates are high or credit facilities are difficult to obtain, consumer expenditure might fall. High rates of interest lead to high mortgage repayments, so a large proportion of consumer expenditure will be on housing costs, leaving less to spend on other consumer goods. High rates of interest are also likely to reduce expenditure on **consumer durables**, such as cars, furniture or electrical equipment, many of which are purchased on credit. Households may also be encouraged by high rates of interest to save a larger proportion of their income, again leading to a fall in consumer spending. On the other hand, if interest rates are low, or if credit facilities are readily available – through the use of credit cards, for example – consumer expenditure is likely to rise. However, some people (e.g. pensioners) may spend less when interest rates are low since a large part of their income might be derived from interest on savings.

Expectation of future price changes

If people expect price levels to rise in the future, they may bring forward their purchasing plans in an effort to beat the price increases, leading to an increase in consumer spending.

The distribution of income

It is not just the level of national income that determines the amount of consumer expenditure, but also how that income is distributed. We described earlier how the mpc of a poor person is higher than that of a rich person. Therefore, if £1000 is redistributed from a rich person who has an mpc of 0.7 to a poor person who has an mpc of 1.0, the rich person's expenditure will fall by £700 but the poor person's expenditure will rise by £1000, resulting in a net increase in consumer spending of £300.

Investment

Investment spending represents spending by firms on capital goods such as machinery and equipment. It is important that we have some understanding of the factors which influence the level of investment as not only is it a component of aggregate demand, but also it has important implications regarding future living standards. The rate of economic growth is very dependent on the level of investment.

As investment adds to the **capital stock** of an economy, it is sometimes referred to as *gross domestic capital formation*. This includes both new additions to the capital stock, and replacement capital to cover **depreciation of assets**. Thus investment may be classified as gross investment, which represents total investment spending, or net investment, which represents only those additions to the capital stock after having made allowances for depreciation. Hence gross investment minus an allowance for depreciation (capital consumption) equals net investment. It is net investment which is important in terms of promoting the growth of the economy.

Over time, the amount of investment spending tends to fluctuate and it is difficult to be certain exactly what determines the level of investment. There would appear to be many different factors which influence the investment decision.

Interest rates

Much investment is made with borrowed money. If interest rates rise it will be more expensive for firms to finance investment, and any given investment project will be less profitable, with those at the margin becoming unprofitable. The relationship between the quantity of investment and the rate of interest is shown in Figure 20.9.

However, the relationship between the level of investment and the rate of interest might not be quite so straightforward. Firms may not be able to cut their investment plans quickly in response to an increase in interest rates due to the long-term nature of much

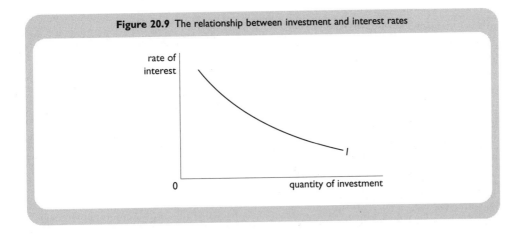

Figure 20.9 The relationship between investment and interest rates

investment. Thus, in the short term in particular, investment is unlikely to be very 'interest-elastic', which means that the demand curve for capital in Figure 20.9 is likely to be nearly vertical. In addition, it is the real rate of interest – that is, the rate of interest in comparison to the inflation rate – which is the most relevant, as opposed to the nominal rate of interest. High nominal rates of interest may, in real terms, be much lower if there is a high rate of inflation.

Business expectations

Business expectations might have more bearing on an investment decision than interest rates. However low interest rates fall, firms might be unwilling to invest if they have little confidence in the state of the economy. Conversely, when firms are confident of buoyant and increasing demand they may be willing to invest even if interest rates are high. Keynes argued that the relationship between interest rates and investment was a highly unstable one, and that business confidence and expectations were far more important in determining the level of investment.

The level of national income and aggregate demand

The higher the level of income and demand, the more *willing* are firms to invest, as they have expectations of high profits, and the more *able* are they to invest, as a high level of demand is likely to mean high profits that can be used to help finance investment.

The rate of change of national income

The **accelerator principle of investment** suggests that it is the *rate of change* of national income and consumer demand that is important in determining the level of investment, rather than the *level* of income and demand. Even when the level of national income and consumer demand is high, if it is at a constant level, then there is no point in firms investing to increase their capacity. Investment will be limited to replacing capital assets as they wear out or become obsolete. In order for firms to have a motive to invest in additional capital equipment, consumer demand has to be rising. The accelerator

Table 20.4 Investment required to match product demand

Year	Demand	Change in demand	Machines required	Net investment
11	10,000	0	20	0
12	10,000	0	20	0
13	11,000	1000	22	2
14	13,000	2000	26	4
15	16,000	3000	32	6
16	19,000	3000	38	6
17	22,000	3000	44	6
18	24,000	2000	48	4
19	25,000	1000	50	2
20	25,000	0	50	0

theory also predicts that an increase in the demand for consumer goods will bring about a much greater change in the demand for capital goods. These points are best illustrated with an example.

Assume a firm faces a demand from consumers for 10,000 units. Its machines are capable of producing 500 units each per annum, hence it must have 20 machines to accommodate the necessary output. Table 20.4 illustrates the investment required by the firm as the demand for its product increases. In years 11 and 12, demand remains constant, as it has for the previous ten years. The firm is therefore not required to undertake any additional investment; it just needs to replace worn-out machines. However, from year 13 demand begins to increase. In years 13, 14 and 15, demand increases at an escalating rate and so investment increases; in years 16 and 17, demand increases at a constant rate and the amount of investment per year remains constant; and in years 18 and 19, demand increases at a slower rate and the amount of investment per year falls. Thus in year 20, the level of demand is as high as it has ever been, and yet net investment is zero. This then illustrates that it is not the *level* of demand that is important in determining the amount of investment, but the *rate of change* of demand. In order for there to be rising investment, demand must rise at an increasing rate, while for net investment to remain constant, demand must rise by the same amount each year. If demand increases, but at a declining rate, investment will fall.

There are, however, a few limitations to this theory of investment. It assumes, first, that firms are operating at full capacity, so that if there is an increase in demand, they will need to invest in new capital; but second, if they are operating below full capacity, they may be able to meet the increase in demand with their existing capital stock. It assumes that firms are confident that any increase in demand will be permanent. However, just because demand increases, firms do not immediately increase their productive capacity; they appreciate that demand might fall again the following year. Thus expectations and business confidence play an important part.

Third, the accelerator theory also assumes that the capital goods industry, those who supply the machinery, has the spare capacity to supply the extra machines on demand. Fourth, that the capital-output ratio is constant: that is, that there is a fixed proportional relationship between the level of demand and the amount of capital stock required.

In our example, we have assumed a constant capital-output ratio of one machine for every 500 units.

The accelerator theory on its own does not provide a complete explanation for variations in the level of investment. Changing expectations in an uncertain environment are perhaps a better explanation as to why firms' investment spending is so prone to fluctuation, as opposed to the rather mechanistic explanation of the accelerator concept. Nevertheless, empirical evidence would seem to suggest that there is an accelerator-type relationship between changes in demand and changes in investment. Moreover, the theory does help to explain why there are such large fluctuations in the level of investment from year to year and why, as consumer demand changes, investment changes at a much faster rate.

Exercise

With reference to Table 20.5, examine the extent to which the accelerator principle could be used to explain fluctuations in the level of investment in the UK between 1987 and 1996.

Table 20.5 UK consumer and investment expenditure, 1987–96 (1990 prices)

Year	Consumer expenditure (£m.)	% change on previous year	Investment expenditure (£m.)	% change on previous year
1987	311,234	+5.3	92,339	+10.3
1988	334,591	+7.5	105,164	+13.9
1989	345,406	+3.2	111,470	+6.0
1990	347,527	+0.6	107,577	−6.2
1991	340,037	−2.2	97,403	−9.5
1992	339,652	−0.1	95,973	−1.5
1993	348,015	+2.5	96,586	+0.6
1994	356,914	+2.6	99,417	+2.9
1995	363,810	+1.9	99,306	−0.1
1996	374,811	+3.0	100,324	+1.0

Source: Adapted from *Economic Trends*, May 1997, annual supplement 1996/97, table 2.2.

Other factors which can influence investment decision are as follows:

- **The cost and efficiency of capital equipment** If the cost of capital equipment falls, firms will be more willing to invest as the return on capital will increase. Likewise, if machinery becomes more efficient, the return on investment will increase. Investment will probably fall, however, if the cost of capital equipment rises.

- **Availability of finance** When firms find it easy to obtain finance for investment, they are more likely to invest. In the past, small firms have often complained that banks are not always very willing to provide funds for investment. This point is discussed in Unit 18.

- **Technological change and the rate of obsolescence** If there is rapid technological progress, firms will find it necessary to replace capital equipment more frequently, and even before it has come to the end of its working life, in order to keep up with their competitors. This will particularly be the case if the industry in which the firm operates is very competitive.

- **The rate of depreciation/capital consumption** The faster the rate of depreciation, the more investment is required to replace worn-out capital stock.

- **Government policy** The government can influence investment in various ways. It can help directly by offering grants or tax incentives on investment. In addition, of course, much investment is carried out by the public sector. The government can also promote investment indirectly, by creating a favourable economic climate which increases business confidence and expectations.

The measurement and use of national income statistics

We now turn to look in more detail at the measurement and use of national income statistics. There are many different terms and definitions used in the measurement of national income, and these require clarification.

Gross domestic product (GDP) is the value of output produced within a country, usually measured over a year. However, some of this output will have been produced by foreign-owned resources. For example, many of the car plants in the UK are foreign-owned. In addition, the citizens of a country may own resources that produce goods and services outside their national boundary. Earnings from production carried out overseas, less earnings from production carried out at home by foreign-owned resources, is referred to as *net property income from abroad*. Gross domestic product plus net property income from abroad is equal to **Gross national product (GNP)**. Some of the output produced during a year will be to replace assets that have depreciated. If we make an allowance for depreciation, or 'capital consumption', the value of output is referred to as **Net national product (NNP)**.

The value of output may be measured according to the prices actually paid for the goods and services. This is referred to as measuring output at *market prices*. However, it is likely that this price will include a sales tax, which will have the effect of raising the price, or the price might include a government subsidy, which lowers the price. This could give misleading results: for example, an increase in a sales tax such as VAT would raise GDP at market prices, but real output would not have changed. Therefore, we ought to subtract taxes from and add subsidies to the valuation at market prices, measuring the value of the output *at factor cost*. The relevant measure for calculating national income is to take net national product at factor cost.

To summarise:

GDP + net property income from abroad = GNP
GNP − depreciation = NNP
NNP at market prices − taxes + subsidies = NNP at factor cost

The level of national income gives us some indication of living standards within a country. The success of an economy is usually judged by looking at how quickly national income is growing. There are, however, difficulties when using national income statistics to measure changes in living standards over time, or when making comparisons between countries, as highlighted in the commentary at the start of this unit, and we shall now examine these difficulties:

- National income is measured in money terms, but over time, money loses its value due to inflation. When comparing national income in different years, it is therefore important to make allowances for inflation, and to measure the real change that has occurred, rather than merely the change in money national income. For example, if national income has risen in money terms by 3 per cent over a year, but prices have also risen by 3 per cent, the real value of national income has not risen.

- The size of the population may also vary over time, so it is also necessary to measure national income per capita (per head). This also applies when making comparisons between different countries.

- Measuring national income per capita still does not take into account the distribution of the income throughout the country. A country may have a high national income per capita, but if there is a very unequal distribution of income, the majority of the population might be on income levels well below this figure. For example, in many South American countries, GDP per capita is relatively high, but this conceals the fact that a few people are extremely rich and many people very poor.

- The accuracy of the information gathered is often questioned. Measuring the total value of income, expenditure or output of a country is an extremely complex task. Much economic activity occurs that is not officially recorded. This is often referred to as the **black (or underground) economy**; people may work for 'cash in hand' and may not declare their income to the authorities. Estimates of the size of the black economy in the UK vary from an extra 3 per cent to 10 per cent on top of the official national income statistics. In other countries, it may be even larger; certainly in Italy it is estimated to be an additional 15 per cent of GDP. If the size of the black economy within a country varies over time, it makes measurement of changes in living standards difficult, while where the size of the black economy or the accuracy of measurement varies from one country to another, it lessens the usefulness of official national income statistics as a method of comparing international living standards.

- Much production and output within an economy may not be traded. For example, if an economy has a high degree of self-sufficiency where people produce goods and services for their own consumption and do not trade them through the market, then these will not be recorded in the official statistics and living standards will appear to be lower than they actually are. Thus someone decorating their own house would not be recorded; neither would housework. Some claim that this devalues the work of women, who do most housework.

- Different countries value their GNP in their own currency, so conversions have to be made, but fluctuations in the exchange rate will cause complications and distortions.

- National income/output figures ignore the composition of the output produced. One might argue that the provision of consumer goods adds more to living standards than the provision of defence equipment. The citizens of those countries that devote a high proportion of their national income to defence expenditure might experience lower living standards than if the composition of output had been different.

- National income statistics also ignore externalities or social costs, as highlighted in the introductory news item. Is it right to measure living standards simply in terms of income and output? There are drawbacks to rapid rates of growth in national income. The pollution associated with high levels of output is considered by many to represent a lowering of living standards and an allowance ought to be made for this in the official statistics.

- The compilation of national income statistics ignores the amount of leisure time that people in a country may have. It may be possible to increase national output and national income through working longer hours, but the reduction in leisure time could reduce the quality of life.

- The needs of people differ from one country to another and this means that making direct comparisons can be misleading. To take an example, countries have differing climatic conditions. A country might have a high national income, but if the climate requires that a large proportion of that income be spent on keeping warm, the disposable income of the people may be much lower than in other countries which have a lower national income per head.

For all these reasons, national income statistics need to be treated with some caution.

Summary

National income can be measured in three ways: by totalling incomes, output or expenditure. The size of the flow of income is determined by injections into and withdrawals or leakages from the circular flow. Injections consist of investment, government spending and exports, while the leakages are savings, taxes and imports. A change in any of the injections or leakages will produce a larger change in the level of income, due to the multiplier process. The government may try to influence the level of income in order to control the level of employment and inflation. Any changes in the level of income will have important implications for businesses. The level of income has an important influence on the levels of consumer expenditure and investment, which, in turn, affect the level of income. National income statistics are used as a guide to living standards within an economy, although they are not a complete or accurate guide to the level of human welfare.

Review questions

1. Name three approaches to the measurement of national income.
2. Identify the three categories of injections into the circular flow of income.

3. Identify the three categories of withdrawals, or leakages, from the circular flow of income.

4. Sketch a diagram to represent the circular flow of income, including the injections into and the withdrawals from the circular flow.

5. State whether the following are injections into, or withdrawals from the circular flow of income:
   (a) the purchase of an imported car by a UK citizen;
   (b) the imposition of VAT on books and newspapers;
   (c) the purchase of plant and machinery by a firm;
   (d) government spending on education;
   (e) households placing money in a building society account; and
   (f) the sale of defence equipment overseas.

6. If injections are greater than withdrawals, what will happen to the circular flow of income?

7. What are the four types of spending that make up aggregate demand?

8. If British consumers show a preference for purchasing imported cars, what effect will this have on the British economy?

9. Explain the effect that the closure of a university in a provincial town would have on the local economy, identifying in particular the impact on the demand for goods and services and the effect on local employment.

10. Explain the key points of the *permanent income hypothesis*.

11. Name three factors, other than income, that might affect consumer spending.

12. What is the difference between gross investment and net investment?

13. Outline five factors that might influence the level of investment.

14. Why does investment expenditure tend to fluctuate more over time than consumption?

15. What three adjustments need to be made to convert gross domestic product at market prices to net national product at factor cost (i.e. national income)?

16. What is the 'black' or 'underground' economy?

Essay questions

1. How does the 'hidden' or 'black' economy affect the level of national income? What do you see as its advantages and disadvantages?

2. Why might national income statistics be an unreliable guide:
   (a) as a measure of human welfare within an economy; and
   (b) as a means of comparing living standards between countries?

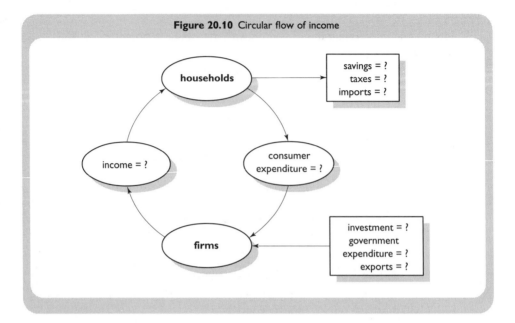

Figure 20.10 Circular flow of income

Exercise

1. Use the following information to complete Figure 20.10:
   Household income = £100bn
   Investment expenditure = £10bn
   Government expenditure = £20bn
   Exports = £20bn
   Consumption on domestic output = 50 per cent of household income
   Savings = 10 per cent of household income
   Imports = 20 per cent of household income

2. Calculate the size of the multiplier.

3. Investment spending now rises to £20bn. Remembering the multiplier effect of a change in an injection, draw a new diagram to show revised values for income, consumer spending, savings, taxation, and imports.

Reading 20.1

The investment puzzle

The economic recovery of the mid-1990s owed much to a rise in exports rather than the more usual explanation of an increase in consumer spending. Investment spending also played little part, and was even lower than it had been at the start of the recovery. This was particularly surprising as conditions existed which were thought to be conducive towards investment spending, namely:

1. above trend economic growth;

2. strong company profits;

3. lower long-term interest rates;

4. lower capital costs; and

5. increased use of existing capacity by firms.

However, the Bank of England believed that firms might have been unwilling to invest, even if it meant losing future sales, for fear of not recovering the costs of the investment, while a CBI survey indicated that inadequate returns on investment and uncertainty about future demand prospects were inhibiting investment. Research carried out jointly by Lloyds Bank and the Engineering Employers Foundation suggests that factors such as market expectations and competitor behaviour are among the most important influences on investment. 'Economic uncertainty' was perceived as an especially important barrier to investment. The sources of uncertainty – for example, about future interest rates, future prices or costs, future demand, future taxes and regulations – can be much more important determinants of investment than current interest rates.

What, then, can the government do to encourage more investment? Interest rate reductions may have little effect unless they make businesses more confident about the future. Indeed, an interest rate *increase* might be more effective if it led businesses to conclude that the recovery was likely to be more sustainable!

Source: Adapted from Lloyds Bank *Economic Bulletin No. 4*, September 95.

Questions

1. Explain why one might expect each of the five points listed at the beginning of the article to lead to higher levels of investment.

2. What could the government do to encourage investment, other than adjustments to the interest rate?

Management of the economy

If the Treasury were to fill old bottles with banknotes, bury them at suitable depths in disused coalmines which are then filled up to the surface with town rubbish, and leave it to private enterprise on well-tried principles of *laissez-faire* to dig the notes up again, there need be no more unemployment and, with the help of the repercussions, the real income of the community would probably become a good deal greater then it actually is. It would, indeed, be more sensible to build houses and the like; but if there are political and practical difficulties in the way of this, the above would be better than nothing.

Source: John Maynard Keynes: *The General Theory of Employment, Interest and Money,* Macmillan Ltd, 1936, chapter 10.

We used to think that you could just spend your way out of a recession and increase employment by cutting taxes and boosting government spending. I tell you, in all candour, that that option no longer exists, and that in so far as it ever did exist, it worked by injecting bigger doses of inflation into the economy. And each time that happened the average level of unemployment has risen. Higher inflation followed by higher unemployment. That is the history of the last twenty years.

Source: Extract from speech by James Callaghan, UK Prime Minister, 1976.

In the previous unit, we examined a model of the economy and looked at some of the factors that determine the level of national income. In this unit we shall look at the macroeconomic objectives of government and the methods that governments can employ to help them achieve these objectives. Although most accept that there is a case for some government intervention to help control the economy, the extent and type of intervention is very much open to debate. The first extract which opens this unit, from *The General Theory of Employment, Interest and Money* by John Maynard Keynes, suggests that governments can and should play an active role in helping to influence macroeconomic variables such as the level of unemployment and the real income of the community, while the second extract, from a speech by James Callaghan when he was UK Prime Minister, highlights some of the problems that may result from government intervention.

The choice and effects of government macroeconomic policies are of great significance to the business community. The measures that the government uses to control the economy are likely to have a major impact on the degree of success or failure of a firm, although of course not all firms will be affected in the same way, depending on factors such as the size of the firm, the type of product it produces, and the degree of competition that exists in their industry.

As you might expect, there are many different opinions as to what the role of government should be in attempting to control the economy. These opinions, however, can be divided into two broad camps. There are those who believe that the economy should be left as much as possible to the workings of the market. Those who follow this line of thought believe that government measures should be limited to helping to ensure that the market is allowed to operate as freely as possible. The merits of the free market were discussed in depth in Unit 7. Others believe that there should be much more government intervention in the running of the economy. We saw in Unit 7 that one of the problems of the free-market system is that it can be unstable with periods of boom and periods of recession. On occasions, it fails to ensure full employment of resources, leading to the unemployment of labour. At other times, there may be inflationary pressures. Therefore, many have come to accept that governments have a role in attempting to

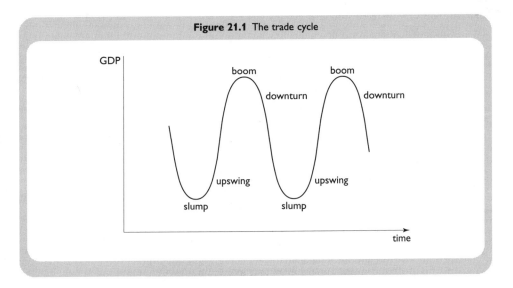

Figure 21.1 The trade cycle

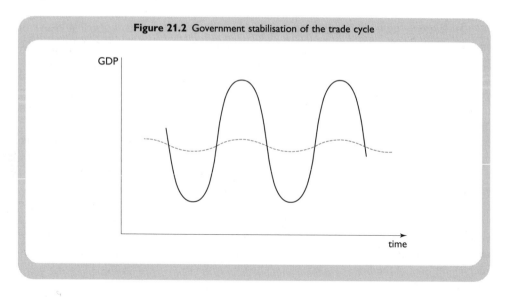

Figure 21.2 Government stabilisation of the trade cycle

manage the economy in order to try to avoid the problems associated with booms and recessions. Figure 21.1 illustrates the pattern of the **trade cycle**, showing the four main stages of slump, upswing, boom and downturn. Figure 21.2 demonstrates the effect of government policy in 'smoothing out' the trade cycle; the broken line represents the path of the economy as a result of successful government intervention, thus reducing the extent of the problems associated with periods of slump and periods of boom. It is argued that if the government is able to manage and stabilise the economy, this will provide firms with a strong and confident economic environment in which to operate.

Macroeconomic goals

Governments are usually recognised as having four major macroeconomic goals or objectives, as follows:

1. To achieve and maintain *stable prices*, or at the very least, low rates of inflation. This has been a key objective of governments in recent years. The problem of inflation is examined in depth in Unit 22.

2. To achieve and maintain *full employment*, or, at the very least, low levels of unemployment. Full employment does not mean that there is *no* unemployment, but it does mean that unemployment levels are very low. In the 1950s and 1960s, an unemployment rate of below 3 per cent was regarded as 'full employment', but governments today would probably gladly settle for an unemployment rate considerably above this level. The problems and costs associated with unemployment are examined in Unit 23.

3. To achieve *balance of payments stability*. A balance of payments deficit occurs when the amount spent on imported goods and services exceeds the revenue gained from selling home-produced goods and services overseas. This represents a net flow of money and wealth overseas and cannot be maintained indefinitely. The

Table 21.1 Key economic indicators (UK)

Year	Inflation (annual % change in RPI)	Unemployment (as a % of the labour force)	Balance of payments (current a/c) (£m.)	Economic growth (annual % change in GDP at factor cost, 1990 prices)
1980	18.4	6.8	+2843	−2.1
1981	13.0	10.4	+6748	−1.1
1982	12.0	12.1	+4649	1.8
1983	4.9	10.5	+3529	3.7
1984	5.1	10.7	+1482	2.0
1985	5.0	10.9	+2238	4.0
1986	5.5	11.1	−864	4.0
1987	3.9	10.0	−4813	4.4
1988	3.3	8.1	−16475	4.9
1989	7.5	6.3	−22398	2.3
1990	7.7	5.8	−19293	0.6
1991	9.0	8.1	−8533	−2.1
1992	4.1	9.8	−10133	−0.5
1993	1.6	10.4	−10756	2.2
1994	2.4	9.4	−2419	3.9
1995	3.5	8.2	−3743	2.5
1996	2.4	7.6	−14	2.3

Source: *Economic Trends*, CSO, various years.

government therefore aims to achieve equilibrium, or even a surplus, on the balance of payments over a number of years.

4. *Economic growth*, which is measured in terms of a rising real national income per head, and which implies rising living standards for the citizens of a country. It has come to be expected that living standards rise over time, with governments typically aiming for a growth rate of 3 per cent per annum.

Table 21.1 outlines the extent to which these objectives have been achieved since 1980. It is possible to extend this list of objectives to include others such as a more equal distribution of income and wealth throughout the economy, or a better regional balance. Moreover, some economists, for example 'greens', would not aim to maximise economic growth. But these four objectives have generally come to be regarded as the main macroeconomic goals of governments.

Unfortunately, these objectives may conflict with each other, which has meant that, over the years, governments have experienced great difficulty in achieving all these objectives simultaneously. Attempts to achieve one objective are likely to have adverse effects on one of the other objectives. Perhaps the most widely recognised conflict is that which occurs between attempts to maintain low rates of inflation together with low rates of unemployment. This was documented through the **Phillips curve**. The Phillips curve and the relationship between inflation and unemployment are examined in more detail in Unit 23. There are, however, conflicts between the other objectives. Attempts to reduce the levels of unemployment might lead to a balance of payments deficit; if more people have jobs, this is likely to lead to an increase in imports. Similarly, attempts to restrict price increases by damping down the level of demand in the economy might have adverse effects on the level of economic growth.

These conflicting goals mean that governments have to prioritise their objectives and decide which are the most important. One or more objectives may have to be sacrificed in order to achieve another. The priority given to each objective changes over time according to economic conditions and the priorities of the government in power. Over the last two decades, control of inflation has been the primary objective of government.

Aggregate demand and aggregate supply

In order to illustrate and explain government management of the economy, we can use the concepts of **aggregate demand** (**AD**) and **aggregate supply** (**AS**). These are the macroeconomic counterparts of the demand and supply models which were introduced in Unit 6. In that unit, we examined how changes in demand or supply affected the price and output of a particular product. In this unit we shall look at how changes in aggregate demand and aggregate supply affect the price level and the level of output in the economy.

Aggregate demand represents the total level of demand within the economy. This demand is derived from consumer spending, investment spending, government spending, and spending by foreigners (i.e. exports) minus any expenditure on imports. The **aggregate demand curve** in Figure 21.3 is downward sloping from left to right as we can assume that the quantity of products that will be bought depends on the price level. The higher the price level, the lower the quantity of products that will be bought, and hence the lower the level of aggregate demand. Just as the demand curve for an individual product shifts to the left or the right, so the aggregate demand curve also shifts. If there is an increase in any of the components of aggregate demand (i.e. consumer spending, investment, government spending or exports) or a fall in imports, then the *AD* curve will shift to the right.

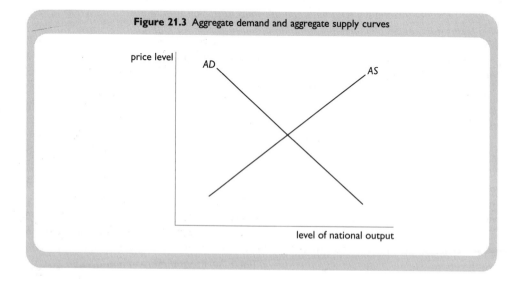

Figure 21.3 Aggregate demand and aggregate supply curves

Table 21.2 Factors causing shifts in the AD and AS curves

Aggregate demand	*Aggregate supply*
Any change in the components of AD:	Any change in:
● consumer spending	● the costs of production
● investment spending	● the size of the workforce
● government spending	● workers' preference for work or
● exports or imports	leisure
These will be influenced by changes in:	● the efficiency of the workforce
● tax rates	● the size of the capital stock
● interest rates	● the state of technology
● business expectations	

Aggregate supply represents the total supply of goods and services by all firms within the economy. The **aggregate supply curve** is often shown as upward sloping from left to right, as in Figure 21.3, since firms will find it more profitable to increase production as the price level rises (other things remaining equal). However, the actual shape of the curve is a matter of controversy, and if the resources of the economy are fully utilised so that firms cannot produce more goods whatever the price, then the *AS* curve will be vertical. Any changes in the conditions of supply will cause the *AS* curve to shift. Thus an increase in wage levels or any other cost of production will shift the *AS* curve to the left. An increase in the size of the workforce or a fall in the costs of production will shift it to the right.

Table 21.2 provides a summary of the major factors that might lead to a shift in either the aggregate demand curve or aggregate supply curve.

We can now use this *AS/AD* model to illustrate the behaviour of the economy and the effects of government intervention. We shall divide the instruments of macroeconomic control into demand-side measures and supply-side measures.

Demand management

If the aggregate demand for goods and services in the economy is too high, in the sense that the economy is unable to supply all the goods and services demanded, prices will be bid upwards, leading to inflation. On the other hand, the aggregate demand for goods and services in the economy might not be high enough to ensure that all resources are fully utilised, resulting in unemployment of some of the labour force. Therefore, in order to try to avoid inflation and unemployment, and the problems which they create, the government could try to control the level of aggregate demand, attempting to reduce it when it is too high and thus avoid inflationary pressures, and increase it when it is too low and thus minimise unemployment.

Demand management can also be used to influence the balance of payments and the rate of economic growth. A reduction in aggregate demand is likely to lead to an improvement in the balance of payments, as the resultant fall in the level of national income will lead to a fall in the level of imports, while increases in aggregate demand lead to an increase in national income, thus improving living standards.

This policy of demand management is associated with the economist John Maynard Keynes and his *General Theory of Employment, Interest and Money*, published in 1936. Traditional economic theory took the view that unemployment would not remain a problem since it would not persist for very long. It predicted that, in the long-run, the economy would settle at an equilibrium level which would ensure that the demand for labour equalled the supply. (This point is examined in more detail in Unit 23.) However, the experiences of the 1930s, when unemployment persisted at very high levels, led Keynes to investigate how the economy works and how the government could intervene to stabilise economic fluctuations and therefore avoid the problems of unemployment.

Keynes and his followers argue that the economy might settle at an equilibrium at which there is significant unemployment. There is no reason why general equilibrium of the economy should mean equilibrium in the labour market. Indeed, it would be very unlikely that all the spending plans of all the millions of individuals and firms in the economy would result in a total level of spending which was just sufficient to ensure jobs for everyone. Therefore, the argument goes, the government should try to influence the general level of spending in the economy so that it is maintained at a level which moves employment as close as possible to full employment.

There are various ways in which the government might try to influence the level of spending in the economy – through fiscal policy, monetary policy, direct controls, or exchange rate adjustments – and we shall now look at each in turn.

Fiscal policy

Fiscal policy is one of the main methods that a government can use to influence the level of aggregate demand and the flow of income. It involves the use of government expenditure and/or taxation. Since government expenditure is a component of aggregate demand and therefore an injection into the circular flow of income, an increase in government spending will have a direct effect on the level of demand. There will also be the subsequent multiplier effects on national income, as described in the previous unit. Keynes strongly favoured fiscal policy as a means of increasing aggregate demand, arguing that during a recession, the government should take the lead by embarking on a public works expenditure programme, for example on roads or houses (see opening extract to this unit). This would create jobs in the construction industry, and the additional income earned by workers in this industry would be spent on other goods and services, thus creating employment in other sectors of the economy. Conversely, if the level of aggregate demand was too high, the government could reduce its own expenditure. This would cause a direct reduction in the level of aggregate demand, and also have additional downward multiplier effects.

Alternatively, instead of using government spending, the government could use taxation to influence the level of demand. A decrease in tax rates would increase the disposable income of households, which will lead to a rise in consumer expenditure, while lower tax rates might also encourage investment spending by firms whose expectations might be raised by the fall in tax rates.

Originally, arranging the budget of the government was a pure accounting exercise, where the government decided the level of its spending and calculated how it would raise revenue to cover that expenditure. The budget was always expected to balance; an

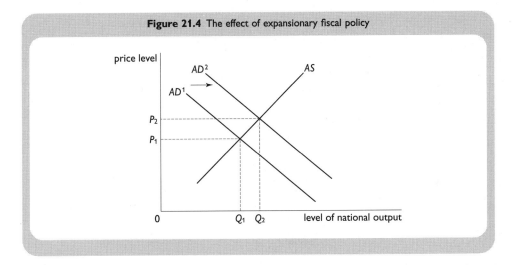

Figure 21.4 The effect of expansionary fiscal policy

unbalanced budget was considered to be bad housekeeping and indicated that the government had miscalculated. However, Keynes said that the government should use the budget as an instrument of economic policy: that is, the government should deliberately unbalance the budget in order to influence the level of aggregate demand. If there is a lack of demand resulting in unemployment, the government should plan for a **budget deficit**, which occurs when government spending exceeds tax revenue. This is referred to as an 'expansionary' or 'reflationary' fiscal policy. Such a policy should help to pull the economy out of a recession, since it will lead to an increase in aggregate demand, as shown in Figure 21.4. As a result of the rise in aggregate demand from AD^1 to AD^2, national output and income has risen from Q_1 to Q_2.

A problem arises, however, in that attempts to reduce the level of unemployment through increasing aggregate demand will probably stimulate inflationary pressures within the economy. As aggregate demand rises, some firms, some sectors and some regions of the economy will start to experience bottlenecks and shortages. Thus prices in these firms, sectors and regions will start to rise. The closer the economy approaches the full employment level, the more difficult it is to increase output and the more likely it is that increases in aggregate demand will result in a rise in the price level. Thus the AS curve could be as shown in Figure 21.5. Initially, an increase in aggregate demand from AD^1 to AD^2 has a sizeable impact on the level of output and employment, without producing much of a rise in the price level. This is because spare capacity and underemployment of resources exist throughout much of the economy. However, if aggregate demand is raised from AD^3 to AD^4, the level of output and employment does not rise by much, but there is a considerable increase in the price level. This happens because the economy is approaching the full employment level.

If the levels of aggregate demand are too high, resulting in inflationary pressures within the economy, the government should plan for a **budget surplus**, which is when tax revenue exceeds government spending. This is referred to as a 'contractionary' or 'deflationary' fiscal policy and would be shown by a shift in the AD curve to the left.

Demand-management policies have therefore often followed the pattern of increasing aggregate demand when it is too low and there is unemployment, until a

Figure 21.5 The impact of fiscal policy dependent on the gradient of the AS curve

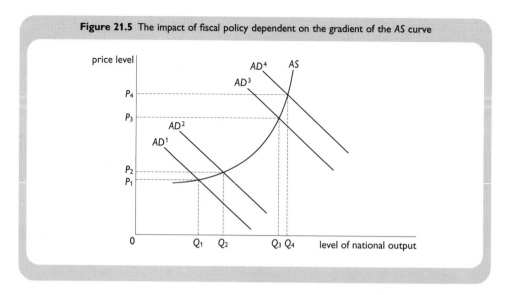

point is reached when the rate of increase of prices is deemed to be becoming too high, at which stage the government would then reverse the policy, dampening down demand so that inflationary pressures are eased. Aggregate demand would continue to be reduced until unemployment again began to rise to unacceptable levels, when the policy would be reversed yet again. For this reason, the strategy of demand management is often referred to as a **stop-go policy**.

This analysis also highlights the conflict that governments face in trying to control both the rate of inflation and the level of unemployment. Nevertheless, these Keynesian ideas were used successfully by governments for three decades after the Second World War. The government increased aggregate demand if unemployment started to rise to unacceptable levels, and then cut back on demand if inflation rates started to rise, and, throughout this period, they managed to ensure that both unemployment and the rate of inflation remained at acceptable levels.

Advantages of fiscal policy
The main advantages of fiscal policy are as follows:

- Changes in fiscal policy have a direct effect on the level of aggregate demand as well as subsequent multiplier effects.

- It can be targeted at specific regions, or specific industries, that are most in need of remedial action. For example, if the rate of unemployment is heavier in one region of the country, the government can direct any increase in its spending to that particular region. Likewise, if one or more industries are suffering particularly badly from a recession, government spending can be directed towards those industries.

- It can be used to influence the composition of demand, as well as the level of aggregate demand. For example, if the government wishes to reduce the level of aggregate demand through raising taxation, it can increase the sales tax on

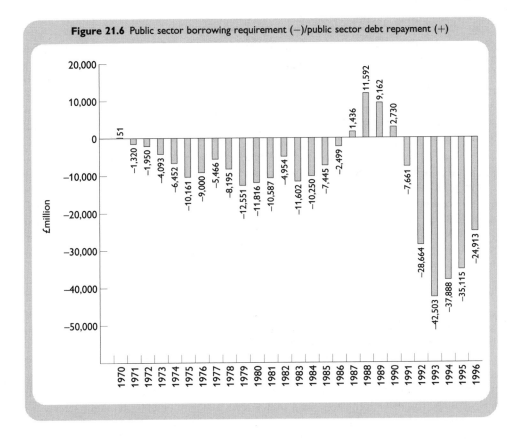

Figure 21.6 Public sector borrowing requirement (−)/public sector debt repayment (+)

some products more than on others and so influence consumer expenditure patterns. Thus leaded fuel might be taxed more highly than unleaded fuel.

● Fiscal policy can also be used to achieve other objectives, such as a more equal distribution of income. This could be achieved through targeting any increase in government spending at the poorer members of the community, or by focusing tax increases on those who earn most.

The public sector borrowing requirement (PSBR)

If the government does operate a budget deficit, this gives rise to the **public sector borrowing requirement** (**PSBR**). This represents the difference between what the public sector plans to spend in a year and what it raises in revenue, and this difference has to be met by borrowing. The accumulated amount that the government has borrowed is referred to as the **national debt**. If the government operates a budget surplus, then this contributes to the **public sector debt repayment** (**PSDR**), which is used to help pay off some of the national debt. Figure 21.6 shows the size of the UK PSBR/PSDR since 1970.

Problems of fiscal policy

Although fiscal policy can be very useful in helping the government to achieve its objectives of stable prices, full employment, balance of payments equilibrium and economic growth, it does have its drawbacks, as follows:

- **Government expenditure is not always flexible**. Much of it is long-term expenditure and cannot be changed easily: for example, public works investment programmes which cannot simply be turned on and off like a tap; roads, hospitals and the like will be at various stages of construction and cannot be stopped in mid-stream. Likewise, the government cannot keep adjusting tax rates, as this would be an administrative nightmare. Changes in the rates of tax also require parliamentary approval, which delays and may limit the options open to the government. Tax rates and government expenditure plans are usually reviewed annually, so changes in fiscal policy can only really occur once a year – as opposed to, say, monetary policy, where interest rates can be changed much more frequently. A further complication is that there is often a public outcry if the government decides to raise taxes or cut back on public expenditure, whether it be on health, defence, education, or old age pensions. Therefore political considerations and the desire to be popular with the electorate may override economic considerations. The desire to be re-elected may deter the government from cutting its spending, even if economic conditions so dictate.

- **Time lags**. Eventually government expenditure and taxation can be changed, but there will be time lags. There will, for instance, be a time lag due to the time it takes the government to recognise that there is a problem with the economy, which is due in part to the length of time required to collect economic statistics. There is also a time lag between the government initiating a policy and when it begins to take effect. These time lags indicate, first, that fiscal policy is not a very flexible policy instrument, and secondly, that it is difficult for the government to judge the effectiveness of any policy which it implements. It might decide to reinforce a policy that appears not to be having much effect, when in fact what is really happening is that the policy is working but is just taking time to have an effect. This can mean that the government policy might actually have a destabilising effect, making fluctuations in the trade cycle worse, rather than stabilising them by overreacting to any problem.

- **Incomplete information and statistics** can lead to difficulties: for example, the government may not know the exact size of the multiplier effect. Any change in government spending or taxation will result in larger changes in the level of national income, due to the multiplier. However, if the government cannot accurately predict the size of the multiplier, it will not know by how much to adjust its level of spending or taxation and will not be able to forecast the eventual change in the level of aggregate demand.

- **Problems of fine-tuning**. Fine-tuning is where frequent but minor adjustments are made to economic policy in order to help the economy settle at exactly the desired level of income. Although fiscal policy is useful for helping to stabilise the economy and for removing heavy and persistent unemployment and inflation, the problem of time lags, ignorance of the size of the multiplier effect, and the inflexibility of government expenditure and taxation means that it can be rather clumsy in its effect and is not very good for fine-tuning the economy. Critics also point to the damaging effects on confidence and long-term investment plans that the 'stop-go' nature of the policy can have.

- **'Crowding out' effect**. In recent years, an argument that has often been employed against the use of government expenditure to increase aggregate demand is **crowding out**. This argument is based upon the premise that any increase in government spending will lead to an equivalent reduction in private sector investment spending: that is, the private sector is crowded out by the expansion of the public sector. This might occur if the economy is making full use of all its resources. If full employment exists, the only way that public sector industries can expand is by attracting workers and other resources from the private sector, thus starving the private sector of those workers and resources. This is known as *'resource' crowding out*. However, Keynesian demand management policies advocate an expansion of government spending only if there is unemployment of workers and resources are standing idle. Thus this type of crowding out is unlikely to occur.

  However, even if there are unemployed workers and resources within the economy, there might still be *'financial' crowding out*. If the government borrows money to finance a budget deficit, this represents an increase in the demand for funds. This increase in the demand for funds may well push up interest rates as the government, as well as private firms, will be in competition for the available funds. This increase in interest rates will crowd out private borrowing and lead to a fall in investment spending. In the extreme case, the increase in public sector spending might be cancelled out completely by a decrease in private sector investment spending. Furthermore, if the country has a system of flexible exchange rates, the higher interest rates might lead to a rise in the exchange rate. This higher exchange rate makes it more difficult for domestic firms to sell their products overseas and at the same time makes imported products cheaper. As a result, private sector firms will suffer a drop in sales which again will cancel out the expansionary policy of the government. In order to avoid an increase in interest rates as a result of the government borrowing, the government could increase the money supply. The larger supply of money means that interest rates should not rise, but the drawback of this is that the increase in the money supply could be inflationary (see Unit 22). Evidence seems to suggest that some crowding out occurs as a result of expansionary government fiscal policies, although the extent of the crowding out is limited.

Automatic fiscal stabilisers

Even if the drawbacks of fiscal policy cause governments to abandon the use of discretionary fiscal policy, it is worth noting the existence of automatic fiscal stabilisers. These stabilisers are mechanisms which automatically help to reduce fluctuations within the trade cycle. Even if the government does not deliberately pursue a budget deficit or a budget surplus, it will find that during times of recession there will be a tendency for it to run a budget deficit, which will help to boost aggregate demand and the level of income. During a recession, government expenditure will tend to rise because it is paying out more in unemployment and other benefits, while it will be receiving less revenue from income tax as fewer people will be working, less revenue from sales taxes as fewer goods and services will be purchased, and less revenue from corporation tax as company profits will be lower.

Exercise

When an economy is booming, unemployment might fall, but inflation is likely to accelerate. Explain how automatic fiscal stabilisers might operate in order to help stabilise the economy.

The impact of fiscal policy on firms

We shall now look specifically at how the government's fiscal policy might affect firms:

- Fiscal policy affects the level of consumer spending and the level of income. The impact that this has on firms will depend on the type of goods and services they produce. If the demand for their product is income elastic, as is the case for consumer durables where demand is responsive to changes in income, the impact will be much greater. A change in the level of income will have a large impact on the demand for the product. For products such as milk or bread, however, changes in the level of income brought about by changes in fiscal policy are unlikely to have much impact on demand.

- In addition to having an impact on firms through changes in the level of income, changes in government spending and taxation can also have a much more direct impact on firms. Government spending comes in many forms. It may be in the guise of regional assistance, where the government might spend money in an attempt to achieve a better regional balance. Firms in the regions which have been targeted might benefit from an investment grant. Alternatively, the government might increase its spending on training and education. Schemes like the Youth Training Scheme (YTS) can help to subsidise a firm's training and wages bill, while an increase in government spending on education would benefit the publishers of textbooks and other suppliers of educational equipment. Two industries in particular rely on the public sector as purchaser of their goods and services and are worthy of a special mention. First, the government is usually the chief purchaser of defence equipment in any country, and in this role, it provides a large amount of revenue for some of the large manufacturing firms in the country. Any reduction in defence spending would therefore have significant implications for these firms. Secondly, the state is the principal purchaser of construction services such as road and house building and repair. If a government decides to trim back its capital investment programmes, the construction industry will suffer from a severe drop in orders.

- Specific tax changes may also have a direct impact on some firms. If the government decides to increase its tax revenue by abolishing income tax relief on mortgage payments, this will have a serious impact on the housing market and construction firms. One of the taxes that the government might adjust in its pursuit of fiscal policy is corporation tax, which is a tax on company profits. A reduction in the rate of corporation tax would mean that firms would have more money available for investment, which might lead to a fall in the amount of borrowing that they would have to undertake, or alternatively, they might decide to distribute more dividends to shareholders.

● The stop-go nature of fiscal policy causes uncertainty for firms. It may make them reluctant to commit themselves to long-term investment plans as demand for their product might keep fluctuating in response to changes in the government's fiscal policy. If the problem of time lags causes fiscal policy to exaggerate the trade cycle rather than to stabilise it, then this will not be in the interests of firms. However, the mere fact that the government is intervening and doing something about the economy might boost the expectations of some firms and instil confidence.

Exercise

In an attempt to reduce the rate of inflation and improve the balance of payments, the government has taken the following decisions: (a) to raise the rate of VAT from 17.5 per cent to 20 per cent; and (b) to reduce its expenditure on defence.

Questions

1. Explain why these measures might lower the rate of inflation and improve the balance of payments.
2. Consider the impact of these measures on businesses.

Monetary policy

An alternative, or complementary method of influencing aggregate demand is the use of **monetary policy**. This involves control of the money supply and the rate of interest. In the 1950s and 1960s, monetary policy took second place to fiscal policy as a method of controlling aggregate demand in the UK. From the 1970s onwards, however, more importance has been attached to the use of monetary policy. This was partly because fiscal policy no longer seemed to be able to provide the answers to high unemployment and high inflation, but also because monetary policy was perceived as being less interventionist than fiscal policy and therefore fits in with the ideology of those who favour the free-market approach to the control of the economy.

There is much controversy concerning the role and effectiveness of monetary policy as an instrument of macroeconomic policy. Keynesians see the role of monetary policy as one of helping to control the level of aggregate demand. If the money supply is allowed to increase and interest rates fall, aggregate demand should rise. Households will find it cheaper to borrow money, hence consumer expenditure will rise. Those households who have mortgages will pay less on mortgage repayments and will have more to spend on other items. Low interest rates should also encourage an increase in investment spending by firms, again adding to aggregate demand. On the other hand, if growth of the money supply is restricted and interest rates rise, this should reduce consumer spending, since, after higher mortgage repayments, they will have less disposable income. It also makes it more expensive to take out loans, so consumers will be deterred from borrowing money, which again will lead to a fall in consumer spending, particularly on those products which are often bought on credit. There should also be a fall in investment spending by firms. Higher interest rates might also encourage an increase in saving, as the reward gained from saving will be greater, again leading to a fall in the level of spending. All these factors should lead to a fall in aggregate demand and thereby reduce inflationary pressures within the economy.

An advantage of using monetary policy to influence aggregate demand is that it is more flexible than fiscal policy. Taxation and government spending plans are only usually reviewed once a year, while changes to the interest rate can be made more quickly and more frequently and can be used to influence aggregate demand between budgets. However, the link between interest rates and aggregate demand is weak and uncertain. We saw in the previous unit that the link between interest rates and investment spending is unpredictable. Evidence seems to suggest that investment is more responsive to business confidence and expectations; it is not just dependent on the cost of borrowing. In addition, there is much doubt over the government's ability to control the money supply (see Unit 17). For these reasons, monetary policy is viewed by Keynesians as supplementary to, but not as powerful or reliable as, fiscal policy.

Monetarists reject the use of monetary policy as a short-term instrument used to control aggregate demand. Instead, they focus on the link between the money supply and the price level, with the belief that there is a causal relationship between the growth of the money supply and the rate of inflation. (This relationship is explained and examined in Unit 22 on inflation.) They see the role of monetary policy as being one of helping to promote and maintain a stable economy through strict control of the money supply. Long-run stability and low rates of inflation will then provide an environment in which private enterprise can flourish and prosper.

A problem with interest rates is that they cannot be used discriminately. Changes in fiscal policy can be targeted at those parts of the economy where attention is most needed, but changes in interest rates are applied indiscriminately across the entire economy. If interest rates are lowered, this lower rate applies across the whole country, even though economic conditions in one part of the country might be much more favourable than in other regions. A further problem is that monetary policy is conducted through financial institutions. This makes it more difficult for the government to control the implementation of the policy; in the past, financial institutions have found ways of circumventing restrictions on lending which the government has imposed on them.

A change in interest rates will also affect the foreign exchange value of sterling. A rise in interest rates will increase the value of the pound, which will make UK goods less competitive overseas and make imports more attractive. This, however, will also help relieve inflationary pressures as there will be less demand for exports, while import prices will be lower.

The impact of monetary policy on firms

Changes in the rate of interest are likely to have some impact on the demand for a firm's product depending on the nature of the product. Higher interest rates will dampen down consumer demand, so firms may suffer a drop in sales. The construction industry, estate agents and removal firms are likely to be particularly affected by a rise in the mortgage rate, which would result in a fall in house sales, while those firms which sell consumer durables that are often bought on credit (e.g. cars) will suffer a drop in demand. Changes in the interest rate will also affect the cost of borrowing for firms, with a rise in the rate raising the cost of financing borrowing. This will particularly affect small firms who are more dependent on bank loans as a source of finance than larger firms who may be able to raise

Table 21.3 The effect of change in the exchange rate on import and export prices

A UK firm exports a product to Germany for £2000, while another UK firm imports German-made components for DM 12 each.

If £1 = DM 2:

The UK product sells for DM 4000 in Germany, while the imported components cost £6 each.

If £1 = DM 3:

The UK product now sells for DM 6000 in Germany, while the imported components now cost only £4 each.

share capital. An increase in interest rates might also lead to a fall in a company's share price, as investors may be attracted to invest their funds elsewhere, such as government securities, which will now be earning higher rates of interest. In order to stop the share price falling and to retain shareholders, a company may have to pay out higher dividends.

Direct controls

The government might try to control the economy through the use of direct controls. These include such things as an incomes policy, which is discussed in more detail in Unit 22, and import controls such as tariffs or quotas, which are discussed in Unit 24. Direct controls are associated more with interventionist governments.

Exchange rate policy

The government might use the foreign exchange rate as an instrument of economic policy. A rise in the exchange rate will make imports cheaper and exports more expensive, both of which will help to reduce aggregate demand and relieve inflationary pressures. A fall in the exchange rate will make imports dearer and exports cheaper, both of which should lead to an increase in aggregate demand as both UK and overseas consumers will be attracted towards UK goods, thereby helping to increase employment. Table 21.3 summarises the effect of a change in the exchange rate on import and export prices.

The option to use exchange rates as a policy instrument depends on whether the economy is party to an exchange rate system. Between 1990 and 1992, the UK belonged to the European **Exchange Rate Mechanism**, which limited the government's ability to use exchange rates as a policy instrument since the extent to which fluctuations in the rate were allowed was limited. The creation of a single European currency will also remove the exchange rate as a policy instrument. Exchange rates and the impact of changes in the exchange rate on firms are covered in detail in Unit 25.

Supply-side economics

From the mid-1970s the UK economy started to experience rising inflation and rising unemployment simultaneously. This meant that Keynesian demand-management policies no longer seemed to be able to provide the answer to macroeconomic problems, and

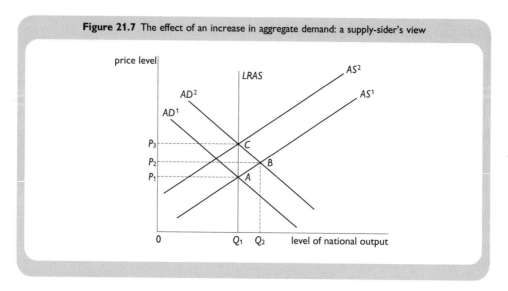

Figure 21.7 The effect of an increase in aggregate demand: a supply-sider's view

indeed, some claimed that demand-management policies were the cause of the problems, as the extract from a speech by James Callaghan at the start of this unit indicates. They attributed the rising inflation and unemployment to the high levels of public spending and government borrowing that had been carried out by successive governments in their attempts to stimulate aggregate demand and thus keep down unemployment. This group of economists, who we can refer to as 'supply-siders', argue that aggregate supply will not respond to changes in aggregate demand, or, if it does, only in the short run. Consider Figure 21.7. In the short-run, an increase in aggregate demand from AD^1 to AD^2 may lead to an increase in output and employment from Q_1 to Q_2. However, as a result of the higher price level at P_2, workers will demand higher wages. This increase in wages will shift the aggregate supply curve to the left, from AS^1 to AS^2, so that the final equilibrium is at point C, with output and employment back at the original level of Q_1, but now with a much higher price level. The long-run aggregate supply curve (LRAS) is therefore vertical, and, in the long-run, any increase in aggregate demand will not lead to an increase in either employment or the national output of the economy, but will simply generate higher prices.

Supply-side economists therefore favour measures that increase aggregate supply, as a means of increasing the output and employment of the economy, rather than demand-management policies. Many modern Keynesian economists would also support some of the methods used to shift the AS curve. The effect of successful **supply-side policies** can be shown through the movement of the AS curve to the right, which results in an increase in the level of output and employment, but a lower price level, as illustrated in Figure 21.8.

The government of Margaret Thatcher which came to power in the UK in 1979 advocated minimal government intervention based on the belief that the free-market system is the key to the long-run success of an economy. It felt that the role of government should be one of allowing and enabling market forces to work as effectively as possible, rather than direct intervention through demand-management policies. While the objectives of government policy did not change, the methods of attaining them did.

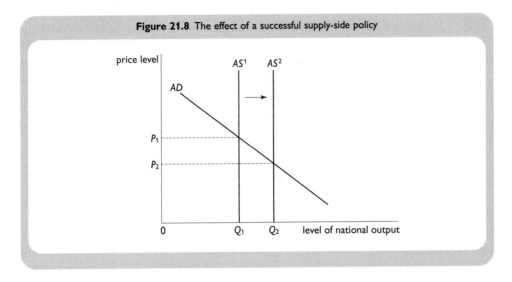

Figure 21.8 The effect of a successful supply-side policy

The government rejected the belief that unemployment could be reduced in the long run through demand-management policies. Any attempt to increase aggregate demand would merely result in inflation, and inflation was felt to be a major cause of unemployment. The best way to reduce unemployment in the long term was to eradicate inflation. Thus the control of inflation became the most important objective, and supply-side policies were an important part of this.

Supply-side measures

Tax reductions

It was argued by the government that high taxes were a disincentive to work. Reductions in income tax would provide people with more incentive to work, as the financial reward from employment, in terms of take-home pay, will be greater. With more people entering the labour force, and those already working willing to work longer hours, this would have the effect of shifting the *AS* curve to the right. Reductions in corporation tax – the tax on company profits – enables firms to plough more of their profit back into investment, again increasing the potential output of the economy.

Reform of trade unions

Many measures were introduced in the UK which resulted in a reduction of trade union power. The effect that trade unions have upon wage levels was examined in Unit 15, but the belief of the government was that trade unions distort the workings of the labour market by forcing up wage levels. If the power of trade unions is reduced, this should relieve pressure on wage levels and again shift the *AS* curve to the right.

Deregulation of the labour market

The government argued that people are sometimes reluctant to set up in business and firms are sometimes deterred from employing workers because of all the rules, regulation and red tape which they encounter and the high costs associated with employing workers. Therefore the removal of bureaucratic regulations and deregulation of the labour market, such as reducing employee rights to redundancy pay, should make it easier and cheaper for firms to employ workers, again shifting the *AS* curve to the right.

Reform of social security and unemployment benefits

High levels of unemployment benefit might deter unemployed workers from seeking employment. By reducing the number of people entitled to claim benefits and lowering the levels of benefit, the unemployed should have more incentive to seek work as the gap between paid employment and state benefits will be much wider. Lower benefits should also help to keep down wage levels, again shifting the *AS* curve to the right.

Privatisation, deregulation and contracting-out

These measures (which were examined in Unit 12) reduce the role of the state and help to increase competition. **Deregulation** has allowed increased competition in previously regulated industries such as bus services and opticians, while the contracting-out of local government services such as refuse collection and the provision of school meals has increased competition and lowered costs. The revenue generated from privatisation also helps in the reduction of income tax thus encouraging incentives.

Retraining

If workers do not have the skills that are in demand, no amount of manipulation of aggregate demand will create job opportunities for them. There will be a mismatch between the demand for workers and the supply. In this situation, it is necessary to make changes to the *supply* of labour through retraining programmes, so that those who are unemployed have the necessary skills to enable them to secure employment in those industries which require workers.

Educational reforms

The government has introduced many reforms to the education system with the aim of introducing more vocational training, rather than having purely academic education. The introduction of schemes such as Technical and Vocational Educational Initiatives (TVEIs), National Vocational Qualifications (NVQs) and General National Vocational Qualifications (GNVQs) is intended to try to make the workforce of the future more skilled and adaptable, which again will shift the *AS* curve to the right.

Regional policy

The government aims to correct regional imbalance by making wages more flexible between regions. Locally negotiated wages as opposed to national wage agreements should ensure that wage levels reflect local labour market conditions.

Profit-sharing and share ownership schemes

Schemes for profit sharing and share ownership involve workers in the success of their firm and help provide an incentive to work, improve productivity and improve industrial relations.

Although demand-side and supply-side policies are often put forward as two completely different and alternative policies, many policies will have both demand-side and supply-side elements to them. For example, government spending on training and education has a demand-side element, since the increase in government spending represents an injection into the circular flow of income, thereby increasing aggregate demand, while the retraining of the labour force makes changes to the supply of labour. Supply-side and demand-side policies should therefore be regarded as complementary to each other, rather than alternative policy options.

Summary

The state of the economy and government attempts to regulate the economy can have a great impact on firms. The major economic problems that the government attempts to address are inflation, unemployment, balance of payments problems and economic growth. There is disagreement as to how these problems should be tackled. Demand-side policies involve regulating the level of aggregate demand, primarily through the use of fiscal policy, which involves manipulating the level of government spending and taxation, and through the use of monetary policy, which involves regulating the money supply and interest rates. Supply-side policies are based on the free-market philosophy that governments should intervene as little as possible in the running of the economy and involve removing any obstacles and obstructions that may prevent the free market from functioning efficiently. While demand-side policies seemed to be unable to deal successfully with the problem of high inflation and rising unemployment in the UK in the 1970s, supply-side policies have also had a mixed record. Although, at the time of writing, inflation has fallen to acceptable levels and the productivity of industry has improved, the level of unemployment has remained high and the balance of payments has experienced record deficits.

Review questions

1. What are the four main macroeconomic objectives of government? Explain briefly why it might be difficult for the government to achieve all these objectives simultaneously.

2. What is meant by fiscal policy?

3. Why is fiscal policy not very useful for 'fine-tuning' the economy?

4. Identify the ways in which changes in fiscal policy might affect firms?

5. What is meant by 'crowding out'? Why might it occur?

6. What is meant by monetary policy?

7. Distinguish between demand-side and supply-side policies, giving examples of each.

8. Illustrate, using an aggregate-demand and aggregate-supply diagram, the effect of each of the following measures:
   (a) an increase in government spending on public sector wages;
   (b) the reduction of the powers of trade unions;
   (c) an increase in government spending on the training of workers; and
   (d) a reduction in corporation tax.
   Explain your answers.

Essay questions

1. How might the government use taxation and its own spending to influence the level of economic activity? With the use of examples, explain how individual firms might be affected by such a policy.

2. Assess the effectiveness of the supply-side policies which have been used in the UK since 1980, and examine the impact they have had on the business community.

Reading 21.1

'Britain is becoming more efficient!'

A report published in 1995 claimed that the UK has become more efficient at manufacturing since 1979, closing much of the productivity gap that existed between itself and countries such as France and Germany, although it continues to lag some way behind the leading Western European economies and Japan. The increased productivity improved Britain's competitive position, and the report claims that, aside from exchange rate movements, this was due to the following four main developments:

1. privatisation;
2. substantial investment;
3. a shift towards smaller businesses; and
4. a more efficient labour market.

Privatisation, it is claimed, improved productivity in the previously nationalised industries. New technology, deregulation, and lower tax rates have encouraged more investment and the creation of small firms, while legislation aimed at reducing the power of trade unions has virtually eliminated industrial action.

Questions

1. The passage identifies four major developments, aside from exchange rate movements, which have contributed to an improvement in Britain's competitive position. Explain why each of these developments would have led to an improvement in Britain's performance.

2. How might exchange rate movements improve Britain's competitive position?

3. Would you classify the developments which are discussed in this report as 'demand-side' or 'supply-side' measures? Explain your answer.

Inflation and its effects on firms

The UK government has been guilty of using several different ways of presenting inflation statistics in an attempt, some claim, to make the rate of inflation appear lower. The traditional measure of inflation used in the UK has been the retail price index, or RPI. But when the government reduced the rates of income tax, it decided to put more emphasis on the tax and price index as a measure of inflation. This took into account changes in income tax and national insurance contributions. They later switched to a measure known as RPI(X). This method excluded mortgage interest payments from the calculation of inflation rates, just at a time when mortgage interest rates were at their highest level for years. When, however, increases in indirect taxes led to a rise in the inflation rate, the government decided to introduce RPI(Y), a method of calculation which excluded indirect taxes as well as mortgage interest payments from the rate of inflation.

So just what is the correct measure of the rate of inflation?

Inflation can be defined as a general and persistent tendency for prices to increase. It does not mean that all prices are rising: the price of some products may remain stable, while some prices may even be falling. On average, however, prices are increasing over a period of time. As prices are increasing, inflation also means that money loses its value; you would need much more money today to buy the same goods which you could have purchased ten years ago.

Maintaining stable prices, or at least, a low rate of inflation, is one of the crucial macroeconomic objectives of governments. Since the late 1970s it has come to be regarded by many as *the* central objective. What exactly is meant by a low rate of inflation is open to argument, although a rate below 3 per cent per annum seems to be acceptable to most governments.

Inflation is present throughout the world. Most countries experience an upward movement in their general price level and, since the Second World War, inflation has been a feature of most European economies. In the UK in the 1950s and the 1960s, it could be referred to as 'creeping inflation', as it remained less than 5 per cent per annum throughout these two decades. The UK government therefore appears to have been relatively successful at controlling inflation at this time, as indeed it was at achieving full employment. The policies of Keynesian demand management (outlined in the previous unit), which were accepted by governments of both main political parties, appeared to be working successfully. In the 1970s, however, inflation in the UK was generally worse than in other European countries. For much of the decade it was above 10 per cent per annum, reaching 25 per cent in 1975. At the same time, unemployment was rising, so people began to question the use of demand-management policies. UK inflation fell in the 1980s but rose again to reach almost double figures by the end of the decade, although in the 1990s it has remained at relatively low levels (see Figure 22.1).

When inflation reaches very high rates, it is referred to as hyperinflation. When this arises, money loses its value very rapidly, to the degree that people lose confidence in money and are reluctant to use it as a means of exchange. Hyperinflation occurred in Germany, which had a *monthly* inflation rate of 322 per cent in 1923 and where prices rose by ten thousand million times between August 1922 and November 1923. Inflation on this scale also occurred in Hungary in 1945, and, in more recent years, inflation has

Figure 22.1 Annual change in the UK retail price index, 1972–96

Source: Employment Gazette, December 1991 and February 1996.

reached extremely high levels in several South American and Latin American countries, in Poland, where prices quadrupled in four months in 1989–90, and in Angola in 1996 where inflation reached over 4000 per cent per annum.

Measuring inflation

It is relatively easy to see how the price of one product has changed, but it is much more difficult to measure the general movement of prices. There is such a large range of goods and services on sale in the economy that their prices are likely to be rising at different rates, and the prices of some products may even be falling. Therefore we need to examine what is happening to the prices of a cross-section of products, and to take an average.

Construction of a price index

A price index examines what is happening to the prices of a representative sample of products over a period of time. This sample of products is referred to as a *basket* of goods. To simplify the construction of our index, we will include just three items in the basket. In the year in which our index is started, the price of Product A is £1, the price of product B is £5, and the price of Product C is £10. We will call the first year of our index the 'base' year, and so will allocate each of these prices the index number of 100. The following year, the price of Product A has risen to £1.10, that of Product B to £5.25, while the price of Product C has fallen to £9.70. This information is shown in Table 22.1, together with the index numbers for Year 2.

The price index in Year 2 is 104, which indicates that the rate of inflation has been 4 per cent over the year. However, this index is rather simplistic, not merely because we have limited the number of items to three products, but because we have assumed that products A, B and C are all of equal significance. However, if Product A were a loaf of bread, while Product B was a pen, changes in the price of bread are of far more concern to most people than changes in the price of pens. Therefore, an allowance for the relative importance of each item needs to be built into our index. We do this by allocating 'weights' to the items in the basket, based on the proportion of total expenditure that they account for. In the weighted index in Table 22.2, Product A has been allocated a weight of 5, Product B a weight of 3 and Product C a weight of 2. To calculate the **weighted index**,

Table 22.1 Price index for three products

	Year 1			Year 2	
	Price (£)	Index		Price(£)	Index
Product A	1	100		1.10	110
Product B	5	100		5.25	105
Product C	10	100		9.70	97
		300 ÷ 3			312 ÷ 3
	Price index in base year = 100			Price index in Year 2 = 104	

Table 22.2 Weighted price index for three products

	Weight	Price (£)	Year 2 Index	Weighted index
Product A	5	1.10	110	550
Product B	3	5.25	105	315
Product C	2	9.70	97	194
				$1059 \div 10$

Weighted index in Year 2 = 105.9

the index number for each item is multiplied by its weight, and the sum of the weighted index numbers is divided by the total number of weights, in this case 10.

Using a weighted index, the rate in inflation over the year is 5.9 per cent. This is higher than our previous figure of 4 per cent because this time, more emphasis has been placed on the product that has the biggest weight and which, in this case, had the greatest percentage price increase.

Exercise

In Years 3 and 4, the prices of Products A, B and C were as follows:

	Year 3	Year 4
Product A	£1.20	£1.30
Product B	£5.50	£5.75
Product C	£9.70	£9.80

Keeping Year 1 as the base year, and using the weights as given in the worked example above,

1. Calculate weighted price indexes for Years 3 and 4.
2. What is the percentage rate of inflation between Year 1 and Year 4?
3. Calculate the percentage rates of inflation between (a) Year 2 and Year 3; (b) Year 3 and Year 4.

Retail price index (RPI)

The main measure of inflation in the UK is the **retail price index** (**RPI**). This examines what is happening to the price of 600 separate items. These items and their weights are chosen to represent the expenditure pattern of an average household, and are revised each year to reflect the changes in expenditure patterns. Table 22.3 shows the retail price index from 1987, while Table 22.4 shows the weights attributed to each category of household expenditure in 1987 and in 1997. From the change in the weighting of each

Table 22.3 Retail price index, annual average (Jan. 1987 = 100)

Year	Average	Year	Average
1987	101.9	1992	138.5
1988	106.9	1993	140.7
1989	115.2	1994	144.1
1990	126.1	1995	149.1
1991	133.5	1996	152.7

Source: Labour Market Trends, June 1997.

category, we can see that food, fuel and light represented a smaller proportion of expenditure for the average household in the 1990s, while housing costs and leisure services represented a much larger proportion.

The RPI provides just one measure of inflation, and is sometimes referred to as the 'headline' inflation rate, but it is not necessarily the best measure of inflationary pressures within the economy. The news item at the start of this unit gives an indication of the range of inflation measures that the government has used. The RPI includes, for example, mortgage payments, local authority taxation (the council tax), and the effect on prices of changes in the rate of VAT. The government claims that it is not a very good measure of the 'underlying' inflation rate, as the inclusion of these items can distort the rate of inflation by causing erratic movements in the RPI. A further complication is that other countries tend to use a different method of measuring housing costs, making the RPI a poor method of comparing inflation rates between countries. The government therefore publishes other measures of inflation: 'RPI(X)' excludes mortgage interest rate payments from the calculation of the inflation rate, while 'RPI(Y)' goes one step further by excluding

Table 22.4 Retail price index weights

	1987	1997
Food	167	136
Catering	46	49
Alcoholic drink	76	80
Tobacco	38	34
Housing	157	186
Fuel and light	61	41
Household goods	73	72
Household services	44	52
Clothing and footwear	74	56
Personal goods	38	40
Motoring expenditure	127	128
Fares and other travel	22	20
Leisure goods	47	47
Leisure services	30	59
	1000	1000

Source: Labour Market Trends, June 1997.

the effects of VAT changes. These measures are perhaps a better guide than the RPI to the inflationary pressures which exist within the economy.

There are also many other price indexes. The *index of producer prices* is a measure of price changes which producers face, and this is perhaps a better measure of the underlying inflation rate, as well as giving us a guide as to what is likely to happen to retail prices in the future. Individual industries also construct their own price indexes, made up of products that are of relevance to their particular industry. Thus the construction industry uses a price index which examines what is happening to the prices of building materials.

It is therefore important to realise that there is not just one measure of inflation. Every individual purchases a different combination of goods and services, and so experiences a rate of inflation unique to themselves. Similarly, each sector of the economy is subject to a different rate of inflation, and different regions of the country are likely to experience differing rates of inflation also.

Causes of inflation

There is much debate and disagreement between economists over what causes inflation. In the two or three decades after the Second World War, inflation in the UK was usually categorised as one of two types: **demand-pull inflation** or **cost-push inflation**. The rise of monetarism in the late 1970s however disputed these labels, and put forward just one main cause of inflation, that of allowing the money supply to grow too rapidly.

Demand-pull inflation

Demand-pull inflation arises when there is too much demand in the economy for the available output. Just as an increase in demand for an individual product causes its price to rise, so a high level of aggregate demand in the economy will cause upward pressure on prices. Figure 22.2 illustrates the effect on the price level of an increase in aggregate demand.

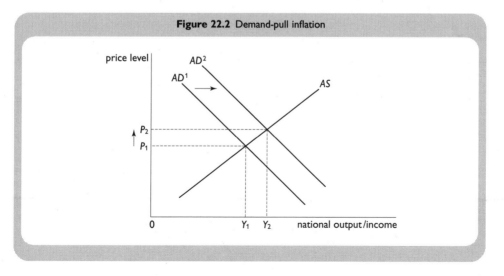

Figure 22.2 Demand-pull inflation

The high level of demand may originate from consumers, from firms, from overseas or from governments. Indeed, demand-pull inflation has often been blamed on governments who, in pursuing Keynesian demand-management policies to keep down the level of unemployment, have injected too much demand into the economy resulting in price rises. A cut in income tax, for example, will increase the spending power of consumers, raising the level of aggregate demand. While this may stimulate employment, output may not be able to increase sufficiently to accommodate the higher level of demand, resulting in price increases.

Cost-push inflation

Cost-push inflation arises when the costs of production rise independently from the level of demand and these increased costs are passed on to the consumer in the form of higher prices. The effect of this is shown in Figure 22.3. The *AS* curve shifts to the left as firms are less willing to supply goods and services as a result of the increased costs of production.

Cost-push inflation has often been blamed on trade unions who negotiate large wage increases for their members independently of the demand for labour, thus increasing the costs of production for firms (wage-push). The effect on prices will be particularly marked in those firms where wage costs represent a high proportion of total costs. In addition, this type of inflation can be self-sustaining and can lead to a rapid escalation in prices as a 'wage–price spiral' develops. In this situation, having achieved a wage increase, workers then discover subsequently that prices have also risen, so that in real terms they are no better off. They therefore demand another wage increase to keep up with or keep ahead of inflation, which in turn leads to even higher prices, and so the spiral continues.

Increases in the costs of materials or commodity prices can also cause cost-pull inflation. When these products are imported from abroad – as was the case for the oil price rises in the 1970s – there is often very little that governments can do to counter the effects of the inflation as it originates from a source external to the national economy. There may also arise 'profit-push' inflation, where firms, perhaps because they have

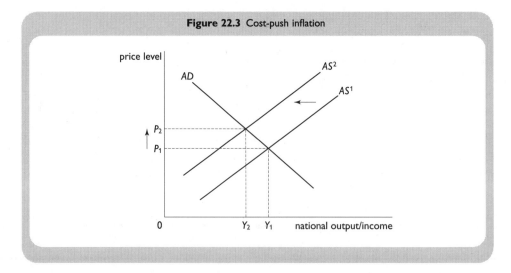

Figure 22.3 Cost-push inflation

obtained a degree of monopoly power, are able to set their own prices independently of consumer demand and raise prices in order to increase profit margins. An increase in indirect taxes such as value added tax (VAT) may also contribute to cost-push inflation.

The monetarist theory of inflation

The **monetarist theory of inflation** regained favour in the late 1970s. It claims that categorising inflation as either demand-pull or cost-push ignores the main cause of inflation, namely, allowing the money supply to grow faster than output. 'Inflation is always and everywhere a monetary phenomenon,' claimed Milton Friedman, indicating a belief that inflation always originates from monetary growth, and nothing else. This is based on the belief that money is just like any other commodity. If the supply of potatoes increases, their price will fall. If the supply of money increases, its price, or *value*, will likewise fall, and if the value of money is falling, this means that prices are increasing.

The origins of this theory, the *quantity theory of money*, date back to the nineteenth century and can be illustrated through the use of the **Fisher equation**, which states that:

$$MV = PT$$

where:

M = the stock of money in an economy;
V = the velocity at which it circulates;
P = the price level; and
T = the number of transactions which take place, which is dependent on the output of the economy.

It is necessary to include the velocity of circulation of money, as each unit of currency can be used many times over in a given time period.

What this equation shows is that the amount of money spent in the economy (MV) is equal to the value of products purchased (PT). For example, if $M = 3000$, $V = 2$, $P = 10$, and $T = 600$, then:

$$M(3000) \times V(2) = P(10) \times T(600)$$
$$(MV)6000 = 6000(PT)$$

This is in fact two ways of saying the same thing. However, monetarists claim more than this. They claim that there is a causal link between the two sides of the equation. They believe that, over time, the velocity at which money circulates remains relatively stable, and that, in the short run, it is very difficult to increase the output of the economy, so the number of transactions will also remain constant. Therefore, if V and T remain constant in the above equation, any increase in the money stock (M) must be accompanied by an increase in the price level (P), in order that the two sides of the equation remain equal. Thus a 10 per cent increase in the money supply will cause a 10 per cent rise in the price level.

So, if M rises to 3300, and V and T remain constant, then:

$$(M)3300 \times (V)2 = P \times 600(T)$$

and P must rise to 11 to balance the equation.

Keynesians tend to disagree with this analysis. They do not agree that the velocity of circulation necessarily remains constant. Nor do they agree that the output of the economy cannot be increased. If the economy has spare capacity, they argue, increases in the money supply could result in an increase in output rather than an increase in prices.

We shall examine the implications of these differing viewpoints for the control of inflation later in this unit.

Government measures to control inflation

Just as there is disagreement between economists as to the causes of inflation, there are differing views as to what policies the government should adopt in their efforts to control inflation (see Table 22.5).

Measures to control demand-pull inflation

If it is believed that the primary cause of inflation is excess demand in the economy, the government can introduce measures to reduce the level of aggregate demand. It can use fiscal policy, increasing taxes and/or reducing government expenditure, or it may decide to use monetary policy, restricting monetary growth and raising interest rates. Alternatively, it could use the external exchange rate as a policy instrument to reduce aggregate demand. By raising the **exchange rate**, this reduces the competitiveness of exports and lowers the price of imports, thereby reducing the demand for home-produced goods from both overseas and domestic consumers.

Measures to control cost-push inflation

If the primary cause of inflation is thought to originate from cost-push pressures, then any policy which helps to reduce production costs will help to reduce the inflationary pressures, although, depending on the origin of the increased costs, there may be little that the government can do. If the higher costs originate from increased import prices (e.g. for oil) the ability of the government to control the inflation is limited. However, one of the major causes of cost-push inflation is often thought to be rising wage costs and, in this case, the government is able to exert some influence. It may try to weaken the power

Table 22.5 Anti-inflation policies

Theory of inflation	Policy measures
Demand-pull	Fiscal policy: raise taxes and/or lower government spending
	Monetary policy: restrict money supply and raise interest rates
	Raise exchange rate
Cost-push	Incomes policy
	Reform of labour market
Monetarism	Strict control of money supply

of the trade unions and reform the labour markets in an effort to make them more competitive and hence ease upward pressures on wage levels, or it may try to increase productivity. It might also decide to introduce an **incomes policy**.

Incomes policy

An incomes policy involves direct intervention by the government to control the level of wage settlements rather than allowing them to be freely determined through the forces of demand and supply. If wage rises can be controlled, it is hoped that this will reduce cost-push pressures in the economy. Incomes policies are seen by many as an attractive alternative to the control of inflation as, unlike policies to reduce the level of aggregate demand, they enable a reduction in inflation without a resultant rise in unemployment. (The trade-off between inflation and unemployment is examined in more detail in Unit 23.)

It is difficult, however, to judge and estimate the impact of any incomes policy, as one does not know what would have happened to wage levels had there not been an incomes policy. Certainly, their record has generally been rather mixed due to the many difficulties that arise when they are used.

First, incomes policies are very difficult to enforce. Wage settlements that firms are awarding are difficult to monitor and police. Moreover, if it is found that a firm has broken the incomes policy, what sanction can be taken against it? There are also many loopholes whereby firms can get round an incomes policy: for example, by redefining a job so that, say, a technician becomes a senior technician and hence receives a pay increase, even though the demands of his job do not change. Alternatively, a firm may keep basic pay rises within the maximum allowed, but the worker may be able to supplement his basic pay with bonuses or overtime pay. Or if firms find that there is a limit to the pay rise that they can award, they may reward employees in other ways, through the granting of perks or fringe benefits such as a company car.

It is because incomes policies are so difficult to enforce that governments have in the past adopted the practice of using 'voluntary' incomes policies, where firms are simply requested to keep within the government's guidelines on pay increases, rather than having a statutory incomes policy where pay increases are restricted by law. The one area where incomes policies can be enforced is in the public sector, where the government controls the purse strings, but this then gives rise to another problem. Public sector workers have their pay restricted but those working for firms in the private sector do not, leading to unequal treatment of workers and the claim that public sector workers' incomes are falling behind those of the private sector.

Incomes policies usually operate through having a maximum recommended pay increase, but the danger here is that this maximum then becomes the norm. For example, if the government says that pay rises should be limited to a 5 per cent increase, everyone then expects to receive 5 per cent, whereas some workers might previously have settled for less. Furthermore, if the limitation on the pay increase is a fixed amount, for example £10 per week, as opposed to a percentage, this causes the problem of eroding pay differentials between workers. The difference in pay between skilled and unskilled workers is reduced, which might result in a fall in the supply of skilled workers.

Incomes policies also interfere with the role of the market in allocating resources. Those industries which are expanding and those firms which are efficient cannot attract more workers through offering higher wages, while contracting industries, which would normally be experiencing declining wage rates, feel obliged to pay the norm specified by the incomes policy, thus resulting in a misallocation of resources. From time to time there will arise under an incomes policy, a situation where a group of workers, for example nurses or fire fighters, claim that they are a special case and ought to be exempt from the policy. Their argument might be very persuasive, and indeed, they may represent a special case, but once an exemption is made for one group of workers, other groups of workers then decide that they too qualify as special cases, and so the incomes policy begins to collapse. The determination of governments to rigidly enforce an incomes policy is also tempered by political considerations. If a general election is approaching, governments might be tempted to relax an incomes policy to improve their chance of re-election. Defeat for both Conservative and Labour governments in elections in the 1970s were partly blamed on their tough line taken on wage increases.

Experience also seems to indicate that incomes policies are only effective in the short term. Workers may be prepared to accept wage restraint for a year or two, but eventually the incomes policy breaks down and is followed by a 'catching-up' period. Thus critics claim that in the long run, an incomes policy has no effect on the level of wages.

In more recent years, incomes policies have been based on productivity deals, where workers are granted pay increases provided that they can demonstrate a rise in productivity. A problem with this approach, however, is that it is extremely difficult to measure productivity for those workers involved in industries such as health, education or the police.

Despite the problems associated with the use of an incomes policy, many still see them as an important instrument in the control of inflation. Even if they break down in the long run, the short-term benefits may still be worthwhile, and although they have their problems and may create a misallocation of resources, it is claimed that the costs of inflation are far greater than the costs associated with the implementation of an incomes policy. One criticism with the use of incomes policies is that they have often been introduced as a last resort, as a response to high inflation once the crisis has arisen, rather than as a preventative measure. Those who support the use of incomes policies say that if they were a more permanent feature of economic policy, then they might have more success.

Monetarist measures to control inflation

The monetarist approach to the control of inflation is strict control of the money supply. As explained earlier in this unit, this is based on the belief that the primary cause of inflation is that of allowing the money supply to increase too rapidly. If monetary growth (M) is restricted to the rate of growth of output (T), then, provided that the velocity of circulation (V) remains constant in the equation $MV = PT$, prices (P) will not rise. However, this policy has its problems. First of all, if the money supply is to be controlled, it is necessary to identify what exactly is meant by money. As outlined in Unit 17, there are many different measures of the money supply, ranging from the narrow measure of M0 to much broader definitions such as M4 and M5. The government may have difficulty in identifying what is the appropriate definition of the money supply to target. It clearly is not sufficient to simply control the amount of notes and coins in the economy, as bank deposits are the chief component of the money supply. But which bank deposits should the government control? Just 'instant-access' accounts, which people tend to use for carrying out day-to-day transactions? Or should savings accounts also be included in the target?

Once governments have identified a suitable measure of the money supply, experience has shown that they have had great difficulty in controlling its growth. Over the years governments have used many different methods to try to control monetary growth, with mixed success. The fact that money can be created by banks limits the government's ability to control its supply.

Due to these difficulties, governments have, in fact, turned to policies to influence the demand for money through interest rate adjustments, rather than controlling the supply of money. The reasoning here is that if interest rates rise, this reduces the demand for borrowing, and so banks will create less money. However, even if they do manage to restrict the growth of the money supply, Keynesians claim that the velocity with which it circulates might increase in order to compensate for the reduced monetary stock. Although governments in the UK since the mid-1970s have been strongly influenced by monetarist theories to control inflation, there still remains some doubt over the statistical link between increases in the money supply and increases in the rate of inflation.

Consequences of inflation: effects on the firm and the economy

Why is low inflation such an important priority for governments? What problems does inflation cause? One might argue that it does not really matter for individuals if the prices of products are increasing, as long as our wages are increasing at the same rate. However, inflation can have important implications for the individual, the firm and for the economy as a whole.

Fear of escalation

One of the dangers of inflation is that it has a tendency to escalate quickly. While inflation rates in single figures may not be too damaging, once inflation increases it can be very difficult to control and, if hyperinflation develops, it can lead to the breakdown of the economy as people lose confidence in money as a means of exchange. It is therefore felt to be vital that we keep on top of inflation and restrict it to very low rates.

Increased production costs

Inflation will lead to an increase in the costs of production for firms, as prices of raw materials and components, and wage levels, rise. This will result in falling profit margins, unless the firm raises prices to compensate for the increased production costs. Higher prices, however, may lead to a fall in demand, depending on the elasticity of demand for the product and the state of competition. The less elastic the demand, the more firms will be able to pass on the rise in costs to the consumer.

Loss of international competitiveness

If the inflation rate in the UK is higher than that of our competitors, UK firms will become uncompetitive and suffer from reduced sales as our prices will be rising more quickly than the prices of overseas products. If a country has a system of **floating exchange rates**, exchange-rate adjustments should help to compensate for the higher inflation rate, but under systems of controlled or managed exchange rates, the exchange rate may not be allowed to adjust sufficiently to compensate for the differing inflation rate. (See Unit 25 for an explanation of exchange rate systems.) Loss of international competitiveness will mean that employment in those industries which rely on export orders will be particularly affected, but other industries are also likely to suffer as consumers will be drawn towards substituting home-produced goods with imports that will have become relatively cheaper, resulting in unemployment and a trade deficit.

Redistributive effects

Inflation hits different groups within the economy in different ways. Some suffer more from inflation than others, and some may even benefit, thus resulting in a redistribution of income and wealth. Those who have savings will find that, in real terms, the value of their savings falls as money loses its value. Likewise creditors, those who are owed money, will also suffer, since when they are paid back, the value of the money will be worth less, while debtors, those who owe money, will benefit. Higher interest rates will help to compensate for these problems, but in times of high inflation the interest rate may not rise sufficiently, with the possibility that 'real' interest rates may even be negative. It is worth noting that as the government is the largest borrower, through the national debt, it gains most during inflationary times. Those workers who belong to strong unions may find that their pay manages to keep pace with inflation, but non-unionised workers who lack bargaining power may find that the real value of their wage falls. Pensioners and those who receive benefits from the government will also have to rely on the government increasing their benefits in line with inflation if they are to have the real value of their income protected. Those on fixed incomes (e.g. some pensioners), who are dependent on interest from savings as a source of income, will also suffer.

Uncertainty

One of the main problems of inflation is the uncertainty that it causes. If the rate of inflation could be predicted in advance, allowances could be made for it. It is therefore unanticipated inflation that causes the most problems and undermines confidence. The uncertainty that inflation creates is likely to influence the behaviour of firms. They may be reluctant to plan ahead and take long-term decisions regarding investment, as they are unable to predict their future costs and revenue. Firms who negotiate long-term contracts are particularly at risk from unanticipated inflation. If firms are able to fully anticipate future price increases, then contracts can be drawn up to take such increases into account, and interest rates charged on loans, for example, can reflect the rate of inflation. But where the rate of inflation cannot be fully anticipated or where firms have differing expectations about the future rate of inflation, it becomes more difficult to settle on the terms of a contract. The reluctance of firms to invest will have adverse effects on the economy as a whole, restricting economic growth.

Menu costs

Inflation also imposes additional administrative tasks on firms. Prices will need to be readjusted more frequently, price lists and catalogues reprinted, vending machines altered, all putting increased pressure on the resources of the firm.

Accounting implications

The accounting function of the firm is also affected by inflation. Budgets will soon become inappropriate if there are high rates of inflation, and amendments will have to be made to the methods used to value the firm's stock and other assets. Assets may be valued at historical cost – that is, at what the firm paid for them – but this will soon become outdated after several years of inflation and their book value will underestimate their current market worth. Firms will therefore have to adopt accounting procedures to cope with the inflation, such as flexible budgets and valuation of assets at current cost.

Wage negotiations

Firms may find that they have to spend more time negotiating with workers during inflationary times, as workers will be determined to secure wage increases that protect their real earnings. The workforce may also become dissatisfied if wage increases are subject to limitation imposed on them by an incomes policy.

This leads us on to the fact that it is not only the inflation itself that causes problems for firms, but also the government measures that are intended to try to reduce the level of inflation, as follows:

- The government may raise interest rates in their efforts to restrict the growth of the money supply and reduce the level of aggregate demand in the economy. This will affect firms in several ways. Those firms who have borrowed money will find that interest payments increase, which will be particularly damaging to small firms, who, not being able to raise finance through the issue of shares, tend to rely more on borrowing as a source of finance. Those firms who do have access to the capital market may decide to opt for lower gearing: that is, relying on share capital as a source of finance, rather than loans. Higher interest rates will also reduce consumer demand. Those firms who produce consumer durables, the purchase of which is often financed through credit agreements, are likely to experience decreased sales, as will those firms in industries connected with the housing industry, where higher mortgage rates are likely to depress the housing market.

- Higher rates of taxation may also be introduced by the government in their attempts to reduce aggregate demand and thus relieve inflationary pressures. These higher rates of tax will leave consumers with less disposable income, leading to a decrease in the demand for many firms' products.

- The government might decide to reduce its own level of spending in an attempt to reduce aggregate demand. This may have particularly damaging effects on firms who rely heavily on central government or local government contracts: for example, those firms in the defence, construction, education and health industries. The reduction in aggregate demand may also damage firms' confidence, as they anticipate a slowdown in economic activity. Firms may therefore decide to postpone or even abandon expansion decisions, which means that those firms who produce investment goods will suffer a drop in sales.

Exercise

As a result of promising sales figures over the previous two years, Coverdale Clothing Limited believed that they had hit upon a successful range of clothing designs. In response to the increase in demand for their products, therefore, they had decided to expand their production capacity. However, shortly after the increase in capacity, there was a marked change in the economic climate with a substantial increase in the rate of inflation, which resulted in unfavourable business conditions for the company. They were particularly hit by the rise in interest rates that the government had implemented. In addition, they were disappointed to see the value of the pound rise on the foreign exchange markets, as this too damaged their trading position.

Questions

1. Why would the government have raised interest rates in response to the increase in the rate of inflation?
2. Outline reasons why the higher interest rates might have caused problems for the company.
3. Why do you think that the exchange value of the pound increased?
4. Outline reasons why the rise in the value of the pound might have damaged their trading position.

Benefits of mild inflation

Although inflation can have many undesirable consequences, it is possible for a firm to derive some benefit from a low and stable rate of inflation. Inflation is likely to increase the turnover and the profit levels of a firm. This will look more impressive, even though the values have not risen in real terms. Likewise, workers may feel happier having received a pay rise, under the illusion that they are better off even though their real wage has not increased. Firms may find that there is less resistance to them increasing the price of their product, even though their costs may not have risen to the same extent, as, in an inflationary climate, people are anticipating price rises. Many firms borrow money to invest in capital equipment, and during inflationary times, the real value of their debt decreases, thus giving a slight advantage to those entrepreneurial firms who have taken a risk by borrowing to finance expansion. In fact, although it is often argued that inflation is likely to reduce investment by a firm, inflation will reduce the real rate of interest which firms have to pay and so might encourage firms to invest. House price inflation can also have positive, confidence-boosting effects on consumers, resulting in an increase in demand for products. Indeed, it is generally far better to have mild inflation rather than deflation. Deflation, where the price level is falling, can create a potentially dangerous situation, as occurred during the depression of the 1930s.

Case study

Making allowances for inflation

A firm's sales turnover may have increased from £200 million in 1987 to £320 million in 1997. However, much of this increase will have been due to the effect of inflation and we need to adjust the figures to take account of the inflation. To do this, we can measure the sales in 1997 at 1987 prices. Using information from Table 22.3, we can see that the RPI increased from 100 in January 1987 to 152.7 in 1997. To find the real increase in sales, we need to deflate the 1997 sales, as follows:

$$320 \times \frac{100}{152.7} = 209.6$$

Thus although sales increased from £200m. to £320m., an increase of 60 per cent in nominal terms, in real terms they only increased from £200m. to £209.6m., an increase of less than 5 per cent.

Summary

Inflation can be described as a persistent increase in the price level. There are differing views as to the causes of inflation, but the main explanations are increases in the level of aggregate demand (demand-pull inflation), increases in the costs of production (cost-push inflation), and that of the government allowing the money supply to expand too rapidly. Measures to control inflation include using taxation, interest rates or exchange rates to reduce the level of aggregate demand, control of the money supply, direct controls over wage increases, or measures to improve the flexibility of the labour market.

Inflation causes uncertainty in the business community and can lead to a fall in investment. It imposes additional burdens on firms and leads to resources being used to offset the effects of inflation. Firms may find that their international competitiveness suffers if our inflation rate is in excess of our competitors. Inflation also has a redistributive effect on income and wealth, with some benefiting from the effects of inflation at the expense of others.

Inflation will affect firms in different ways, as will the government measures which are introduced to tackle the inflation. It depends on factors such as the size of the firm, the type of market they operate in and the nature of the product. Small firms are often among the hardest hit, due to their reliance on bank loans as a source of finance and the higher interest rates which usually accompany inflation. Some firms, however, may even benefit from inflation.

Review questions

1. Outline three explanations of inflation.
2. In the Fisher version of the quantity theory of money equation, $MV = PT$, what does each letter stand for? Explain why MV must equal PT.
3. Name three possible causes of demand-pull inflation.
4. Name three possible sources of cost-push inflation.
5. Explain the monetarist theory of inflation.
6. In what ways might the government cause inflation?
7. What problems might a government encounter in trying to impose an incomes policy on workers?
8. What are the undesirable consequences of inflation?
9. How might inflation threaten the level of unemployment?
10. In what ways might inflation affect investment?
11. In what circumstances can inflation be considered as beneficial to firms?
12. Why are price indexes only an approximate guide to the rate of inflation?

Essay questions

1. Outline the measures that have been taken by recent governments to control inflation, and consider the consequences of these measures for the business community.
2. 'It doesn't matter what the rate of inflation is in one country provided that it is the equivalent of the rate of inflation in other countries.' Do you agree with this statement? Explain your answer.

Reading 22.1

A fall in the rate of inflation, whether it be the headline rate or the underlying rate, is good news for firms. Falling rates of inflation also raise hopes of a reduction in interest rates, which is also good news for business. However, in such a situation, the Bank of England often urges caution, warning the government against stoking up demand. Interest rate cuts would increase domestic spending which in turn could lead to the damaging long-term effects of higher inflation.

Questions

1. What is the difference between the 'headline' inflation rate and the 'underlying' inflation rate?

▷

2. Explain why (a) a lower inflation rate, and (b) a lower rate of interest, is good news for firms.

3. Explain why a reduction in interest rates might lead to the risk of higher inflation.

4. Why might the government be interested in 'stoking up' demand, despite the risk of higher inflation?

Unemployment and its effects on firms

ECONOMICS IN THE NEWS

What level of unemployment should we aim for?

What can be considered a satisfactory level of unemployment? Some people think there should be a job for all, and that we should aim for zero unemployment. Others regard an unemployment rate of around 3 per cent of the workforce as 'full employment'. Economists often talk about the natural level of unemployment. If unemployment rises above this natural rate, the economy is said to be in recession, but if it falls below this rate, the economy is in danger of overheating. But we should not be resigned to accepting the natural rate of unemployment as something that is beyond our control. The natural level itself can be lowered through government policy.

Unemployment can be defined as a situation wh[...]
work cannot find employment. However the fig[...]
employed may be misleading. Different countries u[...]
unemployed, hampering international comparisons, [...]
calculating the number unemployed might change ove[...]
one of the government's macroeconomic objectives was[...]
However, the concept of full employment does not necessarily[...]
and can mean different things to different people. Nevert[...]
government remains that of trying to ensure that unemployment is [...]

The costs of unemployment

Economic costs

Resources are limited, yet people's wants are unlimited, creating the economic problem of scarcity. Unemployment represents a waste of resources. Every day, millions of hours of work are wasted and potential output is lost. The national income and output of the economy is therefore less than it could be.

Financial costs

Unemployment represents a financial cost to the country in terms of the benefits that have to be paid out by the government. Not only is there the cost of the benefits, however, there is also the cost in terms of tax and national insurance receipts that the government would otherwise have been receiving had each unemployed person been working. If many of the unemployed were in work, the government would receive more income tax, more national insurance payments and more VAT, assuming that more goods and services would be bought. There is also the financial cost of unemployment to the individual, this being the difference between what they could have earned had they been in employment and the amount they receive in benefits. While some people might be better off receiving unemployment benefits than working, most people will be considerably poorer, and this is particularly the case in those countries where there is little welfare provision for the unemployed.

Social costs

In recent years, there has been much debate about the social costs of unemployment. There is no doubt that unemployment is a serious social problem. To be unemployed, particularly if this extends over a period of time, can have a demoralising effect on people, bringing them personal suffering, depression and distress. There is evidence to suggest that if someone remains unemployed for a long time, they lose the 'work habit' and find it very difficult to get back into full-time employment. The health of those who are unemployed also suffers; on average, the health of the unemployed is worse than that of those in employment. There is also possibly a link between increases in unemployment and increases in crimes such as theft and vandalism. High levels of unemployment also widen the inequalities in society between the 'haves' and the 'have-nots'.

...and breakdown of unemployment statistics

...rnment uses the number of people who claim unemployment-related ...official measure of the number of people unemployed. The figures are ...oth in terms of the number unemployed, and as a percentage of the ... The method of measuring the numbers unemployed has been criticised for ...estimating the true number of people seeking employment, with claims that the ...ernment is deliberately underestimating the extent of unemployment for political reasons. If an unemployed person does not claim or is not entitled to benefit, she will not be included in the official statistics. Examples of people who might be excluded from the figures include those who only work part-time but would like full-time employment, housewives looking for employment, students who stay on at college but would prefer to be in employment, and those on training schemes such as YTS. On this basis, one could justifiably claim that the true number of people unemployed is considerably higher than that suggested by the official statistics. However, to counter this, it is probable that some people who claim benefit for being unemployed may actually be working in the 'hidden' or 'black' economy.

An alternative way of measuring the number of people unemployed is to carry out a survey of households and the labour force to find out how many people are actually seeking employment. This gives a more accurate picture of the number of people who are actually looking for employment, as opposed to those claiming benefit, but again the figures have to be treated with caution as they are derived from just a sample of households and the labour force.

Unemployment statistics can therefore be a little misleading, and this is particularly the case when making comparisons between different countries which may use different methods of calculating or estimating the number of people unemployed. Figure 23.1 gives

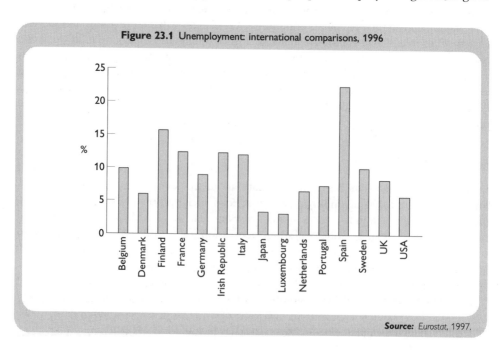

Figure 23.1 Unemployment: international comparisons, 1996

Source: *Eurostat*, 1997.

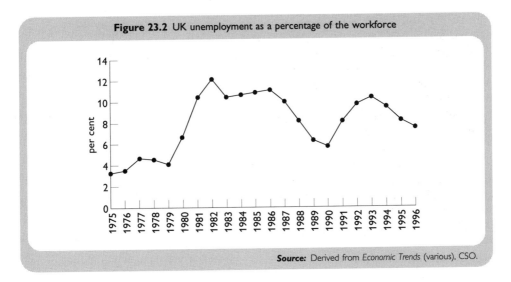

Figure 23.2 UK unemployment as a percentage of the workforce

Source: Derived from *Economic Trends* (various), CSO.

an indication of unemployment rates in different countries and shows that unemployment is not just a problem unique to the UK. In fact, the UK is about average in comparison with other European countries, where the spread in 1996 was from a rate of only 3.1 per cent in Luxembourg to 22.3 per cent in Spain.

Figure 23.2 shows the rate of unemployment in the UK from 1975 to 1996. Although this gives us a guide to the trend in unemployment rates, the aggregate rate of unemployment fails to provide us with a complete picture of the problem of unemployment and it is necessary to break down the aggregate figure to achieve a more meaningful picture. The aggregate figure fails to give us any insight into, for example, what type of people are unemployed or how long they have been unemployed. It is useful, therefore, to break down the aggregate unemployment figure to look at details such as the age, the sex, and the ethnic background of those who are unemployed, in addition to the regional rates of unemployment and the length of time that people have been unemployed. Some disaggregation of the statistics is provided below, but further details and the breakdown of unemployment statistics in the UK can be found in *Labour Market Trends* (formerly *Employment Gazette*) published monthly by the Office for National Statistics.

Figure 23.3 shows regional unemployment rates in the UK and how they have changed over a ten-year period. Regional disparities in unemployment rates have persisted for many years in the UK, with the North of England, Wales, Scotland, and Northern Ireland consistently experiencing higher than average unemployment rates, although we can see from the data that there seems to have been a convergence of regional unemployment rates in the 1990s.

We ought also to examine whether it is it always the same people who are unemployed. If unemployment last month was one million, and is again one million this month, is it the same one million people who have remained unemployed, or have those that were previously unemployed now found employment and a different group of people become unemployed this month? It is useful to find out whether the unemployment figures represent a large pool of people who remain unemployed for a long duration, or whether each month there is a large 'inflow' of people joining the statistics

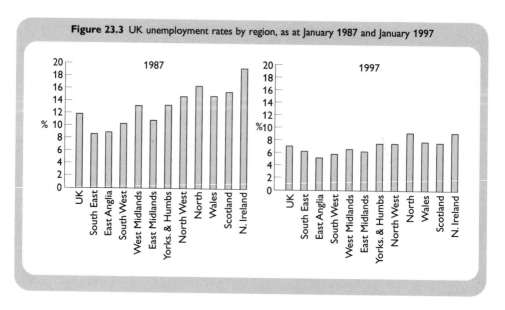

Figure 23.3 UK unemployment rates by region, as at January 1987 and January 1997

and, at the same time, a large 'outflow' of people leaving. If people are unemployed for only a short time and soon manage to find a job again, this is not so much of a problem nor so costly to the economy or to the individual as long-term unemployment. Long-term unemployment is particularly damaging to the morale and self-respect of the individual. For younger people, it may mean that they do not gain the experience of being employed after leaving school, and the longer they remain unemployed, the more difficult it is for them to gain employment, so that they may eventually become unemployable. Figure 23.4 gives an indication of the length of time people remain unemployed and shows that 36 per cent of those who were unemployed had been so for over a year.

Figure 23.5 provides a breakdown of unemployment between the sexes in the UK. Female unemployment is significantly lower than that of men. This is due partly to many unemployed women not being included in the official unemployment statistics. Even taking this factor into account, however, female unemployment rates are still lower.

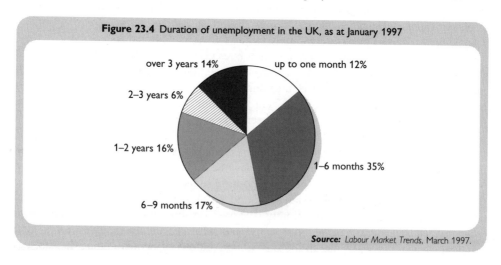

Figure 23.4 Duration of unemployment in the UK, as at January 1997

over 3 years 14%   up to one month 12%

2–3 years 6%

1–2 years 16%

1–6 months 35%

6–9 months 17%

Source: Labour Market Trends, March 1997.

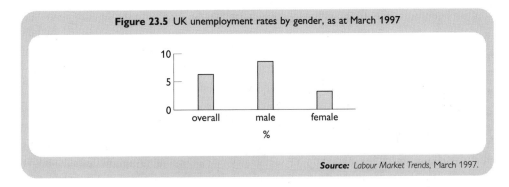

Figure 23.5 UK unemployment rates by gender, as at March 1997

%

Source: *Labour Market Trends*, March 1997.

We can see from Figure 23.6 that unemployment rates among the young (particularly the 18–24 age group) are higher than the average for the UK. This is also true for those aged 50 and over, although early retirement schemes mean that the official statistics do not necessarily reflect this.

Looking at unemployment rates among different ethnic groups (see Figure 23.7), a person is more likely to be unemployed if they are part of an ethnic minority group, regardless of their age, sex, or educational qualifications. However, there are considerable differences between different ethnic minorities: for example, Chinese and descendants of former Ugandan Asians have very low unemployment rates.

In terms of occupation, a worker is more likely to be unemployed if he/she is a manual worker or unskilled as opposed to a non-manual or skilled worker. Similarly, those with high levels of education are less likely to be unemployed. Some industries are also more susceptible to the trade cycle, with, for example, the construction industry usually experiencing large increases in unemployment during times of recession.

Finally, unemployment figures need to be seasonally adjusted. They are adjusted to take into account that, at certain times of the year, we would expect unemployment to fall or to rise. For example, if in the winter months we would expect unemployment to be 10 per cent higher than in the summer months, but in one year it is only 5 per cent higher, then taking into account the seasonal adjustment, the unemployment position has actually improved.

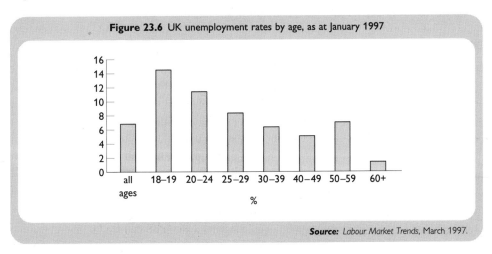

Figure 23.6 UK unemployment rates by age, as at January 1997

%

Source: *Labour Market Trends*, March 1997.

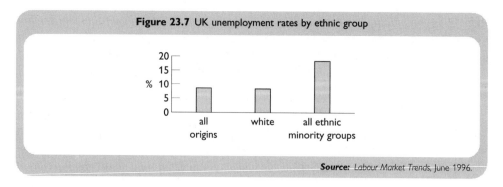

Figure 23.7 UK unemployment rates by ethnic group

Source: *Labour Market Trends,* June 1996.

Exercise

From the data provided on unemployment, construct a profile of a person who is at most risk from unemployment. Does it matter that some sections of the community are more likely to become unemployed than others?

Causes of unemployment

Classical view

The classical view of unemployment is that, in the long run, it should cease to be a problem, because the workings of the market should ensure that the demand for labour equals the supply of labour and therefore all unemployment should disappear. Wages represent the price for labour, and the market for labour is just like the market for anything else. Unemployment might occur if the wage level is above the equilibrium wage, as there will then be an excess supply of labour. However, if this is the case, the

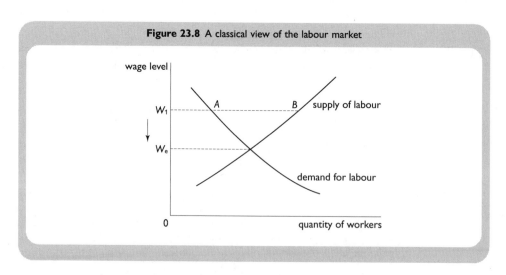

Figure 23.8 A classical view of the labour market

price of labour will eventually fall until equilibrium in the labour market is reached where demand equals supply and unemployment ceases to exist.

In Figure 23.8, if wages were at W_1, there would be an excess supply of labour and unemployment, represented by the distance AB. However, the workings of the price mechanism mean that the wage rate would fall, and as it falls, the demand for labour rises while the supply of labour falls, until we reach a situation where the wage settles at an equilibrium wage of W_e, where the demand for labour equals the supply of labour and there is no unemployment.

Criticisms of the classical view

The classical view of unemployment is not very realistic. A major problem is that the market for labour is not just like any other market, and there are many reasons why it may not settle at an equilibrium level where the demand for and the supply of labour are equal, as follows:

- All workers are not alike. There is not just one labour market, but many different labour markets according to the occupation and skills of the worker or even the region of the country that they come from. For example, a shop assistant in Manchester and a bus driver in London are competing in completely different labour markets. If there was a shortage of bus drivers in London, a shop assistant from Manchester could not simply offer their services as a bus driver in London. Workers are not homogeneous, and this means that the labour market is not as flexible as classical theory suggests.

- The demand for labour is a derived demand. Firms employ workers only if there is a demand for the product they are producing. Thus the demand for car workers is derived from the demand for cars. Therefore, just because the wages of car workers fall, it does not mean that car manufacturers will necessarily employ more workers, as classical theory predicts.

- Workers are also consumers as well as producers. If wage levels fall, the income of consumers will fall, which might lead to a fall in demand for goods and services. In this case, there is no point in firms employing more workers, even though wage costs have fallen.

- Wages are not as flexible as the prices of goods in other markets. Wage levels are not so dependent on demand and supply as the prices of other products. In particular, they tend to be inflexible downwards. Wages are often determined through collective bargaining: that is, through negotiations between groups of employers (employers associations) and groups of workers (unions). The wage rate is usually decided according to the relative strength of each side in the bargaining process, not simply by the forces of demand and supply. Thus wages may persist at a level above the equilibrium wage, despite an excess supply of labour. The government also frequently intervenes to influence the level of wages, particularly for public sector workers, so again, wages are not settled solely by the workings of the free market. The wage paid to a person is normally specified in an employment contract, which is generally a fixed contract, often lasting at least one year. Wages cannot therefore always be lowered in the short term if there is an excess supply of labour.

- Even if there is an excess supply of labour, firms might be concerned as to the effect that a lowering of wages would have on the morale of the workforce. A lower wage could affect their motivation and productivity, or lead to the possibility of an industrial dispute. The firm might therefore decide not to lower wage levels.

- It is expensive for firms to recruit and train new workers. Thus, though there might be an excess supply of unemployed labour outside the firm, these unemployed workers do not really represent perfect substitutes for those already employed by the firm. Despite the existence of unemployed workers, therefore, the wage rate may not fall, as the firm will probably be willing to pay its existing workforce a premium. There are, in fact, two separate labour markets. An internal labour market – that is, those who already work for the firm – and an external labour market – that is, those who are unemployed – and they are not in direct competition with each other.

For all these reasons, the price mechanism does not work very well to clear the labour market when there is an excess supply of labour. It is unrealistic to assume that, even in the long run, an equilibrium will be reached where the demand for labour equals the supply of labour and unemployment ceases to exist. Even in the long run, unemployment will persist.

Types of unemployment

Assuming we can accept that unemployment is likely to persist even in the long run, one of the ways of analysing unemployment is to categorise it according to the factors that have caused it to arise. Identifying the cause of the unemployment should give the government some guidance as to the measures that should be taken to solve the problem.

Demand-deficient unemployment

During a recession, unemployment may persist at high levels. Keynesians refer to this as **demand-deficient unemployment**, in that it is caused by a deficiency of aggregate demand (see Figure 23.9). There is simply not enough demand in the economy to provide jobs for everybody who wants one. It is also sometimes referred to as cyclical unemployment as it occurs during the slump phase of the economic cycle.

As wages are not very flexible in a downwards direction, when there is a decrease in aggregate demand, wages do not fall to compensate for the lower demand for labour, and the labour market remains in disequilibrium with an excess supply of labour. In Figure 23.10, the demand for labour curve (D^1) has shifted to the left (D^2) as a result of the fall in aggregate demand. As wages are not flexible downwards, they have remained at W_1, with the result that there is unemployment represented by the distance Q_1Q_2.

Even if wage levels did fall, there is the problem that the income of workers will fall, which could lead to yet a further fall in aggregate demand and a downward spiral.

Structural unemployment

Structural unemployment is where there is a mismatch between the demand for and the supply of labour. At any one time in the economy, the structure of industry will be

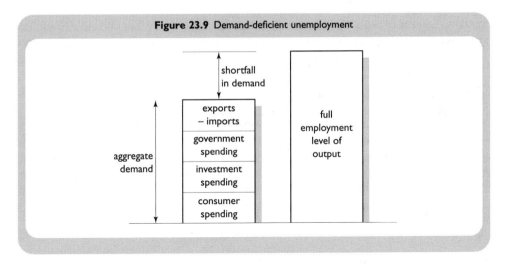

Figure 23.9 Demand-deficient unemployment

changing. Some industries will be in decline, while others will be expanding. Job vacancies exist in the new expanding industries, but workers who become unemployed as a result of other industries declining do not have the necessary skills to work in these jobs. Structural change may occur because of changes in demand patterns: for example, the shift away from coal towards gas and other sources of energy. It may also occur due to the onset of foreign competition: for example, the import of textiles has led to unemployment in the cotton industry in the UK. Where workers have lost their job due to new technology, this is sometimes referred to as technological unemployment, but it can also be regarded as a type of structural unemployment. The new technology may mean that a worker's skills have become redundant as mechanisation and automation have replaced the need for the worker. For example, in the printing and publishing industry,

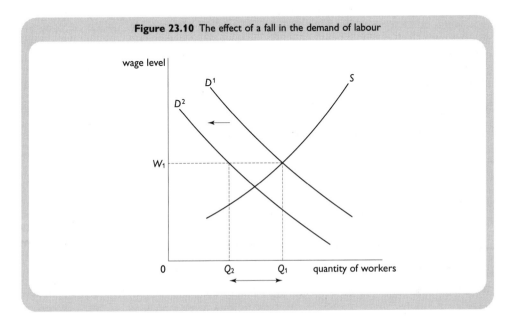

Figure 23.10 The effect of a fall in the demand of labour

the development of word processors and computers have meant that occupations such as typesetters are now redundant. Structural unemployment persists because workers are not occupationally mobile and are not able to transfer easily from one occupation to another.

Regional unemployment

Structural unemployment often leads to regional unemployment. Because an industry that has gone into decline may be heavily concentrated in specific regions of the country, the decline in that industry will result in above average unemployment in that region, as happened to the Northeast of England with the decline in shipbuilding, and South Wales with the decline in coal mining. Regional unemployment persists because workers are not geographically mobile and cannot transfer easily from a job in one part of the country to a job elsewhere.

Frictional or search unemployment

Frictional unemployment refers to those people who are temporarily unemployed because they are in the process of changing jobs or looking for a new job. People are not always able to transfer smoothly from one job to another. It inevitably takes time for workers to look for employment – perhaps because of a lack of knowledge about job opportunities – and for the formalities of appointing them to take place. **Search unemployment** is very similar. It refers to those workers who may have the opportunity of employment, but have declined the offer of a job in the hope of receiving a better offer in the future.

Seasonal unemployment

Some types of employment are dependent on the season or time of year. For example, agricultural workers may find themselves unemployed in winter. Other occupations affected by seasonal factors include those in the construction industry and tourism. We saw earlier in this unit how the unemployment figures are adjusted in order to take these seasonal variations into account.

Both seasonal and frictional unemployment are short-term, and are not regarded quite so seriously as other types of unemployment.

Unemployment – the monetarist view

The monetarist view of unemployment returns to the classical view of unemployment, and a belief in the workings of the market. If the labour market is allowed to operate freely, wage adjustments should ensure that the market settles at an equilibrium where the demand for labour equals the supply of labour. But monetarists acknowledge that there are various factors which prevent the wage level falling, thus allowing the excess supply of labour to persist and resulting in unemployment. Therefore, they claim that among the main causes of unemployment are excessive wages and the factors which prevent the wage level falling. This may be due to trade unions, who manage to maintain wages at

Figure 23.11 Involuntary unemployment

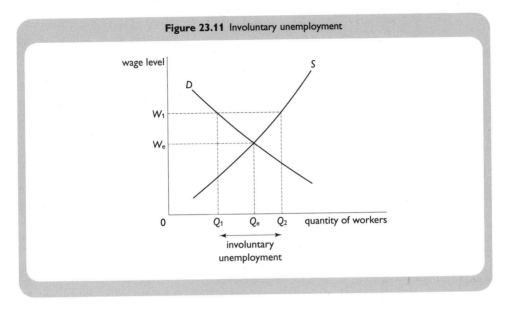

artificially high levels above the equilibrium wage, or the government, who might impose a minimum legal wage above the free-market equilibrium. They are to blame for creating this type of unemployment.

In Figure 23.11, if the wage settles at W_e, the demand for workers equals the supply of workers willing to accept a job at that wage. The labour market is in equilibrium with the level of employment at Q_e. If, however, wages are not flexible downwards, and stick at W_1, some workers who would like a job at this wage cannot find one. Thus unemployment is represented by the distance Q_1Q_2. These people are sometimes referred to as being **involuntarily unemployed** as they are willing to work at the existing wage rate but cannot find employment.

However, the difference between the monetarist view and the classical view is the monetarists' recognition that even if the labour market settles at an equilibrium level, some unemployment may still exist. This they refer to as the **natural rate of unemployment**.

Consider Figure 23.12. While the supply curve for labour (S) shows the number of people actually willing to accept a job at each wage, the curve represented by L shows the number of people who consider themselves as part of the labour force at each wage. (As you would expect, and as explained in Unit 14, the higher the wage, the more people there are who are willing to enter the labour force.) Thus, even at the equilibrium wage of W_e, there is still some unemployment (represented by distance Q_3Q_4), as some people in the labour force do not wish to accept a job at this wage although they are part of the labour force and looking for employment. This could be as a result of search unemployment – people looking for jobs but holding out for a better offer – or frictional unemployment – those between jobs. The distance Q_3Q_4 therefore represents the natural level of unemployment, and these people could be referred to as being voluntarily unemployed, as they are content to hold out for an offer of a better job. Also included in this category of **voluntary unemployment** is regional and structural unemployment, the argument here being that if people were prepared to move out of a region of heavy

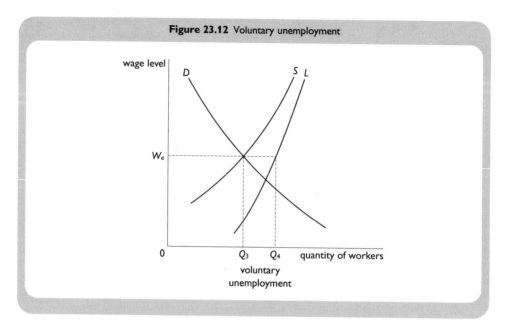

Figure 23.12 Voluntary unemployment

unemployment, or if people with redundant skills in declining industries were prepared to retrain or accept an unskilled job on a lower wage, then they would find employment. One could also add seasonal unemployment to this category of voluntary unemployment.

Frictional, search, structural, regional and seasonal unemployment can therefore be considered to make up the natural rate of unemployment. In other words, natural unemployment is that which remains when there is no demand-deficient unemployment and when the labour market is in equilibrium. The amount of natural unemployment does not remain constant, but fluctuates depending on factors such as the structure of the labour market, the mobility of labour, and the level of taxation and benefits. Policy measures designed to reduce the rate of natural unemployment are looked at in the next section.

Although the natural rate of unemployment is nowadays a widely used and accepted concept, some have criticised this approach to the problem of unemployment. The term 'natural' rate of unemployment somehow suggests that it is inevitable and unavoidable. Those who support the concept assume that the labour market eventually settles at an equilibrium level, and that once this occurs, the government no longer has any role to play in stimulating the economy and the level of employment through increasing aggregate demand. There is also disagreement over the actual amount of natural unemployment that exists, with estimates in the UK varying from 2 per cent to over 10 per cent.

Policies to reduce unemployment

In order to reduce demand-deficient unemployment, governments in the past have followed Keynesian principles of attempting to increase aggregate demand through such measures as fiscal policy and monetary policy (see Unit 21). A problem with this method, however, is that it may result in a rise in inflation and balance of payments problems.

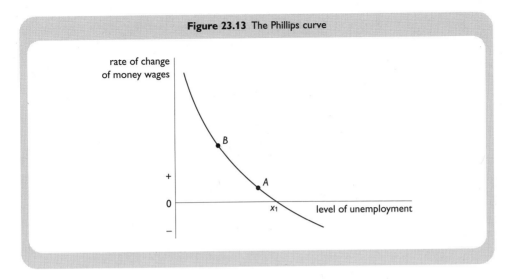

Figure 23.13 The Phillips curve

The conflict between unemployment and inflation has been demonstrated through the **Phillips curve**. In the 1950s, A.W. Phillips made a historical study comparing the rates of unemployment and the rates at which money wages changed between 1861 to 1957. As there is a strong link between the rate at which money wages change and the rate of inflation, the study was used to demonstrate the incompatibility of low unemployment rates with low rates of inflation. The Phillips curve demonstrates the trade-off which was thought to exist between inflation and unemployment. If the economy was in a position represented by point A in Figure 23.13, but the government wanted to reduce the level of unemployment through demand-management policies, it would have to accept that a cost of this is a higher rate of increase in money wages (and therefore inflation), a position represented by point B on the diagram.

Monetarists reject demand-management policies as a solution to unemployment and also reject the trade-off between inflation and unemployment that the Phillips curve displayed. They claim that unemployment cannot be reduced below its natural level through policies of demand management. If unemployment is at its natural level, this would suggest that the unemployment that exists is mainly structural or frictional. Hence any attempt to reduce unemployment through increasing aggregate demand would not decrease unemployment, but would cause inflation to rise. Monetarists therefore believe that in the long run, when the labour market has settled at an equilibrium, there is no trade-off between unemployment and inflation. In Figure 23.14, any attempt to reduce unemployment through increasing aggregate demand would just lead to higher and higher rates of inflation, without increasing the level of employment. The rate of unemployment that exists at X_1 is the natural rate of unemployment.

The natural rate of unemployment has also come to be known as the **non-accelerating inflation rate of unemployment (NAIRU)**, as the rate of inflation will remain constant at this rate of unemployment, but will start to accelerate if the government attempts to reduce unemployment below this level through increasing aggregate demand. In order to reduce unemployment below the natural level, which consists of structural and frictional unemployment, the government should use supply-side policies. The effect of a successful

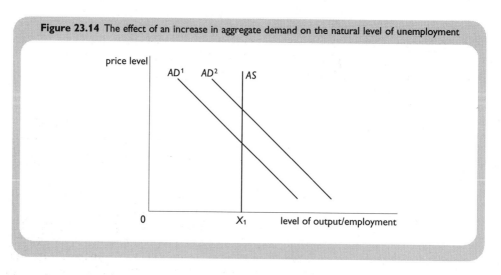

Figure 23.14 The effect of an increase in aggregate demand on the natural level of unemployment

supply-side policy can be illustrated by a move of the *AS* curve to the right, as shown in Figure 23.15.

Supply-side policies aimed at reducing unemployment

Supply-side policies that are intended to reduce unemployment are as follows:

- **Reduction of benefits** A reduction in unemployment-related benefits would reduce search and frictional unemployment, as those who are unemployed would reduce their search time and seek work more urgently if their benefits were significantly reduced.

- **Lowering tax rates** It is argued that high rates of personal tax reduce the incentive to work, as the difference between pay from employment and the amount received in benefits is reduced by high rates of income tax. Lower tax rates for firms might also increase investment and expansion, creating more employment opportunities.

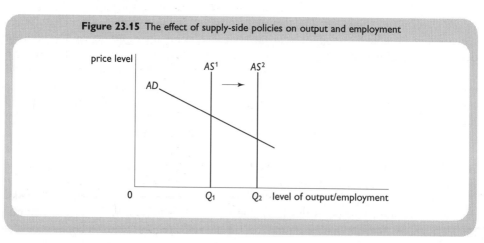

Figure 23.15 The effect of supply-side policies on output and employment

- **Improving information flows** Unemployed workers have imperfect knowledge regarding job vacancies. If information flows concerning job vacancies can be improved, this will reduce the amount of frictional or search unemployment and help the labour market work more effectively. In recent years, the use of new technology has helped employment exchanges and job centres to keep the unemployed better informed.

- **Reform of trade unions** It is argued that trade unions push wages up above the free-market equilibrium level. Higher wages mean firms restrict their demand for labour. Reform of trade unions and a reduction in their power should therefore help to reduce unemployment.

- **Reduction of firms' costs** It is argued that much of the legislation and regulations that exist add to firms' costs and that if these can be reduced, existing firms are likely to employ more workers, while others will be encouraged to set up new firms. For example, a law that says that employers must make redundancy payments to workers that it may make redundant in the future might discourage the firm from taking on employees in the first place. The employers' national insurance contribution, which could be viewed as a 'tax on employment', might also discourage firms from employing additional workers.

- **Improving occupational and geographical mobility** Measures that help improve occupational and geographical mobility of labour will help to reduce structural and regional unemployment. Retraining schemes should enable those with inappropriate skills to acquire the skills that will help them to secure employment. Keynesians and interventionists would also support measures to improve the occupational and geographical mobility of labour, but the essential difference is that supply-siders, who support the use of the free market, believe that government intervention should be limited and that much of the responsibility for becoming occupationally and geographically mobile lies with the individuals themselves – that is, people should be more willing to accept retraining, to accept a job with lower wages, or to travel around the country looking for work. The Keynesian approach is more interventionist and includes, for example, encouraging firms to set up in areas of high unemployment.

Monetarists are also keen to ensure that the labour market operates as freely as possible so that equilibrium in the labour market can occur, and involuntary, or disequilibrium, unemployment disappears. If a labour market is competitive and has flexible wages, wages should adjust to clear the market and remove any excess supply of labour. Again, supply-side measures, such as reducing the monopoly power of trade unions, or abolishing minimum wage agreements, should help to make wages more flexible.

Unemployment and the firm

Unemployment is generally regarded as an undesirable condition for the economy, and it can have adverse effects on a firm. A high level of unemployment reduces the purchasing power of consumers and may lead to a fall in demand for a firm's product, depending on the nature of the product and its income elasticity of demand (see Unit 6). The reduction in sales might mean that firms have to rationalise in an attempt to reduce their costs.

Alternatively, the firm might seek other markets in which to sell its product: for example, it could switch to overseas markets in order to try to maintain sales, although obviously much will depend on whether the unemployment is an international problem.

In certain circumstances, unemployment can be turned to a firm's advantage. During times of unemployment, the surplus of workers will influence wage demands. The bargaining position of trade unions is weakened as, with many workers seeking employment, unions will not be in a position to demand large pay increases for their members. Firms will therefore be able to offer lower wages and will not have to offer so many incentives in order to retain workers. It should also be easier for the firm to fill any vacancies that arise, as there are likely to be plenty of workers seeking employment, although the uneven spread of unemployment may present the firm with a problem in recruiting skilled labour. In addition, the administrative work associated with recruitment may increase as the firm is likely to get many more applicants for each job vacancy. Firms may be able to take advantage of government strategies to reduce unemployment: for example, regional aid, investment grants and retraining schemes. Although unemployment might result in a fall in sales for some firms, those firms who produce products for the cheaper end of the market might find an increase in sales as consumers switch down to purchasing cheaper varieties of products. In this case, other firms might try to adapt their marketing strategy and reposition their product in the market.

Summary

Unemployment exists when there are people who are willing and able to work but who cannot find employment. The official unemployment figures in the UK are based on the number of people claiming unemployment-related benefits. This is not necessarily the same as the number of people unemployed. The costs of unemployment include the loss of potential output in the economy, the financial cost to the government and the individual, and the social costs. The classical view of unemployment assumes that wages are fully flexible, and that the workings of the free market should ensure that any excess supply of labour eventually disappears. In practice, however, wages are not fully flexible and adjust only slowly, resulting in prolonged periods of unemployment. This may occur if there is a fall in aggregate demand, referred to as demand-deficient unemployment. Unemployment can also be classified as structural, regional, frictional or seasonal. When unemployment occurs because the wage level is above the labour market equilibrium, this is referred to as involuntary unemployment. Any unemployment which occurs when the labour market is in equilibrium is referred to as the natural rate of unemployment, and can be termed voluntary unemployment. Demand-side policies aim to reduce demand-deficient unemployment. A drawback of this strategy is that it is likely to lead to an increase in the rate of inflation. Monetarists and supply-siders dispute that unemployment can be reduced in the long run by demand-side measures; all that will happen, they argue, is that there will be increasing rates of unemployment. Instead, they support the use of supply-side measures aimed at raising the equilibrium level of employment and reducing the natural level of unemployment.

Review questions

1. Outline the costs of unemployment.
2. Why might the official government figures for unemployment (a) underestimate, and (b) overestimate, the number of people seeking employment?
3. Distinguish between 'structural' and 'frictional' unemployment.
4. Suggest reasons why the rate of unemployment varies between regions.
5. Why might excessive wages cause unemployment?
6. Why does unemployment arise even if wages are flexible?
7. What is meant by the 'natural' rate of unemployment?
8. Why does the natural rate of unemployment fluctuate?
9. What policies might be used to reduce the 'natural' rate of unemployment?

Essay questions

1. How might a firm be affected by a rising rate of unemployment in the economy? What strategies might it adopt in order to lessen the impact of the rise in unemployment?
2. Would a reduction in unemployment benefit reduce unemployment? What other measures might the government adopt in order to try to reduce unemployment levels?

Reading 23.1

A headline in the *Financial Times* in 1996 announced 'US markets in turmoil after sharp rise in jobs'. One would have thought that an increase in employment would have been good news. But perhaps the US financial markets shared the same views as Karl Marx who, more than a hundred years earlier, had claimed that the capitalist system could only operate efficiently with a 'reserve army of unemployed'.

Economists nowadays talk of the natural rate of unemployment, or the non-accelerating inflation rate of unemployment (NAIRU). It was felt by many that the natural rate of unemployment in the UK at this time was around 8 per cent, and there were fears that as unemployment dipped below this figure, inflationary pressures would build up. Others, however, felt that unemployment could fall well below this level, and that if the government continued to reform the labour market, the natural rate of unemployment could be reduced to as low as 2 per cent. ▷

Questions

1. As reducing unemployment is one of the primary macroeconomic objectives of governments, why do you think the US markets reacted as they did following the improvement in unemployment figures?

2. In what ways might an economy benefit from the existence of unemployment?

3. How might firms benefit from the existence of unemployment in the economy?

4. Why is it important for policymakers to identify the natural rate of unemployment?

5. What are the dangers if the government attempts to reduce unemployment below its natural rate?

6. How might governments attempt to lower the natural rate of unemployment?

The international environment

After reading this module you should be able to:

- explain why international trade takes place;

- discuss the reasons for, and methods of, restricting trade;

- recognise the international organisations which seek to promote trade;

- analyse a balance of payments account;

- identify measures that governments can take to reduce a balance of payments deficit and assess the impact these measures may have on firms;

- understand the workings of the foreign exchange market;

- appreciate the impact that exchange rates have upon business;

- have an insight into the European Union; and

- appreciate the implications that membership of the European Union has for businesses.

International trade

Under a system of perfectly free commerce, each country naturally devotes its capital and labour to such employments as are most beneficial to each ... It is this principle which determines that wine shall be made in France and Portugal, that corn shall be grown in America and Poland, and that hardware and other goods shall be manufactured in England. ... If Portugal had no commercial connexion with other countries, instead of employing a great part of her capital and industry in the production of wines, with which she purchases for her own use the cloth and hardware of other countries, she would be obliged to devote a part of that capital to the manufacture of those commodities, which she would thus obtain probably inferior in quality as well as quantity.

Source: David Ricardo, *The Principles of Political Economy and Taxation*, 1817, chapter 7, republished in Pelican Books edition, 1971, pp. 152–3.

International trade is becoming increasingly important for firms. Firms cannot simply think of their environment in national terms, but must be aware of the international environment. Production has become increasingly 'internationalised', with firms taking advantage of cheaper sources of materials and labour from overseas. Sales have also become internationalised, with multinational firms selling their products in many different markets around the world. Overseas markets represent an opportunity for firms to export, but international trade also represents a threat to firms, in terms of increased competition from abroad.

Many economists favour international trade without restrictions, arguing that countries will gain from the benefits of specialisation, while consumers should benefit from cheaper prices and enjoy a greater variety of products. Critics of free trade highlight some of the problems that it can cause, with competition from overseas leading to the closure of domestic firms and unemployment of workers. They argue that the government should intervene to protect domestic industries by limiting the amount of international trade.

The case for free trade

One reason why international trade takes place is because resources are unevenly distributed throughout the world and some countries do not possess the necessary minerals or raw materials to produce certain goods. Copper and some types of timber, for example, are not indigenous to the UK and it is necessary to import them into the country. However, a further justification for international trade is that it is based upon the principle of specialisation. If, as individuals, we all tried to be self-sufficient, aiming to provide all the goods and services that we needed for ourselves, we would experience a very low standard of living. As individuals, it is reasonable for us to specialise and to trade with others, buying those goods and services that we require in exchange for money earned through specialising at a particular job. International trade is simply an extension of this at an international level. It makes sense for countries to concentrate on the production of those goods and services at which they are most efficient, and then to exchange these with goods and services which other countries are better at producing. It would, for example, be perfectly possible for a country such as the UK to produce bananas, by growing them in hothouses. However, this would result in these bananas being extremely expensive, and probably not of a very good quality, and would represent an inefficient use of the country's resources. The UK therefore concentrates on producing other goods and services to which it is more suited and exchanges these for bananas from those countries which are more suited to growing bananas.

Absolute advantage

The theory of international trade has it roots in Adam Smith's *Wealth of Nations*, published in 1776, and his recognition of the importance of specialisation. Smith argued that if two countries specialised in producing those goods in which they had an **absolute advantage**, and then traded with each other, both countries would benefit. A country is said to have an absolute advantage in the production of a good when it is more efficient in the production of that good than the other country. Table 24.1 shows the number of units of wine and cheese that each country can produce assuming that each country has

Table 24.1 Absolute advantage: output without specialisation

	Wine	Cheese
Country A	200	1500
Country B	1000	300
	1200	1800

Table 24.2 Absolute advantage: output after specialisation

	Wine	Cheese
Country A	–	3000
Country B	2000	–
	2000	3000

the same amount of resources and each devotes half of its resources to wine and half of its resources to cheese. Country A has an absolute advantage at producing cheese while Country B has an absolute advantage in the production of wine. The combined total production of the two countries amounts to 1200 units of wine and 1800 units of cheese. If, however, Country B concentrated all its resources on producing wine, while Country A concentrated on producing only cheese (see Table 24.2), total output would rise to 2000 units of wine and 3000 units of cheese. The total output of both goods has increased. If the countries exchange some of their production for the other good, they can both benefit from the principle of specialisation.

Specialisation between countries therefore enables an increase in the amount of goods and services produced, thus increasing wealth and living standards. In addition, specialisation provides opportunities for businesses to gain from the internal economies of large-scale production, which help to bring down the cost per unit and, therefore, prices. Furthermore, external economies, such as the sharing of ideas and information and access to specialised facilities, can be enjoyed by businesses located in an area of specialisation.

Trade between countries also increases competition, reducing any monopoly power that domestic firms may have, which should further promote an improvement in efficiency and encourage firms to keep down prices. At the same time, non-economic advantages can accrue from trade: for example, trade between countries helps to promote understanding and good relations between countries.

Comparative advantage

What if a country finds that it has an absolute advantage in the production of most goods and services? You might assume that it could not be to that country's advantage to trade with a country that is less efficient in the production of these goods and services. David Ricardo however, in *Principles of Political Economy and Taxation*, published in 1817,

Table 24.3 Comparative advantage: output without specialisation

	Cars	Wheat
Country X	2000	2000
Country Y	500	1000
	2500	3000

extended the theory of international trade to show that even if a country has an absolute advantage in the production of most goods, it is still beneficial for that country to specialise in producing and exporting some goods, while importing other goods. The country should specialise in the production of those goods in which it has a **comparative advantage**, and should import those goods at which it is comparatively less efficient, even though it may still be *absolutely* more efficient at the production of the goods it imports.

Consider the example in Table 24.3. If we again assume that each country has the same amount of resources and each devotes half its resources to the production of each good, we can see that Country X has an absolute advantage in the production of both cars and wheat. However, comparatively, Country X is better at producing cars, for it can produce four times as many cars as Country Y with the same amount of resources, while it can only produce twice as much wheat as Country Y. Likewise, although Country Y is less efficient than Country X in the production of both goods, comparatively it is better in the production of wheat. Thus Country X has a comparative advantage in the production of cars, while Country Y has a comparative advantage in the production of wheat.

Ricardo's law of comparative advantage shows that two countries can gain from trade if each concentrates on the production of those goods in which it has a comparative advantage. Table 24.4 illustrates the gains that can be made if specialisation takes place in this example. Country X has switched *half* of its resources which were producing wheat to the production of cars, while Country Y has switched all of its resources which were producing cars to the production of wheat. The end result is that the total output of cars has risen by 500, without there having been any decrease in the total output of wheat. This represents the gain from specialisation and trade.

The principle can be further explained by examining the opportunity cost of producing the goods in each country. In Country X, the opportunity cost of producing one car is one unit of wheat. In Country Y the opportunity cost of producing one car is two units of wheat. Therefore, the opportunity cost of producing cars is reduced if Country X concentrates on car production. In Country Y, however, for every unit of wheat it

Table 24.4 Comparative advantage: output with specialisation

	Cars	Wheat
Country X	3000	1000
Country Y	–	2000
	3000	3000

produces it has to sacrifice half a car, while in Country X, for every unit of wheat it produces, it has to sacrifice one car. Thus the opportunity cost of producing wheat is minimised if Country Y concentrates on the production of wheat.

Criticisms of the theory of comparative advantage

Ricardo's model is rather a simple one. It only considers trade in two products between two countries. However, it would be possible to extend this model to encompass more products and more countries. Of more concern, however, is the theory's assumption that a country's factors of production are occupationally mobile and can be switched to producing those products in which the country has a comparative advantage. In reality, resources are not so mobile: for example, labour might need extensive retraining. The theory fails to recognise the problems that might be encountered by switching production to certain products and relying on other countries to produce other products: for example, high levels of unemployment might occur if a country ceases to produce certain products. Moreover, severe unemployment could occur in a country if there is a fall in demand for the products in which it has a comparative advantage, hence the dangers of over-specialising on a narrow range of products. The model also ignores other factors (e.g. transport costs) that might reduce the gains to be made from trade. Thus, while free trade should in theory increase world living standards, not everyone in an economy necessarily benefits from freer international trade.

Nevertheless, despite these criticisms, the theory of comparative advantage has come to be regarded as a convincing argument in favour of international trade, and it still retains much of its validity. India and other countries in Southeast Asia, who have an abundant supply of relatively unskilled labour, have a comparative advantage in the production of those goods that call for an abundance of unskilled labour. Other countries such as Germany and the USA, who have a relative abundance of capital and skilled labour, have a comparative advantage in the production of capital intensive goods. It is important to realise, however, that comparative advantage can change and does not remain static. Countries can acquire new areas of comparative advantage through technological developments or through changes in labour costs. Equally, entrepreneurial activity or even government policy can help change a country's comparative advantage. The UK used to have a comparative advantage in the production of manufactured goods, but changes have meant that it now imports large quantities of manufactured goods and concentrates more on the provision of services.

Case study

The terms of trade

International trade is influenced by changes in the relative prices of goods. The **terms of trade** measure changes in relative prices, and show the relationship between the average price of a country's exports and the average price of its imports. It is calculated through the formula:

$$\frac{\text{Export price index}}{\text{Import price index}} \times 100$$

In the base year, the terms of trade will be 100, as both the export price index and the import price index will be 100. If export prices increase faster than import prices, the terms of trade will rise above 100. A rise in the terms of trade is described as an improvement, as it means that more imports can be bought in exchange for a given amount of exports. However, a rise in the price of exports might mean that the demand for exports falls, so an improvement in the terms of trade might not necessarily be favourable for a country, the impact depending on the price elasticity of demand for exports and imports.

Arguments against free trade

In view of the advantages of free trade, why then are there often calls to place restrictions on international trade? Various reasons have been put forward to justify limiting the amount of this type of trade, a policy which is often referred to as '**protectionism**'.

To protect infant industries

This argument applies particularly to developing countries. New **infant industries** which have not yet established themselves will find it very difficult to compete with established industries from other countries. They will probably still be trying to cover their high initial start-up costs and may not yet have reached the stage where they can benefit from economies of scale. Costs per unit are therefore likely to be considerably higher than their international competitors. Therefore, it is argued, these industries should have protection from foreign competition, at least until they have established themselves in the marketplace, and have expanded output sufficiently to enable them to take advantage of economies of scale and to compete on an equal footing with their international competitors. Malaysia, Indonesia, China and Brazil have all used the 'infant industry' argument to support the development of car manufacturing in their economies. One problem with this strategy, however, is deciding when the protection should be removed. At what stage can the industry be considered to have 'grown up'? The industry itself is likely to demand protection from foreign competition for as long as possible!

To protect depressed or declining industries

This is similar to the infant industry argument. It too says that there may be a case for giving temporary protection to these industries, in this instance because they are in a depressed state and are no longer competitive in international markets. Temporary protection would, for example, provide them with an opportunity to reinvest in new machinery in order to become more efficient before being exposed again to international competition. The Multifibre Agreement, which came into effect in the 1970s, aimed to protect the textile industries of developed economies by limiting the import of textiles from newly industrialised and developing countries. However, the fact is that the loss of an industry's competitiveness may be the result of a change in a country's comparative advantage, and, in such a case, temporary protection is not the solution as the industry may not be able to regain its competitiveness. One possible argument in favour of temporary protection is to allow the decline of the industry to take place gradually, thus giving its workers time to retrain and move into new occupations, though the decline of an industry may take place over many years, as in the case of the British textile industry, and protection can therefore become a permanent feature.

To reduce the level of unemployment

While the two arguments above argue for the protection of specific industries, this argument for protection is on a macro level, advocating protection on a much wider scale and arguing that restriction of foreign trade is required in order to help reduce the domestic level of unemployment. By reducing the level of imports, people would be encouraged to buy domestically produced goods, thus creating employment opportunities. A problem with this approach is that domestic firms may become complacent in the face of reduced competition from overseas, and their costs per unit may rise in consequence. Therefore, it is only, at most, a short-term solution, and does not address the problem of why domestic firms cannot compete in the first place. This approach can also be criticised for 'exporting unemployment': that is, unemployment might be reduced at home, but at the cost of increased unemployment overseas.

To alleviate a balance of payments problem

If a country has a severe balance of payments problem, it might seek to redress this imbalance by limiting the amount of imports into the country. Balance of payments problems may arise if the government is attempting to expand and reflate the economy. Measures such as lowering interest rates or tax levels in an attempt to reduce the level of unemployment by boosting aggregate demand are also likely to lead to a situation where more imports are demanded. Therefore, it has been argued, notably by the Cambridge School of economists, that protection from imports should be used alongside any policy which aims to increase aggregate demand to avoid possible balance of payments problems. However such a policy would face difficulties because of agreements made under the General Agreement on Tariffs and Trade (GATT), and membership of the European Union (EU) and the World Trade Organisation.

To counter unfair trade practices

Countries may consider it is necessary to restrict international trade if they believe that their competitors are competing unfairly. **Dumping**, for example, is a practice whereby countries sell exports at subsidised prices, sometimes even below cost price, making it very difficult for firms from other countries to compete. The EU has investigated charges that Norway has been selling salmon on European markets at below production prices and has proposed imposing a minimum import price to counter this dumping. Although GATT and its successor, the World Trade Organisation, have worked hard to reduce tariff barriers, they acknowledge the problems caused by dumping, and sanction the use of tariffs to counter their effects.

To protect a source of revenue

Tariffs represent a source of revenue to the government. Free trade denies them this revenue, which may be an important source of income to countries with low incomes or who have difficulty in raising revenue in other ways.

For strategic and security reasons

Some argue that specialising in some products and relying on other countries to produce other goods places a country in a vulnerable position. If a country finds itself at war with another country and yet relies on that country for the supply of certain goods, it is likely to find that the flow of these goods into the country is disrupted. Hence, for strategic reasons, countries may attempt to continue to produce goods such as steel, rather than import them from overseas.

Exercise

The USA has complained in recent years that subsidised and 'dumped' steel imports from the countries in the European Union were unfairly driving US steel plants out of business.

Questions

1. Explain precisely what is meant by 'dumping'.
2. What actions could the US government take to prevent the so-called 'dumping'?
3. Examine the impact that subsidised steel imports might have on (a) US firms, and (b) US consumers.
4. Why do you think that European governments might wish to subsidise the export of steel?

Types of protection

Tariffs

A **tariff** is a tax on an imported product. By raising the price of imports relative to the price of home-produced goods, countries hope that demand will be diverted away from imports towards domestically produced goods and services. Tariffs might be based on a percentage of the price of the import (**ad valorem**), or on a fixed, specific amount per unit.

The degree of success that a tariff has in restricting trade depends on the price elasticity of demand for imported products. If an imported product has an inelastic demand, then an increase in price will not have much effect on the demand for that product, and the level of imports will remain largely unchanged (see Figure 24.1). If, however, the demand for the import is price elastic, a tariff will reduce the amount of the product imported considerably (see Figure 24.2).

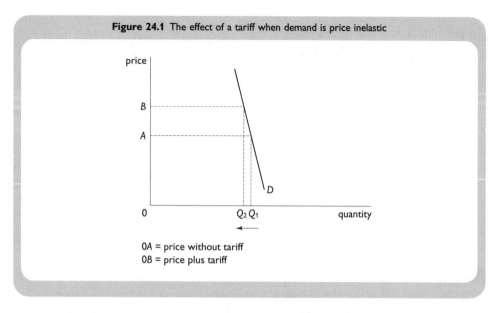

Figure 24.1 The effect of a tariff when demand is price inelastic

OA = price without tariff
OB = price plus tariff

Tariffs may be used in a non-discriminatory way through being applied to all imports. Alternatively, governments might decide to be more selective, applying tariff barriers to certain industries or products only. In either case, however, a country which imposes tariffs may find itself subject to retaliatory measures, so that although the country might be successful in limiting imports into the country, it may also lose some of its export markets. A further complication is that tariffs may well be inflationary, as the price of imported products will have risen, leading to cost-push inflation, while the increased demand for domestically produced goods might lead to demand-pull inflationary pressures. Firms which are protected by a tariff barrier are also likely to become inefficient and uncompetitive as they are allowed to operate behind the protection of the tariff. This will also lead to a rise in costs and prices. An important element of the EU's Common Agricultural Policy (CAP) is the imposition of tariffs on imported foodstuffs.

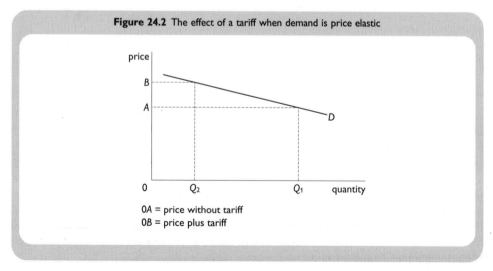

Figure 24.2 The effect of a tariff when demand is price elastic

OA = price without tariff
OB = price plus tariff

Exercise

Imagine a situation in which the car manufacturers in the UK persuade the government to place high tariffs on imported cars.

Questions

1. Examine the effects that this is likely to have on the UK car industry.
2. How might UK consumers be affected?

Import quotas

An **import quota** is a numerical limit on the amount of a product that is allowed to be imported into a country over a period of time. It is therefore a far more direct policy than a tariff, which merely attempts to discourage the import of products through higher prices. One effect of the quota, however, through reducing the supply of the product available to the market, will be to raise the price of the import.

The use of tariffs and quotas nowadays is restricted through international agreements drawn up through trading blocks such as the EU or the General Agreement on Tariffs and Trade (GATT). For many countries, they no longer represent a policy option, so countries have had to turn to other methods of restricting trade.

Voluntary export restraint (VER)

Instead of an importing country imposing import quotas, an exporting country may agree, at the suggestion of the importer, to adhere to a **voluntary export restraint** (**VER**), by which it restricts the amount of a product that it exports to that country. One reason for accepting such an agreement is the threat of trade restrictions. For example, the Japanese government has made agreements with the EU and the USA to restrict the amount of cars and other products that it exports to their markets. However, the World Trade Organisation (the successor to GATT) is seeking to remove such barriers to trade.

Subsidising domestic producers

A government can subsidise domestic firms, thus making their prices comparatively cheaper than those of imported products and encouraging consumers to buy domestically produced goods rather than imports. Governments may also show favouritism to domestic firms in the case of public procurement, rather than having open competition. These practices are banned within the EU because they distort competition. However, the EU does, through its Common Agricultural Policy (CAP) provide significant subsidies to the agricultural sector in order to protect European farmers.

Exchange controls

An exchange control is where a government limits the availability of foreign currencies, so restricting the amount of imports that can be purchased. Exchange controls existed in the UK until 1979, when they were abolished.

Administrative barriers to trade

In recent years, following the agreements to remove tariff and other barriers to trade, countries have devised new methods of restricting trade. This range of new methods includes requiring excessive documentation for imported products in order to deter would-be importers, or using other means of preventing imports coming into the country: for example, Germany insisted that beer must be made with pure spring water, which effectively banned many imported beers; and the French government insisted that all imported video recorders pass through a customs depot in the town of Poitiers, which created a backlog and meant that fewer imported recorders were released onto the market. Sometimes these regulations are made on the grounds of health and safety or consumer protection, such as those prohibiting the import of potentially dangerous fireworks into the UK, or the refusal by the European Union to allow the export of British beef which might be contaminated by BSE. Often, however, the requirement to carry out extensive modifications to, or even redesign, a product before it can be imported into a country deters would-be importers. Safety features on cars are a good example, with different nations having very precise regulations about even the smallest of car design features, which necessitates expensive modification before the car can be imported into the country.

International trading agreements

The General Agreement on Tariffs and Trade (GATT)

The 1930s was an era of high barriers to trade throughout the world, as countries raised tariffs in order to try to protect their own employment levels. The end result was less trade, lower efficiency and no more employment. As a response to the problems created by these measures, the **General Agreement on Tariffs and Trade (GATT)** was created in 1947. Under the agreement, GATT countries, who numbered well in excess of one hundred, met periodically to negotiate on matters relating to foreign trade and to agree on reductions in trade barriers. Through these measures, GATT aimed to increase living standards throughout the world and to ensure a more efficient use of the world's resources. GATT was successful in negotiating substantial reductions in tariffs throughout the world, and later turned its attention to the reduction and removal of **non-tariff barriers** to trade.

In 1995 GATT was replaced by the **World Trade Organisation (WTO)**. Its aim is to continue the progress made by GATT in reducing and removing barriers to trade, and, in order to help it achieve its objectives, it has additional powers to enable it to settle trade disputes and enforce decisions.

Regional trading blocs

In addition to GATT, the latter part of the twentieth century has also seen the formation of regional trading agreements around the world. These agreements may take several formats, as follows:

- A **free-trade area** is an agreement between countries to have **free trade** with each other. Each country is allowed, however, to levy its own individual tariffs and place other restrictions on imports from countries outside the area. One of the earliest free-trade areas was the European Free Trade Association (EFTA) which was established in 1960 by those countries in Western Europe who were unwilling to join the more rigid European Economic Community. (In recent years, however, most of the EFTA countries have now joined the European Union.) Similarly, the North American Free Trade Area (NAFTA) is an agreement which allows free trade between the United States, Canada and Mexico, while Australia and New Zealand have entered into a similar agreement that removes restrictions on the trade between these two countries.

- A **customs union** is a free-trade area plus an agreement to establish common barriers to trade, for example, a common external tariff, against imports from non-members.

- A **common market** is a customs union that also has free movement of labour and capital between member states in addition to the free movement of goods and services. We examine the European Union and its implications in Unit 26.

While the formation of these trading agreements can be seen as a step in the direction of free trade between countries, there is concern that some of the trading blocs are very inward-looking and conflict with the principle of multilateral free trade. Certainly, trading blocs promote free trade between member states but they also sometimes develop a fortress mentality, placing quite severe restrictions on trade with non-members. As a result, there is an increase in trade between members within each trading bloc, giving member states the opportunity to purchase products from each other at lower prices because tariff barriers have been removed, but there is less trade with countries outside the trading bloc and between trading blocs. In fact, countries within a trading agreement may find themselves having to buy products from other countries within their agreement, even though cheaper sources might be available from countries outside the agreement: for example, many tropical countries can produce sugar from cane very cheaply, but the EU studiously protects its own sugar beet industry.

Summary

Economic theory shows that, by adopting a policy of free trade, countries can enjoy higher standards of living. However, there are some costs involved. An industry in a country may go into decline in the face of free trade and no protection from foreign competition. The extent of the costs depend on how quickly the workers and resources of that industry can transfer to other, expanding industries. Individual firms and industries will often argue for protection from international trade, ▷

claiming that, for example, they are not able to compete with overseas firms who may be able to take advantage of much lower labour costs. However, it must be realised that these arguments to restrict international trade are often to protect a vested interest. The individual firm might benefit from restricting foreign competition, but a policy of protection imposes substantial costs on the economy and society as a whole. Restriction of international trade means less choice for consumers and higher prices, and is likely to lead to domestic firms becoming less efficient as they are able to operate behind protective trade barriers. The rate of economic growth will probably be slower and the level of national income lower. Protection may preserve jobs in the short run, but, in the long run, it is not generally an efficient method of sustaining employment. Jobs saved in some industries are likely to be offset by jobs lost elsewhere in the economy as a result of retaliation and a general reduction in trade. It is therefore important that we are aware of the overall advantages of trade and the consequences for the economy of restricting trade, rather than just looking at the subject from the point of view of an individual firm. Trading agreements such as GATT have succeeded in lowering tariff barriers and attention is now being turned to the removal of other barriers to trade.

Review questions

1. What advantages are there to be gained from free trade?
2. Distinguish between absolute and comparative advantage.
3. What is meant by an 'improvement' in the terms of trade? Explain why an improvement in a country's terms of trade might not necessarily be favourable for the firms in that country.
4. What measures could a country adopt to protect itself from international trade?
5. Summarise the main arguments in favour of protection.
6. Explain some of the likely consequences if all countries tried to increase their level of employment by imposing large tariff barriers on all imports.
7. What measures can a government take to attempt to increase its country's exports?
8. Explain the differences between: (a) a free-trade area; (b) a customs union; and (c) a common market.

Essay questions

1. (a) Outline the main reasons why international trade occurs. (b) Describe the potential benefits of international trade to a business.
2. If the case for free trade is so convincing, why do some countries seek to restrict the amount of international trade?

Reading 24.1

The Monopolies and Mergers Commission found that car buyers in Britain are paying more for new cars than their continental counterparts, particularly those in Belgium and the Netherlands. One of the reasons for this was the limit placed on the import of Japanese cars. The voluntary export restraint agreement between Britain and Japan limits imports of Japanese cars to 11 per cent of the market. The Commission declared that this represented a serious constraint on trade and recommended that it be removed as quickly as possible. However, the issue was complicated by the deal made by the European Commission to limit the import of Japanese cars into the EU market.

Question

Using information provided in the passage above, discuss the case for and against the restriction of international trade.

Reading 24.2

British Polythene used to manufacture plastic carrier bags in Telford, UK. It now makes them in China, where labour costs are much lower than in the UK. The Chinese workers are paid approximately 50p per hour, compared with the £5 per hour which the British workers were paid. As a result, the price of plastic bags has fallen, admittedly by less than a halfpenny, but for the high-street stores who buy millions of the bags, this represents a considerable saving. Nike trainers used to be made in Oregon, USA, where the company paid wage rates of $12 per hour. Now they are made in Indonesia, where the wage rates are 20 cents an hour. The result is that we get cheaper shoes, while the Indonesians have greater opportunities for employment.

Questions

1. Using examples from the above passage, explain the law of comparative advantage.
2. Is it right for us to buy goods from countries that pay low wages?

The balance of payments and exchange rates

'Falling yen helps Japanese profits'

A 10 per cent decline in the foreign exchange value of the yen against the dollar in 1996 led to a marked improvement in the performance of Japanese exporters. Export successes included electronics companies such as Sony and Matsushita, who both experienced a large increase in profits. Toyota, Japan's largest car company, saw a fourfold rise in profits despite a fall in domestic sales, while the profits of Honda rose by a similar amount.

Car makers who were more oriented to the Japanese domestic market, such as Mazda and Mitsubishi Motors, were unable to improve their performance, while some industries were severely disadvantaged by the fall in the value of the yen. Airlines and power companies, who are dependent on imported oil, reported a sharp decline in profits.

In this unit we shall look at the different components of the **balance of payments** account and at the options open to government to correct a balance of payments deficit. We shall then go on to examine exchange rate mechanisms, and the impact that changes in the exchange rate has upon firms.

The balance of payments is an account which records the income and expenditure resulting from all the international transactions of a country over a period of time. These transactions consist of goods, services and capital flowing into and out of the country. There are two main headings to the balance of payments account: the current account and the capital account (which is now usually referred to in the UK as transactions in external assets and liabilities).

The current account

The **current account** records payments for the purchase of goods and services from overseas (imports) and income received from the sale of domestically produced goods and services to other countries (exports).

The balance of the trade in goods, sometimes called the **visible trade** balance, refers to the trade in physical merchandise. Finished goods, semi-finished goods, raw materials, oil and chemicals are all examples of visible items. The sale of a car manufactured in the UK to an overseas customer represents an export of a good, or a visible export. This would therefore be recorded as a positive entry in the current account of the UK balance of payments as money is flowing into the country. The purchase of timber from an overseas supplier by a UK firm represents the import of a good, or a visible import, and would be recorded as a negative entry since the money is flowing out of the country.

The trade in services between countries is sometimes referred to as the **invisible trade** balance and includes items such as insurance, banking services, shipping, air transport and tourism. Thus an overseas customer purchasing an insurance policy from a UK company would be recorded as an export of a service, or an invisible export, on the current account of the UK balance of payments, while money spent overseas by a UK holidaymaker would be recorded as an import of a service, or an invisible import. The balance of trade in goods and services is sometimes just referred to as the balance of trade. However, the current account also records other income flows.

Investment income consists of interest, profits and dividends flowing in and out of the country. Thus any profits made by a Japanese car plant in the UK and which are sent back to Japan are recorded as a minus under investment income flows, as the money is flowing out of the country, while interest earned by a UK citizen from an overseas bank account would be recorded as an addition. Payments to international organisations such as the European Union and grants to developing countries are also recorded in the current account under the transfers balance.

Table 25.1 shows the Balance of Payments for the UK for 1996, and it can be seen from the table that the balance of trade was −£5597m., while the overall current account balance was −£14m.

Table 25.1 UK balance of payments, 1996 (£m.)

Current account	£m.	£m.
Exports of goods	166,092	
Imports of goods	178,320	
Balance on trade in goods		−12,228
Exports of services	49,103	
Imports of services	42,472	
Balance on trade in services		+6631
Balance of trade in goods and services		−5597
Other income flows:		
Investment income balance		+10,311
Transfers balance		−4728
Current account balance		−14
Capital account		
Transactions in assets:		
UK investment overseas	−87,450	
Deposits and lending overseas	−129,539	
Changes in official reserves	+509	
External assets of central government	−653	
Total transactions in assets		−217,133
Transactions in liabilities:		
Overseas investment in UK	+49,700	
Borrowing from overseas	+165,234	
External liabilities of central government	−748	
Total transactions in liabilities		+214,186
Capital account net transactions		−2947
Current account plus capital account		−2961
Balancing item		+2961
		0

Source: Monthly Digest of Statistics, June 1997; Economic Trends, June 1997.

The capital account

In addition to recording trade in goods and services, however, the balance of payments also records international capital transactions: that is, the acquisition and disposal of assets and liabilities by firms, individuals and governments. Examples of UK external assets include a UK resident buying shares in an overseas company, the building of a factory overseas by a UK company, and a UK bank making a loan to an overseas resident. Examples of UK external liabilities include investments in the UK by firms or individuals from overseas, and borrowing from overseas by anyone in the UK. It is worth remembering that the initial transfer of capital is recorded in the **capital account**, but any interest, profits or dividends resulting from the initial investment are recorded under 'investment income' in the current account. The capital account also records those transactions which are carried out by government to cover any overall deficit or surplus in the rest of the accounts. Such transactions include additions to or subtractions from the official **foreign reserves** and the lending and borrowing of foreign currency. These official, 'accommodating' flows ensure that the balance of payments always balances, although errors and omissions and the difficulties in obtaining accurate figures means that a **balancing item** has to be included to ensure that the account balances. As can be seen from Table 25.1, the balancing item can be very large, reflecting the degree of inaccuracy of the figures.

If the balance of payments always balances, why is it that politicians and commentators in the media refer to a balance of payments deficit or a balance of payments surplus? They are, in fact, referring to the balance on just one part of the account, usually the current account, or even just the balance of trade and services. Although the overall total of payments out of the country must equal the total receipts, specific parts of the accounts do not need to balance. A deficit on the current account has to be compensated by a surplus on the capital account. Thus, when commentators are referring to a balance of payments deficit, they are usually referring to a situation where the value of imported goods and services exceeds the value of exported goods and services. The financing of a current account deficit is recorded in the capital account and can be met by running down the reserves of foreign exchange or by borrowing from abroad.

Exercise

Having identified whether the following transactions would appear in the UK balance of payments account, decide in which section of the accounts they would be recorded:

1. A UK citizen purchases a car manufactured in Sweden.
2. A US citizen stays in a London hotel.
3. An overseas investor purchases shares in a UK company.
4. A UK firm builds a manufacturing plant in Spain.
5. Overseas customers purchase insurance from Lloyds of London.
6. Dividends from a Japanese-owned car plant in the UK are paid to Japanese investors.
7. A UK citizen purchases a ticket from British Airways to go to the Sydney Olympics.
8. A Greek shipping tycoon buys a chain of UK hotels.

Methods of correcting a balance of payments deficit

A persistent deficit on the current account of the balance of payments presents a problem for a country. Eventually, it will find itself with insufficient reserves of foreign exchange and it cannot go on borrowing indefinitely. It will therefore be necessary for the country to take measures to reduce, and eventually eliminate, a current account deficit, and this will have implications for government policy, which in turn will have an impact on the business community. The government might consider the following measures.

Import controls

Protectionist measures such as tariffs and quotas can be used to restrict the number of imports coming into the country. The range and effectiveness of import controls were discussed in detail in the previous unit. The main problem with using measures such as these is that they are likely to provoke other countries into taking retaliatory measures. International agreements also mean that these measures are no longer a realistic policy option for many countries.

Promotion of exports

The government can try to promote the sale of exports to other countries, through extensive marketing campaigns or by subsidising the exports so that they are more price competitive overseas.

Devaluation

A **devaluation** is where the government decides to lower the value of its currency. A **depreciation** of the exchange rate makes imports more expensive and makes exports cheaper for foreign buyers. Consider the following example. A UK car manufacturer produces and sells a car for £12,000. If the exchange rate is £1 = DM 3, a German customer would have to pay DM 36,000 for the car (ignoring transport costs). If, however, the exchange rate fell to £1 = DM 2, the German customer would only have to provide DM 24,000 to buy the car, while the UK car manufacturer will still receive £12,000 for the car. Meanwhile, a UK customer importing a German television priced at DM 600 would find that the sterling price rises from £200 to £300.

Thus a policy of devaluation can be regarded as a 'double-edged' weapon, as it could not only reduce the amount of imports coming into the country, but also it could encourage more export sales. However, the immediate effect of a devaluation, in making imports more expensive, is to worsen the balance of payments, as people are likely continue to purchase imports until they find a suitable home-produced substitute, causing expenditure on imports to rise in the short run. Firms will also require time to adjust supply to meet the new export demand, so increased revenue from exports will not be immediately forthcoming. Thus the pattern of the balance of payments following a devaluation might be as shown in Figure 25.1, which shows the **j-curve effect** whereby the current account of the balance of payments deteriorates before it gets better.

The success of a devaluation also depends on the elasticity of demand for imports and exports. If the demand for imports is price inelastic, the increase in price as a result of the devaluation will not reduce the demand for imports by very much, and total expenditure on the imports will, in fact, rise. Likewise, if the demand for exports is price inelastic, a lowering of their price in overseas markets will not have much effect on demand, and less revenue will be received. Therefore, in order for a devaluation to be successful, it is preferable for both the demand for imports and the demand for exports to be price elastic.

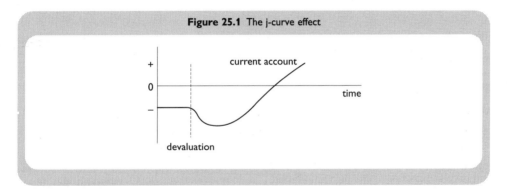

Figure 25.1 The j-curve effect

In other words, it is necessary for the demand for imports and exports to be fairly responsive to the changes in their price. In actual fact, according to the **Marshall-Lerner condition**, provided that the sum of the price elasticities of demand for imports and exports is greater than one, a devaluation should be successful in improving the trade deficit. It is also necessary, however, for the supply of exports to be elastic. There is no point in making exports more price competitive in order to increase demand unless firms and industries have spare capacity and are able to meet the increase in demand with an increase in output.

Devaluation is therefore a suitable policy for those economic conditions which exist when a balance of payments deficit is accompanied by recession and unemployment. Otherwise, there is a danger of inflation, as a result of both the higher import prices and the increased demand for home-produced products from both domestic and overseas customers. The success of a devaluation will also depend on the extent to which exported products have a high import content. The effect of the devaluation is to increase import prices and lower export prices, but if exports contain a high import content, the benefits of the devaluation will be lessened. For example, many cars in the UK are assembled from components imported from overseas. The higher cost of the imported components as a result of the devaluation might cancel out any competitive advantage that the exported cars may have gained.

Domestic deflation

The level of imports depends largely on the level of income. If the government deflates the economy and lowers the level of income, this should mean that the level of imports will fall and will therefore help to reduce a balance of payments deficit. Deflationary measures should also lead to a fall in the rate of inflation, which might make domestically produced goods more competitive overseas. Deflation might be achieved through reductions in government spending, raising taxes or by raising interest rates. Raising interest rates would also encourage an inflow of capital, as investors would be attracted by the higher interest rates. This would help improve the capital account and thus help improve the overall balance of payments.

A problem with a policy of deflation is that in addition to reducing the demand for imports, it also reduces the demand for home-produced products, resulting in a fall in output, a fall in business confidence and investment, and increased unemployment.

However, this reduction in demand at home might encourage manufacturers to switch their sales efforts to export markets, which would further help reduce the current account deficit. **Deflation**, or expenditure dampening, is therefore best used when there is a balance of payments deficit combined with high rates of inflation and overfull employment.

Exchange rates

International trade involves foreign currency. An importer will require foreign currency when it purchases goods from a foreign supplier. On the **foreign exchange markets**, the buying and selling of foreign currencies is done mainly by the banks. The largest foreign exchange market is in London where, in 1996, there was a daily market turnover of up to US$450 billion.

An exchange rate is simply the price of a currency expressed in terms of another currency. Thus, if the exchange rate is £1 = DM 2.50, it means that you would require £2 sterling to 'purchase' DM 5. As the exchange rate is the 'price' of a currency, its value in a free market is determined just like the price of any other product, through the forces of demand and supply. Figure 25.2 represents the demand and supply for pounds sterling. On the vertical axis, we have measured the price of pounds in terms of deutschmarks, and the quantity of pounds is shown along the horizontal axis.

The demand curve for pounds is of a normal shape, sloping down from left to right, since the higher the price of pounds, the less will be demanded, while the supply curve is also of a normal shape, since the higher the price of pounds on the foreign exchange market, the greater the quantity that people will be willing to supply. The exchange rate is determined at that price at which the demand for pounds equals the supply for pounds, which is at the rate of DM 2.50 in our diagram.

If there is then a fall in the demand for pounds, the demand curve shifts to the left and the new equilibrium rate might be DM 2.30. This is illustrated in Figure 25.3. Equally, an increase in the demand for pounds would cause the demand curve to shift to the right,

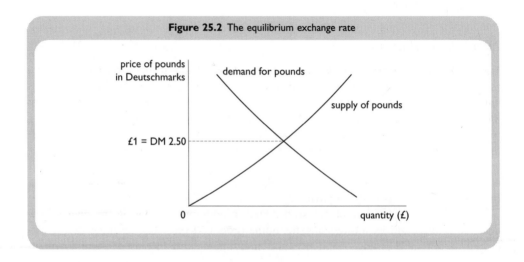

Figure 25.2 The equilibrium exchange rate

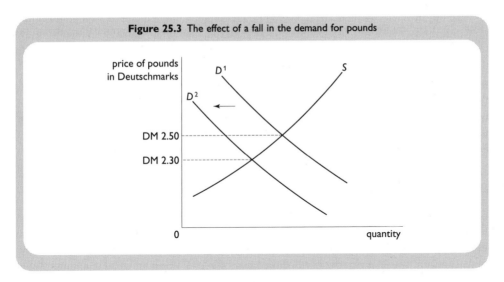

Figure 25.3 The effect of a fall in the demand for pounds

resulting in a higher equilibrium exchange rate. Any change in the supply of sterling would also result in a new equilibrium exchange rate.

In order to determine what causes the exchange rate to change, we need to establish what factors cause the demand for and supply of a currency to change, as follows:

- The demand for foreign currency is derived from the demand to purchase goods and services from that country. If there is an increase in the demand for UK goods and services from overseas customers, there will be an increase in demand for sterling in order to purchase these goods and services.

- The supply of pounds on to the foreign exchange market will be affected by the demand for imports from UK residents. An increase in the demand for imports will lead to an increase in demand for foreign currency, and therefore an increase in the supply of sterling on to the foreign exchange market.

- If the UK has a higher inflation rate than overseas, British goods will become less competitive. This will lead to a fall in demand for UK goods and a fall in the demand for pounds, which will cause the exchange rate to drop.

- If the level of income in the UK falls, the demand for imports will fall. Therefore, the supply of sterling to the foreign exchange market will fall, causing the exchange rate to rise.

- Sterling might also be demanded for investment purposes, for example by multinational companies wishing to build factories in the UK, or by foreign individuals wishing to invest in UK banks.

- A rise in UK interest rates will mean that it becomes more profitable to deposit money in UK banks. The demand for sterling will increase, forcing the exchange rate to rise. On the other hand, a rise in German interest rates will cause the supply of sterling on the foreign exchange market to rise, as people will want to convert into deutschmarks.

● Demand might also be affected by speculators, who might be anticipating a rise or fall in the value of the sterling. For example, in October 1992, speculation that the pound was about to be devalued led to speculators offloading sterling, thus creating an excess supply of sterling on the foreign exchange market that eventually led to a devaluation of the pound.

An exchange rate will only be determined by the forces of demand and supply if there is no government intervention. This will allow the exchange rate to settle at an equilibrium level. This is known as a system of **floating or free exchange rates**.

Managed exchange rate systems

In practice, it is unlikely that a government will allow an exchange rate to float completely freely, and most governments attempt to control the exchange rate in some way. Under a system of **managed exchange rates**, a government only allows the rate to fluctuate by a small amount within a narrow band, either side of a 'par' value, or even maintains it at a fixed level.

We shall now look at the ways in which a government might attempt to control the exchange rate. Imagine a situation in which the government finds that the free market value of its currency is lower and has a tendency to fall below the desired par value. It may take the following courses of action.

Intervention into the foreign exchange market by the central bank

The government can instruct the central bank to enter the foreign exchange market in order to buy the currency in order to remove any surplus that may exist. If the demand for imports into the UK has been greater than the demand for UK exports, there will be a surplus of sterling on the foreign exchange market. Under a system of floating exchange rates, this surplus, or excess supply of sterling, would cause the value of sterling to fall. To prevent this, the Bank of England could enter the foreign exchange market and buy up the surplus pounds, selling its reserves of foreign currency, and this would maintain the value of the pound at the par value. This process is illustrated in Figure 25.4. Conversely, should there be a shortage of pounds on the foreign exchange market, causing its value to rise above the desired level, the Bank of England would sell sterling in exchange for foreign currency. This increased supply of sterling would therefore ensure that the value of the pound again remains at, or close to, its par value.

Intervention in the foreign exchange market by the central bank may be an appropriate policy in the short term, but in the long term, the bank cannot keep supporting the value of the currency as it will eventually run out of reserves. Moreover, speculators may decide that the government is unable to maintain the value of the currency, so they will sell, causing greater falls in the value of the currency. Therefore the government has to resort to other measures to manage the value of the currency.

Adjustment of interest rates

The government can use its interest rate policy to help control the value of the exchange rate. If there is pressure on the UK exchange rate and its value is lower than the par value, the government can raise interest rates. The higher interest rates in the UK will attract capital into the country from individuals who are eager to benefit from the higher returns

Figure 25.4 Management of the exchange rate

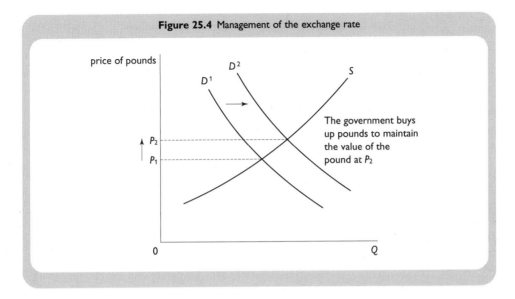

being offered on their investment. In order to invest in the UK, however, these individuals need to convert their currency to sterling, so this will cause an increase in the demand for pounds and will help to maintain the value of sterling at, or around, its par level.

Domestic deflation

The government can pursue a policy of deflating the domestic economy in order to help maintain the foreign exchange value of the currency. If the UK government reduces the level of aggregate demand in the economy, this will reduce the demand for imports into the UK and will therefore help to reduce the supply of sterling released onto the foreign exchange market. Deflationary measures might include raising taxes and cutting back on government spending, or raising interest rates.

Floating versus managed rates

The main advantage of adopting a system of floating exchange rates is that they operate without the need for government intervention. The price mechanism is allowed to operate freely in the foreign exchange market, so that the exchange rate should always settle at an equilibrium level where the demand for a currency equals the supply of a currency. This means that the balance of payments will also always tend towards equilibrium. Figure 25.5 demonstrates the sequence of events which leads to equilibrium in the balance of payments.

As the balance of payments is self-righting under a system of floating exchange rates, the government does not have to worry about taking measures such as deflationary policies to correct a balance of payments deficit. It can concentrate its efforts on domestic problems, such as unemployment and inflation, and its economic policies (e.g. interest rate policy) can be used to address these problems, rather than being used to influence the exchange rate and the balance of payments. There is also no need for a government to hold large quantities of reserves of foreign currency under a system of floating exchange

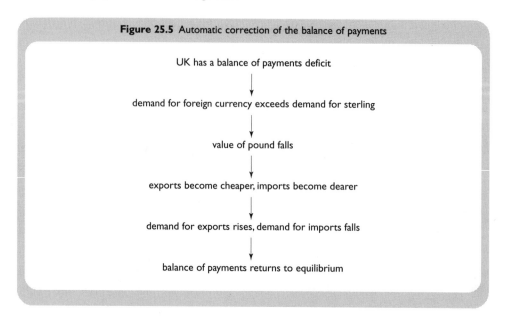

Figure 25.5 Automatic correction of the balance of payments

UK has a balance of payments deficit

↓

demand for foreign currency exceeds demand for sterling

↓

value of pound falls

↓

exports become cheaper, imports become dearer

↓

demand for exports rises, demand for imports falls

↓

balance of payments returns to equilibrium

rates. Under a **fixed exchange rate system**, it uses these reserves to stabilise short-term fluctuations in the exchange rate.

However, critics of floating exchange rates point to the uncertainty that they create. Certainly, the risks for business are increased with the possibility of the exchange rate fluctuating. Traders can never be sure how much they might receive for their products, since the exchange rate might change between signing the contract and receiving payment for the goods. A change in the exchange rate will cause the price of imported raw materials and components to vary, making production costs difficult to predict. These added risks might deter firms from participating in international trade. Figure 25.6 illustrates how the value of the pound fluctuated against the Deutschmark over the

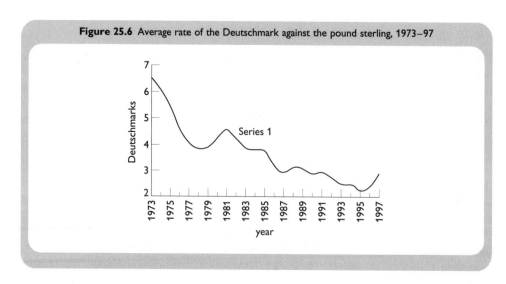

Figure 25.6 Average rate of the Deutschmark against the pound sterling, 1973–97

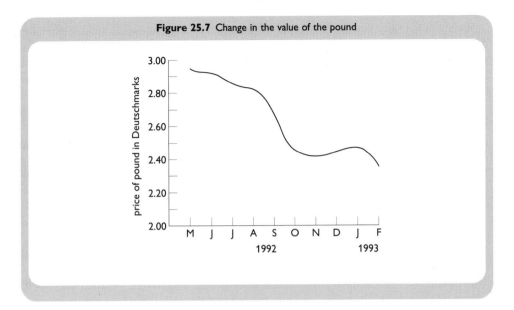

Figure 25.7 Change in the value of the pound

twenty-five years from 1973 to 1997. Figure 25.7, which covers the period when the pound left the European Exchange Rate Mechanism and reverted to floating, shows that even in a relatively short period of time, the exchange rate can change considerably.

International trade flourishes best in conditions of certainty. The risk associated with fluctuating exchange rates can be reduced, however, by firms buying or selling currency on the **forward currency market**. Through the foreign exchange market, a firm is able to make a contract to buy or sell foreign currency on a date in the future at a specified exchange rate.

A fluctuating exchange rate also has an impact on the economy as a whole, with the possibility of adverse effects on the levels of inflation and unemployment. When an economy such as the UK imports such large amounts of food, raw materials and manufactured goods, a fall in the exchange rate and the consequent rise in the price of imports can have quite severe inflationary effects. Although the example given in Figure 25.5 demonstrates how a floating exchange rate can lead to a self-correcting balance of payments, if the demand for imports is price inelastic, an increase in the price of imports, resulting from a fall in the exchange rate, will only increase the demand for foreign currency, as consumer expenditure is greater at a higher price when demand is price inelastic. Thus the balance of payments is not always self-correcting under a system of floating exchange rates and might actually get worse rather than righting itself. The overall balance of payments, and the demand for and supply of currency, is also dependent on capital flows. Thus, although a country might have a deficit on the current account, the value of its currency might not fall, since the deficit on the current account might be counterbalanced by a surplus on the capital account, allowing the current account deficit to persist.

A further criticism of floating exchange rates is that it encourages speculators to trade in currencies, and the extent of their activities can have a destabilising influence on the exchange rate.

Many would argue that the drawbacks of floating exchange rates provide a justification for having a system of managed exchange rates, where the government limits the extent of the fluctuations or even fixes the exchange rate at one level. The great advantage of a fixed exchange rate system is that it removes the uncertainty associated with floating exchange rates. Firms will be more willing to negotiate long-term contracts with overseas customers and to undertake long-term investments overseas. Fixed exchange rates should therefore help to promote international trade.

If exchange rates are more stable, there is likely to be less speculation. If the exchange rate is fixed, then there is no point in speculating on the possibility of an exchange rate rising or falling in value. However, should it become apparent that the authorities are having difficulty in maintaining the exchange rate at the par value, then speculation is likely to become widespread. Indeed, speculators may actually bring about a change in the value of a currency, as their widespread selling of a currency may mean that the government is no longer able to support the currency.

An additional problem is that a country which maintains its exchange rate at a level which is above the free-market equilibrium level will find that its balance of payments is in disequilibrium. In the first instance, the government will have to use its reserves to support the value of the currency, but these reserves will soon become exhausted. Therefore the government will have to resort to other measures to remove the balance of payments deficit, perhaps by reducing the level of aggregate demand through tighter fiscal and monetary policies, so that the level of imports falls. This, however, will have adverse consequences for most firms, who will be faced with a reduction in demand for their products. Hence fixed exchange rates place a constraint on governments and mean that they have less flexibility in their choice of economic policy.

A further problem with fixed exchange rates, is that countries experience different rates of economic growth and different rates of inflation. In consequence, the par value of a currency may soon become inappropriate, particularly if the rates of inflation differ widely between countries. Thus fixed exchange rates only work well during periods of low inflation. During times of high inflation, there is pressure on governments to devalue their currency to regain export competitiveness. In such a situation, devaluations become frequent, so defeating the purpose of a fixed exchange rate system.

We examine the operation of a managed exchange rate system, the European Exchange Rate mechanism, in Unit 26.

The effect of a change in the exchange rate on business

A change in the exchange rate is likely to have an impact on all businesses, and not just on those who participate in international trade. We shall now summarise some of the main effects.

Export prices

For a firm that exports products, a change in the exchange rate will change the price that the overseas customer has to pay for the product. We saw in an example earlier in this chapter: as a result of a devaluation of the pound from £1 = DM 3 to £1 = DM 2, a German customer was able to purchase a car manufactured in the UK priced at £12,000 for only DM 24,000 instead of DM 36,000. If, however, the exchange rate rose to £1 = DM 4, the German customer would now have to pay DM 48,000 in order to buy the car. Thus, a rise in the exchange rate increases the price of exports in overseas markets, while a fall in the exchange rate makes exports more price competitive. You should note that in practice, it is unlikely that the overseas price would change every time the exchange rate fluctuates; instead, in the short run, the export price is likely to be held constant and the difference taken out of, or added to, the exporting firms profit margin. For those firms who rely on export markets for their sales, unfavourable changes in the exchange rate can have a severe effect on sales and profitability. Jaguar sells over half of its output to the USA and an unfavourable movement in the sterling-dollar exchange rate would reduce their profits considerably, as happened in the late 1980s. The launch of Euro-Disney near Paris in the early 1990s was adversely affected by the rising value of the French franc against other currencies; people found the prices too high and there were initially far fewer visitors than had been projected. On the other hand, the fall in the value of the yen in 1996, as outlined in the news item at the start of this unit, led to increased profits for Japanese firms such as Sony and Toyota who now found themselves more competitive in world markets.

Cost of imported raw materials and component parts

A change in the exchange rate will affect the price that a firm has to pay for imported materials and components. If a UK firm imports a component from Germany which costs DM 12, and the exchange rate is £1 = DM 3, the UK firm would have to pay £4 for the component (ignoring transport costs). If the exchange rate rose to £1 = DM 4, the price of the component would fall to £3, but if the exchange rate fell to £1 = DM 2, the price of the component would rise to £6. A rise in the exchange rate therefore results in lower production costs for those firms who rely on imported components or materials, while a fall in the exchange rate increases the costs of production. This explains why Japanese airlines and power companies, which were referred to in the opening commentary, suffered a fall in profits as the cost of imported oil rose following the fall in the value of the yen.

Penetration of the domestic market

A change in the exchange rate affects import prices, and this will have a knock-on effect on the competitiveness of overseas firms who import products into the country. A rise in the exchange rate lowers the price of imports, making it easier for importers to penetrate the domestic market and, at the same time, more difficult for domestic firms to compete in their home market. A fall in the exchange rate raises the price of imported products, thus making it harder for importers to compete with domestic firms.

Case study

Exchange rate changes and price elasticity of demand

The extent to which changes in the exchange rate affect demand for imports and exports depends on the price elasticity of demand for products: that is, how sensitive the demand is to changes in price. The demand for products may not be particularly price elastic, but may depend on other factors such as design, quality, marketing, and after sales service. In such circumstances, changes in the exchange rate might have only a very limited impact on the demand for imports and exports.

Exercise

The chairman of the Downturn Trading Company Limited blamed their low level of profits last year on the rise of the value of the pound on the foreign exchange market. Meanwhile, the chairman of the Ace Manufacturing Company Limited explained that their improved results and high level of profits were also a result of the higher value of the pound.

Questions

1. How do you explain the contrasting fortunes of each company?
2. What strategies could a company adopt in order to counter the adverse effects of a rising exchange rate?

Uncertainty

A fluctuating exchange rate causes uncertainty among those who participate in international trade. Contracts are usually made on the basis of the exchange rate prevailing at the time that the contract is drawn up, and most international transactions are carried out on a credit basis. Thus any change in the exchange rate between the time the contract is made and payment for the goods will cause one or other of the parties to suffer. Figures 25.6 and 25.7 provide examples of how the value of the pound has fluctuated against the Deutschmark, and fluctuations such as these may deter firms from participating in international trade because of the added risks involved.

Inflationary pressures

A fall in the exchange rate could initiate cost-push inflationary pressures within the economy, adding further to a firm's production costs. As a result of these inflationary pressures, the government might feel obliged to introduce counterinflationary policies, which would depress demand in the home economy. The implications of inflation for a firm were examined in Unit 22.

Summary

International trade requires the exchange of currencies. The balance of payments account records all the income and expenditure resulting from international transactions carried out by firms, households and the government. While the overall balance of payments must balance, any component part may be in deficit or surplus. A persistent deficit on the current account of the balance of payments cannot be sustained, as a country's foreign exchange reserves will eventually be exhausted. Methods to improve a current account deficit include imposing protectionist measures to decrease imports, devaluing the foreign exchange value of the currency, or taking deflationary measures in the domestic economy. ▷

An exchange rate is the price of one currency expressed in terms of another currency. The exchange rate is determined by demand for and supply of the currency. However, under a system of fixed or managed exchange rates, the government intervenes in the foreign exchange market to maintain the exchange rate at, or near to, an announced par value.

Review questions

1. What is meant by the balance of trade?

2. Outline the main factors which influence the demand for and the supply of foreign exchange.

3. Under a system of floating exchange rates, explain the effect that each of the following events would have on the value of sterling, using demand and supply diagrams to illustrate your answers:
   (a) a rise in UK interest rates;
   (b) an increase in the demand for holidays in the UK from US citizens;
   (c) a fall in the demand for UK goods from overseas customers;
   (d) an increase in the quantity of oil imported into the UK;
   (e) a rise in US interest rates; and
   (f) a fall in the level of income in the UK.

4. Outline the possible effects on a UK firm of an increase in the value of the pound against other currencies.

5. What advantages would a fall in the value of the pound have for UK firms?

6. Explain why a business might prefer a system of fixed exchange rates rather then one of flexible exchange rates.

7. If the balance of payments always balances, why do we hear about deficits and surpluses?

8. Outline the various policies that might be pursued by a government to remove a large deficit on the current account of the balance of payments.

9. Explain the cause of the *j-curve effect* following a devaluation.

10. How do deflationary measures help to eliminate a balance of payments deficit?

Essay questions

1. (a) Explain why a government might wish to devalue its currency, and discuss those factors that will determine the success of such a policy.
   (b) Consider the implications of a devaluation for the business community.

2. (a) Distinguish between fixed and floating exchange rate systems.
   (b) Discuss whether a fixed or a floating exchange rate would be more beneficial for businesses.

Exercise

A UK clothes manufacturer has a contract to supply a Spanish importer with 500 dresses for a price of 3 million pesetas. The cost of supplying the order is £12,500 and, at the time of the contract, the exchange rate is £1 = 200 pesetas. The Spanish firm has been allowed 3 months' credit.

Questions

1. What is the expected profit for the firm if the exchange rate remains the same?
2. What would happen to the expected profit if, after 3 months, the exchange rate had changed to (a) £1 = 250 pesetas, and (b) £1 = 150 pesetas?
3. What measures could the UK firm take to minimise the risks associated with a fluctuating exchange rate?

Reading 25.1

'Sterling soars as exports reach new high'

In 1996, record-breaking exports from the UK to her European partners were announced, despite near-recessionary conditions on the Continent. This resulted in a substantial rise in the value of the pound on the foreign exchange markets. However, the danger was that if the rise in sterling continued, the improvement in the UK's trade performance would soon come to an end.

Questions

1. Explain why record-breaking exports from the UK should have resulted in an increase in the value of sterling.
2. The passage says that exports to Europe rose despite near-recessionary conditions on the Continent. Why might you expect recessionary conditions overseas to lead to a fall in UK exports?
3. Explain why it was feared that the improved trade performance might soon come to an end if the value of sterling continued to rise.

The European Union

The European Union is irreversibly on track towards a single currency which will be good for jobs and Europe's economies.

Source: Jacques Santer, President of the European Commission, 15 December 1995.

Table 26.1 Members of the European Union

Austria	Finland	Greece	Luxembourg	Spain
Belgium	France	Ireland	The Netherlands	Sweden
Denmark	Germany	Italy	Portugal	United Kingdom

In Unit 24, we made reference to regional trading agreements. In this unit, we shall look in detail at the European Union (EU), and assess the impact that it has on the business community.

The European Union (formerly the European Community) was established in 1957 by the Treaty of Rome. At the time of writing, 15 countries are members (see Table 26.1), although it is probable that additional countries may join in the future, including those from Central and Eastern Europe.

The EU is not just a customs union, it is also a common market: that is, there is free movement of goods, services, labour and capital between member states, in addition to a common external tariff which is applied to imports from countries outside the Union. In recent years, there have also been moves towards creating an **economic and monetary union** (**EMU**). The Delors Plan, devised by Jacques Delors, viewed the creation of EMU as an evolutionary process, and identified three stages:

1. The completion of the single market and improved monetary cooperation and coordination between member states.

2. The convergence of European economies.

3. The creation of a single currency and a **European Central Bank**.

In February 1992, member states signed the **Maastricht Treaty**, which represented a commitment towards greater economic, monetary and social union, although the UK government negotiated the right to opt out of some aspects of the treaty.

We shall now examine several of the main features and issues of the EU and examine their implication for firms.

The Single European Market

The Single European Act, which came into force in 1987, set the end of 1992 as the date by which the European Union was to become a **single market**. Before this date, much progress had been made towards bringing about freer trade between member states with the abolition of tariff barriers. However, by the end of 1992, not only should all tariff barriers have been removed, but also any non-tariff barriers which might have prohibited free trade between member states. From that date, there should have been free movement of goods and services, labour and capital. Examples of non-tariff barriers which needed to be abolished were: technical barriers, such as national specifications for products, that made it difficult for firms to sell their products in other countries; public procurement policies which tended to give preference to home-produced goods and services; and fiscal barriers, where different rates of taxation inhibited trade between member states.

A problem, however, was that the non-tariff barriers were much more difficult to identify than tariff barriers, and countries used many different arguments in an attempt to retain some of the barriers.

Implications of the Single European Market

The Single European Market provided countries with the opportunity for greater specialisation and firms with an increased opportunity to take advantage of the economies of large-scale production. In Unit 24 we discussed the theory of comparative advantage and demonstrated how free trade and specialisation between countries results in a more efficient use of resources. The removal of all barriers to trade, both tariff and non-tariff, gives countries more scope to specialise and to exploit their comparative advantage more fully. In a fragmented Europe, firms only had free access to a relatively small domestic market, in comparison with the much larger 'home' markets available for US and Japanese firms. Hence European firms were not able to exploit fully the economies of large-scale production, and, as a result, incurred higher per unit costs than their American or Japanese competitors. With the removal of trade barriers between member states, firms now had a much larger 'domestic' market in which they could sell their products, providing them with more scope to take advantage of the economies of scale. Thus for UK firms, the 'domestic' market increased from a population of 56 million to more than 350 million.

The implications of this development were that firms had to consider their capacity and ensure that they had the ability to meet any increase in demand which resulted from the larger 'home' market. The creation of the single market made it easier for firms from other countries to launch takeover bids and for there to be cross-border mergers, as well as facilitating participation in joint ventures by firms from different member states. There were also marketing implications for firms. Although the fifteen countries comprise a single market, they are made up of very different social, cultural and economic backgrounds. Firms have therefore had to consider and amend their approach to the marketing of their products. A successful marketing strategy in the home market will not necessarily be an appropriate strategy for other countries in the Union. At the very least, the firm will have to revise the language used in any campaign. There are also other implications involving language. A firm has probably had to increase its training budget in order to train its staff to be multilingual. One alternative would be for the firm to recruit foreign nationals to help them come to terms with the many different languages throughout the Union, remembering that the free movement of labour within the European Union has made the recruitment of workers from other member countries much simpler. On the other hand, some firms may have found it necessary to offer greater incentives just to retain staff, who were now free to seek employment anywhere in the European Union.

Expanding sales into Europe also has transport and distribution implications. The firm will have had to revise its methods of distribution. It may have formed a division to develop business with Europe, and may even have considered relocating in order to be closer to the European market, or to take advantage of, for example, cheaper labour costs that exist in some countries of the European Union. Furthermore, the removal of customs formalities should have helped to reduce prices as cutting out frontier delays and excess bureaucracy diminished costs.

Products may need to be modified, or even redesigned, before they can be exported in order to comply with the various requirements and specifications of the different member states. At one time, it was intended that a European-wide specification should be adopted for all products to enable firms to fully exploit the economies of large-scale production. However, the substantial costs and difficulties associated with this has meant that the European Union has now adopted a system of 'mutual recognition' of each other's laws. This means that if a product is legitimately on sale in a member country, another member cannot prevent the import of the same product into its country, unless it is on health and safety grounds.

However, creating a single market throughout the European Union not only gave firms the opportunity to expand their sales, but also increased competition. For consumers, this implied more choice and lower prices, but for firms, it represented a threat. Throughout the Union, firms were now able to export products without having to confront any trade barriers. Companies therefore had to take steps to defend their home market and to become more efficient in order to survive the increasingly competitive environment. An example of this increase in competition was in the area of public procurement: instead of national governments being able to favour businesses established in their own country when awarding contracts, they now had to invite tenders from throughout the European Union. The creation of the single market combined with the common external tariff has also led to an increase in investment in Europe from Japanese and US multinationals in order that they can claim a share of the European market. This too has sharpened the competitive environment.

Becoming more efficient as a result of the increased opportunity for economies of scale and the increased competitive environment should better equip firms to compete in world markets, selling products to countries outside the EU. Thus the overall balance of trade between the European Union and the rest of the world should improve. The increased efficiency and reduction in costs should help to reduce prices, stimulating demand and therefore creating more employment opportunities throughout the European Union.

We should appreciate, however, that different firms are affected in different ways by the creation of the single market, depending on factors such as the size of the firm, the industry in which it operates, and the skills, abilities and aptitudes of its managers. Not all sectors of the economy are likely to benefit. In 1989, Lloyds Bank predicted that those industries in the UK which were most likely to gain from the creation of the single market were pharmaceuticals, insurance and airlines. These industries would be able to take advantage of their relative strength and expand their activities into Europe. Nonetheless, in order for some firms to achieve the gains from increased economies of scale, other firms are going to close, and redundancies are bound to occur. The extent of the hardship will depend on how mobile the labour force is, and on the speed with which change can take place.

A fear was also expressed by some that certain countries would be in a better position to benefit from the single market than others, notably those countries which had relatively cheap labour costs. Thus, for example, textile firms in countries such as Greece and Portugal, where labour costs are lower, might threaten the existence of textile firms in countries where labour costs are higher, such as Germany and the Netherlands.

A further issue which we need to address, and which has been referred to in Unit 24 in our discussion of trading blocs, is that of 'trade creation' versus 'trade diversion'. The removal of barriers between member states may lead to an increase in trade (trade creation) and provide an opportunity for the most efficient firms within the EU to flourish at the expense of the less efficient firms, thus making more efficient use of the resources within the EU. At the same time, however, the common external tariff imposed on countries outside the EU has resulted in less trade with these countries (trade diversion), which may entail production being transferred from efficient low-cost producers outside the EU to less efficient producers within the EU.

An attempt to quantify the potential gains of the single market were made in the Ceccini Report published in 1988. It predicted that, as a result of the single market, within a period of five years output within the EU would rise by approximately 5 per cent, consumer prices would fall on average by 6 per cent, employment would increase by 1.8 million, and there would be an improvement in Europe's trading position with the rest of the world. However, although significant progress has been made towards achieving a single market and many barriers have been removed, it was unrealistic to expect the formation of a single market overnight. Therefore, there still remain some barriers to trade and obstacles to the creation of a truly single market, as follows:

- Technical standards – for example, covering quality and safety – have not been fully harmonised. Countries still impose different product specifications and different standards, which make it difficult to achieve completely free trade in goods and services. The British use of the three-pin plug is a good example.

- The cultural diversity of the countries within the European Union means that tastes and preferences differ from country to country. To a degree, therefore, the market is still fragmented and that the potential gains from the economies of large-scale production are difficult to realise because firms are not at liberty to supply identical products throughout the whole of Europe. The market for food, for instance, is highly fragmented and there are very few 'Euro products'. Even Nescafé is produced in a variety of strengths and flavours to cater for national and regional differences.

- Countries do not always give full recognition to educational and vocational qualifications gained in other countries, and many professions only recognise their own national qualifications. This obstructs the supposedly completely free movement of labour between member states.

- Some governments still subsidise firms from their own country, through grants and tax concessions. The airline industry is a good example. The governments of France, Portugal and Spain have continued to support their national airlines through subsidies. These subsidies are the equivalent of protectionist measures and prevent free competition between firms.

- Public procurement, the granting of public works contracts, is supposed to be competitive and open to all firms throughout the Union, but governments may still occasionally be tempted to buy from their own national industries, particularly, for example, in industries such as defence equipment.

- A single market should ideally have common rates of tax. While there have been some moves to harmonise the rate of VAT, there still remain considerable differences between the rates imposed by each individual member state. Some countries place much higher excise duties on alcohol, tobacco and petrol than others. Non-wine producers tend to have high excise duties on wines. Those countries within the Union who produce wine claim that this distorts competition and represents an unfair barrier to their exports. The Italian government has been pressured into repealing a new luxury-car tax, which virtually excluded Jaguar cars from Italy. There are also differences in the levels of company taxation. This can affect a firm's ability to invest, and companies are being treated differently in different countries.

● Even many years after the creation of the single market there still remains the problem of fluctuating currencies and the need to convert different currencies between member states, which represents a deterrent to trade. Until a single European currency is introduced, and while the Exchange Rate Mechanism allows currency fluctuations, firms face an added risk when trading with other member states.

The European Monetary System (EMS)

The EMS was formed in 1979. An important element of the EMS was the European **Exchange Rate Mechanism (ERM)**. Its aim was to reduce the level of fluctuations between the currencies of the member states by linking them together, and it was in effect a fixed exchange rate system within the European Union. Each member's currency was fixed against the European Currency Unit (ECU), which, in turn, was determined by a weighted basket of the currencies of the member states, although the system was very dependent on the German mark as this was the strongest currency. Each currency was then allowed to fluctuate by plus or minus 2.25 per cent, although some countries were initially allowed a wider band of plus or minus 6 per cent with the intention that they too would later conform to the 2.25 per cent band. Member countries were obliged to take whatever measures were necessary in order to ensure that their currency kept within the agreed limits. The system is illustrated in Figure 26.1.

The linking of the exchange rates was intended to encourage trade between member countries, as the risks of foreign trade were reduced through stable exchange rates. Although realignments of currencies were quite frequent in the early years of the ERM, during the late 1980s the stabilisation mechanism seemed to work well and it promoted confidence amongst traders. The UK, however, was reluctant to be part of the ERM and

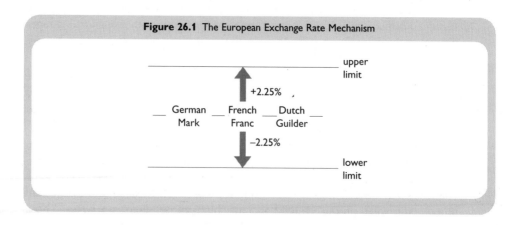

Figure 26.1 The European Exchange Rate Mechanism

did not join until 1990. The reasons put forward for the delay in joining the mechanism were varied:

- The UK had tended to suffer from higher rates of inflation than most of its European partners. This meant that it would be more difficult to keep the value of the pound within the prescribed bands, and realignments would regularly be required.

- Sterling was regarded as a 'petro-currency' because the UK was a net exporter of oil. The value of sterling was therefore very dependent on the price of oil, and any change in the price of oil caused a fluctuation in the value of the pound.

- Domestic economic policy at that time centred on the control of the money supply, but joining the ERM would have meant that interest rates would have to be set to regulate the exchange rate, regardless of the needs of the domestic economy. There was a sizeable body of opinion in the UK that this represented an erosion of national sovereignty, as Britain would no longer be free to decide her own economic policies. It would be forced to pursue certain fiscal and monetary policies simply to keep the exchange rate within its specified band.

- The UK government of the time also believed very much in the workings of the free market, and interventionist policies to control the price of the pound went very much against their philosophy.

By the late 1980s, however, the UK inflation rate had fallen and was very similar to that of her European partners, oil was no longer such an important component of the UK's balance of payments, and it was increasingly felt that exchange rate fluctuations were undesirable and that the pound ought to have some stability against other European currencies. The UK therefore joined the ERM in October 1990. Unfortunately, by September 1992, the authorities were unable to support the pound above its ERM floor, and the UK was forced to suspend membership. This was partly due to the fact that the pound had probably entered the system at too high a rate in the first place, but in addition, high interest rates in Germany meant that capital flowed towards Germany and out of the UK, decreasing the demand for sterling. The activities of speculators who were selling large amounts of sterling also undoubtedly undermined the value of the pound. After Britain's exit from the system the value of the pound depreciated, from £1 = DM 2.95 to as low as £1 = DM 2.20. Other countries also suspended membership, while others had their margin of flexibility increased to 15 per cent, which signified that the principles of ERM had to all intents been abandoned. However, by the end of 1997, all but three countries (Greece, Sweden and the UK) were back in the ERM, albeit at the wider rate of plus or minus 15 per cent. One reason was that membership of the ERM was a requirement for entry into economic and monetary union.

Advantages of the ERM

The main argument in favour of the Exchange Rate Mechanism was that it should encourage trade, as it removed the risk and uncertainty associated with fluctuating exchange rates. Firms could now be confident that exchange rates between member states would remain stable, only fluctuating to a minimal degree. The ERM also placed greater pressure on governments to keep inflation under control. Previously, countries which suffered from high rates of inflation could devalue their currency to regain competitive-ness. The requirement to keep the exchange rate within the permitted band, however, meant that the problems of inflation could no longer be solved through devaluing the currency.

Drawbacks of the ERM

Membership of the ERM meant that a country had less independence to carry out its own fiscal and monetary policy. Some regarded this as an erosion of national sovereignty because it surrendered of the right of a country to determine its own economic policy. For example, interest rates had to be used to ensure that the exchange rate stayed within its permitted bands. If an exchange rate was getting close to its upper or lower limit, the government tended to use interest rate changes to move the currency in the opposite direction. The interest rate may therefore have had to be set at a high level in order to attract funds in to the country and support the value of the currency, but this might not have been in the best interests of the domestic economy, since it led to increased costs for firms, a reduction in demand and increased unemployment. To take an example, after Britain joined the ERM in 1990 the British economy went into recession. There were many calls for the interest rate to be lowered in order to stimulate aggregate demand and help pull the economy out of recession. However, the government was unable to make substantial cuts in interest rates at this time, as it would have caused the value of the currency to fall below its permitted band. Therefore interest rates remained high and the recession continued. Under ERM, taxes may also have to be set at a level which ensures a reduction in aggregate demand in order to keep the exchange rate within its permitted band, since a reduction in tax might encourage an increase in imports and therefore pressure on the exchange rate.

Having the exchange rate fixed within a narrow band also takes away, of course, the option of using the exchange rate as a policy instrument. The government was no longer able to use devaluation as a policy to tackle unemployment and/or a balance of payments deficit.

Moreover, there is an argument that, however appropriate the agreed exchange rate was at the time of entering the exchange rate system, it is inevitable that sooner or later it will become inappropriate, because the economies of countries grow at different rates, which causes a divergence. Hence it will become increasingly difficult for governments to keep the exchange rate within its permitted band, and realignments will, sooner or later, be inevitable, which defeats the whole purpose of ERM.

The power of speculators to undermine the system is an added problem. In theory, the stabilisation of exchange rates should mean that speculators cannot profit as the currency no longer fluctuates. If a realignment is in any way suspected, however, the might of speculation can place great pressure on a currency and bring about a situation where that realignment becomes inevitable – as the UK found out to its cost in September 1992.

In the case of Britain, it was felt by many that the exchange rate chosen by the government when it entered the ERM was too high. Consequently, it was forced to pursue deflationary policies such as high interest rates to maintain the currency at this level, which resulted in a rise in unemployment. This affected firms who suffered from decreased demand for their products as a result of the recession. The overvaluation of the exchange rate also had a particular impact on exporting firms, making their goods more expensive to foreign customers, and on firms who were vulnerable to competition from imports, which became relatively cheaper as a result of the high pound.

The ERM can therefore be seen as a mixed blessing for firms. The increased stability it brought to exchange rates removed the uncertainty and risks associated with fluctuating rates and encouraged firms to participate in international trade. However, the fact that the government had to pursue economic policies that were aimed at managing the value of the currency, rather than policies that were in the best interests of the domestic economy and its firms, can be regarded as a disadvantage.

Economic and monetary union (EMU)

The next stage in the development of European integration is economic and monetary union (EMU). Despite encountering problems in their progress towards EMU, there is a determination within the EU that a group of core countries should realise monetary union in 1999. There are three main aspects to EMU:

1. **A single European currency** It is intended that those members of the EU who have fulfilled certain criteria should adopt a common currency (the 'Euro') by the year 1999. However, at first the euro will only be used in large transactions; domestic shoppers will continue to use domestic currencies for some time after this date.

2. **A European Central Bank** The European Central Bank would conduct monetary policy for those countries which had agreed to full economic and monetary union and would take on much the same role as the central banks of each individual member state (see Unit 17 for a detailed discussion on the role of a central bank). It would have the sole right to issue bank notes and would control the money supply, therefore determining interest rates for member states, and would take over the foreign reserves of each member state and use them to support the euro on the foreign exchange markets. It is intended that the European Central Bank would be independent from governments. This should mean that the bank can act independently of political considerations, instead of, for example, lowering interest rates when an election is approaching. An independent bank can take a longer-term view and does not have to worry about its popularity with the electorate, which, it is argued will better equip the bank to deal with the problem of inflation.

3. **A centralised monetary policy** Instead of each member state pursuing its own monetary policy, a centralised monetary policy would be applied across all countries within the European Union.

Advantages of EMU

- A saving in transactions costs. With a single currency, there is no need to convert currencies. There would therefore be a saving of all the money, time and resources used up in changing currencies (although banks would earn less commission from foreign exchange business!).

- The uncertainty and risk associated with exchange rate fluctuations will be eliminated. This should improve business confidence and encourage firms to participate more in international trade, causing the volume of trade to rise. The rise in confidence could lead, in turn, to an increase in investment by firms, which should promote economic growth within the EU.

- A single currency removes the opportunity to speculate on exchange rate variations between members' currencies. These speculative pressures caused great problems for the ERM from time to time.

- A single currency may also result in an increase in competition, as any price differential on products will be more noticeable.

- An independent European central bank should result in greater macroeconomic stability as it will not be influenced by political considerations.

- Monetary union will force a convergence in inflation rates. Just as the inflation rate between different regions in a country are the same, so inflation rates between different countries within the Union will be the same. For the UK, this means that the inflation rate should fall to German levels.

- A single currency should result in lower interest rates throughout Europe, which will act as a stimulus to the business community. The strength of the euro as an international currency should make it less vulnerable to speculative attacks, so there will be less need to keep interest rates high to support the currency. In addition, the elimination of the risk of fluctuating exchange rates between member states should also lead to a fall in interest rates.

- Economic and monetary union should prompt an increase in investment in Europe from the rest of the world, attracted by a large single market with a common currency and greater macroeconomic stability.

Drawbacks of EMU

- Each member state's government loses its autonomy over domestic monetary policy. Governments are no longer able to set their own interest rate. This is seen by many as a vital surrender of national sovereignty.

- Governments are no longer able to use the exchange rate as an instrument of economic policy. This is of major significance to those countries who find themselves less competitive than the rest of Europe. They will no longer be able to use devaluation of their currency as a means of regaining competitiveness. These countries might then develop into the depressed regions of Europe.

- A single currency also reduces a government's ability to use fiscal policy as an instrument of economic policy. Although governments will still be able to make use of fiscal policy, there will be a limit on the amount of public borrowing permitted. While previously a budget deficit could be financed by increasing the money supply or 'printing money', this option will no longer be open to governments because monetary policy will be in the hands of the European Central Bank. Therefore, any government borrowing will have to be financed through borrowing from the capital market, making it more difficult for governments to pursue a

Table 26.2 Maastricht convergence criteria

1. A stable exchange rate that has been within the agreed band of the ERM (now at plus or minus 15 per cent) for at least two years.

2. The rate of inflation for member states should not exceed the average of the three states with the lowest rates of inflation by more than 1.5 per cent.

3. The interest rate should not exceed the average of the three countries with the lowest interest rates by more than 2 per cent.

4. The budget deficit should not be more than 3 per cent of the GDP of the country.

5. The national debt should not be more than 60 per cent of the GDP of the country.

budget deficit. Yet fiscal policy is likely to play an even more important role under EMU. For those countries who are uncompetitive, a fall in the exchange rate is no longer a method of regaining competitiveness.

● There may have to be a more centralised fiscal system redistributing income from richer areas of the Union to the poorer regions. The decision to adopt a more interventionist regional policy is a political one, and may come up against some resistance.

● A further drawback of EMU is the transition that countries have had to go through before they can qualify for membership. To arrive at a position where monetary union is possible, countries have had to pursue unpopular policies in order to try to meet the **convergence criteria** (see Table 26.2). The requirement, for example, to reduce the budget deficit to 3 per cent of GDP and the national debt to 60 per cent of GDP has led to reductions in public spending, rises in unemployment, and even social unrest in countries such as France.

Convergence criteria

The Maastricht Treaty, signed in 1992, set out a timetable and clarified how economic and monetary union was to be achieved, detailing the key criteria that were necessary before EMU could be achieved. In order that EMU should be successful, it was decided that the economies of all member states should have similar economic conditions before they joined. The economies of the member states therefore had to converge and Maastricht identified the 'convergence criteria', as outlined in Table 26.2. However, the treaty said that these conditions could be relaxed in certain circumstances, for example if there was evidence that progress was being made towards convergence.

The period from 1994 onwards was supposed to be a transition period, with countries attempting to meet the convergence criteria and join EMU by 1997. By November 1995, though, it was realised that the convergence criteria were unlikely to be met by this date by many countries, so the date was pushed back to 1999. Those countries who have met the criteria by 1999 can embark upon economic and monetary union. The current position is that any country not meeting the criteria would not participate in full economic and monetary union, but would continue to work towards meeting the criteria, upon which time they would be admitted to EMU. Monetary union is therefore likely to be created on a 'two-tier' basis, with a group of core countries entering at the initial stage, and a second group of countries outside EMU, but with the possibility of joining later.

The Maastricht Treaty was not without controversy. The French people voted only narrowly in favour of it in a referendum; Denmark originally voted against it before approving it in a second referendum, but, like the UK, has negotiated an agreement that it shall not be obliged to enter into economic and monetary union. In 1997 the UK government announced its policy towards EMU. This was that it was in favour of entry in principle, but would not join in 1999. One reason was that interest rates in the UK were much higher than those in Europe. Cutting interest rates to the European level would over-stimulate the economy. Hence the UK will retain its own independent monetary policy, its own currency, and the ability to set its own exchange rate, although it is hoped that the currencies of those members outside full EMU will shadow the euro. Indeed, this may be a requirement for those countries outside EMU, first, in order to qualify for eventual admission to EMU, and second, because, if they do not shadow the euro, those countries outside EMU could devalue their currency against the euro and gain what could be considered to be an unfair competitive advantage.

Although the ability to continue to use an independent monetary and exchange rate policy has its advantages, opting out also has its drawbacks. By being on the outside, the UK will not be in a position to influence the policies of EMU, and it is quite natural that those within EMU will operate the system to their own advantage. British firms and individuals will still face the costs involved in converting currencies and they may still face the uncertainties of fluctuating exchange rates. Both the CBI and the TUC in Britain have expressed their support for UK entry into EMU. The head of British Aerospace, a firm which participates in joint projects with other European aircraft manufacturers and which relies heavily on overseas markets, has stressed the importance of the UK being an integral part of Europe, and has warned that the adoption of an isolationist stance would have dire consequences for the economy and industry. Meanwhile, multinational firms such as Unilever and Toyota have stated that they would have to reconsider future investments in the UK if it failed to take part in EMU, because the UK might then no longer be regarded as a suitable country for inward investment. The situation may therefore arise in which the UK simply could not afford to be left out.

European social policy

The Maastricht Treaty also contained a **Social Chapter** covering social policy throughout Europe. This made reference to the social rights of citizens and workers, and its objective was to improve living and working conditions throughout the EU. For the single market was not only intended to benefit the business community: there were to be **social benefits** as well, and the intention was that there should be consistency in this respect between all member countries. This would help to avoid the problem of **social dumping**, a process whereby countries can make themselves attractive locations for firms by offering low wages and minimal social protection for workers. Firms who locate in these countries would then have a competitive advantage over firms in other parts of the EU, distorting competition. The aim was to create a 'level playing field' throughout Europe. Different conditions of work between countries would also represent a barrier to free movement of labour.

Table 26.3 The main points of the Social Chapter

1. Freedom of movement of workers.
2. Fair remuneration (i.e. a decent wage).
3. Improvement of working conditions: for example, hours of work and the right to paid holidays.
4. Social protection.
5. Right to belong to a trade union.
6. Right to vocational training.
7. Equal treatment of men and women.
8. Right to information, consultation and participation of workers in company policy.
9. Protection in the workplace (i.e. health and safety).
10. Protection of children and adolescents at work.
11. Rights for the elderly (e.g. pensions).
12. Rights for the disabled.

The rights of workers were grouped under twelve headings, which are summarised in Table 26.3. Examples of issues covered include the entitlement to paid holidays and a maximum working week.

The UK government of the time negotiated an opt-out of the Social Chapter on the grounds that they believed the measures it proposed would increase firms' costs of production, make products less competitive in comparison with production in the rest of the world, and lead to an increase in unemployment. This meant that businesses in the UK were not bound by the agreement, although the UK already met some of the criteria, for example equal treatment of men and women. By opting out of the Social Chapter, it was hoped that UK firms would have a competitive advantage over firms throughout the rest of the EU. It was also hoped that the opt-out would attract inward investment from multinational companies who would not have to abide by the principles of the Social Chapter if they set up in Britain. The refusal of the UK to adhere to the Social Chapter therefore caused some annoyance among other member states, although it has to be appreciated that, partly due to cultural differences, working practices still vary widely between countries.

UK businesses were divided on the implementation of the Social Chapter. Some agreed with the government and saw the opt-out as an opportunity to gain a competitive advantage over firms in the rest of the EU. Other companies voluntarily agreed to adhere to the principles of the Social Chapter, even though they were not required to do so by UK law, arguing that they were likely to see a rise in productivity rates in return for greater social benefits. There was the further complication that many firms have subsidiaries in different EU countries, and, in order to ensure consistency throughout the organisation, they felt it necessary to apply the same standards in their UK plants as in other plants. Thus, despite the opt-out obtained by the UK government, many UK firms do adhere to the principles of the Social Chapter. Moreover, from 1997, and following a change of government, it is intended that the UK should drop its opt-out from the Social Chapter.

Exercise

European labour markets are paralysed by restrictive practices, by social security systems that encourage dependency and by social laws that pile up costs on business.

Source: Kenneth Clarke, Chancellor, Conservative Party Conference 1993.

Questions

1. Identify the additional costs that the Social Charter might impose on business.

2. In what ways might a firm benefit by adhering to the principles of the Social Charter?

The Common Agricultural Policy

The **Common Agricultural Policy** (**CAP**) was established to provide support for farmers and agricultural workers within the European Union. When the CAP was established, agricultural workers represented approximately 20 per cent of the workforce within the EU, and an improvement of the depressed agricultural sector was high on the list of priorities. Today, 7 per cent of the EU workforce is engaged in agriculture, although the figure for the UK is only 2 per cent. The aim of the CAP is to limit the import of agricultural produce into the EU and to try to make the EU self-sufficient in as many agricultural products as possible. This will then help to ensure reasonable incomes for farm workers, who generally earn less than industrial workers.

The scheme operates by setting a target price for farm produce. This price is set at a level which covers the costs of production of the highest-cost producers within the EU, plus an allowance for profit. The authorities then intervene to buy up any surplus produce to prevent the price falling below the target price. (An explanation of how price stabilisation schemes operate is given in Unit 8.) This policy, however, has resulted in the accumulation of large surpluses of, for example, dairy products, beef and cereals, as production has consistently exceeded consumption. Reforms introduced since 1992 have regulated the amount that farmers could supply by issuing output quotas for certain products (e.g. milk), and have helped to reduce the size of the surpluses.

While the CAP has succeeded in some of its objectives – such as raising productivity in agricultural produce, achieving EU self-sufficiency in many products, and helping to ensure a reasonable standard of living for the agricultural community who might otherwise be unemployed – it has proved to be a very costly system. CAP frequently absorbed up to three-quarters of the EU budget, and, despite reforms, it continues to represent approximately half of EU expenditure. Consumers continue to pay higher prices than if a free market existed for agricultural products, which has the effect of transferring resources from the consumer to the producer. The large surpluses that have been accumulated are costly to store, and much has had to be wasted. There has been an inefficient allocation of resources, as land is being used to produce output at a high cost instead of utilising low-cost production outside the EU. The 'trade diversion' effects mean that countries outside the EU – including Third World countries who rely on agricultural exports as their main source of earnings – suffer a loss of trade, as they are no longer able to export their produce to countries within the EU.

European regional policy

European **regional policy** is perceived as becoming increasingly important, particularly as the introduction of the single currency will leave those countries who find themselves uncompetitive with fewer policy options to improve their position. The regional problem is therefore a problem for the European Union as a whole to address, rather than a series of problems for each individual member. Figure 26.2 illustrates the GDP per capita for each member state. The figure for Portugal is only 30 per cent of the Danish figure, and although, as we saw in Unit 20, GDP per capita is not always an ideal guide to living standards, it does demonstrate the wide differences that exist in regional incomes within the EU. The disparities will become even greater should countries of Eastern Europe join the EU. Hungary, for example, had a per capita GDP of $4477 in 1995, less than half that of Portugal.

The free-market approach to the European regional problem would be that in the long run, regional disparities would disappear, for the following reasons:

1. Firms would relocate to the poorer regions where wage levels would be significantly lower than in the more prosperous regions.

2. Workers from the low-wage regions would move to those regions where wage rates were higher.

These two flows would eventually eliminate disparities in income and unemployment between regions. However, in order to induce firms to relocate to the poorer regions, wages might have to fall to levels which would be regarded as socially unacceptable

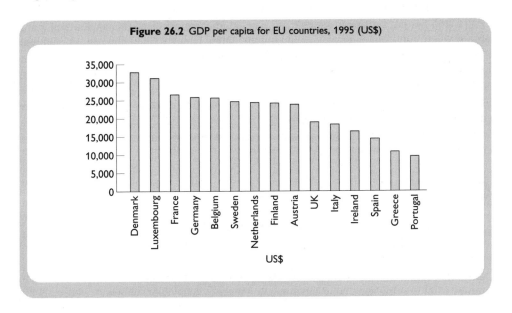

Figure 26.2 GDP per capita for EU countries, 1995 (US$)

within the European Union. In addition, although there exists free movement of labour throughout the Single European Market, language and cultural barriers mean that labour remains relatively immobile throughout Europe. Thus it is doubtful whether the free-market approach would eliminate regional disparities within Europe, and a more interventionist approach is therefore required.

Regional policy accounts for approximately one quarter of the current EU budget. The four countries with the lowest GDP per capita (Portugal, Greece, Spain and Ireland) receive aid from a 'cohesion fund' in order to help them achieve the convergence criteria necessary for economic and monetary union. There also exist 'structural funds', which provide assistance for regions throughout the EU that suffer from high unemployment and low average incomes, such as underdeveloped regions, regions experiencing industrial decline, and rural areas in need of development and structural adjustment. However, although EU regional policy has probably resulted in regional income differentials being less than they would otherwise have been, it is felt by many that the extent of the intervention is insufficient to prevent the differentials becoming even wider.

European Union: the future

Although it is likely that the European Union will continue to move towards greater economic and political union, there will continue to be disagreement and conflict between member states. Although much progress has been made towards creating a single market, there still exist many non-tariff barriers, and governments might continue to find ways to prevent free and open competition. A determined effort is being made to achieve monetary union by 1999, but it remains to be seen whether it will be achieved by this date. Certainly, some countries within the Union are unlikely to fulfil the conditions required to join monetary union by this date, while other countries might exercise their right not to join. It seems likely that there will be a two-tier union, with some members joining EMU but other members remaining outside.

Membership of the EU will probably increase. In addition to Cyprus and Malta, several Central and Eastern European states have applied for membership. This would give firms access to an even larger market, but, on the other hand, it might represent a threat through increased competition. The larger the EU becomes, the more difficult it will be to get agreement between member states, and the more difficult it will be to achieve economic and monetary union. This is especially the case because the countries who are likely to join have a significantly lower GDP per capita than existing members, and, under existing funding rules, would therefore be recipients of substantial net transfers. This would place additional pressure on the EU budget, and would be to the detriment of existing members such as Portugal and Greece.

Summary

The European Union is more than a customs union that promotes free trade between member states and imposes a common external tariff. It is also a common market in which, in addition to free trade in goods and services, there is also free movement of labour and capital. However, although much has been done to remove ▷

barriers to trade, there still exist some non-tariff barriers which prevent the EU from being a truly single market. Nevertheless, the creation of the single market has had a major impact on the business community, particularly in terms of a larger market and increased competition.

Economic and monetary union throughout the EU implies a common currency, a European Central Bank, and a common monetary policy. This will result in a loss of sovereignty for states, as they will no longer be able to pursue an independent monetary or exchange rate policy, and it may mean that regional policy within Europe becomes more important in order to assist those countries who find themselves disadvantaged. The gains anticipated from monetary union include a more stable monetary environment, the elimination of the costs incurred in converting currencies, and the removal of the uncertainties associated with fluctuating exchange rates. It still remains to be seen whether EMU can be successfully implemented, and some countries such as the UK and Denmark have reserved the right not to participate in monetary union. The UK has also in the past expressed mixed feelings over European social policy believing that the principles of the Social Chapter of the Maastricht Treaty would increase firms' costs and make them uncompetitive in comparison with production in the rest of the world.

The Common Agricultural Policy is a long-established feature of the EU which seeks to provide farmers with a reasonable level of income and to make the EU self-sufficient in as many agricultural products as possible. Although it has had some success in achieving its objectives, it has proved to be a very costly system and has resulted in a large accumulation and subsequent wastage of many products.

Review questions

1. Outline the benefits which firms can obtain from the creation of a Single European Market.

2. What problems are firms likely to face as a result of the creation of the single market?

3. Explain why multinational companies from countries such as the USA and Japan are keen to establish production outlets in Europe.

4. Outline the factors which may continue to hinder free trade between member states of the EU, despite the removal of tariff barriers.

5. Explain how the European Exchange Rate Mechanism (ERM) operated.

6. Define the conditions that were regarded as necessary for economic and monetary union to take place.

7. What are the advantages and disadvantages for a British manufacturing firm of full UK membership of the EMU?

8. Why is it necessary for monetary union to be accompanied by a European regional policy?

9. How do you think that the levels of employment might be affected by the implementation of the principles of the Social Chapter?

10. Outline Britain's current position on EMU membership.

Essay questions

1. 'A single currency throughout the EU removes much of the uncertainty that is associated with international trade and is good for the business community.' Discuss.

2. Consider the implications for firms in Western Europe of the expansion of the EU to incorporate the countries of Central and Eastern Europe.

Reading 26.1

Advocates of a monetary union imply that the adoption of a single currency is necessary to perfect the single market's free trade in goods and services. I am an enthusiastic supporter of the attempt to achieve a Single European Market for goods and services. Although such a free-trade zone, even if it involves no increases in external tariffs, could in theory have trade-diverting effects that decrease world welfare, I believe that the weight of evidence points clearly to a net positive effect from trade creation.

But the creation of a single market for goods and services does not require a monetary union. It is possible to have all the benefits of free trade without a common currency. The United States has recently established a free-trade agreement with Canada and Mexico, yet nobody seriously suggests that the United States, Canada and Mexico should form a currency union.

Source: Adapted from an article by Martin Feldstein in *The Economist*, 13 June 1992.

Questions

1. What does the author mean when he speaks of the 'trade-diverting' effects of the European Union?

2. What 'positive effects' are likely to result from 'trade creation'?

3. What do you think the benefits of a common currency would be?

4. What are the arguments against the implementation of a common currency?

Glossary

Absolute advantage A situation in which a country is more efficient in the production of a good or service than another country.

Accelerator principle of investment This principle states that it is the rate at which income changes rather than the level of national income that determines the amount of investment.

Ad valorem tariff A tariff which is calculated as a proportion of the price of the import.

Aggregate demand Aggregate demand represents the total level of demand in the economy. It comprises spending by consumers, firms and government, plus spending on exports minus any spending on imports. The formula is $AD = C + I + G + X - M$.

Aggregate demand curve This illustrates the relationship between the price level and the aggregate demand for goods and services.

Aggregate supply The aggregate supply represents the total supply of goods and services by all firms within the economy.

Aggregate supply curve The aggregate supply curve illustrates the relationship between the price level and the output of the economy.

Ansoff matrix A model to illustrate four alternative growth strategies available to a firm.

Automatic stabilisers Fiscal changes which help to reduce fluctuations in aggregate demand. They operate through (a) tax revenues rising and government spending falling when the economy is booming, thus helping to dampen down aggregate demand, and (b) tax revenue falling and government spending rising during a recession, thus helping to increase aggregate demand.

Average cost Total cost divided by the quantity of goods produced.

Average fixed cost The fixed cost per unit of output. It is calculated by dividing the total fixed cost by output.

Average product Average product measures how much output, on average, each unit of the variable factor is producing. It is calculated by dividing total output by the number of units of the variable factor.

Average revenue Total revenue divided by the quantity of goods sold.

Average total cost The cost per unit. It is calculated by dividing the total cost of production by output.

Average variable cost   The variable cost per unit. It is calculated by dividing the total variable cost by output.

Balance of payments   A record of a country's financial transactions with the rest of the world.

Balance of trade   The value of a country's exports of goods and services minus the value of its imports of goods and services.

Balancing item   A statistical adjustment which is made to ensure that the two sides of the balance of payments account balance.

Barriers to entry   Barriers to entry are market conditions that make it difficult for new firms to enter an industry.

Black economy   Illegal economic activity which is not recorded in the official national accounts.

Black market   A situation where goods are traded illegally at prices above the maximum ceiling price imposed by the government.

Bond   A bond is a legally enforceable obligation to pay specified sums of money at a specified date.

Breakeven period   The period it takes for an investment to cover its costs.

Budget deficit   A situation where government expenditure exceeds its revenue from taxation.

Budget surplus   A situation where revenue from taxation exceeds government expenditure.

Capital account (transactions in external assets and liabilities)   That part of the balance of payments which records movements of capital between countries.

Capital stock   The stock of plant, buildings, vehicles and machinery.

Cartel   A cartel is an agreement between firms to limit output and fix prices.

Ceteris paribus   All other things remaining constant.

Clearing bank   A bank that is a member of the London bankers' clearing house, which clears cheques owed by customers of one bank to those of a different bank.

Collective bargaining   Collective bargaining occurs when workers and employers negotiate wages and conditions of employment for whole groups of workers (as opposed to individual negotiations).

Collusive tendering   Collusive tendering occurs when two or more firms get together to arrange the price of tenders.

Command economy   *see* **Planned economy**.

Commodity bundling   Commodity bundling occurs when a firm sells several products as a single whole.

Commodity money   A physical commodity that is valued in its own right and which is also used as money (e.g. gold).

Common Agricultural Policy (CAP)   This is a scheme which seeks to provide farmers throughout the EU with a reasonable level of income and to make the EU self-sufficient in as many agricultural products as possible.

Common market A customs union which allows free movement of workers and capital between member countries, in addition to free movement of goods and services.

Comparative advantage A situation where a country might be more efficient than another in the production of two or more products, but is relatively more efficient in the production of one of those products. The *law of comparative advantage* states that trade can benefit all countries if they specialise in the production of those goods and services in which they have a comparative advantage.

Competition policy Competition policy is the policy of government to limit the undesirable effects of monopoly.

Competitive labour market A market which replicates the conditions of a competitive goods market (e.g. no individual firm or worker can influence the price of labour).

Concentration ratio A five-firm concentration ratio measures the share of output taken by the five largest firms in an industry.

Conglomerate merger Where a firm expands into a new industry.

Consumer durables Products which are bought by consumers, such as cars, furniture and washing machines. The benefits of the product are expected to last over a number of years.

Consumer sovereignty Consumer sovereignty refers to the process where the output decisions of producers are determined by consumer demand.

Consumption expenditure Expenditure by households on goods and services.

Contestable markets Contestable markets, strictly defined, are markets with zero entry and exit costs, but the idea is extended to include markets which are open to new entrants.

Convergence criteria The conditions which each country of the EU has to meet if it wishes to participate in economic and monetary union.

Cost-benefit analysis Cost-benefit analysis involves comparing all the costs and benefits of a proposed investment.

Corporation tax A tax on company profits.

Cost pass through When fixing prices, regulators sometimes allow privatised utilities to raise prices by more than that indicated by the RPI(X) formula because the firm has no control over some costs (e.g. the British Airports Authority has little control over security costs).

Cost-push inflation Cost-push inflation is caused by increases in the costs of production, independent of demand.

Cross-elasticity of demand Cross-elasticity of demand measures the responsiveness of the demand of one product to a change in the price of another product. It is calculated by dividing the percentage change in demand for one product by the percentage change in price of a substitute or complementary product.

Cross-subsidisation Cross-subsidisation occurs when a loss-making good or service is subsidised from profits made in another part of the firm.

Crowding out A theory that an expansion in government spending results in the reduction – or crowding out – of investment by privately owned firms.

Current account That part of the balance of payments which records trade in goods and services plus transfers of income received from and paid to foreigners.

Customs union A group of countries who agree not only to have free trade among themselves, but also to impose common external barriers against imports from the rest of the world.

Debentures Debentures are debt securities usually carrying a fixed rate of interest issued by a company and secured on its assets.

Deflation A policy of reducing aggregate demand, usually in an attempt to control inflation.

Demand Demand is the quantity of a product which consumers are willing and able to buy. Demand is usually inversely related to price: as price rises, demand falls.

Demand curve A diagram which shows the relationship between price and the quantity demanded. The demand curve will shift if there is a change in any of the conditions affecting demand, such as advertising or income.

Demand for money *see* **Money demand**.

Demand-management policies Policies which focus on influencing the level of demand within the economy in order to help control macroeconomic variables such as inflation and unemployment.

Demand schedule A table which shows the quantities of a product that are demanded at different prices.

Demand-deficient unemployment Unemployment that arises due to insufficient aggregate demand in the economy. It is sometimes referred to as *cyclical unemployment* as it fluctuates with the trade cycle.

Demand-pull inflation Inflation caused by increases in the level of aggregate demand.

Depreciation (of an asset) Where the value of an asset is reduced as a result of wear and tear.

Depreciation (of a currency) Where, under a system of floating exchange rates, there is a fall in the value of a country's currency.

Deregulation Deregulation occurs when government regulations are replaced by market forces.

Devaluation Where the government deliberately lowers the value of the exchange rate.

Diminishing marginal returns A situation where the marginal output of the last worker employed is less than that of the second-last worker employed.

Discounting Discounting the future means that future cash flows are worth less than money now.

Diseconomies of scale Diseconomies of scale occur when an increase in the size of the firm results in a decrease in efficiency.

Dumping A practice of selling products overseas at subsidised prices.

Duopoly An industry with only two firms is called a duopoly.

Economic and Monetary Union (EMU) An EU objective that implies a single currency, a European Central Bank and a single monetary policy throughout the member states.

Economically active The economically active are the labour force in employment (including those employed, self-employed, those participating in training programmes, and persons doing unpaid family work) plus the unemployed.

Economies of scale The advantages gained from producing goods on a larger scale, resulting in a reduction in the average cost of production.

Economies of scope The ability of a firm to produce several different outputs from a common set of resources.

Elasticity of demand A measure of the responsiveness of demand to a range of variables such as price and income.

Elasticity of supply A measure of the responsiveness of supply to changes in the market price.

Entrepreneur An entrepreneur is a decision maker and risk taker in a firm.

Equilibrium price That price at which the quantity demanded equals the quantity supplied.

Equity finance Money obtained by firms through the sale of shares.

European Central Bank The bank responsible for carrying out monetary policy for those countries which have agreed full economic and monetary union.

Exchange rate The price of one country's currency expressed in terms of another currency.

Exchange Rate Mechanism (ERM) A system used by the European Union to limit the extent to which each member's currency fluctuated against other currencies within the mechanism.

External economies of scale The benefits which a firm enjoys as a result of being part of an established, or growing, industry.

Externalities Externalities arise when there is a difference between private costs and social costs, or between private benefits and the social benefits of production.

Factors of production The inputs used in the production of goods and services. They are usually classified as land, labour, capital and enterprise.

Fiat money A commodity which has little value on its own, but which is accepted as money (e.g. notes).

Firm A firm is an organisation consisting of one or more individuals working as a decision-making unit to produce goods or services.

Fiscal policy Policy that involves the management of aggregate demand through the use of government expenditure and/or taxation.

Fisher equation ($MV = PT$) This equation states that the quantity of money (M) multiplied by the velocity at which it circulates in the economy (V) must equal the general price level (P) multiplied by the level of output (T).

Fixed costs Those costs which remain the same in the short run as output varies.

Fixed exchange rate system Where the government takes whatever measures are necessary to maintain the exchange rate at a stated fixed level.

Fixed factor An input that cannot be increased in the short run.

Floating (or free) exchange rate system Where the exchange rate is determined by the forces of demand for and supply of a currency, with no government intervention to control the rate.

Foreign direct investment This involves the creation and maintenance of real productive assets overseas.

Foreign exchange market The market in which currencies of different countries are bought and sold.

Foreign reserves Stocks of gold and foreign currencies held by central banks which may be used to help manage the foreign exchange value of the currency.

Forward currency market A market which exists to help reduce the uncertainty involved under a system of floating exchange rates. A contract is made for the purpose of buying or selling currency at a given future date at an agreed rate of exchange.

Free trade Free trade occurs when international trade is unrestricted by barriers such as tariffs, quotas or any other trade restriction.

Free-trade area An agreement between countries to abolish barriers to trade between member states, while each country is free to set its own barriers to trade against other countries outside the agreement.

Free-rider Someone who is able to consume a product without paying for it.

Frictional unemployment Unemployment that arises as a result of the time it takes for workers to find jobs, even when there are vacancies.

Game theory Game theory analyses the range of best moves available in a situation of mutual interdependence where the participants lack full information.

General Agreement on Tariffs and Trade (GATT) An intergovernmental body whose objective is to reduce trade barriers.

General training General training improves workers' productivity in many firms; specific training only increases productivity in the form which provides the training.

Government failure Government failure refers to the problems which arise from government intervention in the market.

Gross domestic product (GDP) A measure of the total value of output produced within a country.

Gross national product (GNP) A measure of the total value of output of a country produced by the resources owned by that country.

Horizontal differentiation Horizontal differentiation refers to the choice of where to locate a business.

Horizontal merger Where a firm expands within the same industry and at the same stage of production.

Human capital The human capital approach analyses investment in people in the same way as investment in physical capital.

Human resource planning Human resource planning (formerly manpower planning) involves action, usually by government, to ensure an appropriate supply of trained workers in the future.

Import quota A numerical restriction placed on the amount of a commodity that is allowed to be imported over a given time period.

Income effect The income effect is the effect of a change in income on consumption.

Income elasticity of demand Income elasticity of demand measures the responsiveness of demand to changes in income. It is calculated by dividing the percentage change in quantity demanded by the percentage change in consumers' income.

Incomes policy An incomes policy is a strategy used by governments to restrict the extent of pay increases in an effort to control inflation.

Incorporated business An incorporated business has a separate legal identity from its owner.

Indivisibilities Indivisibilities exist when an asset cannot be divided up.

Infant industry An industry which has not yet established itself and still faces high per unit costs as a result of still having to cover its start-up costs and not yet being able to take advantage of the economies of scale.

Inflation A persistent increase in the level of prices.

Injection Injection is any expenditure that originates from a source external to the circular flow of income. The three injections are investment spending, government expenditure and exports.

Insider trading Trading in shares by insiders, such as company directors, who make profits on the transaction through the illicit use of information not known to outsiders.

Internal economies of scale Economies that arise as a result of an individual firm increasing its scale of operations.

Internal rate of return The internal rate of return is the rate of return of an investment at which the net present value is zero.

Investment The purchase of new buildings, plant and equipment.

Invisible trade The trade in services and intangible items such as insurance and banking.

Involuntary unemployment Unemployment which occurs when workers are willing to accept but cannot find employment at the existing wage rate.

J-curve effect Where a devaluation causes the balance of payments to deteriorate at first before it starts to improve.

Kinked demand curve In some theories of oligopoly the demand curve has a kink. Above this kink, demand is elastic; below it demand is inelastic. This makes firms reluctant to change prices.

Laissez-faire system An economy which operates without any government intervention.

Law of diminishing returns The law of diminishing returns predicts that as output is increased in the short run, there comes a point when the return to the variable input diminishes.

Leakage (or **withdrawal**) Any expenditure that leaks out from the circular flow of income and which is not spent on domestically produced goods and services. The three leakages are savings, taxes and imports.

Limited liability   Limited liability means that the owners' private assets are not at risk to pay the debts of a company in which they have shares.

Liquidity   Liquidity refers to the ease with which assets can be turned into spending power. Money is the most liquid asset; buildings are very illiquid.

Long run   The long run is that period of time during which it is possible to vary all inputs and thus change the scale of the firm.

Long-run average cost curve   A curve which shows how the cost per unit varies with output when the scale of operations is varied.

M0   A measure of money supply, largely consisting of notes and coins held by the public and by banks and building societies.

M4   A measure of money consisting of currency held by the public plus deposits at banks and building societies. It is much larger than M0.

Maastricht Treaty   Signed in 1992, this treaty set out a timetable and clarified how economic and monetary union was to be achieved.

Managed exchange rate system   A system whereby the government may intervene to influence the level of the exchange rate, rather than leaving it to be determined entirely by market forces.

Marginal cost (MC)   The extra cost incurred when producing one more unit.

Marginal physical product (MPP)   Marginal physical product is the physical quantity of goods produced by the employment of an additional worker.

Marginal product   The additional output produced as a result of employing an extra unit of a variable factor.

Marginal propensity to consume (mpc)   The proportion of any additional income that is spent on consumption.

Marginal propensity to import (mpm)   The proportion of any additional income spent on imports.

Marginal propensity to save (mps)   The proportion of any additional income that is saved.

Marginal propensity to tax (mpt)   The proportion of any extra income that is taxed.

Marginal revenue (MR)   The increase in revenue when the firm sells one more item.

Marginal revenue product (MRP)   Marginal revenue product is the revenue resulting from employing an additional worker. It is calculated by multiplying the marginal physical product (MPP) by the price of the product.

Market economy   An economy where the resources are allocated through the workings of the price mechanism.

Market failure   Market failure arises when the market mechanism fails to produce an efficient allocation of resources.

Market structure   Market structure is those organisational features of a market which have a significant effect on competition.

Marshall-Lerner condition   This theory states that a devaluation of a currency will lead to an improvement in the trade balance provided that the sum of the elasticities of demand for imports and exports is greater than one.

Merit goods Goods and services which are of benefit to society as a whole, as well as to the individual who consumes them. Merit goods tend to be underprovided by the market mechanism.

Minimum efficient scale (MES) The size of a firm which is required to gain maximum benefit from the economies of scale. Beyond this level, the long-run average cost stops falling.

Monetarist theory of inflation A theory that inflation is solely due to the expansion of the money supply.

Monetary policy The management of the economy through the control of the money supply and interest rates.

Money Money is anything which is generally acceptable as a means of exchange.

Money demand Demand for money refers to the people's decision to hold money rather than other assets.

Monopoly Monopoly exists when there is only one firm in an industry.

Monopoly profit A monopoly profit is the money received by a monopoly because of its control over price and output (i.e. profit over and above that which would be obtained by a firm in a perfectly competitive market).

Monopsony Monopsony occurs when there is only one buyer.

Multinational (MNC) An MNC is one which owns or controls production or service facilities in several countries.

Multiplier effect The multiplier process magnifies the effect of any change in injections into or leakages from the circular flow, so that the eventual change in the level of income is greater than the initial change in the injection or leakage. The multiplier can be calculated by using the formula $1/(1-mpc)$.

National debt The accumulated debt incurred by the government as a result of persistent budget deficits.

National income A measure of all the incomes obtained from the production of goods and services in a country throughout the year.

Nationalised industry A nationalised industry is one that has been brought under state ownership and control.

Natural monopoly An industry that is characterised by high fixed costs and low marginal costs, and where competition would be wasteful and inefficient.

Natural rate of unemployment That level of unemployment that exists when the labour market is in equilibrium.

Net investment Total investment minus an allowance for depreciation.

Net national product (NNP) GNP minus depreciation.

Net present value The net present value of an investment is the present value of future income produced by an investment less its cost.

Non-accelerating inflation rate of unemployment (NAIRU) NAIRU is that rate of unemployment that is consistent with a stable rate of inflation. Any attempt to reduce unemployment below this level through increasing aggregate demand leads to increasing rates of inflation.

Non-tariff barriers   Barriers other than tariffs and quantitative restrictions which hinder trade between member states, such as differences in national product specifications and regulations.

Normal profit   The level of profit needed to keep a firm in business. It is the profit which would be made by a typical firm in a perfectly competitive industry.

Normative economics   Normative economics is concerned with values, that is, what *ought* to be (e.g. 'the rich should pay higher taxes').

Oligopoly   Oligopoly exists when there are only a few firms in an industry.

Open market operations   Open market operations are purchases or sales of bonds by the government to increase or reduce the money supply.

Opportunity cost   The opportunity cost of an action is the cost of the best forgone alternative action.

Optimum output   That level of output at which the average total cost is at a minimum.

Ordinary shares   Owners of ordinary shares own the company and receive dividends which vary with the level of profits. Such shares can rise or fall in value.

Overdraft   An overdraft is a permission to overdraw the money in a bank account for a certain period of time. The interest charged may vary during this period.

Partnership   An association of two or more people who are co-owners of a business.

Payback period   The expected number of years of operation needed to recover an initial investment.

Perfect competition   Perfect competition exists when there are many buyers and sellers, an identical product, and participants have perfect knowledge of the market. The firm is a price taker.

Phillips curve   A Phillips curve is a diagram that illustrates the possible trade-off which exists between inflation and unemployment.

Planned economy   A planned economy is an economy in which resources are usually owned by the state and where production decisions are made by state planning rather than by the market mechanism. Also known as a *command economy.*

Portfolio investment   This is the purchase of financial assets such as shares.

Predatory pricing   Predatory pricing occurs when a firm attempts to weaken actual or potential competitors by measures such as cutting prices.

Preference shares   Preference shares are fixed-interest securities, the holders of which have a prior claim over ordinary shareholders in any profit distribution.

Present value   The value today of a sum of money to be received in the future.

Price control   Where the government or some other authority places a *maximum price* or a *minimum price* on a product. In the case of a maximum price, or a ceiling, the price is not allowed to rise above this level. In the case of a minimum price, or a floor, the price is not allowed to fall below this level.

Price cap   A price cap is a price limit imposed by the regulator in some privatised monopolies.

Price elasticity of demand   A measure of the responsiveness of demand to changes in price. If demand is responsive to changes in price, it is said to be *elastic*, while if demand is unresponsive to changes in price, it is said to be *inelastic*.

Price discrimination   Price discrimination exists when a monopolist can charge different prices for the same service.

Price elasticity of supply   A measure of the responsiveness of supply to changes in price.

Price maker   A firm is a price maker when it can decide the price at which it sells its goods.

Pure monopoly   Pure monopoly exists when there is only one firm in the industry.

Price taker   A firm is a price taker when it has to accept the price determined by the market. Most consumers are price takers.

Principal–agent   The principal–agent problem arises when principals (e.g. owners) have differing interests to their agents (e.g. managers).

Private benefits   The private benefits of production are those that accrue to the firm that makes the product, or to the consumer that uses it.

Private costs   Those costs which are borne by an individual or firm in the carrying out of some activity.

Privatisation   Privatisation is the selling off of publicly owned assets to the private sector.

Product differentiation   Product differentiation occurs when a firm makes many varieties of a basic product.

Product life cycle   The stages through which a product might move from its introduction to its decline.

Production function   A production function summarises the relationship between outputs and the inputs necessary to produce them.

Profit   Profit can be defined as the difference between total revenue and total cost.

Protectionism   The term given to a policy of restricting the flow of imports into a country.

Public goods   These are goods and services that have the features of non-rivalry and non-excludability. This means, first, that the consumption of the product by one person does not reduce the quantity available for other consumers, and second, that it is impossible to exclude non-payers from consuming the product. These products will not be provided privately through the market and therefore have to be provided by the state and paid for collectively through taxation.

Public sector borrowing requirement (PSBR)   The amount by which the expenditure of the public sector (mainly central government) exceeds its revenue in a year and therefore has to be borrowed.

Public sector debt repayment (PSDR)   The amount by which the revenue of the public sector exceeds its expenditure in a year and can therefore be used to repay some of the national debt.

Regional policy   A policy which aims to reduce disparities, such as those of income and unemployment, between regions.

Regulatory capture   Regulatory capture occurs when a regulator becomes too sympathetic to the problems of the firm being regulated.

Restrictive trade practices   Restrictive practices are devices by firms to influence various aspects of the market.

Retail price index (RPI)   The main measure of inflation in the UK. It measures the average level of prices of goods and services consumed by a typical household.

Rights issue   The name given to shares sold to existing shareholders by a firm in order to raise more money.

Search unemployment   Unemployment which arises when unemployed workers delay accepting employment opportunities in the expectation of a better opportunity arriving.

Seasonal unemployment   Unemployment which is associated with those industries where employment opportunities are dependent on the time of year.

Segmented labour market   A segmented labour market exists when the labour market is divided (e.g. between insiders who have good jobs and outsiders who find it difficult to get good jobs).

Semi-variable costs   Those costs which have a tendency to increase as output increases, but which do not vary greatly with output.

Sensitivity analysis   Sensitivity analysis involves changing the parameters of an investment decision in order to estimate their effects.

Shadow prices   Shadow prices are estimated prices used as substitutes for market prices.

Short run   That period of time during which the firm is unable to alter the scale of its operations.

Sight deposits   Deposits in banks and building societies which can be withdrawn immediately.

Single market   A single market means that there is free movement of goods, services, labour and capital between member states.

Social benefit   The social benefit of production is the private benefit plus the benefits to other individuals or firms from the production.

Social Chapter   A section of the Maastricht Treaty which made reference to the social rights of citizens and workers throughout the EU.

Social costs   The social costs of production are the private costs plus the cost to society of any activity. The costs to society could include pollution, danger to health and other disadvantages incurred by individuals or firms as a consequence of the production.

Social dumping   A process whereby a country seeks to make itself an attractive location for firms by offering lower wages, and lower levels of social protection for workers, than other member states.

Stop-go policy   A situation where the government alternately pursues reflationary and then deflationary policies in an attempt to tackle macroeconomic problems.

Structural unemployment Unemployment that arises as a result of a change in the structure of the economy. Those who work in declining industries become unemployed and are not able to transfer to jobs in the expanding industries due to lack of occupational mobility.

Subsidy A payment paid by the government to the producers of goods and services.

Substitution effect The change in demand for a good caused by a change in the relative prices of goods rather than by a change in income (e.g. if the price of apples rises, some people will buy more pears).

Supply The quantity of a product which firms are willing and able to sell. In most cases, the quantity supplied rises as the price rises.

Supply curve A diagram which shows the relationship between price and the quantity supplied. The supply curve will shift if there is any change in the conditions of supply, such as a change in the costs of production.

Supply schedule A table which shows the quantities of a product supplied at different price levels.

Supply-side policies Those policies aimed at increasing the supply of goods and services by removing any obstacles that may prevent the free market from working as efficiently as possible.

Tariff A tax placed on an imported good with the aim of restricting imports and/or raising revenue.

Term loan A term loan is one for a fixed period of time.

Terms of trade The terms of trade is a format that compares the price of exports relative to the price of imports. It is calculated by dividing the export price index by the import price index and then expressing the result as a percentage.

Time deposits Deposits in banks and building societies which can only be withdrawn after a period of notice.

Total costs The sum of total fixed costs and total variable costs.

Trade credit Credit given by one firm to another (e.g. when a retailer need not pay the wholesaler on delivery).

Trade cycle The periodic fluctuations of national output.

Trade union An association of workers formed in order to improve the conditions of their working lives.

Transactions costs Costs which are incurred when goods and services are bought.

Transfer prices These are the prices which are charged on transactions that take place within the company (i.e. on intra-company transactions).

Transnational (TNC) This is sometimes used interchangeably with multinational, but, more narrowly, it can refer to a company which operates in only two countries.

Treasury bills Treasury bills are short-term (usually 3- or 6-month) IOUs sold by the government each week.

Unemployment A situation in which workers are willing and able to work but cannot find employment.

Unincorporated business An unincorporated business is one in which there is no legal difference between the owner and the firm.

Variable costs Costs which vary as output varies.

Vertical differentiation Vertical differentiation occurs when goods are differentiated by quality.

Vertical merger Where a firm expands in the same industry but at a different stage of production, either 'backwards' towards the raw material or 'forwards' towards the end product.

Visible trade The trade in tangible items or goods.

Voluntary export restraint (VER) An agreement by an exporting country to limit the quantity of a product which it exports to another country.

Voluntary unemployment Unemployment which occurs when workers are not willing to accept wages at the current wage rate.

Weighted index An index where each item is ascribed a weight according to its relative importance.

World Trade Organisation (WTO) This organisation replaced GATT, and is committed to reducing and removing barriers to trade.

Index

FINANCIAL TIMES

Supplement

How to read the Financial Times

Philip Coggan, Markets Editor, Financial Times

The Financial Times was founded in 1888 and has been known for a century for its distinctive pink paper (an early marketing technique that stuck).

The paper is split into two, with the first section broadly covering politics, economics, social developments and industrial trends and the second section covering individual companies and stock, currency, bond and commodity market movements.

Pages covering UK and international companies

The UK results coverage includes an important feature in the form of comments on the figures. The aim is to guide investors through the morass; for example, to point out when profits have been boosted by one-off factors such as asset sales; when the trend in profits growth is slowing; when a healthy profits figure masks a weak cash position; when the performance is strong, but the shares already reflect all the good news.

Valuing shares

There are a number of techniques for valuing shares, based on the assets, profits, dividends or cash flow of a company. *Net asset value (NAV) per share* is calculated by adding up the value of the tangible assets of a company, deducting the debts, and dividing by the number of shares in issue. It can be a good way of assessing the value of some companies; if the share price is 80p and the NAV per share is 100p, it would in theory be possible for a predator to buy up the company and sell off the assets at a profit. However, many modern companies are in the service sector and have few tangible assets, so NAV is of only limited use in valuing shares.

The *price–earnings ratio* (P/E) is a method of comparing a company's share price with its profits. The first step is to work out a company's profits, after tax and other deductions. These are known as the *earnings*, which are then divided by the number of shares in issue, to get the *earnings per share*. The last step is to divide the *share price* by the earnings per share to get the P/E ratio. Roughly speaking, this figure represents the number of years' earnings an investor is paying for a share; buying a company on a P/E ratio of 10 means one is paying 10 times current earnings. In theory, the lower the P/E the better. However, the markets are always looking ahead. Companies with a high P/E tend to be ones where investors are expecting earnings to grow quickly; companies with a low P/E are expected to show modest, if any, profits growth.

Another popular valuation measure is *dividend yield*, which shows the annual dividend as a percentage of the share price. Many investors own shares for their dividends, which over the long term make up a significant proportion of stock market returns. An advantage of dividends is that they are real, in the sense that they have to be paid in cash; assets and profits can sometimes be accounting illusions. It would be a mistake, however, to assume that the company with the highest yield is the most attractive. Since the yield represents the dividend divided by the share price, as the price falls the yield rises. Sometimes shares offer a high yield because investors expect the company to cut the dividend, or not pay it at all; in other cases, they expect little in the way of growth. If a share has a low dividend yield, it may be that the company is currently paying only a small proportion of its profits out as dividends, so it can reinvest the money to help its business grow. Fast-growing companies tend to have low dividends; investors hope that eventually both profits and dividends will grow at an above average rate and they are prepared to accept a low yield for now.

The London share service pages, give the P/E and the dividend yield (headed **yld gr s**) for most quoted companies.

Sometimes investors prefer to look at *cash flow*, rather than profits or dividends. In some cases, this may be because it is harder to manipulate cash flow than it is to fiddle the earnings or profits figure. In other cases, a company might look better value on cash flow than on an earnings basis; for example, if the company takes a heavy charge against its profits for depreciation of its assets.

Shares are divided by industrial sectors

so that ratios can be easily compared between, say, Sainsbury and Tesco, or Guinness and Allied Domecq. Other information shown includes the share price, the day's change, the 52-week high and low, and the market capitalization (the value placed by the stock market on the company, calculated by multiplying the share price by the number of shares in issue). Symbols direct the reader to footnotes which show where special circumstances apply.

The stock market

The back page of the UK edition contains coverage of the London stock market. The aim is to explain both why shares in individual companies rise and fall and why the overall market goes up or down. This is a difficult area; shares in, say, Acme Construction may rise on hopes of a bid from Megacorp. Even if the rumour turns out to be untrue, it is still the case that the story lifted the shares and it is our job to report it. One way of assessing the credibility of rumours is to look at the volume of shares traded. If it is greater than normal for that stock, it may indicate that the story has some substance; if volume is low, the chances are that few believe the rumours.

Individual shares may move for a whole host of reasons: stockbrokers' reports; bid rumours; executive departures; adverse press reports; results which beat, or fall short of, market expectations. This last factor is one of the most important. Outsiders are often puzzled when a company which reports a 30% rise in profits sees its shares fall. Markets indulge in what one might call the White Queen syndrome, after the character in Through the Looking Glass. The White Queen screamed before she pricked her finger and when the injury actually occurred, made only a small sigh, as she had got all her screaming over with in advance. Similarly, stock markets are forever looking to the future and anticipating what will happen. Expectations are built into the market; thus if a company is expected to increase profits by 40% and only reports a rise of 30%, its shares will fall.

FTSE

Because there are so many quoted shares, investors use 'benchmarks', in the form of baskets of representative stocks, to track the market's overall movements. The most commonly used in the UK is the *FTSE 100*, which stands for the Financial Times/Stock Exchange 100 index and is designed to show the UK's 100 largest companies. Broader indices, such as the *FTSE All-Share* which includes around 800 stocks and the *FTSE SmallCap* which covers shares in smaller companies, are also used. Companies drop in and out of these indices as their shares rise and fall, or are subject to takeover.

The indices are also used to monitor the performance of fund managers who look after other people's money, whether it be pension funds, charities, or the portfolios of private investors. Experience has found that it is very difficult to beat these benchmarks. In part, this is because the index will inevitably represent the average performance of all shares, and thus all investors; by definition, therefore, half of all investors should not beat the index. On top of that factor is the burden of administrative and dealing costs, which investors have to pay, but the index does not reflect. More fundamentally, it seems as if very few people have the ability to pick successful shares. Academics have argued that this is because markets are efficient; share prices reflect all the available knowledge about a company. What will affect the price, therefore, is future news, which by definition cannot be known.

If picking the best shares is difficult, so is predicting the moves of the overall market. Over the long run, at least, it tends to go up. BZW's Equity–Gilt Study shows that £1,000 invested in equities at the end of 1945 would have grown, with net dividends reinvested, into £218,140 by the end of 1995. The same amount in a building society would have risen to just £10,400. But in the short term, it can fall very sharply. On Black Monday, 19 October 1987, the FTSE 100 index fell by 10.8%, and it then dropped another 12.2% on the following day.

The main factors which cause the market to rise and fall include the following:

Interest rates. Broadly speaking, rising interest rates are bad news for share prices and falling rates are good. Rising rates increase the cost of corporate borrowing and thereby reduce profits. Higher interest rates also increase the attraction of selling shares to hold funds on deposit. Factors which are likely to lead the government to raise interest rates – rising inflation, strong economic growth – are therefore often bad news for the markets.

Profits growth. Equities represent a share of the assets and profits of a company. The faster profits grow, therefore, the better for the markets. Tax changes which eat into profits hit the market.

Supply and demand. Flotations and rights issues increase the supply of shares in the market and drive prices down (other things being equal); dividends, share buy-backs and takeovers for cash increase the funds available for investment and push prices up.

International influences. Increasingly, stock markets are being dominated by global influences as investors move money round in search of the most attractive havens. There is a tendency for share prices to move up and down together; London, in particular, is heavily influenced by Wall Street and a sharp fall in the US market usually has a knock-on effect in the UK.

The global picture

For those who are interested in more than just the UK market, the *world stock markets page* covers the rest of the globe. The aim is to explain why each market rose and fell on the day and to give details of a few substantial movements of individual stocks. As with the UK, Wall Street often sets the tone, although Tokyo follows its own agenda. Having been amazingly strong in the 1980s, the Japanese stock market has been in a slump throughout the 1990s in the face of a sluggish economy and weakened financial system.

Investors are becoming increasingly interested in the so-called *emerging markets* of Latin America and Asia, which have faster rates of economic growth, and thus the potential for greater increase in corporate profits, than the developed world. Liberalization of these markets has also encouraged foreign investors to buy shares.

Bond markets

Daily coverage of the *bond markets* appears on the International Capital Markets page.

Government bond market

The market in government bonds is huge; at the end of 1995, there was some $22 trillion of outstanding debt or around $3,500 for every individual on the planet. Bond markets are curmudgeonly and rather misanthropic sorts; they tend to dislike news that pleases the rest of the population. A fall in unemployment, a pick-up in wages or a strengthening of economic growth will tend to cause the bond markets to fall. This is because the biggest enemy of bond markets is inflation. Even at 5% inflation, prices double every 14 years or so, so the real value of a 15-year bond will halve between issue and repayment. Bond investors tend to believe that strong economic growth (which in developed countries tends to be an annual rate of 2.5% or more) leads to inflation.

Apart from inflation, the other important factor in influencing bond markets tends to be supply. The supply of government bonds depends on the size of the country's budget deficit, so a larger-than-expected deficit tends to depress bond prices. In some countries, particularly the developing world, the debts become so large that countries have little hope of repaying the capital, or even the interest; such was the case during the debt crisis of the early 1980s, which centred on Latin America.

An important note for anyone reading the paper's bond market coverage is the relationship between the *yield* and the *price*. The yield is calculated by dividing the interest rate payable on the bond by the market price; as the price rises, therefore, the yield falls and vice versa.

Primary bond markets

The coverage of primary bond issues on the same page looks at how companies and governments are raising money, how much, at what rate, and in which currency. Trends change as borrowers seek to get the best terms available; it may, for example, be advantageous for a UK borrower to raise money in Australian dollars and convert back into sterling.

Foreign exchange markets

Coverage of the *foreign exchange markets* immediately follows the capital markets page. Here again, the market is huge

with daily turnover of around $500bn in London, and can be turbulent, as when the UK and other currencies were forced out of the Exchange Rate Mechanism in 1992. The main factors affecting a currency are economic; low inflation, a trade surplus, high real (after inflation) interest rates, tend to cause it to rise; high inflation, a trade deficit and low real rates tend to cause it to fall. But on a day-to-day or week-to-week basis, currencies can often move in a contrary direction to that implied by the economic fundamentals.

Commodites

Financial assets have tended to be good investments in the 1980s and 1990s but back in the 1970s, the smart money was in *commodities*. The era of high inflation saw price booms in most commodities, with the most obvious example being oil. Falling inflation, new sources of supply and improved production techniques combined to bring down commodity prices in the 1980s. Interest in the area has recently revived, however, and our commodities page covers the most important developments; the ups and downs of raw material prices can have important effects in individual sectors of the economy. A poor coffee harvest in Brazil, a cold winter in the US, political unrest in the Middle East; all can have knock-on effects which eventually become apparent to the consumer.